ST. MARY'S COLLEGE OF MARYLAND LIBRARY
ST.

W9-CLV-918

RUTGERS UNIVERSITY STUDIES IN GEOGRAPHY
NUMBER ONE

THE INVASION OF NEW ZEALAND
BY PEOPLE, PLANTS
AND ANIMALS

ahc

Decorative invaders grace Hagley Park, Christchurch, in the spring.

33833

THE INVASION
OF NEW ZEALAND
BY PEOPLE, PLANTS
AND ANIMALS
THE SOUTH ISLAND

ANDREW HILL CLARK

GREENWOOD PRESS, PUBLISHERS
WESTPORT, CONNECTICUT

Quotations from the works listed below have been used with the permission of the listed authors or publishers. In addition, previously published material by the author has been used in this work with the permission of *The New Zealand Geographer, The Journal of Economic History,* and the University of California Press (publishers of *New Zealand,* United Nations Series, Berkeley, 1947).

The *Geographical Review* for: articles by Prof. K. B. Cumberland. Oxford University Press, Oxford and London, for: R. G. Stapledon, 1928, *A Tour in Australia and New Zealand: Grasslands and Other Studies;* and J. S. Marais, 1927, *The Colonisation of New Zealand.* Cambridge University Press, Cambridge, for: G. M. Thomson, 1922, *The Naturalisation of Plants and Animals in New Zealand.* George Allen and Unwin, Ltd., London, for: A. J. Harrop, 1928, *The Amazing Career of Edward Gibbon Wakefield;* and J. C. Beaglehole, 1936, *New Zealand, a Short History.* Ernest Benn, Ltd., London, (successors to T. Fisher Unwin), for: G. H. Scholefield, 1909, *New Zealand in Evolution.* Blackie and Son, Ltd., Glasgow, for: J. R. Muir, 1939, *The Life and Achievements of Captain James Cook.* John Murray, Publishers, London, for: W. S. Childe-Pemberton, 1909, *Life of Lord Norton.* G. Houghton Brown, Esq., London, for: A. Defries, 1938, *Sheep and Turnips.* Whitcombe and Tombs, Ltd., Christchurch, N. Z., for: E. J. Wakefield 1845 (1908 ed.), *Adventure in New Zealand;* R. McNab, 1913, *The Old Whaling Days;* J. C. Andersen, 1916, *Jubilee History of South Canterbury;* A. D. McIntosh, editor, 1930, *Marlborough; A Provincial History;* and F. W. Hilgendorf, 1939, *Wheat in New Zealand.* A. H. and A. W. Reed, Dunedin, N. Z., for: J. Deans, editor, 1937, *Pioneers of Canterbury: Deans' Letters 1840-1854.* R. M. Burdon, Esq., Christchurch, N. Z., for: *High Country, The Evolution of a New Zealand Sheep Station,* 1938. The New Zealand Government (through Sir Joseph Heenan, Under-Secretary for Internal Affairs), for: R. Carrick, 1903, *Historical Records of New Zealand South, Prior to 1840;* E. Best, 1924, *The Maori As He Was;* L. Cockayne and E. P. Turner, 1928, *The Trees of New Zealand;* H. G. Philpott, 1937, *A History of the New Zealand Dairy Industry, 1840-1935;* and W. G. McClymont, 1940, *The Exploration of New Zealand.* University of Melbourne Press, Melbourne, Australia, for: Brian Fitzpatrick, 1941, *The British Empire in Australia, An Economic History, 1834-1939.* Longmans, Green & Co., New York, N. Y., for: Lord Ernle (R. E. Prothero), 1912 ed., *English Farming, Past and Present.* Cambridge University Press, Cambridge, England, for: Gordon East, chapter 13 of H. C. Darby, editor, 1936, *An Historical Geography of England Before A.D. 1800.*

Copyright © 1949 by the Trustees
of Rutgers College in New Jersey

Reprinted by permission
of Rutgers University Press

First Greenwood Reprinting 1970

SBN 8371-2982-6

PRINTED IN UNITED STATES OF AMERICA

PREFACE

This book is a report on a revolutionary change in the character of a region, which occurred in a period of less than two centuries. One of the most important factors in the change was the invasion of the area by armies of plants and animals, which, with the help of man, mingled with or displaced the native flora and fauna. Since attention is focused on the complex multitude of elements associated in the area (the things of nature like soils and plants, rivers and mountains, climate and insects, together with man and his impedimenta of institutions, habits, and prejudices), it has seemed to be a useful study for a geographer. Most studies of man are more or less concerned with the milieu of human activity, but those which attempt to describe and explain the blending in area of human culture and natural habitat quality are, perhaps, peculiarly appropriate to geography. The writer would like to go further and hope that this study might be exemplary of the themes of historical geography. The precise taxonomic pigeonhole in which it is placed is, however, unimportant and may be safely left to those with the necessary will and skill in dialectic.

The region treated is South Island, the largest territorial unit of the Dominion of New Zealand. Largely by way of this island did the invasion of New Zealand by exotic plants and animals occur; it was there that the dominant patterns and practices of land use, now common to the country as a whole, were developed. Because South Island is so little known to the world, and has such significant contrasts with the much more widely publicized North Island, it has been necessary to devote a rather large portion of the report to a summary of the physical geography of the area and to those facets of its history which are of most significance to the invasions analyzed. It is hoped that each part of this introduction will serve a purpose in itself, since a full and co-ordinated picture of the natural character of the area has not hitherto been attempted, nor have the historical data, most of them widely known, been arranged and interpreted from this viewpoint. Various historical traditions, often based upon untested assumption, are carefully scrutinized. From a detailed study of the invasions, some conclusions are reached which, if valid, may contribute to a clearer understanding of the present character of the region.

In a very real sense the study is a pioneering venture, both in the nature of the material studied and the methods of research and analysis employed. So far as New Zealand is concerned, it is thought of by the author as an attempt to open up the field, and in a great many parts a major effort remains to be made. Perhaps some students will be encouraged to check the data and conclusions (often very tentative) of the writer, and to conduct the extensive exploration which is here only initiated.

The earlier draft of this report contained a degree of detail in citation and illustration which has partly yielded to editorial pruning. If much remains, it has been left to substantiate the often unorthodox views of a student who spent scarcely two years in the country. The actual field work, which involved a reasonably full coverage of the island, and much of the archival work were undertaken during the years 1941 and 1942. Little attempt to interpret the evolution of regional character beyond the beginning of World War II has been made. The methods employed in the collection and analysis of the evidence are discussed elsewhere.*

This is intended to be the first of a series of studies dealing with similar problems of the development of patterns and practices of land use in mid-latitude areas overseas which were settled by folk from the shores of the North Sea. Most of the evidence for such a study in Maritime Canada has already been assembled, and visits to both South Africa and Australia for the purpose are

---

* Andrew H. Clark, "Field Work in Historical Geography," *The Professional Geographer,* vol. 4, no. 1, pp. 13-22, December 1946.

projected. Interested readers are invited to appraise this report not only in itself, but in the light of these plans.

The plight of the visitor to a strange land, who is most hospitably received and aided by dozens of new friends and then attempts to express public appreciation of such help, is, as most geographers know, beyond solution. To this multitude who cannot be thanked by name, the writer and his wife, through whose joint interest and effort this report appears, extend wholehearted thanks. We cannot refrain from mentioning a few: George Jobberns and George Wilson of Canterbury University College and Kenneth Cumberland of Auckland University College, who were at the time colleagues in Christchurch; Professors Hudson, McCaskill, and Bevin of Canterbury Agricultural College; Sir Joseph Heenan of Wellington, a high-spirited public servant; Ida B. Leeson, then of the Mitchell Library in Sydney; Carl Sauer and John Leighly of the University of California under whose joint guidance a doctoral dissertation,° based on much of this material, was prepared; William Thomas of Rutgers University who has drawn a few of the best maps and advised on others; and Ruth Field of Rutgers University Press whose adroit editorial pencil has so greatly improved successive manuscript drafts, and who has seen the book through the press. Publication has been supported by the Rutgers University Research Council.

The task has been long and exacting, but it has been a most rewarding experience. For the reader we can only hope for some little of the joy of discovery which was ours in exploring a beautiful and unfamiliar land and in trying to find out something of how it came to be what it is today.

A. H. C.

New Brunswick,
New Jersey.
June, 1949.

° Andrew H. Clark, "The South Island of New Zealand; A Geographic Study of the Introduction and Modification of British Rural Patterns and Practices Associated with the Exotic Plants and Animals of the Island," accepted by the University of California at Berkeley and available in the library of that institution.

CONTENTS

IV

THE INVADING PLANTS

V

CONCLUSION

LIST OF ILLUSTRATIONS

I

THE LAND

CHAPTER I

THE PRIMITIVE HABITAT:
SETTING FOR THE INVASION

The several islands which make up New Zealand are distinctly isolated in the great expanse of the southwest Pacific Ocean. The greatest unit, South Island, is diametrically opposed to the Iberian peninsula; the Canterbury plains along its middle eastern shore are the antipodes of the northwestern corner of Spain. More precisely, the exact center of the island is not far from 45 degrees south latitude and 170 degrees east longitude. Together with slightly smaller North Island and Stewart Island off its southern flank, South Island is separated by long distances from the nearest inhabited Pacific islands and lies some twelve hundred miles from the Australian continent.

The significance of the isolated location can hardly be over-emphasized. The highly individualized flora and fauna indicate a period of separation from other land masses which is long in the geologic time scale. The first men (of perceptible record) visited the present islands of New Zealand probably little more than a thousand years ago. These islands were the last considerable land areas, outside of the highest latitudes, to be visited by Europeans. Indeed, by past or present routes of travel, they are the farthest habitable parts of the world from northwestern Europe. It is barely four centuries since the first European brought even a vague report of the island. Known to an apathetic world in the nineteenth century as the most distant of the Australian colonies of Great Britain, New Zealand was literally at the end of the line, a modern *Ultima Thule*.

South Island's location relative to the Polynesian islands on the northeast and the Australian continent to the west has played a highly significant role in the development of its contemporary regional character.[1] Effective European settlement began in Australia some decades before it was extended to New Zealand. Because of prevailing winds, the sailing routes, and indeed the chief steaming routes until the opening of the Panama Canal in 1914, from any part of northwestern Europe to New Zealand ran around the Cape of Good Hope and past Australia. Thus, South Island, and thence the rest of the country, derived the most important elements of its early pastoral and agricultural complex from Australia.

CONTOURS OF THE SURFACE [2]

The area of South Island is about fifty-eight thousand square miles, approximately equal to that of the state of Illinois, or of England and Wales taken together. Elongated northeast to southwest it extends for some six hundred miles between 40 degrees and 47 degrees south latitude. For most of that distance its width varies between a hundred and a hundred and fifty miles. The coastline (*see* end papers) is not greatly indented except in the extreme northeast, where subsidence of the land has drowned old river valleys to form the fretwork of bays and channels of the Marlborough Sounds, and in the fiorded strandlines of the southwestern tip. Rough terrain in the immediate hinterlands of these areas has, however, hampered the development of ports, which have appeared instead wherever they were fostered by economic demand, often in very inferior sites. Elsewhere good natural harbors are confined to inlets eroded from the volcanic debris of the Banks Peninsula, Dunedin, and Bluff areas.

The land forms are built of rocks which vary widely in age and type. Many have not been assigned precise chronological pigeonholes because of the absence of convenient fossil date tags. The surface rocks of Stewart Island, most of Fiordland, and western Nelson are much altered sedimentaries of Palaeozoic or greater age intermingled with granitic intrusions. Covering most of Otago and forming a thin core of the principal mountains through Westland, central Nelson, and into the Marlborough Sounds, are the

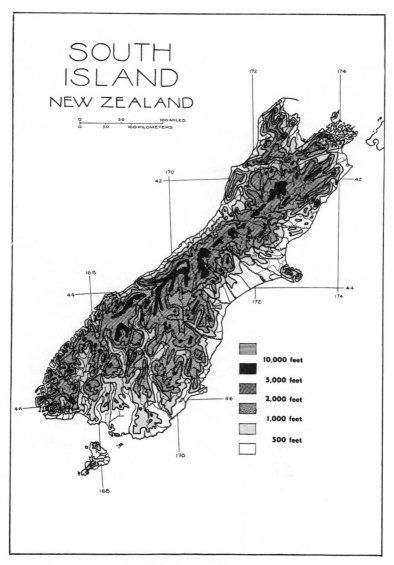

FIG. 1. South Island: Relief by contour lines.

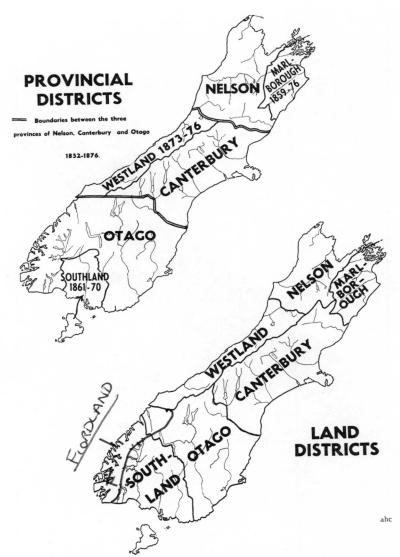

PROVINCIAL DISTRICTS

=== Boundaries between the three provinces of Nelson, Canterbury and Otago

1852-1876.

NELSON

MARL-BOROUGH 1859-76

WESTLAND 1873-76

CANTERBURY

OTAGO

SOUTHLAND 1861-70

NELSON

MARL-BOR-OUGH

WESTLAND

CANTERBURY

FIORDLAND

SOUTH-LAND

OTAGO

LAND DISTRICTS

ahc

FIG. 2. South Island: Provincial Districts, and Land Districts (*see* Appendix A).

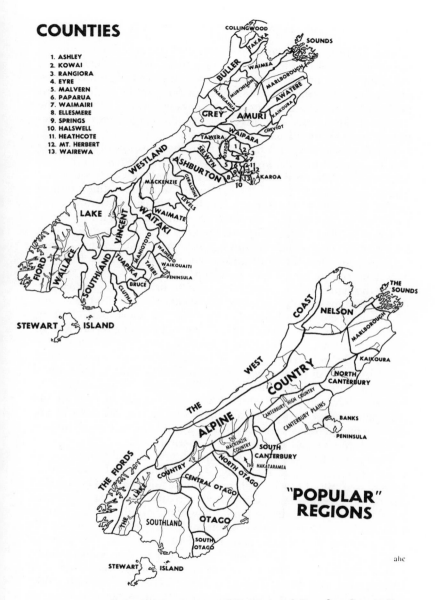

COUNTIES

1. ASHLEY
2. KOWAI
3. RANGIORA
4. EYRE
5. MALVERN
6. PAPARUA
7. WAIMAIRI
8. ELLESMERE
9. SPRINGS
10. HALSWELL
11. HEATHCOTE
12. MT. HERBERT
13. WAIREWA

COLLINGWOOD
SOUNDS
TAKAKA
BULLER
WAIMEA
MARLBOROUGH
MURCHISON
AWATERE
INANGAHUA
GREY
AMURI
KAIKOURA
WAIPARA
CHEVIOT
TAWERA
WESTLAND
SELWYN
ASHBURTON
AKAROA
MACKENZIE
GERALDINE
LEVELS
MALVERN
WAIMATE
LAKE
VINCENT
WAITAKI
MANIOTOTO
WAIHEMO
WAIKOUAITI
SOUTHLAND
TUAPEKA
TAIERI
PENINSULA
FIORD
WALLACE
BRUCE
CLUTHA

STEWART ISLAND

THE SOUNDS
COAST
NELSON
WEST
MARLBOROUGH
KAIKOURA
NORTH CANTERBURY
THE
COUNTRY
CANTERBURY HIGH COUNTRY
ALPINE
CANTERBURY PLAINS
BANKS
THE MACKENZIE COUNTRY
SOUTH CANTERBURY
PENINSULA
THE FIORDS
THE LAKE COUNTRY
NORTH OTAGO
THE HAKATARAMEA
CENTRAL OTAGO
"POPULAR" REGIONS
SOUTHLAND
OTAGO
SOUTH OTAGO
STEWART ISLAND

ahc

FIG. 3. South Island: Counties, and Regions of Popular Conception (*see* Appendix A).

schists. In these, long-continued heat and pressure have reduced the original rocks to a finely foliated mass, which breaks down into thin leaves and in which nearly all clues as to age have been obliterated. Extremely friable, they yet form some of the highest peaks of the Southern Alps (*see* end papers and fig. 1) where the nature of the rock is well advertized in the jagged crestlines between intersecting glacially eroded basins.

Hardly less uniform in character than the schists, and embracing almost as large an area, are the graywackes, of which the hills of Southland and most of the mountain highlands of Canterbury and Marlborough (figs. 2 and 3) are built. Sometimes finer than a typical graywacke, sometimes a rough pebbly conglomerate, these rocks are most commonly a coarse gray sandstone. With little evidence of folding or faulting and in the virtual absence of fossils, interpretations of structure and age remain tentative. It is doubtful, however, that the graywackes were deposited later than the Mesozoic era, and they may be older.

On the flanks of the mountains, chiefly on the eastern margins of the great masses of schists and graywackes, are limited remnants of younger covering beds. Tertiary for the most part, that is, under sixty million years of age, these rocks are softer as well as more varied in character than their older neighbors. From them much of the relatively gentle hill-and-downs country has been carved. Blocks of these newer rocks are also present in the faulted mountain area of the northwest. The large accumulations of gravelly debris and silts which are at the surface in most of the true plains and quasi-plains are hardly to be termed rocks at all; these accumulations were deposited during the last brief million years of the glacial or Pleistocene period.

Five major types of land form are identified in the highly generalized diagrammatic map (fig. 4): mountain highland, Fiordland massif, tilted blocks, hills and downs, and plains. Dominating the island's scenery and occupying a greater area than any other type of land form, the *mountain highland,* built of the schists, graywackes, and older rocks, extends almost throughout its length and, in some places, for more than half its width. The popular geographical cliché "backbone" has comparative validity only if one imagines a sinuous series of bare, knobby, disjointed, and loosely tied vertebrae. The graywacke areas are, in particular, "structureless" in the sense that there is no orderly system of "ranges" or "axes." Where these are described they are usually

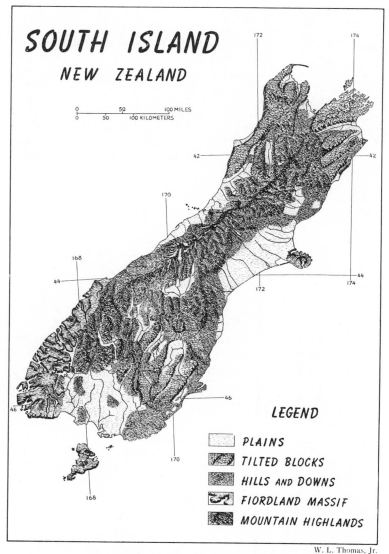

W. L. Thomas, Jr.

Fig. 4. South Island: Land-form areas.

Within the figure:

SOUTH ISLAND

NEW ZEALAND

0   50   100 MILES
0   50   100 KILOMETERS

LEGEND

PLAINS
TILTED BLOCKS
HILLS AND DOWNS
FIORDLAND MASSIF
MOUNTAIN HIGHLANDS

interfluves of haphazard trend. The greatest heights and the most striking evidence of deep-cutting mountain glaciation are in the stretch of a hundred and thirty miles between two relatively easy passes: Arthur's to the north linking tributaries of the Taramakau and the Waimakariri, and Haast to the south which connects the valley of the river of the same name with that of the southeast-flowing Makarora. Here lie the great ice fields from which spectacular valley glaciers cut down through the subtropical rain forest of the west coast almost to the sea. Above the ice, Mount Cook rears its magnificent twelve-thousand-foot peak to dominate the island. However, most of the highland elevations are rather below five thousand feet than above, and passes at between two thousand and five thousand feet are common if not always easily traversed. The highest peaks and, in general, the watershed lie much nearer to the west coast than to the east.

Glacial action has broadened many valleys within the mountain complex. In such a valley Samuel Butler made his homestead in his days of sheep-running on South Island and from it he drew his description of the approach to *Erewhon*. Many, too, are the lakes—Wakatipu, Wanaka, Hawea, Ohau, Pukaki, Tekapo, Rotoroa, and others (*see* end papers and fig. 15)—which are legacies of the overdeepening by valley glaciers or of the damming of drainage channels by piles of morainic debris. Some larger basins which are probably structural also exist, notably the Mackenzie country (fig. 5), its floor smoothed and filled by glacial gravels and occupied by a trio of great glacier-fed lakes.

Fiordland and Stewart Island have not been very thoroughly studied, but the rocks appear to be generally ancient and crystalline. The word *massif* is chosen to describe Fiordland not only because of its geomorphologic connotation of a mass of mountains, but also because of its literal French meaning of a solid block of masonry. The mass has been deeply gouged but there is little evidence of recent major folding or faulting movement. Here, in a region where contemporary precipitation often exceeds three hundred inches a year, the Pleistocene ice accumulations must have been enormous. The ice cap built up on an extensive, rolling, plateau-like surface, and the steep-sided fiords of the southwestern coast, resulted from deep ice-cutting followed by a rise in sea level as the major continental ice sheets the world over melted to release water to the oceans. Indeed the lakes on Fiordland's eastern margin are called "fresh-water fiords" by Jobberns [2] (fig. 6).

New Zealand Aerial Mapping Ltd.

FIG. 5. Bird's-eye view of the Mackenzie Country.

In Central Otago, and in much of Nelson and Marlborough, the structural interpretations suggest a succession of broken, *tilted blocks.* Some slope "regularly" with a sharp fault-scarp face and a gentle back slope, as that between the Wairau and Awatere Rivers. In a few cases, notably the horst between the Takaka and Motueka valleys, blocks have risen relative to neighboring areas with little tipping. The greatest variety in angle and direction of dip of adjacent blocks is found in the Otago region. The schistose scarp ridges are often high, sharp, and jagged, inviting such names as "Raggedy" and "Rough Ridge" (fig. 57). There is a structural resemblance to Nevada's basin-and-range country but Central Otago has a much larger proportion of its area in ranges; the basins are confined to rather narrow flats in the major valleys. Small as these valleys are, they had an important part in the drama of agricultural and pastoral invasion.

South of Central Otago, between it and the sea, lies the southern area of hills, valleys, and *plains* which Jobberns [2] describes as "a maturely dissected upland with residual hills and valley plains." There the most extensive lowlands, and those economically most useful to the agriculturists and graziers, are adjacent to the lower courses of the Taieri, Clutha, Mataura, and Oreti Rivers. Much larger than any of these, and the principal element in the low-

New Zealand Department of Internal Affairs

Fig. 6. Edge of the Fiordland plateau as seen from Lake Manapouri.

land east of the mountains, is the great plain of Canterbury. Its remarkably even coastline of over a hundred miles is interrupted only by Banks Peninsula. Tapering out along the sea at both northern and southern ends, it reaches its greatest breadth of forty miles just inland from the peninsula. The plain is built of coalescing gravel fans, and there is an almost imperceptible rounding up to the heights of the interfluves from the valleys of the mountain-born rivers which occupy the swales (fig. 7). The gravels are extremely porous and the covering soils thin (fig. 22). The great depth of ground water below the centers of the fans has had very important consequences in the utilization of the area.

The transition from mountain to plain is sometimes abrupt (fig. 7), sometimes gradual (fig. 8). In the latter case, the intervening areas, in the east as in the south, are termed *hill-and-down* country. This type of land form reaches the coast, with no intervening plain, east of the mouth of the Clutha, bordering the delta plain of the Waitaki on both sides, and again north of the outlet of the Waimakariri. In among the downs, hills, and low mountains are other plains or flats: the Cheviot, Hanmer, and Culverden basins of North Canterbury are examples. In the northeast the "plains" are discontinuous patches of river valleys and deltas between the tipped blocks. The Nelson plain proper is a narrow band around Tasman Bay, but it is often meant to include the low-lying gravelly Moutere Hills which form a small triangle southward with the true plain as its base.

On the west coast the "plains" are tiny patches interrupted by rocky headlands and backed by high and difficult mountain country as far south as the mouth of the Grey. The peculiar multi-level "plain" of Westland lies south of that river and extends for less than a hundred miles. There may once have been a relatively level or slightly rolling plateau surface at some height above the sea; perhaps the coast has since risen a good deal. The steep slopes of the western mountains and their present heavy precipitation suggest that a great load of detritus would have been available to build such a marginal plain. In this now elevated mass the short, swift, mountain rivers have since cut valleys with the same marked development of terraces which is so generally characteristic of the valleys of the island (fig. 9), leaving terrace remnants which are often more extensive than what is left of the

FIG. 7. The debouchement of the Rakaia River from mountain to plain.

New Zealand Aerial Mapping Ltd.

New Zealand Aerial Mapping Ltd.

Fig. 8. Delta plain of Waitaki River: Panorama of hill-and-dale transition between mountain and plain.

original surface. Progress north or south along the coastal margin is like nothing so much as the alternating ascent and descent of stairs. Even ignoring the tangle of the subtropical rain forest which covers it, this is far from easy country.

Most important of the minor land-form areas is Banks Peninsula. It is essentially a large volcanic island tied in with South Island relatively recently by the advance of the plains. Here, on a basement of rocks like those of the central mountain highland, two volcanoes built up flat cones perhaps as high as contemporary Egmont or Ruapehu on North Island. Figure 10 illustrates well the results of erosion in the subsequent enlargement of the central craters, the development of radial streams, the drowning of their mouths with the formation of bayhead flats, and the faceting of the inter-valley spurs by wave action.

The configuration of the land surface is an extremely important element of the island's geographic character. South Island has its plains, its downs, and its lower hills, and on these areas the major agricultural and pastoral production has taken place; yet, as a shepherd born in the Scottish highlands told this writer once with pride and fondness in his eyes, "There's nowhere ye can go in the island without there's a friendly mountain looking over ye're shoulder." At many times and to many men, however, the mountains were far from friendly.

The size, rugged relief, latitude, and isolated maritime location of South Island all affect the conditions of the air above it. With no considerable body of land nearer than Tasmania, each air mass which moves in over it must have been subjected to oceanic influences in its lower strata for considerable periods. The excessively high rainfall of the west coast, and the advanced rate of accumulation in the snow fields which feed the island's glaciers, are attributable to the universally moist and potentially unstable character of these strata. The significance of the slow oceanic drifts along each coast, with a general direction to the northeast, is not well established beyond a possible lowering of the mean air temperatures.

The oceanic aspects of the climate are, however, much obscured by the effects of the rugged relief. Not only do we have marked rain-shadow effects in the eastern lee of the mountains, but in the same locations moderately high temperature ranges occur, a characteristic usually associated with continentality. Above all, un-

FIG. 9. Terraces in a river valley of North Canterbury.

abc

New Zealand Aerial Mapping Ltd.

Fig. 10. Banks Peninsula from the air.

even terrain creates a sharply varied pattern of climates in limited contiguous areas, contributing to vivid local contrasts in habitat character. Despite this obvious limitation, generalizations must be made, but the implicit qualification should always be recognized.

Since each part of the earth's surface has a unique location, and the controls of climate are precisely repeated in no two places, it becomes a matter of some difficulty to identify "homoclimes" (areas of closely similar but not precisely duplicated climates) of South Island in other parts of the world. Yet there is no more useful way of suggesting the essential character of the regional climate. Although classifications of climate are legion, the system developed by Vladimir Köppen and his associates is both reasonably precise and widely understood, and is particularly useful for climatic comparisons. In South Island all stations with usable records fall within his *Cfb* type; translated from the arbitrary symbols, this indicates a climate of mild to moderately cold winters, warm but not hot summers, and a precipitation regime which has a limited month-to-month variability. Traditionally this is called a "West Coast Marine" climate, and the type areas of the climatologist include coastal northwestern Europe, the state of Washington in the United States, the British Columbia coast, and southernmost Chile. There are areas of the same classification, however, in the northeastern United States, the western Caucasus, northern Honshu, and southeastern Australia.

In a search for similar climatic areas, South Island should be divided along the line of the major watershed. Its excessively humid west coast (the *perhumid* of Thornthwaite's [4] early classification) has its only analog in Chile's southern archipelago. Washington and Oregon have too uneven a distribution of precipitation throughout the year, and the British Columbia littoral too great an annual temperature range, for either to be comparable. More acceptable homoclimes exist for the drier eastern slopes of South Island with their greater extremes of temperature, yet there, too, we can quickly eliminate many possibilities. The northern Appalachians have too great a temperature range, the Biscayan coasts too warm a summer, northern Honshu too severe a winter. Apart from Tasmania, and little-known parts of southern Patagonia, the most nearly comparable area in the world, climatically, with eastern occupied South Island is found in the British Isles. This has been a matter of very great significance to the importation of British people, plants, and animals.

At a much higher latitude than South Island, the United Kingdom and Eire experience days much longer in summer and much shorter in winter. A lower total of sun energy received there directly each year is, however, apparently balanced by the great, poleward-moving oceanic drift of the northeast Atlantic which carries relatively warm water past northwestern coastal Europe. The greatest differences between the climates of South Island and Great Britain seem to be the greater cloudiness and humidity of the latter.

Of the individual climatic elements, little can be said of air pressure in a brief and nontechnical discussion. Pressure fluctuates with the passage of air masses of different character over the island, the fluctuations being associated with differences in the character of each mass and of the "fronts" which form between them. Most rising of air, condensation, and precipitation are associated with these fronts, and general changes in air temperature, as well as pressure, with the transition from one mass * to another.

* Although new basic approaches to meteorological theory are now being widely and rapidly developed, the air-mass concept, implying fronts and zones of discontinuity where the lighter air rises over the denser, is thought to be adequate to the understanding of climatic processes in South Island in general outline.

F<small>IG</small>. 11. Two-story bridge over the lower Awatere River with a windbreak on the upper level.

Careful study of the data of wind direction reveals only an expectable variation from one place to another in an area of such highly broken surface, except for a more than haphazard tendency toward winds from the northwest. Mean velocities appear to be rather lower than in other areas of similar (*Cfb*) climate, a conclusion which contradicts a belief widespread in New Zealand and which is undoubtedly fostered by the existence of certain local wind "funnels" where rather high wind speeds may be reached (fig. 11). Attention should perhaps be called to the phenomenon of the "Nor'wester" of Canterbury, a desiccating wind, in nature comparable to the chinook of the Rocky Mountains or the *föhn* of the Alpine valleys, which blows hot, dry, and sometimes with considerable force across the plains.

The accompanying isothermal maps (figs. 12 and 13) do not show *actual* air temperatures, but rather these reduced to sea-level equivalents. Maps of actual isotherms would be most complicated, due to the normal decrease in temperature of 3 degrees F. for each thousand feet of increased elevation in an air mass, and would become, essentially, relief maps indicating little about the character of the atmosphere. The maps do indicate that the

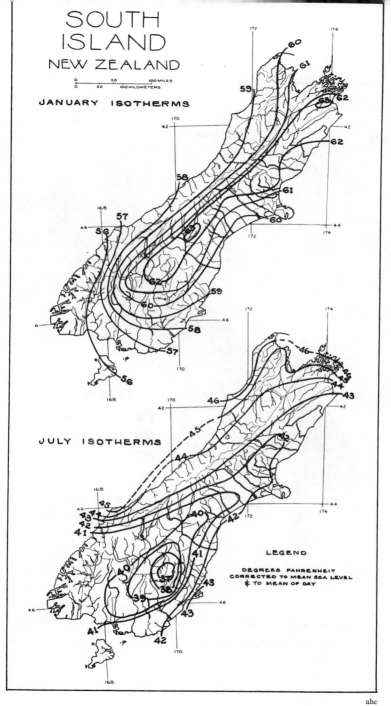

SOUTH
ISLAND
NEW ZEALAND

JANUARY ISOTHERMS

JULY ISOTHERMS

LEGEND

DEGREES FAHRENHEIT
CORRECTED TO MEAN SEA LEVEL
& TO MEAN OF DAY

ahc

FIGS. 12 AND 13. January and July isotherms.

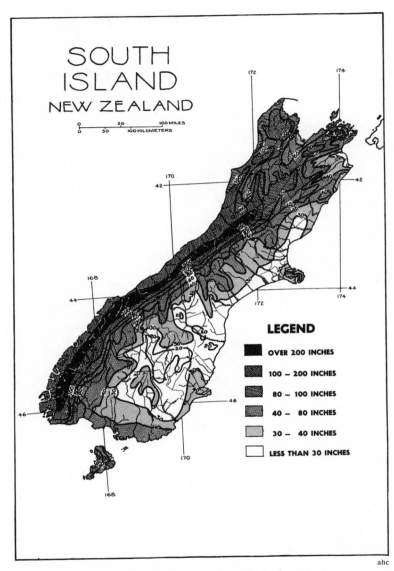

Fig. 14. South Island: Distribution of precipitation.

interior and east coast are much warmer in summer (January) and that the southeast, particularly Central Otago, is decidedly the coldest place in winter (July).

It is important to both plants and animals that the critical winter isotherm of 43 degrees F., and the somewhat less significant summer isotherm of 60 degrees F. both run through the center of the island. The latter isotherm (more precisely that of 57 degrees F. for the three summer months) has long been considered the critical limiting isotherm for the growing of most commercial varieties of wheat. The importance of the 43 degrees F. isotherm lies in the fact that if the average temperature of the coldest month in any place falls below 43 degrees F., a very large number of useful perennials which have no protective devices against frost cannot be grown. It is true that the *actual* isotherms, rather than those shown, would be the significant lines in these respects, but the actual isotherms would almost coincide with the sea-level lines in the chief, low-lying. farming areas.

An examination of actual monthly means for the several stations indicates a very moderate regime with respect to both annual ranges and extremes of temperature. Except in a few interior stations, the actual mean of the coldest month is uniformly above 40 degrees F., and only one known station has a mean monthly winter temperature below freezing. Whereas July is the coldest month throughout the island, the highest temperatures are unlikely to occur before late January, and February is the warmest month in several places. Similar "lags" are noticeable in Norway, for example, and indeed are characteristic of maritime places in general. The warmest station on the island has a summer mean of less than 65 degrees F., yet the lowest summer mean is above 54 degrees F. Briefly, the winters tend to be mild with occasional frosts, and the summers relatively cool.

If the precipitation map (fig. 14) and the relief map (fig. 1) are compared (bearing in mind that most air masses approach the island from the west), intensification of precipitation to the windward of the mountains, with a compensating diminution in their lee, is plainly to be seen. Yearly averages of above two hundred inches, and individual records of nearly four hundred inches on the westerly mountain slopes, are contrasted with long-term means of less than fifteen inches in Central Otago. In 1940 two stations in Otago land district, distant but fifty miles airline, one on the upper western slopes of the watershed and the other pocketed behind the mountains to the east, had a difference in yearly total of 367 inches. Nevertheless most of the occupied area of the island does not experience such extremes; for the most part the variation is between twenty-five and sixty inches. This moderate rainfall is remarkably evenly distributed through the year, the only significant peaks being recorded in the low-rainfall areas of Central Otago in the summer, when convectional precipitation is at its peak. The much greater relative humidity with lower winter temperatures and the consequently increased "efficiency" of the winter precipitation give rise to the general popular impression that winter is much the rainiest season. It certainly is, without question, the *wettest* part of the year. In general, year-to-year variability is thought not to be high, the greatest deficiencies from the normal, as well as the greatest excesses, occurring in the highest rainfall belt. The contemporary irrigation of large areas of Canterbury plains' land is only to a minor degree a matter of insurance; primarily it is designed to step up the total ground water available to grass roots in the summer months. Intensity of precipitation is lower than over most of the United States; the rain tends to fall relatively gently and over long periods. It must be remarked again that in rainfall, as in temperature, South Island offered superb conditions for the pasture grasses of northwestern Europe.

Hail is widely known but is sporadic in occurrence. Snow, on the other hand, does blanket the southern mountain areas for many months at a time (fig. 15) and is perpetual on the alpine ice fields. Around the coast and at lower elevations, however, it is relatively infrequent in occurrence. A ground cover of snow is almost unknown in the lowlands and valleys of Nelson and Marlborough, or anywhere along the west coast except at great elevations. It may lie for a few days at a time on the upper levels of Banks Peninsula, but rarely is it found in Christchurch for more than a day or two each winter, and in many years the city is entirely free from snow. At elevations of five hundred to a thousand feet in Canterbury, and down to sea level in southern Otago and Southland, the snow cover persists for a week to a fortnight each winter. The effect on the occupying culture is only considerable at "high country" sheep stations between one thousand and three thousand feet, where deep snows may cause appreciable stock losses.

Other climatic characteristics will be indicated below in connection with their immediate significance to land utilization. We

ahc

FIG. 15. Early spring snow scene on Lake Tekapo in
the Mackenzie basin.

may simply indicate here that the frost-free period is generally
long, fogs and thunderstorms are relatively rare, and the total of
hours of sunshine is greater than that experienced in England and
less than that common to the east-central United States. Of
greatest importance to the settlers from the British Isles was the
fact that, despite a much rougher land surface and a totally unfamiliar natural vegetation, they found conditions of climate with
which they were generally familiar; the added boon of a greater
amount of sunshine seemed to make man, beast, and plant thrive
better in the new land. Above all, the climate did not demand
houses built to withstand excessive heat or cold, nor was expensive
winter stabling of stock required. The climatic contrasts which
required an immediate technologic revolution in matters of shelter,
clothing, and methods of land use for British and French settlers
in northeastern North America were absent in New Zealand—
notably so in South Island, the cradle of development for the
Dominion's patterns and practices of land use

PRE-EUROPEAN VEGETATION

The sketch map of primitive vegetation (fig. 16) [5] illustrates
the dominance on the island of two major plant associations,
"rain forest" and "tussock" grassland. Both of these, but par-

SOUTH
ISLAND
NEW ZEALAND

LEGEND

■ RAIN FOREST

▓ SCRUB AND BRUSH

▓ SWAMP AND BOG.

▓ TUSSOCK GRASSLAND

□ ALPINE   INCLUDING ICE
            AND BARE TOPS

ahc

FIG. 16. South Island: Distribution of pre-European vegetation.

ticularly the latter, tended locally to blend into associations of scrub and brush. In areas of poor drainage, more usually on the grassland margins, a bog-swamp type occurred.

The grassland occupied the greatest area and upon its resources of food for sheep the first major pattern of land use by the European invaders was established. The tussock cover was remarkably uniform in character. Its general aspect was of a sea of waving bunch grasses dotted sparsely with shrubs or the New Zealand cabbage trees. The tussocks were not contiguous at the roots, as in a turf, but their spreading leaves gave an almost continuous shade cover to the areas not occupied by their bases. In these spaces, enjoying a microclimate far different from that of the exposed tussocks, was a substratum of grasses, herbs, and sedges. The tussocks, largely of the genera *Poa* and *Festuca*, were distinctly xerophytic, and the leaves became hard, tough, and generally unpalatable by midseason. The botanical constitution of the understory of vegetation was certainly much more varied. It is, however, very difficult to reconstruct its character previous to the invasion. It was upon this more succulent lower subassociation that the exotic animals chiefly grazed. A century of attack by the incisors or hooves of the animals (not forgetting the rabbits) and by burning (*see* p. 197) must have greatly changed its character. To this change the deterioration of the sheltering tus-

FIG. 17. Much deteriorated tussock grassland in the middle Awatere valley.

ahc

socks (fig. 17), which once commonly attained heights of two to three feet, must have contributed directly in alteration of the microclimate. Scattered through the grassland were individuals of far different type: a fine-branching small-leaved myrtle, the Maori "manuka" (*Leptospermum* spp.); the "wild Irishman" (*Discaria toumatou*) best known as "matagari," English corruption of the Maori "tumatakaru"; the savanna-like "Spaniard" (*Aciphylla* and *Celmisia* spp.), a spear-grass; occasional clumps of the famous, sword-leaved "New Zealand flax" (*Phormium tenax*), or the "toe-toe" (*Arundo conspicua*) so similar to pampas grass (*Gynerium argenteum*) in appearance as to be indistinguishable from it at a glance; or, finally, an occasional lone "cabbage tree" (*Cordyline australis*), its straight, rough, naked trunk crowned with a tuft of green palm-like leaves at twenty to thirty feet above the ground (fig. 18).

Fᴵɢ. 18. Native *Phormium tenax* ("flax"), *Cordyline australis* ("cabbage tree"), and the invading *Pinus radiata* (Monterey pine) in association along a South Island roadside.

ahc

The existence of such a grassland, so uniform in character over at least twenty-five thousand square miles, in a region well on the moist side of Köppen's grassland boundary, is an anomaly to be compared with the grasslands of the Argentine Pampa or the "prairie peninsula" of North America. The dominance of xeromorphism in the tussocks is thought not to be consonant with the present climate. Suggested explanations * range from a geologically recent period of drought, through matters of edaphic constitution and the effect of the desiccating *föhn* winds, to possible cultural modification of a hypothetical precedent forest by the earliest Maori immigrants. Each suggestion so far advanced has been rather successfully challenged and the mystery remains. Complicating the problem is the successful acclimatization of planted exotic trees which now reproduce naturally in the grassland even under the driest conditions in Central Otago.

Cockayne, master botanist and plant ecologist of New Zealand, has ably defended his apparently daring designation of "rainforest" for the tree-growth which forms the second great association. Herewith is a summary of his meticulous description:

Trees are almost all evergreen and of many genera; some species develop large, plank-like buttresses at the base of the trunk; some species produce flowers on the naked stem or trunk; lianes and epiphytes are physiognomic; tree ferns and herbaceous ferns of many species abound; the forest floor is covered with filmy-ferns, mosses and liverworts; lichens and bryophytes hang everywhere; the undergrowth is extremely dense; the association has many stories—up to six; the growth is extremely luxuriant.[8]

This forest has been greatly altered over much of the area with extensive bush clearing, logging, and the depredations of large numbers of browsing Red deer, rooting porkers, and many other invading animals which have been loosed upon it during the last

---

* Schmieder [6] in discussing a similar problem in the Argentine Pampa, quotes Köppen on the *Cfb* climate, "It produces luxurious forests of high trees wherever tree growth is not restricted by excessive winds or adverse soil conditions" and there is general agreement as to the existence of a distinct anomaly. A leading contemporary New Zealand botanist, Allan [7] indicates that even forest plants tend strongly to "xeromorphic structure not in consonance with the present climate and habitats in which they are found." The most popular explanation for the two anomalous western hemisphere grasslands, firing by the native population for hunting purposes, seems to have little force in New Zealand. The moa could have been the only object of such hunts, and there is no evidence that the Maori so far departed from his usual conservational attitude toward the natural vegetation.

Charles Foweraker

FIG. 19. Rimu (*Dacrydium cupressinum*) dominating an altered stand
of the west coast subtropical rain forest.

century and a half. Enough examples of relatively undisturbed
cover remain, however, to allow even a casual visitor to quickly
verify the elegant description of the botanist (figs. 19 and 20).
The association was almost continuous from the Marlborough
Sounds, around the northern and western watersheds, and along

the southern coasts to the mouth of the Clutha River below Dunedin. It appeared as well on the middle slopes of some mountains of Central Otago, in isolated patches on hill and mountain slopes in South Canterbury, and in larger areas in North Canterbury, almost completely covering Banks Peninsula, and as a coastal strip at the foot of the Seaward Kaikoura Mountains of Marlborough.

Recent writers have been inclined to challenge the term rain forest for the more southerly subassociation which Cockayne called "subantarctic" in distinction to the more hygrophytic "subtropical" stands which fully justify the general description quoted above. Actually the two subtypes blend into one another so gradually that it is almost impossible to fix even approximate boundaries. Dominant in the "subtropical" were broad-leaved dicotyledonous evergreens of the yew family (*Taxaceae*) which are popularly lumped together as "podocarps," although they include *Dacrydium* as well as *Podocarpus* species. Intermingled were various hardwoods (*Metrosideros, Weinmannia, Belschmiedia,* and other genera), no less highly individualized than the

FIG. 20. Subtropical rain forest virtually undisturbed in the middle Buller valley.

ahc

pine-like softwoods, as well as tree ferns and lianas in profuse variety. In contrast, large areas of the "subantarctic" consisted of almost pure stands of the misnamed "antarctic beech" (*Nothofagus* spp.) with its small, round, hard, evergreen leaves and distinctly hard wood.

The minor association of scrub and heath, now so greatly extended by the destruction of the forest and grassland and the spread of the three most aggressive bushy exotics (gorse, broom, and blackberry), was formerly confined chiefly to river beds, hill gullies, and shady slopes within the tussock grassland. Manuka, matagari, and the poisonous tutu (*Coriaria arborea*) were among the chief constituent plants of the association. Around Tasman Bay a fairly extensive area of bracken fern (*Pteridium esculentum*) should be included in this group. Bog-and-swamp formations, more or less equivalent to German *niedermoor* or English fen, occurred in areas of high ground-water and around the shores of lakes and ponds. Largest of the areas with this cover was a wide bordering "collar" between Banks Peninsula and the Canterbury plains proper. Besides the ubiquitous *Phormium tenax*, raupo (*Typha angustifolia*), the New Zealand bulrush, was most typical in the wet lands.

The natural vegetation was a most significant part of the setting for the agricultural and pastoral invasion. On it sheep and cattle were pastured; in it rabbits, deer, wild pigs, and goats made their homes and wreaked their profoundly altering influences; from it the settlers drew their lumber, fence rails. and fuel.

PRE-EUROPEAN FAUNA

Apart from the relatively few rats and dogs which entered the islands with the arrival of the Maori, who in turn preceded the first Europeans by barely a thousand years, the indigenous animal life of the islands was notable chiefly for its birds. Small bats of two species were the only mammals, and of twenty species of reptiles, nineteen were small lizards of the skink or gecko families. The remaining saurian was that curious "living fossil," the tuatara (*Sphenedon punctatus*). It is thought that two species of frogs, New Zealand's only amphibians, were confined to North Island.

Members of the avifauna were thus free of natural enemies except from the insect world or from among themselves. A description of the rich general and specific variety of birds would require a ponderous catalogue. Honey-eating songbirds, hopping parrots, parakeets, hawks, owls, wood pigeon, quail, and a vast number of kinds of sea birds were reported by the early visitors. The penguin was the only flightless sea bird, but flightless land birds, like the penguin important only in the southern hemisphere, were found in abundance. The spectacular *Dinornithiformes* (various genera and species of moa), the greatest land birds of historic times, had been extinguished by the Maori before the arrival of the Europeans. Men, cats, dogs, and pigs quickly took a heavy toll of the remaining land-bound birds. Even the kiwi (*Apteryx* spp.), the national symbol, has almost disappeared. This peculiar individual, with an apparent fur in place of feathers and no outward sign of wings or tail, was described by Wallace as "the most unbird-like of living birds."

The fish, both of fresh and salt water, were of great variety, but there were few firm, fleshy merchantable types to vie with the salmon, cod, herring, sardine, or tuna of northern waters. Sea mammals, which were to prove strong economic magnets, were abundant along the shores and in the neighboring seas. The walrus was absent, but both the "eared" or "fur" seals (sea lions) and the "earless," "true," or "hair" seals (including the so-called sea leopards and sea elephants) were known. The fur seals disappeared earliest under intensive exploitation at the turn of the eighteenth century, but the others soon followed. Of the cetaceans, the "right" or "black" whale of the whalebone (*Mysticeti*) group, and the sperm, toothed, or cachalot whales (*Odontoceti*) were most important. The cows of the right whales came inshore along South Island for calving in early winter and were joined inshore by the males in spring, whereupon the whole group put out to sea for the summer. When near shore in the spring they were fairly easy prey and formed the attraction for the shore-whaling industry which first opened the island to settlement. The sperm whale was taken at sea, and bases for its hunting in New Zealand waters were more closely associated with North Island than with South Island.

SOILS [9]

Charles B. Kellogg, the distinguished soil scientist, once wrote that soil "is the final synthetic expression of the forces in the natural landscape working together." To begin with, there is a certain parent material, lying at a particular slope, in juxtaposition to a given set of regional land forms. The particular local climate will then develop certain drainage and erosional patterns and, together with these, will induce harmonious floral and faunal associations. Each of these local conditions and influences contributes to the local character of the soil which reflects them all. Since climate is perhaps the most pervasive factor, it has been possible to classify a limited number of major zonal, or climatic, soil groups over the world. These groups are described, of course, only in terms of mature soils where similar sets of basic factors have been in operation for a long period. Taking Siberia as an example, we may speak of its "chernozems" (a Russian name for deep, black, fertile soils of temperate grasslands which has been generally accepted) and be sure that our meaning will be understood by ecologists, agriculturists, and geographers in general. Also in Siberia we identify chestnut brown and brown steppe soils, sierozems or desert soils, with similar assurance of being generally comprehensible.

For New Zealand, and particularly for South Island, there are no such satisfactory descriptive devices available. This is partly because formal pedologic study has had so brief a history there, but fundamentally it is because the instability of the surface, both in steep areas of rapid erosion and in flat areas of continued deposition, has not, in general, allowed the particular local complexes of soil-forming processes to achieve their ultimate result of a mature soil.* The resulting immaturity has meant, among other things, great local variability and prevailing thinness.

The soil-forming process generally at work, however interrupted, is that of podsolization which occurs ordinarily in areas of high humidity, under a forest cover, and with moderate to cool summer temperatures. It involves the leaching and washing of clays and soluble compounds from upper to lower layers, and induces a degree of acidity which inhibits favorable bacterial action. Usually confined to forested areas, this process has apparently operated in South Island in many of the regions of tussock grassland as well. As a result, most of the few and limited mature soils, as well as most of the immature skeletal types, are quite acid. Certain areas have been studied in some detail, and these observations are confirmed by the examinations made of such di-

---

* The early stage of pedologic study in New Zealand and the peculiarity of the local conditions, suggests that any attempt to reproduce a map of soils, without detailed elaboration of the categories used, would be to little explanatory purpose.

ahc

FIG. 21. Supposed capping of loess on the limestone hills of
north Otago.

verse soils as: the swampy "pakihi" soils of Westland's multi-level
"plain," which have an impervious clay pan at some depth below
the surface; the peculiar soils developed on the loess-like deposits
which cap both the basalts of Banks Peninsula and the limestone
downs of north Otago (fig. 21); and the thin silt-loam veneer
which covers the gravels of the higher Canterbury plains (fig.
22). Only in some of the driest areas of Central Otago does there
appear to be any eventual prospect of the development of soils
comparable to those of grassland areas elsewhere in similar climates, that is, soils of depth, considerable humus content, of
neutral to basic reaction, and of inherent natural fertility.

A major difficulty in attempting to reconstruct the indigenous
character of the soils is the fact that they must have been profoundly altered over the last century by the invasion of alien flora
and fauna. To this change, fire, plows, stamping hooves, grinding

ahc

FIG. 22. An excavation (*top*) and a stony pasture (*bottom*) near May-field, Canterbury, illustrate thinness of soil on the higher Canterbury plains.

ahc

teeth, drainage ditches, artificial fertilizers, exotic grasses and clovers, crops, and weeds have all contributed. Much of the alteration has been in terms of "culturally accelerated" soil erosion (a term made popular in New Zealand by Cumberland [9]), which will be discussed further in a later chapter as an important corollary of the various phases of the invasion.

The soils were deficient in calcium, phosphorus, and nitrogen, although these deficiencies have been repaired over wide areas by top-dressing with lime and superphosphate or by the sowing of leguminous plants, with roots playing host to nitrogen-fixing bacteria, in the rotational grasslands. There is generally plenty of available potash, but other deficiences in the trace-element category (copper, cobalt, boron, etc.) have been held responsible for nutritional troubles in the flocks and herds.

Perhaps the most important point to make about South Island's soils is that they had no high level of natural fertility. Thin, acid, and low in humus, there was none of that deep reservoir of fertility, even in the grassland areas, which permitted unremitting cropping for decades in the states of Buenos Aires or Iowa, or in the province of Saskatchewan. With whatever other special blessings nature endowed South Island, fertility of soil was not among them.

II

THE PEOPLE

CHAPTER II

POLYNESIAN OCCUPATION AND EARLY
EUROPEAN CONTACTS

THE MAORI *

O ut of the islands we now call Indonesia, at some unknown period in the remote past, the Polynesian peoples came to the mid-Pacific.[1] Indefatigable voyagers and explorers, they penetrated the far reaches of the greatest of oceans but do not appear to have found New Zealand until the tenth century of the Christian era. The Polynesians who settled New Zealand, and are known today as the Maori,† have a well-established tradition that the first discovery of their islands was made by the famous Polynesian navigator, Kupe. Although other scouting expeditions fol-

* Unfortunately for the purposes of this study there is not very much data on which a Maori "geography" of South Island might be based, although there has been a good deal of significant publication concerned with the society and general economy of the Maori. The early omnibus scientists (Dieffenbach, Von Haast, Hector, and Colenso), the "splendid amateurs" (Percy Smith and Eldon Best), and contemporary scholars [Buck (Te Rangi Hiroa), Ernest Beaglehole, Firth, Kiesing, Ngata, Skinner, and Sutherland] have made their several valuable contributions to an understanding of the Maori without showing much curiosity about the habit-habitat relationships, and with little stress on the areal differentiation of Maori culture within the country.

† Maori was simply a Polynesian word meaning ordinary or usual, which was used to distinguish the resident Polynesians from the strange white men in New Zealand. There is little evidence to suppose that there was any Melanesian strain in the Maori, a hypothesis which has suggested to some students a pre-Polynesian population in New Zealand. Certainly the limited amount of archaeological work accomplished so far in New Zealand has disclosed artifacts of only undoubted Polynesian origin.

ahc

FIG. 23. Distribution of Maori in South Island about 1750.

lowed, it was not until the fourteenth century, only six hundred years ago, that a carefully planned colonizing expedition, the "Fleet" of Maori tradition, set out from central Polynesia for New Zealand. The reason generally given for this mass emigration is overpopulation and the resulting social discontent in the home islands (probably the Society group). For some reason yet inadequately explained, all contact of the Maori with other Polynesian groups seems to have ceased until after the arrival in 1769 of the earliest European visitor, Captain Cook, although Cook's Tahitian interpreter was able to speak easily with the Maori.

There is no satisfactory estimate of the size of the fourteenth-century migration and, indeed, rather wide disagreement as to the numbers present in both islands at the time of Cook's arrival. An estimate of fifty thousand in all, with less than ten thousand of these in South Island, would seem to accord best with the known facts.* The Maori in South Island were not only few in number but were also unevenly distributed (fig. 23). The limited archaeological work in location of settlement sites is not too helpful because of the roving nature of the Maori. Most permanent camps are believed to have been on or near the coasts, and from one-third to one-half of the island's population is thought to have been concentrated on the shores of Cook Strait, particularly in the Marlborough Sound area. Scattered camps (rather than settlements) were to be found along the eastern and southern coasts as far as Fiordland. The Maori frequently did move inland on hunting and gathering expeditions, and sometimes large parties reached Westland in search of the prized greenstone (New Zealand jade, a variety of nephrite). The cross-island trails and camp sites so far determined, however, yield no evidence of even semi-permanent occupation of the interior or the west coast. The largest permanent settlement in the eighteenth century, although it may have had a very short history, was at Kaiapoi just north of Banks Peninsula.

Elsdon Best remarks that "in pre-European times the Maori

* Buck [1] would suggest a higher figure; Skinner [2] a somewhat lower one. Duff [2] thought eight to ten thousand reasonable at the time of Cook's arrival, although these numbers diminished rapidly before the double onslaught of muskets and measles. Fenton [2] reports that less than twenty-five hundred were enumerated in South Island in 1858 (in a rather loosely organized census) and nearly half of these were in Marlborough or Nelson. Somewhat higher figures are suggested by Durward [2] for the southeast and by Dieffenbach [2] for the northeast in 1834 and 1840, respectively.

lived in much the same manner as did the neolithic folk of Britain, in communities, the size of which was controlled by the food supply." [3] Although we may postulate other "controls" on the size of the community, Maori culture is well termed "neolithic," lacking metals; also absent, however, were the wheel, pottery, and true weaving. In South Island the reasonably broad base of domesticated plants and animals of Polynesia had been narrowed by climatic exigencies and transport limitations to one plant, the sweet potato (Maori "kumara," *Ipomea batatas*). Other imported plants, including taro and paper mulberry, found their climatic limits not far south of the North Auckland peninsula of North Island. The domesticated dog and rat, both used for food, survived the canoe journey to New Zealand (as pigs and fowl apparently did not), but there is no evidence that they contributed much to the staple diet. Birds and fish supplied the major foods. There was but one general utility fiber, derived from the leaves of *Phormium tenax*, and from it most clothing and nets were made. Stone tools were simple, the basic implement being a stone adze which was morphologically a hoe but functionally an axe.

Some of the buildings, particularly those used for ceremonial purposes or storage, were large, substantial, ornately carved timber structures. Living quarters were simple but, when at least semipermanent, quite adequate. "Furniture" consisted solely of *Phormium* mats. Clothing was chiefly in the form of mats or kilts, again almost always of plaited *Phormium* fibers, and it was unsatisfactory for the damp and chilly winters of South Island. Cooking was done in a pit oven out of doors. Vessels were of hollowed wood or basketry. Food was not boiled but cooked by the worldwide hot-stone, steam-oven technique. Fire was kindled by a primitive fire plow, and food was prepared with shells or small bone, or stone scrapers.

Because the Maori had carried agriculture further poleward in the southern hemisphere than had any other human beings in pre-Columbian times (kumara were grown beyond 44 degrees south latitude on the Canterbury coast), and because the tuber was so important in North Island, its relative rôle as a staple food in South Island has been exaggerated. The climatic hazards of its culture on the island today suggest that it could not have been a real staple but was, rather, a welcome addition to the great variety of food which was caught or gathered. Most important of wild plants was the bracken fern, the roots of which were roasted, peeled, and eaten. It was sufficiently widespread to assure travel-ing Maori of a basic emergency food supply. Less important were the root and blanched heart (hence "cabbage tree") of *Cordyline australis*, the abundant pollen of the raupo (which was made into cakes), and many varieties of seaweed. Although the Maori relished birds' eggs and developed great skill in snaring birds themselves, primary reliance for food in South Island was upon the resources of sea, river, and lake. Not only eels and shellfish but a great variety of sea fish were taken, the latter most effec-tively by the use of canoes and nets. Some of the nets were very big and required a large group to manipulate them. Cook re-ported one net from North Island thirty feet in depth and nearly half a mile in length.

The Maori were among the most restless of primitive peoples and many of their frequent journeys around the country had little apparent economic motivation. By preference they traveled in canoes hollowed out of logs, in the handling of which they had developed some of their highest skills. There was a good deal of foot travel upgrade on inland trails, but these tended to parallel rivers, and the downstream trip was commonly made on rafts constructed of buoyant *Phormium* stalks. Trans-island trails tended to converge on Westland's Arahura valley where the prin-cipal supply of greenstone was located.

Students of Maori culture have found systems of land tenure the most tangled skein they have been called upon to unravel, and there is still little general agreement in this matter among the recognized authorities. It is probable that the basic conception was never "possession" in a contemporary sense, but rather "use." At any rate the claims to "use" were strongly enough voiced and each tribe (*iwi*) or sub-tribe (*hapu*) "held" its lands by a most complex system of "rights" obtained by inheritance, conquest, or in more devious ways. The "title" to every piece of land to which a tribe had ever laid claim seems to have remained valid in the eyes of its contemporary members. In fact, however, "title" was good only so long as any tribe or sub-tribe could maintain it by force. Claims had been extended over such large areas by fre-quent tribal migrations and almost continuous inter-tribal war-fare through the more than four centuries of occupation that there was, literally, no *system* of land tenure when the Europeans arrived.

As an introduction to the European peopling of the island, our interest in the Maori is perhaps primarily concerned with such deformation of regional character as they had achieved in four to five centuries, but there is too little evidence yet for any clear-cut statement. There is no very good reason to believe that they should be charged with any major alteration of the natural vegetation, although it remains a possibility that large areas of eastern South Island were changed by them from forest to grassland. The Maori indisputably extinguished the moa, and perhaps selective hunting changed the character of the avifauna in reducing the numbers of other flightless birds. The use of the soil in South Island was too limited in extent to assume any marked change in soil character. There were extremely few, and no significant, cultural elements in the general landscape as a result of Maori occupance: a few temporary fish weirs, the central buildings of the scattered settlements, some shallow canoe-canals among the distributaries of the lower Wairau—nothing more striking than these. Essentially the Maori are believed to have lived in harmony with the region and to have altered its pristine character little if at all. It is particularly important to remember that in South Island they were few, scattered, and peripheral.

EARLY EXPLORATION AND EUROPEAN CONTACTS [4]

It appears that a European first saw New Zealand when two ships under the command of Abel Janszoon Tasman sighted the west coast of South Island, perhaps just south of Hokitika, in 1642. Tasman was a practical and efficient seaman and his voyage was one of commercial exploration from Batavia for Governor Anton Van Diemen who was actively interested in finding new fields of exploitation for the already fabulous Dutch East India Company. Seventeenth-century science was, however, ably represented on the voyage by the geographer, Francoys Jacobzoon Visscher, whose writings (especially *Memoir Concerning the Discovery of the Southland* which according to Beaglehole [5] was produced in January 1642) and speculations may have prompted the venture.

Tasman skirted the west coast of South Island from his landfall to Golden Bay where an attempt to land a boat's crew ended in the killing of four men by the occupants of a Maori war canoe. Known as Massacre Bay, or as Tasman named it, *Moordenaer's* Bay, it was the effete taste of a recent generation that caused it to be renamed Golden Bay. Although Tasman tacked about in the wide western expanse of Cook Strait to the north, he missed the strait and mapped it as a bay. Tasman and Visscher then sailed up the west coast of North Island and on to discover the Tongan group,[6] although no member of the expedition set foot on New Zealand soil. Hocken, one of New Zealand's great early historians, aptly suggested that the Netherlanders be credited with a "descry" rather than a "discovery." [7]

To that part of the New Zealand coast which he saw, Visscher gave the name of *Staedte Landt*. Its possible extent and content excited the imagination of cartographers, explorers, and chancelleries for the next century and a third. In various imagined contours it appeared in productions of the Dutch schools of cartography and was copied thus into dozens of contemporary European atlases. Most spectacularly it was inlaid with a world map on the pavement of Amsterdam's new Town Hall in 1648. Few Europeans doubted that Tasman had indeed skirted the western shores of a vast continent in the southern Pacific, *Terra Australis incognita,* apparently confirming the earlier representations of Ortelius.

When the British Admiralty dispatched James Cook and his party in the bark *Endeavour* to observe the transit of Venus of June 3, 1768, at King George's Island (Tahiti) in the eastern Pacific, it gave him sealed orders to be opened and followed when that enterprise was concluded. These orders indicated that there still existed in Europe a conviction of the existence of a great southern continent despite lack of corroboration since Tasman's time. The legendary continent was now known as New Zealand; its presumed eastern extension off South America, when proved insular, had kept the name of Staten Land (now preserved in the name of Staten Island, off Tierra del Fuego).

The orders enjoined Cook to proceed southward "in order to make discovery of the continent above-mentioned, until you arrive in the latitude of 40°, unless you sooner fall in with it; but not having discovered it, or any evident signs of it, in that run you are to proceed in search of it between the latitude before mentioned and the latitude of 35°, until you discover it or fall in with . . . land discovered by Tasman and now called New Zealand." [8] The instructions continued in elaborate detail. Following them in his famous painstaking manner, Cook sighted the east coast of the North Island of New Zealand on October 7, 1769.

While Tasman was content with a "descry," Cook was intent on discovery and some exploration; quite probably he was concerned with the possibility of adding to the dominions of his sovereign. After three months spent in exploring the coasts of North Island, the bark finally swung around Cape Egmont from the north and into Tasman's "bay," sighting the north coast of South Island on January 15, 1770. On the following day the anchor was dropped in the lovely harborage of Ship's Cove near the mouth of Queen Charlotte Sound. The first Europeans set foot on South Island that day, and three weeks were spent in careening and scrubbing the bark and replenishing supplies.

Because of the ready availability of various reproductions, none of Cook's charts is given here,[9] but the accompanying map (fig. 24) shows his general course about South Island. On February 6 the *Endeavour* sailed through Cook Strait and proved the insularity of South Island by circumnavigating it, though without again putting a boat ashore. Contrary winds which kept the ship well offshore caused some curious inaccuracies in an otherwise remarkably careful chart of the coast (Banks Peninsula was rated an island and Stewart Island a peninsula). After sighting Farewell Spit again, Cook was off to New Holland and the homeward journey. He made several subsequent visits to Ship's Cove, and in 1772 rested in and charted Dusky Sound, one of the larger fiords at the southwestern extremity of the island. We are interested in these visits from the point of view of any cultural introductions which resulted from them. As for Cook himself, however, New Zealand was to figure in his plans only as a refreshing and refitting station en route to further Pacific voyages.

The vast publicity attending Cook's discoveries and the wide circulation of published accounts, together with the reports of the voyages of de Surville and Marion du Fresne, brought New Zealand to the attention of the world. The climate was described with particular favor and several schemes for colonization were tentatively launched; Benjamin Franklin was associated with one such plan as early as 1771. Yet permanent settlement was slow to develop. The experience of Marion du Fresne and a number of his crew, who were killed and eaten after landing on the North Auckland peninsula, added to the already unsavory reputation of the antipodean area in general in the popular European mind. This reputation had already a connotation of "convict settlements" engendered by the dumping of convicts at Botany Bay (near the

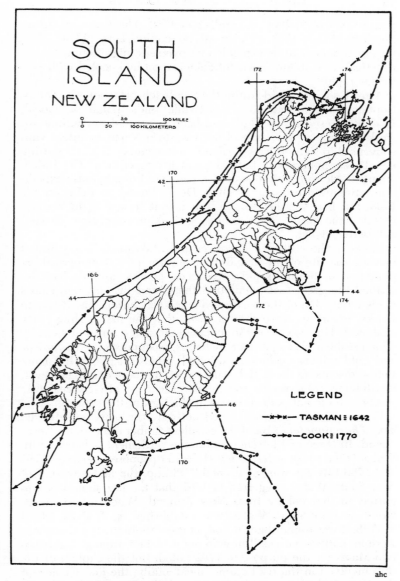

FIG. 24. Routes of the Tasman and Cook voyages of discovery.

present city of Sydney, Australia) in 1788. The European situation from 1770 to 1830, which needs no retelling here, did not allow for much energy to be expended on overseas migration; after the American Revolution, ardor for colonization had cooled with particular rapidity.

After Cook's tragic death in the Sandwich (Hawaiian) Islands, Captain George Vancouver, erstwhile midshipman on Cook's *Resolution* (second voyage), had been appointed to continue his work in mapping the coast of northwestern North America. Vancouver's ship sighted New Zealand on November 2, 1791, putting into Dusky Sound with both ships of his expedition. The Italian scientist, Alessandro Malaspina, in command of a Spanish expedition, attempted to make a call at Dusky Sound on February 25, 1793, but bad weather forced him to put to sea again without entering the fiord. These voyages served to make New Zealand still better known.

Between the visits of Vancouver and Malaspina, Dusky Sound became the site of the first European attempt at commercial exploitation of South Island's resources. Cook's journals had described the great seal population there, and his accurate charts made navigation of the narrow channels less hazardous. It was in Dusky Sound, in November of 1792, that the first sealing party anchored. This was to be the real beginning of a series of steps by which sealers, "flax" gatherers, whalers, pastoralists, agriculturists, and gold miners explored, exploited, and settled South Island. Before discussing the initial sealing party in more detail, however, it will be useful to review some general features of New Zealand's position in the antipodean world at the turn of the century.

Cook's journals had publicized not only the seals but also the flax (*Phormium tenax*) and the excellent timber of northern North Island. In three of the schemes for the settlement of New South Wales (then southeastern New Holland) proposed between 1783 and 1786 this flax was mentioned.[10] Phillip, the first governor of New South Wales, suggested in 1787 that the flax should be imported to that colony from New Zealand. When a settlement, based on New South Wales, was established on Norfolk Island in 1788, it was found that *Phormium* grew there too but that there were no natives with skill in working it. A first attempt to kidnap two Maori for the purpose in 1792 failed, but the captain of the ship involved in the try became, incidentally, the first whaler off the New Zealand coasts. It was a returning ship of Vancouver's expedition which finally succeeded in the abduction of Maori from New Zealand for this purpose. The search for timber began in 1794 with the visit of the brig *Fancy* to collect a load of flax and spars in the valley of the Thames River, to the east of the present site of Auckland; two more ships followed in 1801. The raw material for buildings, as well as that for canvas and rope, was in great demand across the Tasman Sea, the "white pine," or kahikatea, being the earliest timber exploited (the more famous thick-boled kauri did not become a staple until 1820).[11]

Also mainly associated with North Island, but important to the eventual southern settlements, was deep-sea whaling. The first recorded in Australasian waters, in 1791, was undertaken by a fleet of ten transports, some of which were ordinary whalers bound for the western coasts of the Americas after dumping their convict cargoes at Port Phillip (Melbourne). They were satisfied with the first month's fishing in the Tasman Sea, but then, feeling that the weather was becoming too difficult, they left for their original goal. Not until 1798, when rumor reported three Spanish cruisers off Cape Horn as a repercussion of the European war, did three more whalers appear. In the next half century they were followed by increasing numbers which divided their attentions between deep-sea and shore whaling, the latter of much the greater significance to South Island. McNab [12] reports these whalers to have been a cosmopolitan group, two of the eight ships recorded in 1805 having come from New Bedford, Massachusetts.

SEALING AND WHALING ACTIVITIES

The two decades following Cook's discovery and exploration had yielded little knowledge of the country inland from the coasts, but they had served to make these coasts well known. A steady intercourse with the Maori of North Island had begun for supplies, labor, and the gratification of sexual appetites. In the Bay of Islands on the North Auckland peninsula an unstable, rowdy settlement of Europeans grew up. Its reputation for lawlessness was to make the name of New Zealand synonymous with the outermost pale of civilization for many decades. To the south, European settlement was slower to be established and more directly concerned with the immediate economic problems of obtaining seals and whales.

A sealing vessel of 1792 which landed a party in Dusky Sound has already been mentioned. It was apparently the earliest occasion on which a group of Europeans spent so much time on South Island. When the men were picked up a year later, they had built a forty-foot boat (probably the first entirely constructed to European plans of Australasian timber) and had procured forty-five hundred sealskins. Thus was sealing—of such great significance to the subsequent invasion of peoples, plants, and animals—initiated in South Island. Important as it was, however, it was destined to last but little more than a quarter of a century; by 1830 it had virtually ceased on the shores of South Island proper.

In the last decade of the eighteenth century, the area about Bass Strait and the southern shores of Tasmania had been the great sealing grounds of Australasia. Bass himself, one of the most famous of the sealers, who visited Dusky Sound to secure timber, brought back fresh reports of the abundance of seals along New Zealand coasts. This contrasted with the depleted condition of the old grounds. Baudin, commander of the scientific expedition sponsored by Napoleon on the ship *Géographe et Naturaliste*, wrote, in 1802, from King's Island to Governor King of New South Wales:

There is every appearance that in a short time your fishermen will have drained the island of its resources by the fishery of the sea-wolf and the sea-elephant. Both will soon abandon their resorts to you if time be not allowed them to recruit their numbers which have been much diminished by the destructive war carried on against them. They are becoming scarce already and if you do not issue an order you will soon hear that they have entirely disappeared.[13]

No effective heed was given to Baudin's conservational broadside; with this decimation of the quarry in Australian waters, Bass himself led the shift to New Zealand in 1803 (although he and his ship were lost on the first voyage), when one small schooner of thirty-one tons spent three months sealing at Dusky.[14] In 1804 an English whaler, the *Scorpion*, visited Dusky en route to Port Jackson and secured some skins there.[15] In the same year an American whaler first recorded the existence of Foveaux Strait. Advertisements in the *Sydney Gazette* on April 14 and April 21, 1805, speak of vessels frequenting, or occasionally touching at, Dusky Sound and its vicinity (fig. 25). These, it may be suspected, refer to sealers visiting occasionally and whalers regularly, the latter for refreshment.

Sealing by colonial ships based upon Port Jackson had to con-

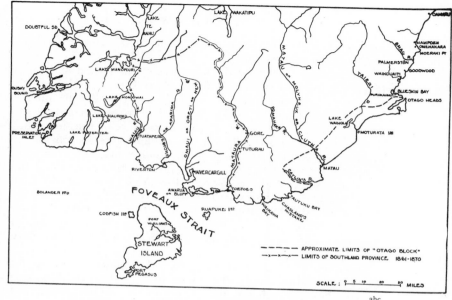

ahc

FIG. 25. Map of South Island's southern shores.

tend with the repressive measures devised by the still powerful
mercantilist groups at "home," particularly in the periods from
1795 to 1801 and from 1805 to 1808; [*] by the end of the second
period, sealing had begun the shift from South Island proper
to Stewart Island and the various antarctic islands (Antipodes,
Bounty, Campbell, Auckland, Macquarie, etc.), most of which
were officially named by 1810. The second decade of the nineteenth century marked the height of the sealing industry in what
were called "New Zealand" waters, and seventy to eighty thousand skins were secured there each year selling in the Sydney

---

[*] New Zealand coastal fishing for whales and seals was placed under the control
of the East India Company by the Board of Trade in 1795, and activity was very
limited as to both whaling and sealing until the war dangers off the American coasts
in 1798 (possibility of apprehension by Spanish men-o'-war) caused the restrictions
to be temporarily lifted. In 1801 the whole southern ocean was opened to fishing,
provided that vessels concerned in such activity turned over their logs and journals
to the Court and Directors of the East India Company.

From 1805 to 1808 navigation of colonial vessels south of 43 degrees 49 minutes
south latitude was forbidden altogether, though it is thought that some colonial
vessels continued to operate in the area, and there was much activity off South
Island by American sealers in these years. Further, in 1810, a duty of twenty pounds
a ton was levied on all oil produced in Australasian waters by colonial vessels.
(See *Historical Records of New South Wales,* vol. v.)

market at fifteen shillings each,[16] but these must have been largely taken to the south.[17]

The primary reason for the shortness of the period of interest of sealers in the Foveaux Strait area (as had been the case in the Bass Strait region earlier) was the rapid decline in number of seals there. Up until 1825 at least, a few sealskins continued to be recorded among mixed cargoes derived from the area, thus precluding any opportunity for the remaining seals—too few to be objects of sealing *per se*—to recruit their ranks. When Captain Benjamin Morell of the American schooner *Antarctic* visited the Auckland Islands and the Snares in the late eighteen-twenties, he could not find one seal on those formerly prolific grounds.[18] In the twenties the decreasing number of sealers became altogether based on Australian ports, as British and American ships joined the rush to the South Shetland Islands following their discovery in 1819.

The mention of traders calling for other cargoes suggests interest in the area beyond the taking of seals. One of these was the continuing search for "flax" (*Phormium*) by the official and mercantile interests of New South Wales. Attempts to rely upon a combination of "imported" Maori labor and Norfolk Island fiber had failed. In 1813 one of the many syndicates formed for the purpose of increasing this supply of raw material for cordage and canvas explored the area around Foveaux Strait very thoroughly. The report of this journey by one Williams, a Sydney rope-maker attached to the expedition as an expert, is most informative.[19] From a base on Stewart Island, now called Port Williams, he crossed to Bluff and penetrated some distance into the Southland plain. He found that the local Maori were growing large crops of white potatoes, which not only formed their own staple food but also gave them a surplus for trade with visiting ships.

The actual evidence of other visits is spotty. In 1808 two ships from New South Wales, the *Pegasus* and the *Governor Bligh*, had officially recorded the insularity of Stewart Island, and in 1809 the *Pegasus* (Mr. Stewart first officer and navigator) returned with the report that "The coasts of Stewart Island were explored by the ship *Pegasus* (Capt. S. Chase) in 1809. The island was then uninhabited, abounding in wood . . . containing several excellent harbours and runs of the finest water. . ."[20] The *Pegasus* then sailed up the east coast of South Island and first recorded the peninsularity of Banks "Island." The *Sydney Gazette* of March 12, 1809, reported that a sealing party abandoned on an islet west of Stewart Island had spent four years in the area, but after the report of Williams' visit in 1813, a period of thirteen years has left scant record.

Then in 1826, William Stewart, late of the *Pegasus* and apparently acting for an English syndicate, directed his attention to the island which bore his name. He first visited the Bay of Islands in North Auckland peninsula. Kororareka on this bay had maintained the reputation for disorderliness established early in the century. A rough, lively, enterprising, undisciplined assemblage of white men, Maori, and half-castes, including ship deserters and convicts, had established a lawless community there. From this motley group, Stewart recruited some Europeans, including two sawyers and two shipwrights. He brought them to Stewart Island and established them at Port Pegasus on the southeast coast to start a small timber and shipbuilding yard. They were shortly visited by two ships sent out by the New Zealand Company of 1825 which were en route to the Bay of Islands. From this trip, leaving his employees on the island, Stewart returned to New South Wales with but four hundred and sixty sealskins and a ton and a half of prepared flax—a very poor cargo. As the project looked increasingly unprofitable, it was abandoned, although the little community thus established on Stewart Island struggled on for some years.

In this fashion did the southern shores become known to sealers, traders, and the officialdom of New South Wales; though little is recorded, a good deal of intercourse with the southern Maori is almost certain to have occurred as ships took seals, refreshed, or traded. Moreover the nature of sealing had required that gangs be left for varying periods of time to conduct the sealing and be picked up later with their catch. Some fought the Maori, some traded with them, some lived with them; in all, the southern shores obtained potatoes, half-caste children, and some rather devastating European diseases, along with some useful metal goods and varied new techniques.

There are at least two good reasons for presenting at such length this rather laboriously culled story of the earliest contacts of Europeans with South Island. In the first place, there has been little emphasis on the degree to which seamen out of Port Jackson were familiar with the shores of South Island in the earliest part of the nineteenth century, and this study will stress the importance of the area's cultural inheritance from the New South Wales. In the second place, Australian knowledge of South Island was largely confined to the cool and rainy southern shores. Half Moon Bay on Stewart Island has some sixty inches of rain distributed over two hundred and twenty-nine days a year; there are many days as well which are cloudy without actual rain. Over the region as a whole the rainfall averages between fifty and one hundred fifty inches a year and is just as evenly spread. Not only does the rain seem virtually perpetual but there are few windier parts of New Zealand than the Foveaux Strait area, a circumstance which created serious navigation hazards resulting in a series of shipwrecks during this period.* Such conditions of climate seemed to be unsuitable for agriculture and sheep-running, and the difficulties of preparing flax due to the unavailability of wood (for heating water) in the areas where flax could be found, discouraged the development of the flax industry. There seemed to be little in this unfriendly coastal environment to encourage permanent settlement.[21]

On the very heels of the departing sealers, however, there came a new group of entrepreneurs who were destined to have a much greater impact on the future cultural life of the island. Shore whaling, developing out of the deep-sea whaling and concentrating on the oil-rich right whale, sprang up rapidly all along the eastern and southern coasts. In autumn the great lumbering cows came into the sheltered bays from the open ocean to deliver their young and were easily taken. Much more elaborate equipment was required than for sealing, and the whaling crews often stayed on the island over the off-season. Permanent houses were built, gardens were started, livestock was imported and, in effect, the first permanent settlements were established at scattered points from the Marlborough Sounds, through Banks and Otago Peninsulas and around the coast, to Preservation Inlet in Fiordland. In a great many ways the sudden appearance of these permanent or semipermanent settlements depended on inheritance from the sealers. Two staples of European diet, pork and potatoes, were now available from practically all of the Maori camps, and little food had to be imported. The Maori had spent a half a century growing more and

---

* One much publicized wreck was that of the *Elizabeth Henrietta*, a flax trader, wrecked on Ruapuke Island, northeast of Stewart Island in 1823, though this vessel was later refloated and returned to Australia with a cargo.

more accustomed to European visits and ways, and becoming more and more dependent upon European goods. This technologic dependence on things obtainable only by trade or labor assured the new settlements of food, laborers, and a minimum of danger from attack.

The earliest sea whaling had been largely sponsored by merchants of Sydney and Hobart Town. Later, English, American, French, Portuguese, and Dutch whalers joined the colonial ships. Even when the shore-whaling establishments were set up, European ships, sometimes by the dozen, anchored in the same bays and competed for the same quarry. But it is of the greatest importance that, except for a very few Americans, only Australians (including Tasmanians) operated from the land. With whaling as with sealing, the predominant influence of the rough-and-ready community across the Tasman Sea was maintained. Largely neither agricultural nor pastoral in origin, that group had in many ways, by trial and error and inventiveness, developed a host of techniques of land use which, while almost entirely based on British domesticated plants and animals, were often considerably different in character from the methods of the mother country. To the South Island of New Zealand they brought what skills they had, and new inventiveness in a still newer environment adapted and changed these once more. It is saying almost too little rather than too much to assert that South Island's agricultural and pastoral development owes a great debt to Australian experience; it is a fact that will bear repeating a number of times.

Detailed word-pictures of the whaling period on South Island shores appear in many of the earliest descriptions by eye witnesses from the late thirties and early forties.[22] Two scientific expeditions of some importance had visited the coasts of South Island between 1820 and 1830. On May 28, 1820, Captain Bellinghausen, the Russian scientific explorer, visited Queen Charlotte Sound; more important from the point of view of information left, was Dumont D'Urville's visit in 1827.[23] Shore whaling started almost simultaneously in the northeastern and southwestern sounds areas, which have harbors superior to the rest of the island. The first station known was on Tory Channel in the Marlborough Sounds in 1827; another, at Preservation Inlet, followed in 1829; still others soon appeared at different points. In a communication of the Governor of New South Wales (Sydney Record Office), dated April 6, 1832, the writer says, "I made strict inquiries as to European settlement in the South. The mate of the schooner in which I sailed to New Zealand had formerly lived for two years in the South Island and had frequently visited the fine bays as far south as Foveaux Strait for the purpose of buying flax and pork. He told me there were Europeans located all along the coast, and that their numbers were rapidly increasing." [24]

It will be most convenient to treat each area separately, and we may arbitrarily begin in the northeast. The first station, organized by a Sydney man, John Guard, was at Te Awaiti ("Tar White" according to whaling vernacular of the time), where his men lived with their concubinous Maori housekeepers. When the whaling season was over, they continued on in houses of their own construction or moved in with the villages to which their women belonged. Often they spent the summer hunting pigs, raising potatoes, or gathering flax for trading purposes. The area around Cook Strait (fig. 26) was still one of great unsettlement among the Maori however, being a focal point of inter-island warfare and a "shatter zone" for groups driven out of North Island. Guard's establishment was nearly destroyed by a marauding Maori band in 1828 and he moved to Kakapo Bay in Port Underwood. Others followed, and in 1830 there were five vessels in Port Underwood: four from Port Jackson and one from Hobart Town.

Guard's first stations were not equipped to save oil but managed to survive with the sale of bone alone. The first cargo of oil that can be identified as coming from South Island reached Sydney on February 3, 1830, although the proportion, if any, from the shore fishery is not known. It consisted of two tuns (420 Imperial, that is, 504 American or British wine measure gallons).* Most of the early cargoes from New Zealand were mixed and most vessels collecting oil and bone for Sydney loaded as well timber, flax, pigs, potatoes, curios (such as mummified, tattooed heads), and even pickled eels and oysters. In return the list of trade goods for the Maori reads very much like the inventory of an early Hudson Bay Company's outpost. [25] A great stimulus to shore whaling and general trade after 1830 was the fact that New Zealand produce was considered in Hobart Town, as previously in Sydney, to be colonial produce and hence free from colonial duty.

---

* The wine measure, applicable to virtually all commodities shipped in casks, was used for oil. Apparently the coopers made few, if any, casks to the Imperial measurements. The American gallon is a unit of the wine measure and, approximately, 1 wine gallon = 1 American gallon = $\frac{5}{6}$ Imperial gallon.

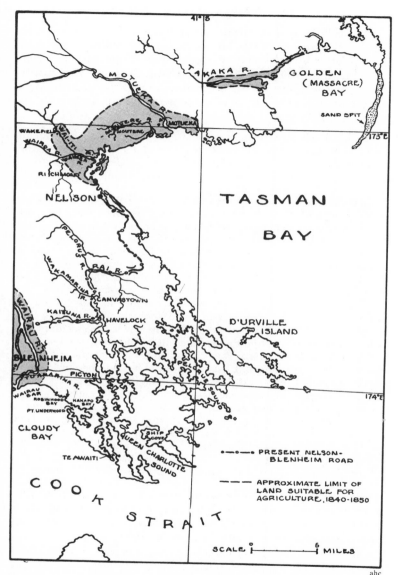

FIG. 26. Map of Cook Strait, Tasman Bay, and the Marlborough areas.

The technique of the fishing is of interest, for it indicates the type and degree of activity on the shores. The following is quoted from a letter by John Bell of Sydney, one of the earliest settlers in Cook Strait, who had resided at Cloudy Bay for seven months during the whaling season of 1840. Although his description is of activity a decade after the beginning, methods apparently did not vary much:

The black whales visit the bays and coasts of New Zealand for the purpose of calving and begin to set in about the beginning of April and remain until about the middle of September. Cloudy Bay in Cooks Straits is considered the best situation on account of its excellent harbour. . .

. . . If the fishing is to be carried on by a shore party, the try-pots and huts are erected on the beach and the vessel which brought the party down is either employed in collecting flax along the coast, or returns to Sydney, and is sent down again at the end of the season to bring them up with what oil they may have caught. The boats are sent out at daylight every morning, and when they are so fortunate as to kill a fish it is towed ashore and flinched and boiled up upon the beach. When the fishing is carried on in a vessel, the blubber is boiled out in try-pots erected on the deck as in a sperm-whaler. From its being tried out immediately after the fish is caught the oil is much purer and free from the rancid smell of the Greenland oil. . . . The whales are seldom killed nearer than two miles from the harbour, and sometimes seven or eight, and if the tide or wind is against them it is a most laborious business to tow such a huge animal. I have known the boats to be out for four-teen hours pulling, except at short intervals, all the time. Indeed, killing the fish is a trifle in comparison with getting it in, our party alone lost seven large fish after they were killed last season. The depth of water in the bays where the whales are killed is from 14 to 20 fathoms. They yield from 2 to 13 tuns of oil, those killed by my party last season aver-aged 6 tuns of oil each and three and a half hundredweight of bone. The cows are generally larger and produce more oil than the bulls, but they get thin toward the end of the season from supporting the calves. . . .[26]

Altogether in 1830, five vessels carried about six hundred tuns of oil and about thirty tons of bone from the region of Cook Strait to Sydney. Successful operations, principally in Cloudy Bay and Port Underwood, continued through the thirties. In 1834, when the first American ship at Cloudy Bay was reported, new Maori depredations all but wiped out the shore establishments. It was in this year that John Bell established himself with assorted do-mestic animals on Mana Island in Cook Strait and became a supplier of food to the whalers. In 1835 the shore stations were re-established and the number of ships continued to increase. In 1836 and 1837 whaling in Cloudy Bay was at its peak. Besides numerous shore establishments based on the Australian colonies, there were, in 1836, eighteen vessels at anchor in Port Underwood, including thirteen American, two English, two Tasmanian, and one French. For 1837, eighteen American ships were listed, and in that year more than 38,554 barrels of oil, valued at over a hundred and thirty thousand pounds were shipped from New Zealand to New England.[27]

The decline of whaling in Cloudy Bay occurred as more southerly locations, later in beginning, reached their peak years. The decrease in oil production is reflected in the more general character of cargoes arriving in Sydney from the Cook Strait area, and the activities of merchants and shipmasters from Sydney became more those of general traders than of whalers. The end of the decade was thus like its beginning, in that pigs, pork, lard, planks, flax, potatoes, and salted fish became of greater value than oil and bone combined, testifying to the spread of pigs and potatoes among the Maori and whalers who lived with them in the summers, as well as to the dissemination of European techniques of preparing and preserving produce.

The whaling declined here, as subsequently elsewhere, from the same causes which had brought sealing to an end. It was said that the decline at Port Underwood was in part due to a scarcity of whale food and to the unfavorable winds of the winter season, which, dominantly southerly or southeasterly, often forced ships and boats alike into the shelter of the port. Fundamentally, however, it was but another case of shortsighted exploitation destroying its own resource, more spectacular than the depletion of vegetation and soil which followed the agricultural and pastoral invasion, but of the same sorry variety. It is of interest that, as in similar cases in other parts of the world, the few voices lifted to question such a vicious mutilation of areal character by the destruction of resources which were potentially permanent, should have passed quite unheeded. New Zealand was still beyond any enforceable law, still the happy hunting ground of those who had had no roots in the past of the area and felt no interest in its future. With so many vessels, each having several boats, the competition became extremely keen, and the result was the virtual extermination of whale cows and calves. Seventy or eighty boats are known

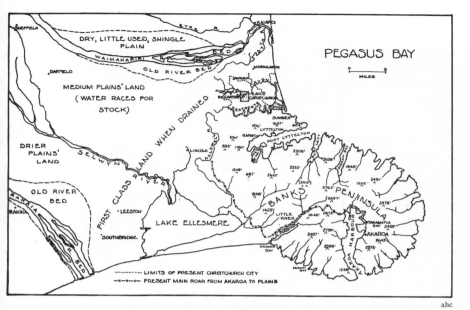

ahc

FIG. 27. Map of area of pioneer settlements in Canterbury.

to have put out after a single whale.[28] While a very little whaling continued after the thirties (indeed a whaling station at Te Awaiti is still, over a century later, in intermittent operation), whaling became of little significance in itself. Its important contributions had been made in the nucleus of European settlement which remained, and in the contacts of European with Maori, which prepared the way for the first organized immigration from the British Isles to the Cook Strait area in the early eighteen-forties.

There was whaling at a great number of places south of Cloudy Bay as well. At Kaikoura it was never very important before 1840, but the establishment of shore whaling in the bays of Banks Peninsula was of great antecedent importance to the opening up of the Canterbury plains to agricultural and pastoral settlement. We do not know just when the magnificent facilities of Banks Peninsula for the refreshment of ships first became known to sealing, whaling, or trading vessels. It seems probable that if Cook had not been blown offshore when nearby, he might have visited it; it is a reasonable speculation, too, that the subsequent publicity might have made it a frequently visited area (fig. 27). It was Captain Chase of the *Pegasus* who first, officially, reported its peninsular character and its sheltering and refreshment possibilities in the twenties. Some rather vague references to visits of ships occur from time to time; one tells of an overland journey from what is now Port Lyttelton harbor to the Maori *pa* at Kaiapoi in 1831.[29] The first project for actual agricultural or pastoral settlement here seems to have occurred in the same year, 1831. One of the many Sydney firms engaged in the New Zealand trade was that of Messrs. Cooper and Levy, in whose honor their agent, Captain Wiseman, named the two principal western harbors of the peninsula Port Cooper (now Port Lyttelton) and Port Levy. They had apparently, in 1830 or before, made some sort of land transaction with the Maori.[30] However, their first shipment of supplies with which to start a permanent agricultural center together with the title to the land was lost at sea with their ship, the *Industry,* off Stewart Island in 1831.*

In the Canterbury Museum at Christchurch is the log of the master of a whaler who began operations around Banks Peninsula in the years between 1835 and 1837. This *Piraki Log*[31] does not make it clear when the writer, one Hempleman, first started operations in Peraki (or Piraki) Bay; McNab believes that they got underway in 1837 with Hempleman, his wife, and eighteen hands forming the first European community in the area.[32] At the same time overseas vessels were whaling in and around the bays, at least twelve American and five British ships making Port Cooper their temporary headquarters in 1836. By 1839 not only had more ships (including many formerly at Cloudy Bay) been anchoring in the bays, but other stations were being established at Ikirangi, Ohahoa, and Island Bays. Possibly one hundred Europeans were in this year residents of the peninsula, mostly at whaling stations. Peraki had twenty-five, Ikirangi thirty-one, and Ohahoa twenty-four. Meanwhile, W. B. Rhodes (a sea captain and associate of the Sydney firm of Cooper and Holt—successors to Cooper and Levy) had become interested in the exploitation of the peninsula by trade and pastoral farming as well as by whaling. On November 10, his manager, Green, landed with Australian cattle at Red House Bay, near the mouth of Akaroa Harbour. With him were his wife and possibly two other men. At this period two adventurers, Angus and Clough, were also living at the head of Akaroa Har-

---

* The evidence here is in part contradictory and probably also in part legendary, but something corresponding to these events seems to have occurred.

bour, and Weller Brothers of Sydney had two coopers making casks at Port Levy.[33]

In April, 1840, a Sydney firm landed six men, two women, and a child at Ohahoa Bay.[34] They were to begin an agricultural settlement on the plains and they eventually settled on the upper Avon at what is now Riccarton, a suburb of Christchurch. With great labor they cleared thirty acres of *Phormium* and tussock, dug it, and planted it to oats. Though they harvested this crop and stacked it, it was nearly destroyed by rats (reputedly Maori rats but as likely Norway greys, which must have begun a rapid penetration of the island, probably from the notoriously rat-ridden whaling ships). This loss, together with fear of the shallow bar of the Avon and of the Maori at Kaiapoi, led them to abandon the project after eight months. They had demonstrated, however, that agriculture on the plains was entirely feasible. Their clearing of thirty acres should have provided ample evidence of the superior suitability for agriculture of the heavier plains lands, as compared with the bush country of North Island or northeastern South Island of which they might have managed to clear an acre or two in the same time. There is reason to suppose that this experience was kept unpublicized by the promoters who hoped to obtain large tracts of land at a small price.

Meanwhile the first organized European immigration to South Island was taking place in the peninsula, and it came from France not England. The rivalry of British and French interests in the southwest Pacific area during this period will be touched upon later in this chapter. There seems to have been one suggestion that the area might be developed as a French counterpart to the Botany Bay penal settlements, and a difference of opinion in England as to whether New Zealand would be harmed or benefited by receiving French political prisoners.[35] In any event a French whaling captain, Langlois, had effected a deed with some Maori at Port Cooper for (as he thought or claimed) the greater part of Banks Peninsula in 1838.[36] Upon his return to France, and after a good deal of government lobbying, he promoted a company for whaling and settlement in the peninsula area. The chief stockholders were merchants of Nantes and Bordeaux, whence it derived the name *Nanto-Bordelaise Cie.* It was then decided to send out a whaling ship under Langlois with an initial contingent of settlers to complete and extend his original land purchase, to establish an agricultural community, and to prosecute the whaling.

This company found it no easier to secure settlers than did the New Zealand Company, which was canvassing at the same time in England, but there were plenty of poverty-stricken people in the French towns and countryside and the promotional propaganda of the company appealed to some sixty-five of them. The terms included free transportation, seventeen months free rations from the date of leaving France, and five acres of land per adult man in the settlement area, provided it was cleared and worked within five years. The company further undertook to transport back to France, free of charge, emigrants "if they had been persuaded in error either about the salubrity of the climate or about the fertility of the soil." [37]

Eventually the sixty-five emigrants were embarked. Among them was one *vigneron* from the Department of the Jura who had experienced three poor vintages in a row. He had decided to emigrate to Martinique, but upon arriving at Rochefort and finding that sailings to the West Indies were closed for the hurricane season, he engaged to join the company with his family. There were, also, carpenters, gardeners, stonemasons, a banker, and a miner, as well as various undifferentiated laborers. [38] Six of the colonists were German-speaking, although their precise origin cannot be traced.

In the interests of protecting the settlement, and especially perhaps the French whalers in these waters which had made Banks Peninsula their chief center of operations, [39] the French Government decided to send out under Captain Lavaud, *l'Aube,* a corvette of thirty-two guns. Lavaud's instructions apparently ordered the policing of the settlement and the hoisting of the French flag at Akaroa. [40] Earlier in the same year (1840) the British representatives and the tribal chiefs signed the Treaty of Waitangi, and British sovereignty over New Zealand was proclaimed. On August 10 the British vessel *Britomart* arrived at Akaroa and the next day the Union Jack was hoisted at Green's Point. It is reasonable to suspect that Lavaud expected this British declaration of sovereignty and, acting on instructions to avoid trouble, deliberately planned that his arrival (August 15) postdate that of the British. At any rate, although he did not immediately recognize British authority, he did work with the British officials.

Langlois' *Le Comte de Paris* arrived with the emigrants on the seventeenth. Two children had died almost at the end of the

voyage and fifty-seven French and six German settlers finally
disembarked (thirty men, eleven women, and twenty-two children). After some further negotiations with the Maori, the laying
out of sections and building of houses began. The first season was
so advanced by the time some patches had been cleared that only
potatoes were planted. A scarcity of land for the five-acre lots
caused the Germans to move over to the first bay north of Akaroa
township, which was promptly dubbed German Bay, a name it
retained until the emotional fever of the First World War caused
it to be changed to Takamatua Bay.[41] Subsequent reports of
government surveyors, and other official or semiofficial visitors
(Felton Mathew in 1841, Captain Mein Smith in 1842, and Captain Wakefield, Mr. Tuckett, and Dr. Monro in 1844), reveal the
slow progress of the inhabitants. Without capital to acquire more
land or animals, they were compelled to depend on a kind of
subsistence horticulture and the sparing assistance of the *Nanto-
Bordelaise Cie.* or French naval vessels, of which there was always
at least one in the vicinity until the end of the decade (although
the dual control of French naval and British civil authorities
ended in 1843 and British sovereignty was recognized by the
French government before 1850).

What happened to the majority of the French immigrants is
still a mystery. Some remained in the area and a dozen or more
French names persist around Akaroa today. Some of the families
received an offer to move to Tahiti and Marquesas, but while the
bald statements that they either did or did not do so are frequent,
there appears to be no conclusive evidence one way or the other.
A resident of Akaroa, writing in the *Lyttelton Times* of November
18, 1854, gives a perhaps unwarrantedly gloomy picture of the
end of this first and only French settlement on South Island; some
of his conclusions certainly are open to doubt:

The French settlers built pretty houses, planted vineyards and flower
gardens, and lived chiefly upon the expenditure of the government
establishment, assisted by whaling vessels frequenting the harbour.
Akaroa was a large restaurant for the South Sea whalers. Whaling was
profitable; money flew about freely [this is contrary to any other
record], and the restaurateurs made little fortunes without the necessity
of engaging in any particular agricultural industry. But times changed.
The French government, finding their political views defeated, with-
drew their support from the place. The *Nanto-Bordelaise Cie.* transferred its interest to other lands. The whales deserted the coast; the

whaling stations were abandoned to the rats; and the whaling ships ceased to frequent the harbour. No more money came to Akaroa. There was no extent of cultivated land, no market for produce, no articles of export. Some of the settlers returned to France, some died, others went to the diggings, none came to supply their place. Those who remained behind, having no motive for exertion, lived quietly on their means [perhaps one or two families did, but the record in general was one of poverty]; houses became deserted, rotten, ruined; the land was allowed to go out of cultivation; the fences disappeared piecemeal; the roads cut by the French government became choked with shrubs and fallen trees, the timber bridges over the creeks rotted unheeded, and so completely did the *laissez aller* system prevail amongst all the parties concerned, that even the fine *magasin*, or store, built by the French and now used by the government as a Post Office and Customs House, had been allowed to fall into a ruinous state of decay.

An historical geographer must emphasize more the French immigrants' lack of the skills necessary for success in a new country, the lack of level land, the difficulty of clearing the bush, the lack of money to buy, and the lack of interest in the husbandry of domestic animals. Some details of their experience in both animal and plant husbandry are given in parts III and IV of this volume. The British settlers were to find that the most profitable activity in the new settlements on South Island was the production of dairy products, draft animals, and wool. Opportunities for such enterprises were, under the circumstances described, largely denied to the French. If this has been a rather full account of the failure of a colonization attempt which grew directly out of the shore whaling activities, it is precisely because of its whaling antecedents, and because of its failure, that it is included here. This study is an interpretation of the history of land use, and we can have few valid judgments as to why settlement in South Island took the particular course it did unless we know something of possibilities alternative to those exploited by the later permanent colonists.

Economically, whaling was of great significance around Banks Peninsula in the years 1838 to 1848. Yet today, beyond a few rusting try-pots, and the contributions which the whalers made to the deforestation of the peninsula, little evidence of the whaling era can be found in the area. On the other hand, the small band of French have left some lasting impressions. The town of Akaroa itself, with its twelve-meter-wide streets, and lots extending to low water (a practice completely foreign to British usage), with its French street names, with shuttered windows, sharp gables, and relic grapevines on its older houses, retains a distinctly French atmosphere. Seen from the top of the first spur to the north in the afternoon sunlight, it has the aspect of a small Provençal town. Only closer inspection reveals English gardens, brightly painted corrugated iron roofs instead of tiles, and English legends above the little hotels and shops.

Interesting as these beginnings in Cloudy Bay and Banks Peninsula are, settlements further south may have been more important. The first was at Preservation Inlet, the most southerly of the southwestern fiords.[42] This started about 1828, initially perhaps as a station for procuring flax or timber. It continued until 1836 at least, averaging about a hundred and fifty tuns of oil per season and the usual five tons of bone for each hundred tuns of oil. According to Williams' claims before the Land Claims Commissioners of 1842,[43] he had erected there in 1830 a dwelling house, a store, six houses for whaling crews, and a boat shed for sixteen boats (although Shortland[44] tells us that the maximum number of boats operating from Preservation was four). In 1832, the same year that John Guard claimed to have "bought" Kakapo (that is, the land around the Port Underwood station) for a hundred pounds' worth of trade goods, Williams claims to have purchased the land from northward of Dusky Sound to the south bend of Preservation Inlet for sixty muskets.[45] This would have been a high price, as Fiordland apparently had a greater population in Williams' day than it has had at any time since (Bradshaw[46] reports twenty-three people and two goats in 1887; in 1941 the record shows twenty people and no livestock). Incidentally the claims of Williams and Guard, if true, represent the earliest conveyances of land to Europeans from natives in South Island.

Local Maori contributed potatoes and flax to the settlements and the trading ships, and supplied an important element of the necessary labor force. Decline of native population with the onslaught of exotic diseases was thus immediately detrimental to the success of the stations. Clarke[47] mentions several epidemics of measles and one of smallpox; the actual journals of the stations record one epidemic which was almost certainly measles, and one of influenza, in 1834. It must be re-emphasized that the Maori population was concentrated near the coast, though "concentrated" may be a poor word for such mobile groups. Certainly after 1830 there seems to have been no settlements further inland than Tuturau (just below Mataura on the river of the same name) and near Lake Waihola on the Taieri plain.[48]

In any event, whether because of fewer whales, fewer Maori, falling markets, or bad management, the Preservation station changed hands in 1834, being taken over by Johnny Jones of Sydney, who was destined to be the greatest entrepreneur on the southern coasts in this period. In a real sense this aggressive businessman deserves as much credit as the "founder of Otago" as do any of the leaders of the Presbyterian settlement at Otago harbor in the late forties. McNab [49] has unearthed the following letter from Jones in reply to a request by Major Gibb, collector of customs at Sydney, relative to New Zealand statistics:

Sir,   Sydney, 24 March 1836

According to your request I beg to transmit you the following information relative to my Establishment at New Zealand. I have 39 men employed in the Fishery which I have carried on for the last 12 months and procured 125 tuns of oil none of which has been exported by me.

I also beg to state that the late Geo. Bunn was in possession of the said Establishment for about six years and procured upwards of 500 tuns of oil during that period.

> I have the honour to be, Sir
> Your obedient Servant,
> John Jones.

Other settlements, in a number of which Jones was interested, existed in the decade between 1835 and 1840 at several points along the southern coast. Some lasted but a season; some were maintained through most of the period. The localities included the mouth of the Omaui (or Oreti) River (now Invercargill), Awarua (Bluff Harbour), Toetoes (at the mouth of the Mataura River), Tautuki Bay, and close to the mouth of the Matau (Clutha) River.

With the station on Moturata Island at the mouth of the Taieri River, the name of Jones' chief competitor, the firm of Weller Brothers of Sydney, appears. It had a station there from 1839 to 1841, but its main interest was in the whaling activities at Otakou (now Otago Heads near the mouth of Otago harbor) and nearby

Purakaunui (better known today as Blueskin Bay). Otakou was in many ways the best base for shore whaling south of Cloudy Bay and had received attention from passing whalers since 1831, in which year Weller Brothers sent their first ship from Sydney to Otago. The outgoing and return cargoes of this vessel show that the earliest interest was as strong in trade as in whaling. The cargoes were [50] outgoing—"6 cases muskets, 62 bbl. gunpowder, 1 case axes, 5 casks beef, 1 case whaling gear, 1 case whaling line, 2 iron boilers, 1 pipe gin, 2 puncheons rum, and 5 kegs tobacco and stores"; return—"100 spars, 10,649 ft. planks, 1,200 trennails, ½ ton flax." The station was burned to the ground in 1832 but in 1833 a more elaborate establishment with a full complement of whaling hands was set up. The cargo sent out in 1833 [51] suggests less concern with Maori trade and more for the serious business of whaling. Going to South Island were: flour, beef, sugar, salt, butter, vinegar, pickles, woolen slops and cotton, tar, pitch, lime, two thousand bricks for the try-works, a hundred and sixty tuns (empty), other casks, brandy and rum. There were four boats engaged the first year; the return cargo, possibly all from this station, included a hundred and thirty tuns of oil, seven tons of whale bone, one ton of flax, eight tons of potatoes, and one cask of seal skins.

In the first years at Otago Heads, the labor force was about half Maori, though their numbers declined in the late thirties for reasons suggested above. The new settlement lived in a constant state of alarm from raids of the Maori with their new muskets and ammunition. Moreover, after 1835, a decline in production set in as more visiting ships anchored in the area for the season. An attempt by the seamen to combine to raise wages (currently three shillings per day with provisions) as the labor supply diminished was rigorously denied by shipowners.[52] Despite the difficulties, however, Otago was receiving very favorable publicity in Australia. The following excerpt [53] is from a letter in the *Australian,* dated January 20, 1837:

... The whaling season commences at Otago the latter end of March, during which whales are in abundance throughout the bay, and often caught within the harbour. In the vicinity the flax plant grows luxuriantly and the fibre is of good quality. Esculents [presumably pork and potatoes] are abundant and obtainable at very low price. Various species of timber grow at, and in the neighborhood of Otago which may be purchased from the natives at an extraordinary low price.

Jones took over a station at Waikouaiti, north of Otago Heads, in 1838, which had been started the previous year; he continued it until 1843 with the usual record of great initial success and rapidly declining returns. Meantime, in 1837, he had established a new station at Moeraki and was now doing a larger business than the Wellers. Before a committee of the Legislative Council of New South Wales, on July 6, 1839, the following evidence was given:

Jones had 280 men employed at 7 stations: Preservation (1), Jacob's River (1), Bluff (3), Waikouaiti (1), and Moeraki (1). Six of the stations had 32 men each and one had 42 men. He had sent cattle to his stations "recently." A block of land had been "purchased" from the Maoris for each station, running up from the beach and five to ten miles wide in each case. The Wellers had the Otago Heads station, and the short-lived auxiliary station at the Taieri mouth, and claimed to have purchased some four hundred thousand acres, including one block of 36 square miles, from the Maori.

This evidence, coming at a time when every trader from New South Wales was attempting to establish the greatest possible validity to land claims in New Zealand, is of course suspect. Auxiliary evidence and other contemporary sources tend, however, to support the claims in general, if not in particular. In 1840 Jones further attempted to consolidate his position and his claims by sending a party of thirty-two people, including ten married couples and eleven children, with twenty head of cattle to establish an agricultural settlement at Waikouaiti. The settlers came from New South Wales and included some recent English and Welsh immigrants to the colony. Some little preliminary agricultural effort appears to have preceded this venture in 1838, when a small farm is reported at Matanaka, two miles up the Waikouaiti River from its mouth.

J. Hughes, of Sydney, ran a station at Onekakara, near Moeraki, from 1836 to 1843.[54] Hughes was also an agricultural and pastoral pioneer. He had been employed by the Wellers at Otago Heads as a "headsman," that is, commander, of a whaleboat. This station had the usual history of miscegenation and its resulting bevy of half-caste children. Besides pigs and goats which soon ran wild, cattle, sheep, and domesticated plants were introduced. Apparently there was a whaling station at Timaru, too, for a short time from 1836 to 1839.[55] Certainly Shortland refers to a location at Hine-te-Kura, a short distance from Timaru where "a few years before, there had been a whaling establishment. Many forlorn-looking huts were still standing there; which, with casks, rusty iron hoops, and decaying ropes, lying about in all directions, told a tale of the waste and destruction that so often fall on a bankrupt's property." [56]

The shore whalers were all recruited in Sydney, which center also supplied the capital and management of the stations. The people who came and stayed seem, from their names, to have represented the blend of Cockney and Irish which dominated the population of New South Wales before the gold rushes. Perhaps ships' deserters figured most largely among the white whaling hands, and there would have been the greatest opportunity to desert from non-British ships. As the shipping in whale fishing was dominantly from northeastern American ports in the last part of the decade, we may suppose, without proof, that some of the earliest white settlers of South Island were of New England origin.

In 1834, a hundred English ships, a hundred colonial ships, two hundred and seventy-three American ships, and fifteen French ships were engaged on the South Seas fishing grounds. [57] American whalers had been known in southern New Zealand waters before 1834, but that was the year in which the first American ship, the *Erie* out of Newport, took up bay whaling on South Island. She was reported at Cloudy Bay June 3, 1834, and reached Newport, Rhode Island, June 11, 1835, with two hundred barrels of "sperm" and eighteen hundred barrels of "black" oil. We can find no evidence as to how much of this cargo originated from the fishing in Cloudy Bay, as of course the sperm oil obviously did not. This voyage with many others led to increasing publicity for New Zealand in New England. The following advertisement appeared in the New Bedford *Mercury* July 20, 1835, and is illustrative of American contacts:

Letter Bags
Ship, *Samuel Robertson*, McKenzie, for South
Atlantic Ocean and New Zealand, August 5th

By 1836, twenty vessels, representing many of the leading whaling ports of New England, were present in South Island bays. New Bedford sent five, Fairhaven five, Nantucket two, Newport two, Warren two, and Newburyport, Poughkeepsie, Bristol, and St. John (N.B.) one each. Thirteen were at Cloudy that season and three at Banks Peninsula. The numbers of American ships fluctuated from year to year. The greatest fleet, thirty-seven ships, visited South Island bays in 1839, but the number then rapidly declined. Even if we eliminate desertions to shore whaling, which, nevertheless, seem probable, the possibility of cultural introductions from New England to the little communities was great.

The French ships tended to concentrate more around Banks Peninsula and were never as numerous. The first recorded French whaler, the *Mississippi*, seems to have appeared off Cloudy Bay in 1836. In 1838 there were fifteen ships in all. The French sailors were more frequent deserters than the Americans, or so Lavaud of *l'Aube* testified in one communication to his ministry of marine.[58] Their lays were much smaller than those of the American and British colonial sailors despite a government subsidy of four pounds per tun to French vessels, and a price in France for oil nearly double that in New England.[59] We do not hear, however, of any remaining for any length of time, and we have not even suspected French origins, attributable to French whaling activity, outside of Akaroa.

Before proceeding to the more orderly and numerically more important later accretions of population, a brief summary of some eyewitness accounts as to details of the settlements themselves may be useful.[60] The largest communities between 1838 and 1840 were at Te Awaiti on Tory Channel, and around Port Underwood off Cloudy Bay. Here lived a cosmopolitan group which, apart from Australian colonials, was chiefly composed of deserters from American, British, French, and occasional Portuguese, Dutch, Danish, or German (Bremen) ships. Te Awaiti was, according to Jerningham Wakefield, who visited it in 1839, the most considerable "town" in South Island, with a population of two hundred forty adults, of whom forty were Europeans, and twenty-five half-caste, as well as many more full-blood, Maori children. Some quotations from Wakefield [61] will be sufficient to indicate the physical nature of the town:

There were about twenty houses... the walls generally constructed of wattled supplejack, called *kareao,* filled in with clay; the roof thatched with reeds; and a large unsightly chimney at one of the ends, constructed of either the same materials as the walls, or of stone heaped together by rude masonry. Barrett's ["head man" at Te Awaiti in 1840] house... was a very superior edifice built of sawn timber, floored and lined inside, and sheltered in front by an ample veranda.

Though it was Sunday, to Wakefield's dismay:

A large gang were busy at the try works. . . . large iron boilers with furnaces beneath. Into these the blubber is put, being cut into lumps about two feet square. The residue is called *scrag* and serves to feed the fires. The oil is then run into coolers, and finally into casks ready for shipping. The men were unshaven and uncombed, and their clothes covered with dirt and oil. . . . they reminded me, as they stoked the furnaces, and stirred the boiling oil, of Retzsch's grim imagination of the forge in the forest, in his outline illustrations of Schiller's ballad of Fridolin. . . . the stench of the carcases and scraps of whale flesh lying about on the beach was intolerable.

The settlements to the south of Te Awaiti in Cloudy Bay were all grouped around Port Underwood. At Robin Hood Bay there was a large Maori *pa*, but no settlement. Ocean Bay had two stations with about thirty Europeans and some hundred Maori. At Kakapo Bay, John Guard, the pioneer, lived with his wife and his children, the first of all-European blood born on South Island; here there lived also six other Europeans, together with an assortment of Maori. In the same bay a Dutchman, James Wynen, kept a store and with him lived his Maori wife and several other natives. Tomkins Bay boasted two stations, six Europeans, and thirty Maori. On the east side of the bay lived one Captain Daugherty with his Irish-Canadian wife, and a Portuguese, John Madeira, who kept a miserably equipped station near the southern headland. One of the whalers in Ocean Bay, a Captain Blenkinsopp, having supposedly bought a large tract of land in the Wairau valley, lost the "deed" by a mortgage to one Unwin of Sydney. The latter sent four men with a herd of cattle to Ocean Bay in April 1840. When the Maori refused to allow them to drive the cattle inland, they were instead driven over to the Sounds, whence they ran wild, spread into the Wairau, and became a real nuisance in the early days of the pastoral penetration of that area.[62] There were many domestic animals and gardens about the settlement.

There is no need to further describe the Banks Peninsula settlements. At Otago Heads, D'Urville[63] reports finding (in his 1840 visit) about a dozen European cottages with gardens full of vegetables, potatoes, lettuce, turnips, and flowers. Two of the cottages were rum shops. Captain Mein Smith[64] reported twenty white men and no women there. In 1844 Tuckett[64] reported a European population of about a hundred at Waikouaiti, though not all of the original ten families of agriculturists brought over by Jones in 1840 still remained. The stations of the extreme south did not achieve either the numbers of population or the permanence of these centers.[65]

Such, then, was the state of settlement in South Island in 1840. Whaling activities have been discussed in detail with deliberate purpose. The people of New Zealand are still, on the whole, very self-consciously British and delight in the title "Britain of the South" for their island country. When New Zealand's centenary was celebrated in 1940 it was a very real fact that their New Zealand had begun in 1840. In that year the imperial government officially assumed sovereignty over the territory, and the first considerable body of settlers arrived directly from the British Isles. With no wish to slow the tide of this sentiment it must be insisted that such a viewpoint has obscured the importance of earlier contacts and settlement, for in 1840 South Island alone had several hundred European residents dotted along the eastern and southern coasts from Cook Strait to Fiordland, some of whom had lived there for a considerable period. Plants and animals had been imported and solid experience in land use had been gained. The experiences of organized settlement after 1840 can be understood adequately only against the background of the previous sixty years of exploration and exploitation.

CHAPTER III

THE FLOW OF SETTLEMENT AFTER 1840

Despite the evidence of continuing and increasing movement of men and skills from the Australian colonies to New Zealand, both before and after 1840, interest in the origin of the earliest organized settlements has been concentrated too closely upon the British Isles. It is essential that we be familiar as well with contemporary circumstances across the Tasman Sea. From 1788 until the eighteen-thirties New South Wales remained primarily, although of course not exclusively, a settlement of deported convicts, former convicts, and their descendants. Van Diemen's Land (Tasmania) had a similar history for the period. O'Brien's thorough and stimulating studies [1] of British social problems in the late eighteenth and early nineteenth centuries, particularly in relation to poverty and penology, provide an excellent background for an understanding of the process by which the hopeless urban pauper-criminals were transported first to the American colonies and then, after a lapse of some years, to the new antipodean possessions. [2] More important, these studies also give us a picture of the essential character of the people themselves from whom a significant proportion of South Island's early population must have been drawn.

It is true that among the few free settlers there were many very industrious merchants, traders, agriculturists, and pastoralists. Even by 1830 large quantities of Australian wool were competing on the British market with the German wools (chiefly

Saxon and Silesian). Within another twenty years Australasia was to become much the largest supplier of wool to the British market, and the demand for Australasian wools was to continue strong for twenty years after 1850, even though the general price of wool declined in the fifties. Moreover commerce was growing; the activities of merchants from Sydney and the newer Hobart Town in Van Diemen's Land along the New Zealand shores have already been discussed. But in the late eighteen-twenties the majority of the population was composed of convict deportees, many of whom had achieved a free status, and their descendants, popularly known as "currency lads." New deportees continued to arrive, in fairly large numbers in the thirties, until deportation was discontinued in 1841. There were many settlers of some considerable social and economic status, but even among the non-convict immigrants, the proportion of urban poor appears to have been very large.

The period in which we must have most interest in New South Wales is that from the early eighteen-twenties until the early fifties when the first gold rushes began. This was an era of continuing social distress and political ferment in England, as it was on the European continent nearby. The unfortunate results of the continuing enclosures and the new industrialism on rural and urban social life had been apparent long before the French Revolution. The inadequacies of the poor laws combined with these fundamental troubles had created hopeless penological conditions when transportation to the North American colonies was cut off, and inadequate jails were crowded to saturation with those whom the administrators of the law classed as criminals. This is no place to discuss the laws themselves, the actual social conditions, or the hopeless dilemma of both the small ruling clique and the great mass of poverty-stricken people it governed. The immediate problem of getting the jails and hulks cleared, so that the punishments which the law provided could be enforced, led to the beginning of shipments to the shores of New Holland. Then came the long-drawn-out wars, and the rise of still more reactionary sentiment in Parliament.

At the end of the wars in the twenties, virtually all the social maladjustments which had existed in Britain at the time the American colonies revolted were still present in aggravated form. Probably instigated by Malthusian views, a new colonizing sentiment blossomed which was concerned not with solving the problems of penology or mercantilist expansion, but with alleviating the plight of the poor. Various groups and societies were formed to promote free emigration; in spite of the fact that government support was slow in coming, emigration was virtually the only escape for the poor from nearly intolerable conditions, and with the thirties a great tide of emigration began to roll. Altogether, from the postwar years of the early eighteen-twenties to the beginning of the fifties some "three million British were expatriated from the cold neighbourhood of the parish or the union to the warmer colonies which offered them work and bread. Of these more than 222,000 sailed to Australasia. The new Poor Law (1834). . . . brought about the dispatch abroad of most of the millions." [3] It should be emphasized again that convict transportation continued through these later years. Of eighty-three thousand persons thus sent to Australian colonies from 1787 to 1841, twenty-seven thousand embarked in the years from 1833 to 1841, joining the ninety-five thousand free emigrants of the same period.

There was some artisan skill and some agricultural experience in this migration, but it was very thoroughly diluted in the large mass of unskilled laborers and the very great numbers of discharged soldiers and sailors who swelled the ranks of relief recipients in the postwar years. They were very raw materials for the peopling of pioneer regions, being often not only unskilled but underfed and disease-ridden as well. Yet they and their children provided the first labor force, and contributed greatly to the ancestry of the self-governing population of the Australasian colonies in the succeeding century. Besides the free immigrants there were also the accretions from the gold rushes in the fifties, but they were in large degree from the same cultural stratum. [4]

The mass of the population seems not, in general, to have been responsible for the invention or introduction of many new techniques; too often its members were unwilling and inefficient hands for the agriculturalist and pastoralist. One of the virtues of such a population, however, was that it had little to unlearn. A dead weight of peasant prejudice which might have blocked the rapid development of new techniques was largely absent. On the other hand, judging from the experience in North America, Australasia has been very much the poorer for its failure to attract large groups of small farmers and peasants from the continent of Europe. A much different attitude toward the land itself and its use or misuse might have been present there today had they come and brought with them the peasant's instinct for the conservation of those resources of the countryside which are potentially permanent. They did not come, however, and all contemporary records suggest the overwhelming urban and unskilled character of the Australasian labor force; although it is a point which has not been stressed, it is, I believe, of great importance in the development of New Zealand.

When the new arguments for colonization by the theorists and reformers began to appear in England in the twenties, New Zealand was frequently mentioned as a possible field to absorb the "redundant" population of the British Isles.[5] Whaling and sealing, missionary contacts with North Island from 1814 on, and the visits of such writers and scientists as Bellinghausen in 1820, Dumont d'Urville in 1825, and Darwin in the *Beagle* somewhat later, had created a good deal of interest in this "backyard" of Australasia. The most aggressively vocal of the colonizing theorists was Edward Gibbon Wakefield.[6] This brilliant, opinionated, persuasive gentleman devoted a tireless energy, in a materially quite disinterested way, to projects first in South Australia and then in both islands of New Zealand. Others had concentrated on New Zealand as a field for emigration while Wakefield's attention was directed farther west, but the failure of the New Zealand Company of 1825, and of Baron Thierry's colony in the Auckland peninsula, are of concern only to North Island. New Zealand as a whole, and South Island incidentally, comes into the picture after the failure of Wakefield's first experiment on the shores of the Australian Bight.

The principal points in Wakefield's theory of colonization were the careful selection of immigrants with avoidance of the great "pauper" class, the retention, otherwise, of all the major features of the contemporary English class system, and a high fixed price per acre for the land. The last feature was to be the keystone of all the various schemes he proposed. It would prevent large aggregations of land and provide funds for the importation of a labor force of carefully selected lower-class emigrants, for the building of churches, schools, and roads, and for the salaries of clerics and schoolmasters. In Christchurch today there are some concrete examples of these not always effective theories; the land endowment of Canterbury University College, for instance, is a direct result of the ecclesiastical and educational provisions in the plans for the Canterbury settlement which Wakefield organized.

In the thirties, Wakefield inspired several successive organizations to petition the government to allow and support the colonization of New Zealand under the regulations of his system. Official Westminster was, however, far behind the sentiment of the people in their reborn enthusiasm for colonization. The Church Missionary Society, championing the idea of New Zealand for the Maori, lobbied powerfully against them. The chief argument of the Wakefield group was that, as a matter of fact, New Zealand was being colonized and the Maori were not only being debauched and decimated but must eventually be dispossessed as well. Wakefield's remarks in his evidence before a House of Commons' select committee in 1836 have been widely quoted:

Very near to Australia there is a country which all testimony concurs in describing as the fittest country in the world for colonisation, as the most beautiful country with the finest climate, and the most productive soil. I mean New Zealand. . . . Adventurers go from New South Wales and Van Diemen's Land, and make a treaty with a native chief, a tripartite treaty, the poor chief not understanding a word about it, but they make a contract upon parchment, and with a great seal: for a few trinkets and a little gunpowder they obtain land. After a time, in these cases, after some persons have settled, the Government at home begins to receive hints that there is a regular settlement of English people formed in such a place; and then the Government at home generally has been actuated by a wish to appoint a Governor and says, "This spot belongs to England; we will send out a Governor." The act of sending out a Governor, according to our Constitution, or law, or practice, constitutes the place to which the Governor is sent a British province. We are, I think, going to colonise New Zealand, though we be doing so in a most slovenly and scrambling and disgraceful manner.[7]

As Marais remarks, "Unfortunately for Wakefield, New Zealand was not in 1836 subject to British Rule." [8] Since the Church Missionary Society, whose opposition has been noted above was more concerned with northern North Island, the Wakefield group emphasized the possibilities not only in southern North Island but also in South Island.

It is difficult to condense sufficiently the confused discussion of sovereignty in New Zealand. There is little doubt that Cook believed he had effectively established British claims to both islands, but his visit was followed by that clearly marked official apathy toward colonial expansion which succeeded the American Revolution. This feeling was further reinforced in another context when sugar prices collapsed after the Napoleonic Wars, and there was much evidence of an official attitude by the associates of the younger Pitt that colonies in general were not worth the cost of administering them. Thus, despite the fact that Governor Phillip's royal commission, when he sailed for Botany Bay with the first convict fleet in 1787, appointed him Captain-General and Governor-in-Chief of New South Wales and its dependencies (which from the latitudes given was clearly meant to include New Zealand), and despite the fact that, following the public proclamation in 1814 that New Zealand was a dependency of New South Wales,[9] Governor Macquarie appointed justices of the peace in New Zealand and enacted laws for the punishment of crime there, the British government yet saw fit to deny sovereignty in the case of the application of the first New Zealand Company of 1825, deferring to, of all things, Tasman's prior "discovery."[10] Then, reversing itself again, a Resident, without power, was appointed in 1832 to try to reason with lawlessness. The appointee, Busby, persuaded the native chiefs to choose a flag (a stars-and-stripes effect suggested by a Yankee whaler was chosen[11]) and to issue a declaration of independence in the name of the "Confederated Tribes of New Zealand." Finally, in 1838, a British Consul was appointed, thus recognizing, in practice, Maori sovereignty. As there was no unity among the Maori tribes and absolutely no intertribal organization, the whole procedure was farcical and apparently intended only for the support of the missionaries against the Wakefieldians on the home front.

The latter too, however, were developing new arguments. In a later work[12] Wakefield apparently abandoned one of his basic principles as to the quality of the laboring emigrants by advancing the thesis that the position of British capital would be improved by this method of exporting the surplus poor. Some highly placed men, many of whom had been banded together in the Colonisation Society of the early thirties, joined the ranks of the colonizers. The various trials and tribulations of the Society are well described by Marais[13]; he discusses the cessation of assisted emigration to Canada and the Cape in 1831, the cost being deemed too high for the results gained. A New Zealand Association was later formed at government request and, against the feeling of the group itself that it should remain financially disinterested, it was forced to become a joint stock company, "The New Zealand Colonising Company." Later it took the name "New Zealand Land Company," incorporating the interests of the New Zealand Company of 1825, and finally it became, simply, the New Zealand Company. In the end the concessions to the government proved futile and the Company's plans for a settlement on New Zealand were left without official sanction. Nevertheless these plans were well advanced and as the Company had recruited a number of land buyers, it determined to go ahead on its own. On May 5, 1839, an advance party of six men was sent out on the vessel *Tory* to make arrangements for buying land and otherwise prepare for the colonists who were to follow. Edward Gibbon Wakefield's brother, a Colonel Wakefield, was in command of this party, and his nephew, whose description of the whaling communities at Port Underwood and Te Awaiti has been quoted above, also went along.

The despatch of the *Tory* and, some scholars believe, the activities of the *Nanto-Bordelaise Cie.* with its threat of establishment of French sovereignty, finally moved the government to take action toward regularizing the juridical status of New Zealand and its white settlers.[14] A Captain Hobson, R.N., was appointed consul, with instructions to attempt to gain the consent of the Maori tribes to the extension of British sovereignty. This completed, the new colony was to be considered a part of New South Wales, and Hobson was to become Lieutenant-Governor under Gipps of that colony. Important in his instructions was that, British sovereignty having been accepted, he was to seek the agreement of the chiefs that "hence forwards, no lands shall be ceded, gratuitously or otherwise, except to the crown of Great Britain." The squatting problem in New South Wales was becoming serious, and a repetition of this practice was to be avoided. As will appear, this intention failed to a large degree in the event. Apparently the Wakefield group had hammered home one idea to the otherwise hostile government, for the instructions proceeded that Hobson was to insist "on a system of *sale*, of which experience has proved the wisdom, and disregard of which has proved so fatal to the prosperity of other British settlements." He was to announce immediately on his arrival that "Her Majesty will not acknowledge as valid any title to land which either has been, or shall be hereafter acquired in that country which is not either derived from, or confirmed by a grant to be made on Her Majesty's behalf." He was however to assure settlers that reasonable claims would be allowed.[15]

Governor Gipps had made the Colonial office aware of a mad scramble for land titles in New Zealand by various speculators (especially traders and whalers) based on any sort of document purporting to have been signed by any Maori. Probably the leading offenders were the "best citizens" of New South Wales and members of its legislative council. Literally hundreds joined in this land title rush. Scholefield quotes McKay, one of the Lands Commissioners subsequently appointed to investigate the claims arising out of the rush as follows:

At the time the land fever, in its different phases of "sharking," jobbing, and *bona fide* speculation, literally raged in New Zealand. Almost every captain of a ship, upon arriving at Sydney from New Zealand exhibited a piece of paper, with a tattooed native head rudely drawn on it, which he described as the title-deed of an estate bought for a few muskets, hatchets, or blankets. Other captains were literally supplied in Sydney with blank deeds of "feoffment" for the use of these purchasers, and as the Government had a fixed price of 5s., and afterwards 12s., per acre on land in Australia, adventurers crowded to New Zealand, hoping there, under cover of the Declaration of Independence, 1835, to pursue their schemes with impunity.[16]

Meanwhile, without waiting to hear how the *Tory* had made out, the Company made the first of its many blunders through haste. The subscribers to land in the scheme were growing impatient, and speed seemed imperative, so the first immigrant ship with 156 colonists was sent off. Colonel Wakefield had arrived in Cook Strait in August 1839 with the *Tory,* and soon afterwards "bought," or so he believed, over twenty million acres from the Maori for nine thousand pounds worth of trade goods, including three hundred red blankets and two hundred irresistible muskets. He believed this land to include a large slice of what was later to become Nelson province of South Island. Ten per cent of the country was to be reserved for the Maori and the enhanced value of this tithe, following upon close European settlement, was held by the promoters to be the real payment for the land.

On January 22, 1840, the first pioneer immigrants of the company arrived at Port Nicholson (the present site of New Zealand's capital city, Wellington, on the southern tip of North Island) expecting to occupy at once acreage equivalent to the money they had invested. Almost immediately, however, on February 3 Hobson arrived at the Bay of Islands, at the other extremity of the island, and proceeded according to his instructions. By May he had concluded the Treaty of Waitangi by which the signatory tribes admitted British sovereignty over all the country. Although the validity of the subsequent proclamation of sovereignty, as applicable to South Island, has been questioned by some students, British sovereignty was, in fact, established by the end of the year over all of what is now known as New Zealand. As Hobson followed his instructions literally, all the settlers and the Company's new immigrants found their supposed title to land in New Zealand null and void until examined by the Crown, nor could new purchases be made except by the Crown. Despite the entreaties of the Company, Hobson established his "capital" at Waitemata Harbour (Auckland) instead of at Port Nicholson.

We cannot report in any detail the tribulations of the Port Nicholson pioneers. The awkward position of the settlers as a result of the firm stand of the Crown on land alienation was relieved partially by the waiving of pre-emptive crown rights over small areas at Wellington and near-by centers where settlement was taking place.* The Company's surveyors had arrived a very short time before the immigrants, and their surveys were slow in progressing. The surveyors were held up by fear of the Maori and by the obstacles of the rugged terrain with its heavy forest cover. In October, 1841, only six hundred of a population of twenty-five hundred, most of whom were company immigrants, were settled on the land.[17] Still the Company sold its scrip in London and poured shipload after shipload into the new colony (New Zealand was separated from New South Wales on Nov. 16, 1840).

THE NELSON SETTLEMENT

At the beginning of 1841, the directors of the Company entered into an agreement with Lord John Russell to waive all claims based

---

* The appointment, and beginning of hearings of the new Lands' Commissioners, who were to adjudicate on the various claims, was slow. Hearings dragged on through two decades. Finally, in 1846, the Colonial Office entered into an agreement with the company, which materially reduced the original twenty-million-acre "purchase." Then in 1847 the Crown gave to the New Zealand Company the entire and exclusive disposal of all Crown lands and the exercise of the Crown's legal right of pre-emption belonging to the southern (that is, New Munster) government of New Zealand. This enabled the Otago and Canterbury settlements to proceed more smoothly and they were able to make satisfactory arrangements with the Crown when the Company folded in 1850. These settlements' claims were absorbed by the new provincial governments in 1852, and by 1856 in fact, and by 1858 in law, the provinces had gained complete control of disposal of their own land.

on purchase from Maori. The Company was to get land at the rate of four acres for every pound sterling it could prove it had expended on immigration. Relations with the government were thus finally regularized, and a charter was issued to the Company on Feb. 12, 1841. The Company was to purchase, acquire, settle, improve, alienate, and mortgage lands, lay out settlements and towns, and work therein all mines, pits, and quarries, all minerals and metals, and make provision for the introduction of immigrants.

Although a site was not yet chosen, plans for a second settlement, to be known as Nelson, were announced, which resulted, largely by accident, in the first organized British settlement in South Island. The new settlement was to consist of 201,000 acres, divided into allotments of one thousand parcels of 201 acres each; each parcel was to consist of one acre in town, fifty suburban acres, and one hundred and fifty acres of country property. Each purchaser was to pay three hundred pounds for each parcel. The company undertook to pay one-half of the money received toward the costs of immigration, one sixth on roads, surveys, and administration, one-sixth on public objects, and to reserve only one-sixth as payment for the land. Of the fifty thousand pounds to be set aside for public purposes, twenty thousand were earmarked for the encouragement of steam navigation, fifteen thousand were to be devoted to religious uses and endowments, and fifteen thousand were to go to the establishment of a college. The expected total income of three hundred thousand pounds was never realized; as late as April 5, 1844, over half of the two hundred and one thousand acres were still unsold.[18]

That land sales for the new project proceeded slowly was hardly surprising, since the site was still undecided and the difficulties of the first settlements around Cook Strait were becoming more widely known. Nevertheless an advance shipload of settlers arrived in the Strait in 1841, and a decision as to location was forced. The administrator of the new settlement, Captain Wakefield, a third brother, thought the Port Cooper plains most suitable. Rumor of the first successful cropping there in 1840 may have reached his ears, and the harbors of Banks Peninsula were a great attraction. Political convenience, however, overruled geographical common sense, and Hobson insisted on the new settlement being no further south than Cook Strait. Colonel Wakefield's chief surveyor, Tuckett, made a hurried reconnaissance survey of the lands around Tasman Bay and reported them quite unsuitable for the venture. Had he known of the plains of the Wairau and their relatively easy accessibility from the head of Queen Charlotte Sound, he might possibly have chosen them. But the only knowledge of the Wairau valley was hearsay from the Port Underwood settlers, and the shallow bar at the mouth of the river made entrance to the area seem entirely too difficult. Over Tuckett's objections and under the lash of an immediate necessity to locate the new immigrants, the shores of Tasman Bay, and especially the limited, lower Waimea valley area, were chosen (fig. 26). A port of a kind, behind a long boulder bank, was found, and there the new settlers were landed. Thus haphazardly and irrationally was the site of Nelson chosen, and its disadvantages have prevented it from taking a really important part in the development of South Island. Its principal assets today are an intensive horticulture and a magnificent climate, which attracts a considerable "retired" population. In 1841 the one valuable asset was the climate.

By May, 1842, almost fifteen hundred emigrants had been landed in the area. Although these included a few "capitalists" or land purchasers, the vast majority of the inhabitants were of the laboring class. The various annual reports of the New Zealand Company provide quite complete records. In all, over a period of nine years, the company sold in Great Britain 442 parcels of land to 315 purchasers of whom only 80, owning 109 allotments, ever set foot in the settlement. In contrast 3100 members of the laboring class, of whom 980 were adult males, were brought to Nelson. Allowing for movement of both laborers and capitalists between the settlements of New Zealand, it is evident that some 90 per cent of the population of Nelson were, upon arrival, penniless or nearly penniless laborers. The record of what skills they had is not very complete. There were some farm laborers among the importees, and no doubt a little managerial skill in agricultural and pastoral pursuits as well. On the whole, however, the immigrants had little knowledge of plant or animal husbandry and were completely unprepared for an agricultural or pastoral life in a new country. There is no indication of any numbers of the yeoman farmer type.

The Company guaranteed to the land owners that the laborers were to be carefully selected, and the Company claims, in all of its records, that this was accomplished. It would be naïve to have expected any other claim, yet most students of the colonization of

New Zealand accept this declaration of the Company without supporting evidence. The regulations with regard to laborers stated that they were supposed to be mechanics, craftsmen, agricultural laborers, or domestic servants. They were to be nominated by purchasers of land scrip, but the company does not even claim that this regulation was followed, and it seems overwhelmingly probable, in view of the confessed difficulty of obtaining laborers and the high degree of absenteeism among the landlords, that it was all but completely ignored. No person resident in a workhouse, or in habitual receipt of parish relief, was to be accepted. There were to be as many women as men, and married couples without children were preferred. No more than two children under seven years of age, per family, were allowed. No adults over thirty-five years were taken unless they were the parents of children over fourteen. Passages were free except for children of one to fourteen years who were charged three pounds each. Laborers had to pay their own way to the home ports. Each emigrant was to provide his own bedding and the tools of his trade.

One wonders what laborers above the class of paupers, or near paupers, could have been induced to go to the much advertised terrors of "cannibal-ridden" New Zealand, where little was known of the country, and where it was planned to preserve all the class distinctions of a system in which these people were very near the bottom. A small sum would buy passage to North America, the attractions of which were well advertised and included a very much shorter voyage in steerage. The patriotic advantage of living under the British flag was equally to be had in Canada, the Cape, or Australia. It simply does not make sense that a superior class of laborers should, of its own free will, have chosen to go in preference to New Zealand. Unless there is proof to the contrary one must assume that the Company simply took what it could get, and that the great majority of Nelson's settlers were culturally and economically from the lowest levels of British society which had a status above that of "criminals." One must certainly doubt the exclusion of paupers. The social conditions of the English poor in the early nineteenth century have been alluded to before and are well publicized in any event. If we add that they were probably mostly townsfolk, some of the major difficulties of early settlement in Nelson, and to a degree later in Otago and Canterbury where the same arguments hold with somewhat reduced force, are more easily understood.

One of the inducements offered to the laborers by the company was that they would be granted continuous work at reasonable wages by the company until they could be used for their intended purpose, that is, to supply labor for the landholders as these developed their allotments. In Nelson the few landholders who came were to be a long time in getting their land. It was August 21, 1842 [19] before an acre of even suburban land, let alone country proper, was open to selection, and by this time the population had swelled to seventeen hundred. Still another season was to pass before use could be made of the fern land which included most of the flat areas not occupied by heavy bush or swamp. According to one of the early laboring immigrants in Nelson, the town site itself was still largely covered with fern two feet high in 1843, and by the end of the year only a half-dozen enterprising men had begun farming operations at "the Waimea," that is, the beginning of the plain, three or four miles south of the town site proper. All the while there were in Nelson a great number of unemployed laborers for whom work had to be made or relief without work given. The whole sorry story of these early years of the Nelson settlement is recorded in detail by a number of the early settlers there,[20] although there may be some doubt as to the complete objectivity of their accounts.

The difficulties were almost inevitable, however, in the circumstances. This community of little agricultural skill was suddenly dumped on an infertile shore fronting a completely unknown wilderness. The harbor proved dangerous for ships. Today, after a century of experiment, the hills around Nelson are used only for rough grazing. The nearest land at all suitable for agriculture was four miles distant, and its use involved either the cutting out of a thick mass of fern roots or, on the swampy sections, of removing a still more formidable tangle of raupo and *Phormium* and providing drainage ditches. In this lowland, and the smaller districts of the lower Moutere and Motueka valleys to the west, there were perhaps sixty thousand acres which might, one day, be agricultural land; less than fourteen thousand acres of this were considered to be potentially first-class as early as 1844.[21] Not only was there a mere fraction of the proposed two hundred and one thousand acres, but that fraction was broken into widely separated pieces. The mountains behind the lowlands were clothed in the heavy, subtropical bush. In such a fashion did the nature of the terrain, which neither the Company nor Wakefield seems to have

held important to the success of this "carefully planned" settlement, effectively nullify the policy of "concentration" of agricultural settlement to promote the "civilized" appurtenances of
contemporary British life. All of Wakefield's plans were thus di-
vorced from considerations of habitat quality. Even with the failure of the Cook Strait settlements, which followed that of South
Australia and within the same decade, Wakefield was once again
to plan a settlement with almost as little regard to site or to the
cultural qualifications necessary to the success of immigrants.

These physical limitations forced the company to develop several projects for the employment of the people. An eyewitness
reported that "The men were sent to work in very large gangs;
on spade, pick and shovel work, at so much per week, the same
price being paid to an able navvy as to a crippled tailor or a soft-
handed music-master. Of course all learned to do the same in-
finitesimal amount of work, and woe betide the man who dared to
do more." [22] The practice of absentee-landlordism also presented
difficulties, some of which are noted in the *Nelson Examiner* of
Feb. 18, 1843:

There are many things which are exceedingly vexatious about the
absentee proprietorship. One's land has to be fenced entirely at one's
own expense; whereas, in equity the outlays should be divided between
oneself and one's neighbours. No assistance can be procured if extensive
draining is required; no help of any sort in the general improvements
by which the occupied land next door is as equally benefitted as one's
own.

By the end of 1843, Fox, who had replaced Captain Wakefield
as the company representative in Nelson when the latter was
killed in the Wairau massacre (*see* p. 90) was spending fifteen
hundred pounds a month on relief with almost nothing to show
for it, an all but intolerable drain on the company's resources.
An attempt to reduce wages gave rise to restlessness and to many
small acts of violence, which, considering the incredible trick
which bad management had played upon them, seems to have
been a mild reaction on the part of the laborers. Even if the rate
of wages was maintained, the food available on which to spend
those wages was tragically insufficient. To obtain more food, at
least one ship was sent to Valparaiso for flour. A Nelson proprietor
of the time wrote in 1849:

At the time of the great distress in 1844-5 .... many families lived
almost wholly on potatoes, and not a great abundance of them, for more

than 12 months. The rural population, especially women and children, looked wretched, pinched, and haggard. They showed in their faces the grievous scarcity which befell them upon the Company's suspension [of relief payments].[23]

It was then necessary to controvert one of the fundamental Wakefield tenets and give land to the laborers to work without any payment for it on their part. Finally a deferred payment plan covering a ten-year period was worked out for small allotments, but the payment was frequently overlooked. In 1851 a select committee of Grey's legislative council reported regarding Nelson:

When the claims to Crown lands were investigated the other day there were only about 50 original purchasers from the company remaining in the settlement but there were more than 200 other persons chiefly of the working class, who, though they had not paid any to the Company were yet prosperous landowners there.[24]

These circumstances initiated a sort of yeoman agricultural class in South Island created from the hungry landless laborers. Wakefield, even before Fox's regime, had started twenty laboring families on "cotter" farms in the Riwaka; these families were given small lots of land, still unsold by the company, and a few seeds, including some wheat and potatoes, free.[25] Others settled near the edge of the bush at Motueka at this time, but these chiefly sawed wood for the Nelson settlement. By 1850, fifty of the Nelson laborers had acquired land,[26] the utilization of which is shown in table I.

TABLE I

LAND USE IN NELSON (1850)

	Total for 50 Laborers	Average per Laborer
Land in crop	402 acres	8 acres
Cattle	589 head	11 head
Sheep	606 head	12 head
Goats	679 head	13 head
Pigs	392 head	7 head

The population of Nelson showed little increase in the first eight years:[26]

1842	1843	1844	1845	1846	1847	1848	1849
2500	2942	3036	2931	2853	2867	3089	3372

Yet it was great enough that the settling of even fifty laborers on the land, even supposing each had a fair-sized family, was not a very complete solution to the problem.

In 1847 the landowners and the company agreed on a plan of resettlement. Its essence was that all unsold sections of the original scheme be suppressed, and that the scrip-holders be granted a right of re-selection in order of original choice. But even this scheme rested on a completely insecure basis of inexact, incomplete surveys, many of the very control points of which had been lost.[27] Grey, New Zealand's somewhat dictatorial governor of the time, attempted to rationalize the chaos by issuing the *New Zealand Land Company's Claims Ordinance*, which allowed settlers to throw up useless sections in favor of scrip claims of a nominal value of a pound per acre on other New Zealand lands. The scrip was valid at any sale of government land in either province (New Ulster and New Munster) into which New Zealand was then divided.

A point of the greatest importance in the breaking up of much of the Nelson settlement into small subsistence farms worked by laborers, was that those men with capital to invest, well aware of the great pastoral expansion occurring contemporaneously on the Australian mainland, decided to reserve their money for sheep farming. Since the price of wool almost guaranteed a rapid increase in capital, such enterprises were preferred to the sinking of capital in a slow methodical development of agricultural possibilities in difficult country. Many of the pioneers of pastoralism in South Island, and for all practical purposes, New Zealand, were men coming from New South Wales; however, Frederick Weld, one of its leaders, was a scion of one of the oldest and wealthiest of England's landed Roman Catholic families and had come directly from "home." The story of the pastoral expansion, as such, belongs in a later chapter, but its connection with the peopling of the country demands mention here.

Shrewd traders very early began introducing cattle and sheep to Nelson from New South Wales. By 1844 there were nearly five thousand sheep and nearly a thousand cattle in Nelson.[28] By 1850 sheep had increased to more than seventy thousand, and in 1856 to over a quarter of a million. Meanwhile, land in crops, not including groves of exotic trees, had increased only from one thousand to five thousand acres, between 1844 and 1856. These figures reflect directly the quick abandonment of an agricultural, in favor of a pastoral, economy. The running of sheep, however, demanded more land and, in general, quite different land from that available in the early Nelson settlement. As early as 1842, Cotterell, a surveyor for the company, seeking additional land to satisfy the plans for the settlement, had made a reconnaissance through the Wairau valley. The following year a party of surveyors was sent into the area which Colonel Wakefield believed he had purchased, but upon which the Claims Courts had not yet ruled. It began the formal survey of sixty thousand acres believed to be available in the Wairau valley and of a hundred and twelve thousand acres in the Awatere valley and along the lower coastal areas toward Kaikoura. The few resident Maori, aware that this land had not yet been awarded to the Company, actively resented the activities of the surveying party. Eventually a fracas resulted in which twenty-two of the Nelson people, including Captain Wakefield, were killed. Though the Land Claims Court threw out the Company's claim to the Wairau in 1844, the Maori, apparently fearing vigilante vengeance, fled, and despite difficulty of access, the "squatters" poured in.

The real difficulty of effecting entrance to this country for men and sheep can be seen by reference to figures 1, 16, and 26. Heavily wooded hills or narrow valleys, choked with brush where not swampy, formed a continuous barrier on the north from Port Underwood to the headwaters of the Wairau River. The harbors on Cloudy Bay were barred by fairly sheer cliffs from the interior. It was to be some years before any but very small boats negotiated the Wairau bar, and there was no good harbor between Port Underwood and Banks Peninsula. Kaikoura was a fair shelter, but it was not easy to travel from there to the Wairau-Awatere area. Eventually a number of routes from Nelson were established, but most of them were through rough country and some were roundabout. The present main highway from Nelson to the Wairau is a rather spectacular, winding, slope-hugging feat of engineering.

The first man to overcome these obstacles to entry with sheep is thought to have been one George Duppa from New South Wales. He had previously, in 1844, squatted with two hundred head of cattle and sheep on unoccupied land in the Wai-iti valley, and his entry into the Wairau (in the summer of 1846-1847) is commonly supposed to have been the first. In 1847, Frederick Weld, who had started to run sheep in association with three friends in the Wairarapa valley east of Port Nicholson in 1844,[29] decided to take up land somewhere in the Wairau area. He and a partner started with a very few horses and cattle and twenty-five hundred sheep. With great difficulty the animals were landed at Robin Hood Bay in Port Underwood; then came the tedious task of swimming the sheep across the Wairau, and, after driving them over the nose of the Vernon Hills by an easy pass to the Awatere, again swimming them across that river. Weld's head-quarters were established a few miles south of the Awatere near Flaxbourne stream, and "Flaxbourne" was to be the name of the station. It became one of the greatest squatting estates, and con-tributed to the creation of one of the largest fortunes in New Zealand. Less than fifty years later the estate became the center of a cause célèbre in the country when the government bought it, broke it up, and resold it for close settlement.

Others with capital, including several men from New South Wales as well as local landholders who preferred this easier way of making money, were quick to import Merino sheep from the Australian colonies and drive them inland to the great expanses of tussock. In 1849 there were thirty squatters in the area, though it was only in that year that Governor Grey bought the area officially from the Maori and proper surveys were begun. The squatters had well calculated that occupation would give virtually unassailable right to the area and had been concerned, at first, only to get the maximum number of sheep into the land, whether they were scabby (see p. 202), in poor condition, or otherwise undesirable. This carelessness was to have rather serious results; though the quality of imports later greatly improved, for the mo-ment quantity was much more important.

By this means virtually all of the possible pastoral land was in skeleton occupation by the time the surveys were completed. To salvage something from this wholesale use of lands now legally its property after Grey's action, the New Zealand Company im-posed the highest rental rates on the illegal occupants that they thought the traffic would stand; actually the rates now seem to have been incredibly low. In the same year of 1849, the Company issued eighteen-month grazing licenses on the basis of occupancy as from January, 1849. This allowed each applicant to describe "his" run, estimate its carrying capacity, pay a five pounds license fee and an additional fee of one penny per sheep and eight pence per head of cattle. By February of 1849, thirty applications were received. Thus a tract of land carrying twenty thousand sheep cost, for rental, about a hundred pounds a year. There were no tithes or poor rates, in fact no taxes of any kind. Though pro-visions were dear, and labor, so the run-holders claimed, asked exorbitant wages of as much as fifty pounds a year plus provisions, the cost of keeping a sheep for a year was reckoned at but two-pence per head. The initial cost of landing a sheep at Nelson was about twelve shillings per head. In 1850, a letter written by Fox, the Company's agent at Nelson, reported yields of four and a half pounds of wool per head from Weld's sheep at Flaxbourne. Earp [30] claimed that, at the then current price of wool, capital would double itself in three years with the sale of wool and the natural increase of the flocks. There was no housing of the animals in the mild climate nor supplemental feeding with the initial light stocking.

This decade ends with reports of good pastoral land to the south in Canterbury, the opening up of a market there for the surplus stock, and the exploration for, and establishment of, stock routes across the intervening mountains for this trade. Discussion of this will come properly, however, later in this volume under the subject of sheep. The *Nelson Examiner's* issue of March 31, 1855, gives figures for the population of Nelson, excluding Amuri, which was economically tied in with the new Canterbury Settlement to the south and from which no returns had been received. In 1848 the population had been 3,089, scarcely 150 more than the 2,942 of 1843, the second year of the settlement. From the *Examiner's* data for 1855, we find the total population (5,801) distributed as shown in table II.

TABLE II

DISTRIBUTION OF WHITE POPULATION IN NELSON (1855)

Location	Male	Female
Nelson township	940	880
Suburban North	109	99
Suburban South	142	117
Waimea East	511	416
Waimea South	382	342
Waimea West	181	151
Motueka	392	382
Massacre Bay	72	49
Queen Charlotte Sound	56	43
Wairau	352	185

One source of the new population is particularly interesting:

This large addition to our numbers had been caused chiefly by immigration which has taken place from the Australian colonies within the last few months, although during the same period there have been numerous arrivals likewise from England.[31]

Still a scarcity of labor persisted, and the new provincial government had voted eight thousand pounds for immigration and sent an agent to London.

Besides centers at Nelson, Richmond, Wakefield, and on Golden Bay, two settlements had begun to the east, one in Queen Charlotte Sound and the other on the lower Wairau. In 1847 James Wynen, the Dutchman previously reported at Port Underwood, moved to a location amid the swamps and distributaries of this river. Because of its marshiness the place was long called The Beaver, though later, as capital of the new province of Marlborough, it was to take and keep the corollary name of Blenheim. Wynen started the first store and soon a nucleus of settlement appeared, mainly "cob" cottages, small huts of mud and straw made into bricks or packed between frames, which were the standard early buildings in the treeless areas. The first agriculturists began operations around The Beaver in 1849, but in all the Wairau area there were only 212 acres fenced and seven acres in wheat in that year. By 1855 this had increased only to 1,006½ acres fenced, with 57 acres in wheat, 52 in oats, 42½ sown to English grasses, and 38 acres in gardens and orchards.[32] An important event of 1855 was an earthquake which not only demolished most of the "cob" cottages, but which apparently depressed the land, causing a flooding and deepening of the Wairau. Small steamers and schooners, instead of only whaleboats, now came into general use on the lower river. McIntosh reports that 103 vessels of ten to fifty tons entered the river in 1857 and took out wool valued at £51,450.[33]

The difficulty of access from the sea had previously caused agitation for the development of a port at the head of Queen Charlotte Sound and a connecting road to the plain. There had long been a Maori settlement on the present site of Picton. An observer commenting on the native cultivation there, in the March 29, 1845, issue of the *Nelson Examiner,* wrote that "The plantation occupied 50 or 60 acres and consisted of potatoes, cabbages, turnips, Indian corn, Kumaras, mellons, pumpkins, etc." An extensive description of the favorable features of site and situation are given on pages 50 to 52 of the *Twelfth Annual Report* of the New Zealand Company.[34] In 1847-1848 the landholders in Nelson were given free a quarter-acre section in the new township established there for each town lot held in Nelson. There was still only one white man there in 1853, but in 1855, thirty-four Europeans, with eight Maori, signed a petition for a road connection to the Wairau as residents of the area. The little village retained its Maori name of Waitohi, despite numerous official fancies, until the new province was formed and it became Picton.

THE OTAGO SETTLEMENT

Meanwhile two more "planned" settlements were being promoted for South Island which depended more intimately on the preliminary pioneering. The first was to be a Scottish settlement, and for its location the hinterland of Otago harbor was chosen.[35] Up until 1847, of 76 vessels dispatched by the New Zealand Company only three had come from Scottish ports, and the proportion of people of Scottish origin in the settlements adjacent to Cook Strait was small. Yet poverty in Scotland was even more serious than in England. Hocken [36] reports that in 1840, in Paisley alone, eleven thousand wage earners (including of course very young children) of a population of forty-four thousand were out of work and starving. For the rest, standard wages ran about seven to eight shillings per week for a sixteen-hour day, six days a week. Most of those who could emigrate followed the beaten tracks to North America or, to a lesser degree, to New South Wales. Of some four hundred thousand leaving the British Isles between 1839 and 1842, only eight thousand went to New Zealand, and of these only five hundred in three ships were Scottish.[36]

The idea of a purely Scottish settlement originated with a Scot named Rennie who had been very much interested in Wakefield's schemes. In some respects he was a good deal more practical than Wakefield, and he planned for a small block of about a hundred thousand acres to be thoroughly surveyed and prepared before the arrival of the settlers. The choosing of land by lot ("parcels" to include different types of land), fixed prices, and indeed all the major Wakefieldian features, were to be included. As the New Zealand Company was in one of its chronic periods of disfavor with the government, Rennie and an associate, Captain Cargill, took their plans to the Colonial Office. They proposed that the New Zealand Company provide the land, transport the emigrants, and arrange for the initial surveys and public works. A Scottish

Association, closely identified with the national church, was to be organized, and it would sell the land, enlist emigrants, and run the settlement. The suggested apportionment of expected revenues was very similar to that planned for the Nelson settlement. *

Then in 1843 came the open break in the established Church of Scotland and the formation of the Free Kirk. One of the leading dissidents joined Cargill and Rennie in the scheme on the understanding that it was to be a Free Kirk colony of which he would be the principal minister. This was the Reverend Thomas Burns, as stubborn and determined a man as oatmeal ever nourished. When he insisted that all educational funds should be under his, that is Free Kirk, control, Rennie sharply disagreed. It is significant that Rennie, not Burns, then resigned from the promotional group. Cargill, hoping to avoid some of the trouble experienced in Nelson, suggested the creation of a landed, if poor, yeomanry by urging that land buyers be encouraged to re-sell lots of ten acres, at two pounds per acre, to be repaid out of income in four yearly installments of five shillings each. It was, however, to be many years, as Cargill was to discover, before a man could make any kind of living for his family out of ten acres in New Zealand, and then only on the best land and in the most favorable situations.

Meanwhile the Company had been going ahead with its search for a suitable locality. In 1842 the Company sent its principal surveyor, Captain Mein Smith, to visit the harbors of the east coast of South Island and report on possible sites for a settlement. He was able to get a good deal of information from the whaling communities, although the land, at any distance from the coast, was still largely unknown. His report favored the Banks Peninsula area and its hinterland, as Captain Wakefield had favored it earlier for the Nelson settlement. His opinion of the land tributary to Otago harbor was not favorable. In this he was supported by Dr. Shortland,[38] sub-protector of aborigines for the New Zealand government, when he passed through the area on his official round of duties. He had a very poor opinion of the Taieri plains (fig. 28) covered as they were with bracken fern and "dry wiry grass growing in tufts." Neither Smith nor Shortland were, of course, thinking of sheep country, but even if they had been, it remained for the adventurous, land-grabbing squatters of the Wairau to prove that the tussock was easily convertible to marketable wool.

* The scheme, however, was less grandiose; the suburban allotments were reduced from fifty to ten acres, and the rural lots from a hundred fifty to fifty acres.[37]

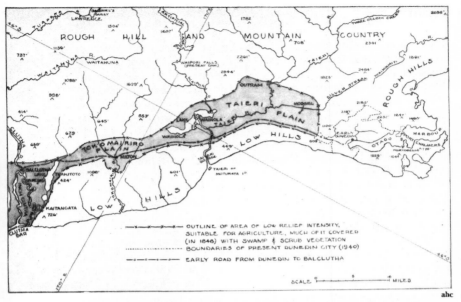

ahc

FIG. 28. Map of Otago peninsula and harbor, including Taieri and Tokomairiro plains.

We have not been able to give space to the long-drawn-out story of the political history of the new colony in these years, nor even to the changing fortunes of the New Zealand Company. When Fitzroy became governor in 1843 he waived the Crown's right of pre-emption over a hundred and fifty thousand acres in South Island for the proposed Scottish settlement, out of such land in that island for which the Crown could arrange to complete purchase from the Maori. The surveyor, Tuckett, who had protested the site of the Nelson settlement and resigned when his worst fears were realized there, was re-engaged to select and survey the land for the new settlement on the understanding that he would have a free hand. An official representative accompanied him to guard the interests of the Maori and the government, and to arrange for purchase from the Maori of the land which Tuckett chose, and the party included one Dr. Monro, a monied Nelson landholder. Tuckett thought most highly of the areas around Moeraki and Waikouaiti, where Jones and Hughes had been conducting profitable agricultural enterprises for some years. Their lack of harbors for shipping, however, ruled them out. Unlike Mein Smith he preferred the area about Otago harbor and the

Taieri valley to the Port Cooper plains. He thought the harbors of Banks Peninsula too open and the Port Cooper plains too swampy.* Monro could assure him from the limited experience in Nelson that land carrying tussock, flax, or fern had agricultural possibilities, and he thought the Taieri plain would be of enormous advantage as a hinterland to Otago harbor, in which judgment he was correct. Indeed he would have located the center of settlement at the mouth of the Taieri but for its treacherous bar. After inspecting the Bluff-Invercargill and Riverton areas he returned to Otago and settled on the upper harbor as the site for the principal town. The first suggestion of a name for the town was New Edinburgh. The happier choice of Dunedin, an old Scottish name for Edinburgh, was first urged in 1843 and accepted in 1846. In June Colonel Wakefield arrived and arranged with the Government representative to purchase four hundred thousand acres, of which a hundred and fifty thousand would be reserved for the settlement. An agreement whereby the remaining two hundred and fifty thousand acres could be used by the settlers until sold was the basis of later depasturage licenses. The company was by then beginning to recognize the inevitability of a pastoral economy.

Then came the news from England of the suspension of the Company's activities due to the almost hopeless financial position into which its ill-prepared ventures had sunk it. Nothing further was done about the Scottish settlement for two years and, undisturbed, the whaling communities along the coast continued in their slow metamorphosis to a direct interest in agricultural and pastoral land use. That at the mouth of Otago harbor held perhaps twenty Europeans. To these were added two runaway sailors on Kaituna creek at the harbor head, where Dunedin was to be established; a further four or five families, who had escaped from the tribulations of the Company's settlements at Wellington and New Plymouth in North Island, settled at different points about the bay.

During this cessation of activity by the Company in 1845, there was a lengthy Commons debate in London on colonies in general and on New Zealand in particular. As a result the British government agreed to lend the Company a hundred thousand

---

* Tuckett had fallen into the Avon en route to the Deans' farm at Riccarton, and his judgment may have involved some personal pique! His experiences on the whole trip are minutely detailed in his diary.[39]

pounds for seven years and to grant it four hundred thousand acres in Otago unconditionally. At the same time Burns and Cargill spread the gospel of a new and fairer Caledonia to be created in the Antipodes. There was no shortage of laborers eager to go, but, as in every other similar scheme and for reasons progressively more apparent, land purchasers were shy. Still the company decided to proceed with the surveys which Tuckett had begun in 1844. One Charles Kettle was dispatched from "home" to carry on and, in Wellington, he picked up a staff of twenty-five assistants, or laborers. The chief recommendation of at least fifteen of them seems to have been that they had indubitably Scottish names. Most of these were to remain and become members of the new settlement. As one of Tuckett's men had continued to live at Otago Heads as a sort of resident watchman, and had used his many months to survey carefully the harbor, work was begun immediately. A port town, the present Port Chalmers, well inside the Heads and just where the harbor narrows sharply, was first laid out. The surveying contract for the main block was let in five sections, and the site of the town established at the harbor head south of the Kaituna stream, which was now picturesquely renamed The Water of Leith. By the middle of 1847 most of the surveys were completed, but when no settlers appeared, the surveying crews and many of those who had gathered in expectation of imminent establishment of the settlement began to leave. On July 24, 1847, Kettle wrote to Colonel Wakefield that "Dunedin is now almost deserted, there being only 5 houses in the town inhabited and we have for the present almost given up hopes of the arrival of the settlers." [40]

Then the floundering company was given another infusion of life by loans from, and arrangements with, the new government of Lord Russell, which succeeded Peel's government in 1847 after the repeal of the Corn Laws. Under the new arrangements a property was to consist of a quarter-acre town lot, a ten-acre suburban lot, and a fifty-acre country lot—the parcel to be sold for £120 10s., or forty shillings per acre. Of the twenty-four hundred properties into which the 144,600-acre tract was divided, only two thousand were for sale; two hundred were reserved for the New Zealand Company as payment for its services (outside of the land), a hundred were to be sold to the future municipal corporation of Dunedin, and a hundred were set aside as special religious and educational endowments. The suburban lots were close to the harbor and on the peninsula; the fifty-acre lots were distributed through the Taieri, Tokomairiro, and Molyneux (Clutha) districts. Of the expected cash yield of £289,200, three-eighths was to be devoted to emigration of laborers, one-fourth was to go to the New Zealand Company in payment for the land, one-fourth was to be devoted to surveys and public works, and one-eighth to endow religious and educational projects.

The sale of properties was vigorously pushed in Scotland, and while by November 16, 1847, only 104 had been purchased, it was decided to proceed with the dispatch of the first ships, which left Britain before the end of the year. Most of the cabin passengers sailed in one ship, the proportion being 24 cabin to 72 in fore-cabin and steerage, while the larger vessel had but 12 cabin passengers to 235 forward. As eight of the cabin passengers on the second ship were Burns and his family, the proportion of proprietors to laborers was, once again, very small. Moreover, on the smaller ship, more than half of the immigrants were English, indicating a breakdown in the national purity of this *Nova Scotia Australia* at its very inception.

The first year was not as pleasant as it had been hoped. It was very bad management to have the ships arrive on this rainy coast just at the beginning of winter, although even a Dunedin winter might have seemed relatively pleasant to Scots. After living for some months in barracks following their arrival early in 1848, the settlers began to fan out in the spring to explore and build temporary homes on their allotments. They made very good use of both the surplus food production and experienced advice of the farming establishments at Waikouaiti and Moeraki. In September and October of 1848, the Reverend Burns, taking his duties as spiritual leader of his people most seriously, carefully recorded the results of his first ministerial visitation. The winter and early spring had been well spent. Ninety-three European families of 444 souls were living in 88 houses; there were, in addition, 166 Maori and half-castes in the area. The European population was thus a hundred more than had arrived on the two ships, further testimony to the considerable previously resident population and to the possibility that many people, particularly of Scottish descent, may have come from other Australasian colonies.

Almost immediately upon the founding of the settlement, the *Otago Daily Times* began publication, and census figures (table III) appeared in the issue of Nov. 10, 1849.

TABLE III
EUROPEAN POPULATION IN OTAGO (1849)

	Male	Female	Total
Town of Dunedin	240	204	444
Port Chalmers	28	10	38
Country	158	105	263
Total	426	319	745

The population of European extraction shows a rather heavy balance in town, though there was a much quicker and more effective spread to the country than in Nelson. The breakdown as to religious profession is shown in table IV.

TABLE IV
RELIGIOUS PREFERENCE (OTAGO 1849)

	Number of People
Presbyterian Church of Otago	476
Church of England	161
Methodist	8
Roman Catholic	7
Independent	1
Unknown	92

The "Unknown" class strongly suggests the pre-1848 population; Burns would certainly have known the religious preferences of the ship's passengers. It is indicative of the difficulty in obtaining the kind of emigrants desired for a church colony, that roughly only two-thirds were professing Presbyterians.

The April 6, 1850, issue of the *Otago Daily Times* furnishes us with further interesting statistics. By April 1, 1850, the population had increased to 1,182, not counting 38 just arrived on an oversea ship. The Presbyterians were still further diluted, numbering only 725 out of 1,172 who stated their affiliation. Of even greater interest is that, within this group, the adherents of the Church of Scotland outnumbered the "Wee Frees" 423 to 302, even if the 111 listed as "other dissenters" may have also been largely Free Kirk. Since the Anglicans were 306 and there was a scattering of other sects, it is obvious that within two years the conception of a Free Kirk settlement had been completely abandoned. The increase of population, too, was much greater than recorded immigration and natural increase combined, indicating further influx from other parts of New Zealand and the Australian colonies. Something of the pattern of difficulties experienced in Nelson was, one feels inevitably, repeated. Too many landless laborers and too few capitalists to hire them was again the theme; stop-gap employment on public works (sawing the timber which clothed the hills above the western shore of the harbor, and making streets and cutting roads) had to be given for many months, as agricultural development and its expected demand for labor was very slow. The wages paid by the New Zealand company of approximately 17s. 6d. for a fifty-five-hour week must, however, have seemed utopian to many of the immigrants. The *Otago Witness* reported on April 5, 1850, that less than two hundred and twenty acres were under cultivation as of April 1.

When the news came, in October, 1850, that the Company had wound up its operations, the sponsoring body (the Lay Association of the Free Church of Scotland) attempted to carry on. The price of land was, however, much too high, and from the demise of the Company until the beginning of 1852 only £3,752 worth of land was sold. Finally on May 17, 1853, the Association itself was dissolved, and the last feeble outside prop for the little settlement vanished. Nor had the population shown any great increase. On January 1, 1854, there were only two thousand Europeans in the block;[41] there were indeed only twenty-four hundred in all the settlements from the Waitaki River to Fiordland. These together made up the Province of Otago, which was established with Canterbury and Nelson as one of the three provinces of South Island in 1852, when representative and responsible government was granted to New Zealand.

In the year 1855, Fitton[42] gave the total provincial population as follows: Europeans 2,852, Half-castes 79, and Maori 505, a total of 3,436. The *Otago Provincial Gazette*, however, proceeded to show the geographical distribution of 3,495 people (table V). There were in all, thirty-six hundred acres in cultivation and another two thousand acres fenced but not yet plowed. A further twenty-one thousand acres, neither fenced nor cultivated as yet, had been purchased. The livestock included four mules, 323 goats, 717 horses, 1,627 swine, 8,496 "cattle beasts," and 75,474 sheep.

The slow agricultural development was, in large degree, again due to the greater lure of sheep-running for those who had money to invest. Much of the land in the block and beyond had been taken up under a system of licensing depasturage, and even as early as January 1, 1854, while only two thousand acres were under cultivation for wheat, oats, and grass, the Otago area was running thirty-five thousand sheep and over five thousand cattle.

TABLE V

GEOGRAPHICAL DISTRIBUTION OF OTAGO POPULATION (1855)

Dunedin and Port Chalmers		1582 (Europeans)
Taieri East	220	
Taieri West	119	
Native village and Waihola	120	
Tokomairiro and Clutha	167	
Total	626	*Including Maori in the Taieri-Tokomairiro-Clutha area*
Waikouaiti	81	
Goodwood	91	
Moeraki	66	
Waitaki	49	
Total	287	*Including Maori along the coasts to the north.*

The first Provincial Council for the new province of Otago, which had control of the disposal of its own lands, met from December, 1853 until April, 1854, thus anticipating the meeting of the General Assembly for the colony as a whole, which met for the first time on May 24, 1854. The fact that the provincial councils got in the first licks at oratory and legislation was one of the many factors encouraging a strongly localized provincial consciousness which was to prevent any concerted action for the development of the colony as a whole for another fifteen to twenty years. The Otago council passed new Land Regulations which required a ten shilling per acre down-payment for land alienated within the block, and annual improvements of ten shillings per acre in each of three subsequent years before full title could be obtained. The price was still too high for the graziers, and they pressed steadily inland in ever greater numbers beyond the confines of the block. The council then, while maintaining a ten-shilling cash and a thirty-shilling improvement regulation for every acre sold within the block, was forced to make easier regulations without. At first, six hundred thousand acres were put on sale without the prohibitive improvement clause, but except for favored areas, such as

homestead sites or bits of river flat, not much was sold. Yet the
squatters continued to graze more sheep on larger acreages until
the interior was effectively "staked out" in runs even beyond the
great lakes and up to the limit of possible grazing in the Southern
Alps.

The measure finally adopted to assert Crown rights to the interior lands and to produce as much revenue as possible, was the
issuance of depasturage licenses, as had been done earlier in the
Wairau. These required from the lessee only that he should maintain a certain minimum stock population in the area held, and
that he pay sixpence per head annually for cattle and a penny a
head for sheep. As in other parts of South Island, the right of pre-
emption on certain acreages (as eighty for a homestead and ten
for each shepherd's hut) was allowed. Under these benign rules,
between 1855 and 1861 the number of sheep in Otago increased
from fifty-nine thousand to six hundred and ninety-four thousand,
and the cattle from sixty-five hundred to forty-four thousand.

The sheep owners, many directly from Australia, began, with
this expansion, to absorb the unemployed men of the settlement.
The early payment of relief, or giving of "made" work, soon
ceased. In 1854 the provincial council authorized the establishment of immigration agencies in both London and Glasgow, an
overwhelming majority of the council opposing restriction to Scottish immigrants.[43] The next two years saw an influx of five hundred a year, mostly from the British Isles. In 1858 the annual total
jumped to twenty-eight hundred, with the aid of a twenty-thou-
sand-pound loan applied to the purpose; more than seven hundred arrived on three ships almost simultaneously in midwinter.*

* The assisted immigrants signed an agreement to repay assistance received in
one, two, or three years after their arrival, but the scheme failed as most such
schemes had failed before. Ten years later, in 1867, thirteen thousand of the twenty
thousand pounds or more thus spent on assisting immigrants was still outstanding.
McIndoe (undated pamphlet in Hocken Library, Dunedin) gives the following
breakdown of Otago population figures from 1853 on:

	Immigration	Emigration	Total Population
1853	471	28	2,391
1854	332	187	2,557
1855	356	133	2,852
1856	671	102	3,796
1857	589	220	4,631
1858	2,821	551	6,995
1859	2,300	515	9,010
1860	3,031	269	12,961

Wages, which had advanced from the early "made-work" level of three shillings per day to seven shillings, largely as a result of the general rise in world prices following the great spate of world gold production in the decade, now dropped back to six shillings.

The population, which reached seven thousand in 1858, and had jumped to thirteen thousand in 1860, was still overwhelmingly of the laboring and poor artisan class. Though the artisan skills were sometimes high, they were often not of great applicability in the new land. The chief occupations open were those of musterers, carpenters, fencers, bullock drivers, and shearers on the big sheep stations, or agricultural laborers on the smaller farms near the coast. Many highland shepherds with their dogs also came at this time, and their special contributions, considered in detail below, were invaluable. There was a continued dribble of population from the Australian colonies (fifty in 1855, for example), which continued up until the great influx from Victoria and New South Wales with the gold rush to Otago in 1861. The influence of this stream was disproportionate to its small size in terms of the capital, chiefly sheep, and the experience of sheep husbandry on great, open, tussock-covered runs, which it brought with it.

The Southern Block, the country forming the plains of Southland between the Mataura River and Fiordland (fig. 25), was included in the boundaries of the new Province of Otago in 1852. Its purchase from the Maori was completed in 1853, and in that year one Alex Sinclair drove a herd of cattle overland from Dunedin.[44] Three run-holders took up land in 1854, five in 1855, and four in 1856. Thereafter they came in greater numbers. They were mostly Scottish in name, although many had had Australian experience. The *Otago Gazette* (vol. 8, p. 158) reported the population of the Southland area as 406 on December 31, 1857. Though the first sheep were imported through Bluff Harbour in 1853,[45] most of them may have been driven overland from Dunedin until Bluff and New River (Invercargill) were declared Ports of Entry in 1857. The same issue of the *Gazette* listed 22,300 sheep, 2,258 cattle, 242 swine, 160 horses, and 67 goats in the area. At the same time, the beginning of 1858, fourteen buildings were reported for the town of Invercargill, with several more on the outskirts.[46]

In Southland, as previously in the Wairau, there were in the late fifties almost completely pastoral communities, lightly peopled and completely dominated by the wealthy sheep owners. Their interests were not those of the towns and villages of Collingwood, Motueka, or Nelson in the north, nor of the string of coastal settlements from Oamaru (with a population in 1859 of only twenty-five people) through Moeraki, Hampden, Palmerston, Waikouaiti, Dunedin, Mosgiel, and Milton to Balclutha, in Otago. In both cases the pastoralists, forgetting that they held the land almost without fee, complained that when they bought land on their runs a *pro rata* share of the proceeds was not spent there but in the provincial centers. Similar complaints appeared in North Island in the late fifties. As the run-holders were the wealthiest, and often the best-educated members of their communities, they tended through the limitations of the franchise to dominate the General Assembly in Wellington, if they failed to do so in Dunedin or Nelson. They succeeded in having passed there a *New Provinces Act,* which received the assent of the Legislative Council and the Governor in 1858. All that was required to create a new province, and thus to put the electors thereof in control of their own land fund, was that a majority of the electors in any block of country exceeding five hundred thousand acres in extent should so indicate their desire. On November 1, 1859, and on April 1, 1861, Marlborough and Southland, respectively, thus came into being.

At the time of its "independence," Southland's 280 electors voted for fifteen hundred people, while Otago's population at the same date, just prior to the big gold strikes, had reached nearly fifteen thousand. Southland had a short life as a province and was reunited to Otago on October 6, 1870, after a hectic financial career in which it endeavored to build a railway from Invercargill north to the gold fields. Marlborough dragged out its separate political existence until 1876 when all the provinces were abolished. One is tempted to use the term "a political abortion," (one that was frequently applied in those vigorous days) to describe either of these adventures.

THE CANTERBURY SETTLEMENT

While organized settlements were thus getting under way to the north and south, activity toward the filling in of the great intermediate plain (fig. 28) on the east coast was also beginning. The settlement of Canterbury had marked advantages over the others. In Nelson, little use seems to have been made of the prior experience of those settlers around Cook Strait who remained from the whaling era. From its very inception, the Otago settlement did have a nucleus of agricultural experience and a source of food inherited from the whaling days. The Canterbury settlement, however, had not only the advantage of a decade of previous agricultural experiment in the very area, but it could also draw upon all the experience of both the Nelson and Otago settlements in avoiding mistakes. Moreover it attracted settlers with practical agricultural and pastoral skill from the earlier settlements on both islands and, to a greater degree even than the older settlements, from across the Tasman sea. It benefited from being able to buy livestock which was acclimatized in the island and accustomed to the food which the tussock lands supplied. Some of Canterbury's more important advantages are mentioned, in order to assess properly the opinion sometimes expressed that the Wakefield system more nearly succeeded there than in Nelson or Otago. There is no satisfactory evidence that it did so, and the fact that the settlement prospered so well is no argument for that thesis.

Edward Gibbon Wakefield seems to have been irrepressible. The failure of the Nelson settlement he blamed on the Company's blundering management. The Otago settlement interested him, but not deeply. He still kept high hope of a reasonable trial for his general system despite the disappointments in South Australia, Wellington, New Plymouth, and Nelson. He still thought that if a true cross-section of English life, less paupers and criminals, could be transported to a new world, a region with all the characteristics which he idolized in his England must result. To achieve this, people must pay high prices for the land, both to keep them on it and to pay for laboring immigrants, public works, schools, roads, and churches. Land must neither be cheaply sold nor cheaply leased. Above all, every attempt must be made to get a full range of members of English society, including yeoman farmers and urban middle-class tradesmen, to enlist. He was, again, asking the extremely unlikely, if not the impossible, and he paid no more attention than previously to the physical character of the setting for his Anglo-Utopia. The settlement succeeded, but in no sense was it a Wakefield settlement in character as it did so.

This time Wakefield hitched his wagon to that brightest star of English upper-class society, the Church of England. An association was to be formed independent of the Company, much like the Lay Association of the Free Church of Scotland. When its membership was announced in 1848 it sounded like the roster of a slightly improved, and more respectable, House of Lords. Named after his see, it included the Primate of the Church of England with five of his bishops and selected members of the higher clergy, as well as assorted peers, distinguished members of the House of Commons, and some eminent business figures. The prospectus, issued June 1, 1848, followed much the same general lines as the Wakefield-patterned plans for the Nelson and Otago settlements. It differed in its larger scope (a million acres), its higher price for land (three pounds per acre), and its more elaborate ecclesiastical plans, which included the erection of residences for a bishop, an archdeacon, and a college principal, and of twenty schools, twenty churches, twenty parsonages, a college, and a chapel. These represented such a heavy cut into the prospective proceeds of the land sale that, from the perspective of a century later, it seems hard to imagine any but a very loyal churchman buying into the scheme, but the strong ecclesiastical flavor was intended to attract the better class of laborers. Not content with being as self-consciously English as the Otago settlement was Scottish, it set out, thus, by the method in which it intended to use the land-sale proceeds, one third of which were to provide for churches and church-controlled schools, to be even more completely a church colony as well. While it seemed advisable for the Canterbury group to dissociate itself as far as possible from the Company whose disasters had been highly publicized, the Company was to arrange for the sale of land to it.

Wakefield had a serious stroke in 1847 and the actual organization of the new settlement fell largely into the hands of one of his most enthusiastic proselytes, a young Anglo-Irishman, John Robert Godley. For some time he had handled the necessary public contacts for Wakefield, whose earlier rather purple personal history might have created antipathies in the ultra-respectable clientele he hoped to attract. Despite Godley's hard work, the land sales were sluggish. First the million-acre goal was abandoned in 1849, and by July 1, 1850, a total of only nine thousand acres had been sold for twenty-seven thousand pounds.[47]

By the late forties the Port Cooper plains seemed more attractive than ever as a site for a settlement, and it was here that the location for this select little England was chosen. Before discussing the early course of the Canterbury Association's settlement however, some of the preliminary pioneering should be briefly reviewed.[48] In 1840, we may recall the new French settlers at Akaroa, and the cattle of Rhodes on the hills to the south of them, the unsuccessful agricultural experiment of the same year on the banks of the Avon stream, and the several bay-whaling establishments. The unhappy course of the French settlement has been briefly discussed. In 1842, Sinclair and Hays, two Scots with some capital who had migrated as landholders to Port Nicholson with their families and had faced the land shortage and Maori threat there, decided to try to find land elsewhere in the colony. After a reconnaissance visit, they decided on Banks Peninsula, and obtained the approval of the Company to settle there and make provisional land selections in satisfaction of their scrip. In 1843, with their families, they settled at the head of Pigeon Bay (fig. 27). In a few years they had become well established with comfortable houses constructed of the plentiful peninsular timber. Considerable stretches of the bay-head flats (fig. 10) were already cleared of big timber by whalers and others, and there they started a small dairying industry, supplemented by some agriculture, with cattle imported from New South Wales via Port Nicholson. They were able to find a ready market for butter and cheese in Wellington and Akaroa. Lumbering was an additional source of income, and the Sinclairs also built some small schooners.

In 1843, before finally sailing to Pigeon Bay, Captain Sinclair had transported two other Scotsmen, William and John Deans, to Port Cooper. These brothers, also unable to find satisfaction for their land claims on North Island and unwilling to occupy their claim in the ill-omened Nelson settlement, had decided to establish themselves in this area. Their published letters [49] describing their early years there are among the most important documents in the historical geography of South Island, and we will draw upon them heavily in discussing agricultural and pastoral beginnings. If we have credited a Welshman, Jones, with laying some of the foundations of the "Scottish" agricultural settlement of Otago, as much credit must be given to these two dour and determined Scots for laying the groundwork on which the Canterbury "pilgrims" were later to build.

They chose a site near a considerable patch of bush along the Avon stream, where the brief 1840 agricultural experiment had taken place, and called it Riccarton. The sixty-four acres of bush were an invaluable asset, one of the few small patches on the plains between Banks Peninsula and the mountains. Part of the original grove is still standing as an untouched native reserve in the Riccarton suburb of Christchurch, a tribute to the Deans' conservational instincts and an indication of how much less vicious the mutilation of the region might have been if the yeoman farmer element had not been almost completely lacking in the people of South Island. For the Deans were true yeoman farmers in spirit—representatives of the few left in England or Scotland who had not been ruthlessly "enclosed" off the land in the previous sesquicentury.

Actually, Wakefield, Governor Grey, and Selwyn, the Anglican bishop of New Zealand, had all visualized a North Island location for Canterbury. Among those suggested were the valleys of the Rangitikei and Manawatu, and the Raumahunga plains of the Wairarapa valley near Wellington.[50] With these especially in mind, a surveyor with New Zealand experience, one Captain Thomas, was engaged by the Association in 1848 to sail for New Zealand to select a site for the settlement and to survey it. He quickly heard of the Deans' brothers success, which directly contradicted the sour report of Tuckett in 1844. A letter from Wellington to London at this time [51] detailed some of the proven advantages of the Port Cooper plains over a North Island location. These included: an excellent port; absence of Maori in any number; and grassland easy to plough and of vast extent, without timber to clear and yet with timber readily available from the nearby heavily wooded peninsula. Captain Thomas' report [52] after his selection of the plains' site was dated May 18, 1849. It provides a well-organized, complete, but concise description of the still virgin plains. In the same year his recommendations were adopted by the Association; approval of the Governor and Bishop followed, though it was not until August of that year that the Port Cooper area was finally purchased from the Maori. This area included the northern section of Banks Peninsula, all of which was exempted from the "purchase" of what is now Canterbury and Otago from the Ngai Tahu tribe in June, 1848: twenty million acres for two thousand pounds. Absolutely essential to the success of the settlement, the peninsular lands brought the Maori two hundred pounds, one of the highest prices per acre which they received.

In the sketch accompanying Thomas' report, the capital city, for which the unquestionably correct Anglican name of Christchurch had been selected, was planned for the head of Port Cooper, with a subsidiary town of Stratford to be located just east of the Deans' farm. The port itself was to be located farther down Port Cooper inlet. Port Cooper and Port Levy were temporarily renamed Victoria and Albert. Later, a similar move to give the names of Victoria and her consort to the Franz Josef and Fox glaciers also failed, and New Zealand today is notable in the British Commonwealth for its singular lack of reminders of the imperial queen in its toponymy. The move to change Maori names, or those applied by the pre-1848 settlers, to ringing English alternatives was only moderately successful. Of six major rivers in Canterbury thus rechristened, three are known today by their original Maori names. The six were, from north to south (the surviving name is in italic); *Ashley*–Rakahire; Courtenay–*Waimakariri; Selwyn*–Waikerikeri; Cholmondeley–*Rakaia; Ashburton*–Akateri; Alford–*Rangitata.*

As the surveys proceeded, it became clear that the present site of Lyttelton would make the best harbor, and that the site projected for the capital city contained too little flat land; the capital consequently displaced Stratford, by the banks of the Avon. By March of 1850, Captain Thomas had surveyed three hundred thousand acres of the plains and pegged out the streets of Lyttelton and Christchurch. The street names of both places were chosen from the list of British episcopal sees. When Godley arrived as executive agent of the Association on April 11, 1850, he found that an immigrant's barracks, a house for himself, and a variety of other buildings had been built in Lyttelton. Finally the first four ships containing the "pilgrims" arrived, three of them together on December 16, 1850, with 791 immigrants in all, and settlement proceeded.

The connections of the Association with the Company were meantime severed when the latter discontinued operations in 1850 and the Crown took over its assets and liabilities. The outstanding debts and claims of the Company were finally settled only in 1857 by the *New Zealand Company's Claims Act* of that year, by which the provinces were induced to accept part of the liabilities as charges against their revenues. After a short period of deputizing for the Crown in the administration of the new settlement, the Association was replaced by the Canterbury Provincial Council, with the operation of the *Constitutional Act* of 1852. This act provided representative (assuming rather severe property qualifications for the franchise) and, by quick evolution, responsible government through an elective general assembly for the colony, and elective provincial councils for the six provinces into which New Zealand was divided. The Otago Association gave up its charter in 1852, and the Canterbury Association did likewise in 1853. The large, empty spaces between the three nuclei of settlement in South Island made it a simple matter to draw bold lines across the map as boundaries between the new provinces of Nelson, Canterbury, and Otago (*see* fig. 2).

As usual, the fundamental principle of the Wakefieldians, concentrated agricultural settlement, quickly broke down in Canterbury. It failed, not because of lack of good agricultural land or markets, for, as we shall see later, both of these existed in good measure, but because a far more profitable alternative use for capital was available. This use had been pioneered in the plains of the Little and Great Karoos at the Cape, whence it had been transferred to New South Wales and vastly altered there with a great deal of original invention. For a period of five years or more before the Canterbury settlement got going, grazing had been demonstrated by the pioneer squatters in the Wairau and Awatere valleys to be a much more profitable activity than agriculture. A contemporary writer, who shall be nameless, punned that Wakefield's schemes had "died in the wool."

The beginnings of pastoralism in South Island in the late forties were closely connected with contemporaneous difficulties of over-expansion in the wool-growing industry in New South Wales and with the falling price of wool. Between 1841 and 1844 that colony had endured a severe economic crisis [53] which was to continue, though with steady abatement, until the gold strikes of the end of the decade. Sheep with eighteenpence-worth of wool on their backs were sold for less than a shilling.[54] The Australian story is not to be retold here, but with the difficulty of easily finding new land, with sheep to be had for the asking, and with millions of open grassy acres available in New Zealand within reasonable transportation distance for large "mobs" (or flocks) of sheep, the result was perhaps inevitable. Capital from England was converted to sheep in New South Wales or Victoria before reaching the new colony, or, even more largely, Australian entrepreneurs who had escaped with something of their original capital in the slump, moved across the Tasman Sea to begin anew.

When Canterbury was opened, there was already, then, a large sheep population in the Wairau-Awatere, and the squatters there and in New South Wales were casting covetous eyes southward to those great expanses of tussock on the edge of which the little. community of the Church of England was tentatively establishing itself. Already the sheepmen were forcing a passage through the weak defenses of the settlement in coastal Otago to the open lands of Central Otago and the Southland plain, converting most of those with capital there, including Cargill himself, to this newer and quicker method of financial advancement. One of their representatives, Rhodes, who with his brothers had pioneered Australian pastoral squatting [55] had, as we have seen, pioneered the introduction of cattle to Banks Peninsula. To these he soon added sheep, establishing his first station on the southern shores of what was to be Lyttelton Harbour. Moreover, even the Deans brothers, hard-headed businessmen above all else, had begun to run sheep up-country before the pilgrims arrived. More of the Australians followed on the heels of the pilgrims and the great race for land was on. In Canterbury, as in Otago and Nelson, the landholders with capital easily forgot the high principles of Wakefieldism, and instead of spending their money on agricultural development, they joined in the new rush.

They could not afford to buy the land at three pounds an acre for their purposes, and could not even buy much at the cheaper rate of ten or five shillings per acre which Grey set in 1853 for wastelands outside the blocks, though some large alienations of better, more accessible, land were made under these rules, notably by one Moore from Van Diemen's Land. Though the Canterbury Association's block had been increased to two and one-half million acres from the original one million, the three pounds per acre regulations for sale therein were long continued, and there was many times more acreage available beyond its limits. Although not all of the nine and one-half million acres of Canterbury which lay to the east of the divide were suitable for sheep, for various reasons of relief, vegetation, or climate, there were at least five million acres of fair to good virgin tussock land open to the squatters.

To the purchase of an acre in the block for three pounds was soon added the right to graze five unoccupied acres in the block at a rate of 18s. 6d. per hundred acres per year, as the Association attempted a feeble compromise to save its position. Even this compromise, however, did not hold the sheepmen in the block. The Imperial Government's *Australasian Land Sales Act of 1842* [56] was made the authority for the fourteen-year-leasehold provisions

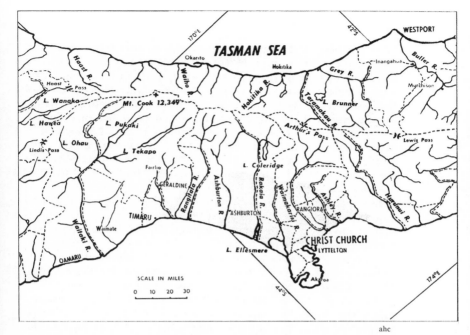

ahc

FIG. 29. The waist of South Island: The plains of Canterbury in relation to the mountains and west coast (principal area of plains shaded).

of 1851, which have already been mentioned in connection with the Otago expansion. The regulations made it easy for the squatters to control effectively the land they leased. Indeed, within a decade, in Canterbury, Marlborough, and Southland, they *were* the government, for all practical purposes, operating through the provincial councils which had successfully wrested the control of disposal of the public domain from the general assembly. The sheep owners were to dominate the general assembly itself, even after the abolition of the provinces in 1876, until the great social, political, and land-tenurial revolution of the last decade of the century. By right of pre-emptive purchase, they could largely fend off challenges to their position, and quickly became, based on their control of most of the public domain, the chief vested interest in all occupied parts of the island. The use of the land for sheep meant that it could not be used for closer settlement, even where that became of fairly obvious necessity. Within a decade South Island's tussock lands, virtually to the farthest limits of possibility, became a gigantic sheep farm (fig. 30). A century later the best description of the island is still "sheep country," though the relative importance of the sheep industry was to be threatened by competition of gold-seeking, agriculture, and dairying at different times, and though the techniques and products of the industry, as well as the sheep themselves, were to change greatly. Some of the argument of later chapters has been anticipated here, but just as an understanding of the invasion of plants and animals demands some background knowledge of the peopling, so it is difficult to discuss the influx and settlement of people without consideration of some salient points with regard to land-use history.

In contrast to the implications in North America of the term "squatter," it implied in Australia large-scale capital and operations; from there it migrated with the sheep, and often the squatters themselves, to New Zealand. The "squatocracy" (a term later applied in opprobrium) of Canterbury was a blend of such Australian immigrants with entrepreneurs from the mother country. The building of a station house in the center of a wide reach of pasture land, with its dependent colony of servants and laborers, suited the Australian squatter economy and Canterbury social pretensions alike. The squatter taught the English gentleman the economic rules of the game and often gained social acceptance (if he were not of the same class) by learning the social rules in return. Actually, a rather high proportion of the Australian squatters were of Scottish origin, and Scottish names are predominant among those who came to New Zealand, so far as Nelson, Marlborough, Otago, and Southland are concerned, though the nature of the settlement may have attracted a higher proportion of English to Canterbury.

Canterbury's population increased more quickly than had that of Nelson or Otago, despite heavy losses to the Australian gold diggings in the early fifties. Paul mentions that five vessels with 580 emigrants arriving in 1852 were estimated to have just replaced those lost to the Victorian gold fields.[57] In November of that year there were thirty-four hundred Europeans and two hundred Maori in the province. In 1855 [58] the principal agricultural district stretched from the river Ashley to the river Halswell, about twenty miles long and six miles wide. The population was congregated thickly around Christchurch, but the new township of Kaiapoi (the old Maori *pa* of that name had been further north near the sea) was forming on the left bank near the mouth of the

Joyce Finney

FIG. 30. Mouth and bar of the Avon stream with Banks Peninsula to
the left and Christchurch in the background.

Waimakariri River where it is joined by the Cam stream from
the north. The port town of Lyttelton had about nine hundred
people and was connected with Christchurch and Kaiapoi by small
vessels of from fifteen to twenty tons which could negotiate the
bars of the Avon or the Waimakariri (fig. 30). There was also a
bridle track over the Port Hills from Lyttelton to the rest of the
settlement; the *Lyttelton Times* of March 17, 1857, announced
the first use of a new cart road by a wheeled vehicle making the
trip from Lyttelton to Christchurch.

Around the bays of Banks Peninsula the chief activity was the
cutting of timber for the plains, a practice that denuded that area
of trees in a few decades. In 1855, although sheep farming was
the principal topic of interest in the settlement, more of the population was engaged in agricultural pursuits. The population included 2,196 males and 1,699 females, of whom no less than 565
had been born there.* Seven thousand two hundred and twenty-
one acres of land had been fenced, chiefly by ditch, post, and rail,
though quicks and gorse had been introduced; of this: 2,920 acres
were in crop, including 807 in wheat, 802 in oats, 287 in barley,

---

* These official statistics published in the *Canterbury Provincial Gazette* (July 1,
1854) perhaps refer to children born in the "colony" instead of the "settlement";
in any event such early statistics are of dubious accuracy.

364 in potatoes, 289 in "artificial" grass, 227 in orchards or gardens, one acre in maize, and 143 in other crops. The stock included 20 asses or mules, 396 goats, 596 horses, 4,391 pigs, 6,363 head of cattle and 99,245 sheep. Except for wool, the exports of 1853 consisted of sawn timber and house frames, potatoes, oats, and cheese to a value of £3337. On December 16, 1854, the *Lyttelton Times*, celebrating the fourth anniversary of the landing of the "pilgrims," estimated the value of wool exports as about twenty-four thousand pounds. The Custom House records for the period from January 1 to November 30, 1855,[59] show the export items listed in table VI which had a value above a hundred pounds.

TABLE VI

EXPORTS FROM CANTERBURY VALUED ABOVE £100
(Jan. 1 to Nov. 30, 1855)

Articles Exported	Coastwise (i.e. New Zealand)	To Sydney	To Melbourne	Total Value
Butter	6,720 lb.	1,568 lb.	3,024 lb.	£ 707/ –/–
Cheese	48,720 lb.	10,955 lb.	14,100 lb.	3,688/15/–
Barley	1,719 bus.	463 bus.	524 bus.	711/16/–
Oats	3,441 bus.	3,008½ bus.	3,651 bus.	2,612/12/9
Wheat	2,829 bus.		859 bus.	2,212/16/–
Flour	26½ tons		1 ton	1,015/ –/–
Potatoes	128½ tons		590¾ tons	6,834/ –/–
Timber (sawn) .	5,100 feet	50,000 feet		551/ –/–
Wool	28,448 lb.	399,308 lb.		21,387/16/–

Total (including ale and beer, bacon and hams, butter, carrots, bran, sharps, firewood, whale oil, onions, building stone, etc.) value = £40,037 15s. 1d. The wool formed more than one-half the value of exports.

According to the *Lyttelton Times* of Dec. 16, 1856, by that time the whole of the "available" country in the province was "beneficially" occupied by sheep and cattle farmers beyond the narrow belt of agricultural land around Christchurch, which, by 1858, included but fourteen thousand acres in cultivation. In 1859, by the official statistics of the colony, the population of Canterbury was estimated to have risen to 12,784, surpassing that of Otago (9,010) and even that of Nelson (10,178). Agricultural settlement was reaching into what are now Rangiora, Springs, and Ellesmere counties. North of the Waipara and south of the Rangitata to the Waitaki, the great tussock areas were not yet agriculturally occupied, but were dotted with sheep stations. South of the Rangitata, Canterbury province contained in 1858 only 349 people (280 males and 69 females) and a new townsite was just beginning at Timaru, but with no less than 144 houses including two of stone. There were but 122 acres in cultivated crops in the southern area, but there were 152,885 sheep.

THE ENTRY OF THE "DIGGERS"; SOUTH ISLAND'S GOLD RUSHES OF THE SIXTIES

Much of the story of the peopling of South Island to the end of the fifties has not been easily available hitherto, and a good deal of what has been said above represents new evidence or new interpretation of known facts. There is much less that needs to be said here about the subsequent course of the peopling, which has been effectively and elaborately treated by a number of writers.[60] Some brief outline of that course must, however, be set down as a prelude to a discussion of the plant and animal invasions as such.

The period of initial heavy import of population between 1840 and 1850 had seen little export of goods; it must be thought of as a period of self-sufficiency, or of import of capital. In the fifties, heavy imports of capital, especially in terms of sheep, continued, but were partly balanced by growing exports of wool. Though wool was to be overshadowed by gold in the sixties, to be supplemented by both gold and wheat in the eighties, and again by frozen meat and dairy products in increasing degree in the nineties and into the new century, wool production was to remain of basic if slowly diminishing importance as a directive of land use.

When the gold rushes to California and Australia were receiving their greatest publicity just at the mid-century mark, South Island lost, temporarily we may suppose, a certain amount of venturesomeness in immigrant character and liquid capital that it might otherwise have drawn. The opening of a market for agricultural produce in New South Wales and Victoria, however, helped to maintain some agriculture around the nuclei at Nelson, Christchurch, and Dunedin. The magnet of gold did draw off labor, but disappointed gold seekers also moved into New Zealand to make up this deficiency. Soon, however, the population in this land of tentative agricultural beginnings and large-scale pastoral occupation was to feel the economic and social intoxication of alluvial gold mining on its own soil.

Gold had been reported in New Zealand at various times in the first decade of organized settlement.[61] Captain Wakefield had found traces of gold on his expedition from Nelson to Massacre

(Golden) Bay in 1842. Other reports followed, but little interest was attached to them until after the California finds of 1848. With the Australian rushes of 1851, a good deal of gold fever was beginning to appear, and in 1852 a small rush set in to Coromandel peninsula on North Island, which was later to become the chief New Zealand center of "reef," or hardrock, gold mining of the colony. More intensive prospecting was stimulated, and by 1856 the first alluvial gold field on South Island was proved on the Aorere River. The town of Collingwood on Massacre, or Golden, Bay was thus established, but its glory was brief and it has never attained again its population of the eighteen-fifties. Quite a few disappointed prospectors from California and Victoria moved in, but there was no large-scale desertion of other activities in the established settlements, and no real "rush" occurred when gold discoveries were announced on the Buller River, in the same area, in 1859.

Though Canterbury's graywacke mountains and the gravelly plains derived therefrom were barren of gold, it had been reported from several places in the Otago schist country in the fifties.[62] In 1861 a certain Gabriel Reid made the first big strike in a gully (Gabriel's Gully) along a tributary of the Tuapeka stream in Tuapeka county. Reid had learned his techniques in California and Australia. The fluid alluvial-gold-mining population, faced with declining yields elsewhere, found its imagination captured, and a very large rush set in. The population of Otago rose from

FIG. 31. Increase of population in Otago (1853-1875) when immigration far exceeded emigration.

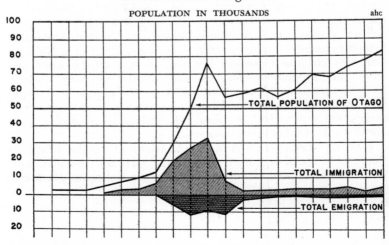

POPULATION IN THOUSANDS   ahc

TOTAL POPULATION OF OTAGO

TOTAL IMMIGRATION

TOTAL EMIGRATION

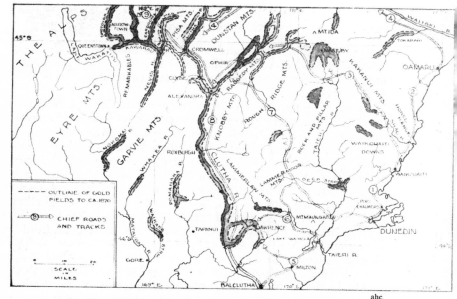

Fig. 32. Routes of entry to the Otago gold fields.

12,691 in 1860 to 30,269 in 1861.[63] The tremendous, abrupt rise in population (fig. 31) was mainly attributable to a mass movement from Melbourne to Dunedin, and so inland, via the lower Taieri plains, to Lawrence. Within a very few months the rush of people had greatly outnumbered the total previous influx of population to the island from the time of the earliest sealing shore parties.[64]

Other finds took the miners progressively farther inland until camps were spread all over what is now Central Otago and northern Southland (fig. 32).[64] These reached even into Lake County northeast of Lake Wakatipu. In the first two years an average of twelve thousand active miners had recovered over a million ounces of gold by the crudest of hand methods. Up to 1872 from Otago alone over three million ounces were exported to a value of approximately twelve million pounds.

Meanwhile the visiting geologist, Hochstetter,[65] had published a report in 1859 which led to further prospecting in the Nelson area. Minor finds were made in the Marlborough Sounds region in 1860, but not until 1864 did a small rush to the Wakamarina set in. Though this field was to bring four thousand men to the diggings temporarily (to found the town of Havelock and the present crossroads of Canvastown and to yield a hundred thousand pounds worth of gold in a year), the field was to prove a very temporary one, when, later in the same year, word came of strikes on the west coast.[66]

Up to this point in the current chapter there has not been any occasion to mention the west coast of the island between Farewell Spit and Fiordland. Its character as to land forms, vegetation, soils, and climate may be quickly gathered from the relevant sections above. The rainfall is excessive, the jungle of the subtropical rain forest all but unbroken, and there is no extensive area of plains. The only "harbors" were the limited estuaries of the rushing mountain rivers, which had very difficult, shallow bars and were often choked with cross-timbers brought in by spring and summer freshets. McClymont,[67] Harrop,[68] and Lord [69] have each reviewed the earliest exploration, which was of extraordinary difficulty. Brunner and Heaphy had followed the coast down from West Wanganui inlet as far as the Taramakau in 1846, and only the still-disputed possibility that some of the settlers who had run a sealing station at The Steeples from 1836 on had crossed the bar in 1844 suggests any earlier contacts.[70] Their report was, understandably, very pessimistic about future settlements along the coast, confirming Cook's off-shore judgment: "an inhospitable shore, unworthy of observation." Brunner, however, continued his explorations in 1846, 1847, and 1848, including one remarkable journey lasting many months in which he was accompanied only by a few unenthusiastic Maori and which he survived by the eating of fern root and the wearing of sandals of *Phormium.*

For another nine years European contacts with the coasts were infrequent, though some more knowledge of the upper and mid-Buller areas was gained. The final agreement for the purchase of the west coast from the Maori was drawn up in March 1856,[71] but it excluded the Arahura district. McKay, the Government Land Purchase officer who had reached the headwaters of the Aorere and Karamea Rivers in 1856, and Mawhera *pa* at the mouth of the Grey in 1857, did not complete the purchase of the Arahura area until 1860. There was, in fact, no apparent urgency for doing so.

One result of the desultory, if widespread, prospecting initiated by the Coromondel and Aorere rushes, was a visit in 1857 by three adventurers from Port Lyttelton, the brothers Oakes, who sailed on the *Emerald Isle* around the southern end of South Island and up the west coast. They got good prospects of gold at Jackson's Bay and at the mouth of the Grey, whose bar they may have been the first Europeans to cross. There was a general impression that the known antipathy of the Canterbury provincial government (which controlled the coast from the mouth of the Grey to Fiordland) to discovery of a gold field in the province led to lack of publicity for, if not direct suppression of, their reports. In this same year of 1847, Harper and Locke made the first Canterbury trans-Alpine expedition by Europeans and also reported gold discoveries. Leonard Harper (a son of Bishop Harper, one of the early leaders of the Canterbury settlement) pushed south along the coast below the Franz Josef and Fox glaciers. In a letter of July 20, 1861, his brother, Archdeacon Harper, reported that Leonard considered the west coast uninhabitable. These were followed, in 1858, by the adventurous G. W. H. Lee, a sheep owner whose explorations had aided in the opening up of the stock route from Marlborough to Canterbury. Accompanied by two Maori he visited the Lake Brunner area, where the forest had a few more openings in it, and decided to take up a run there. When he shortly did so it was the first, and for long the only, pastoral run on the western side of the main Alpine divide, though hardly in typical "coast" country. The Maori accompanying him reported quantities of gold from the left bank of the Buller.[72] The first generally believed reports of gold from the coast were, however, those by John Rochfort, who accompanied James McKay, and who is credited with the location of the Old Diggings field on the Buller in November of 1857.

In 1860, McKay's party met the official geological exploration party from Christchurch under von Haast at Mawhera *pa*. With these more official visits and reports, with the subsequent strikes in Otago, and with Nelson-Canterbury rivalry as between the Buller area (Nelson) and the area south of the Grey (Canterbury), activity in the exploration for gold increased, though still without encouragement from Christchurch. As more evidence appeared that a profitable field might be established, however, the provincial government sent more explorers and, especially, surveyors to lay out a few roads. It was felt that land transport was vital, for, though many small vessels were crossing the bars of the Buller and the Grey, the percentage of wrecks was high. Attempts to cross the lower courses of the rivers by the land route along the shore cost seven lives in 1863. Yet despite the difficulties (and the official apathy or opposition), the popular pressure on the provincial government for more action to open up the coast was becoming too difficult to withstand. The *Lyttelton Times* had editorialized on July 30, 1864:

> If a gold field is, after all, to be forced on Canterbury, without the consent and contrary to the expressed desire of the settlers, they must, nevertheless, submit to fate; and should the natural feelings of discontent, swelling up in their prudent bosoms when Fortune's golden favours are thrust into their hands, be somewhat hard to subdue, the consolation exists that the gold field had turned up in the remotest corner of the province.

This was probably not hypocrisy. Through the fifties, great efforts, to a degree successful, had been made to introduce a better type of laborer to Canterbury, and to preserve the social system so satisfactory to the squatters. The rebellious, democratic reaction to "squatter" government on the part of the Victorian diggers had been highly publicized. It is perhaps significant that the more business-minded government of Otago had evidenced no such viewpoint.

This opinion was published after a modest strike on Greenstone Creek early in that year. As in Otago, more and richer strikes were successively made, and all the auxiliary phenomena of a major gold rush developed. By September of 1865 there were eight to ten thousand people south of the Grey. Towns of some permanence began to rise as sawmills appeared. By December of 1866 the *Nelson Examiner* estimated a population of thirty thousand, and Harrop [73] gives fifty thousand for this date, though whether either of these figures includes the population within Nelson province at the mouth of the Grey and, especially, on the Buller, is not certain. By comparison, The *Official Statistics* for New Zealand for 1853-6 (Auckland, 1858) records that, in 1856, some ten years before, there were just over seventeen thousand people in all of the island. In late 1866, the booming social and economic capital of the area, Hokitika, according to advertisements in old circulars, had at least a hundred taverns in operation. In one day in 1867, forty-one different vessels, of the widest variety as to sort and description, were anchored in the harbor within the bar. In the best year, 1866, over two million pounds worth of gold (552,572 ounces) were recovered.

ahc

Fig. 33. Remains of gold miners' huts in Central Otago: (*top*) high in the mountains, and (*bottom*) down in a valley (near Ophir).

When gold production in Otago declined and was restricted more and more to the techniques of dredging and reef-mining, which needed much capital but little labor, the boom towns of course declined in size. Many, however, did not quite die; they maintained themselves as commercial centers for the pastoral industry and the small extent of irrigation-nurtured agriculture and horticulture which grew out of the techniques of alluvial gold mining. The roads and communications which the gold rush had built helped to compensate for the great areas of valley tailings, the pitted hillsides, and the broken water races which the search for gold left as scars on the countryside (fig. 34). Queenstown, Arrowtown, Cromwell, Alexandra, Roxburgh, and Lawrence rather quickly subsided, but they have managed to hang on as towns. Others like Clyde and Naseby dwindled to mere sleepy villages; Ophir, to a crossroads (fig. 33). Their former populations had been absorbed by coastal towns and countryside, or they have left the colony, but there were, and are, no real "ghost towns" in Otago.

The decline on the west coast was more rapid and more disastrous, for there was no pastoral or agricultural cushion to soften the shock of the dwindling gold returns. However, there was coal on the coast, mined on the banks of the Grey as early as 1865, and a great wealth of timber. To coal-mining and timber-cutting, the few of the population who stayed were to turn; and amid these activities, together with a little tourism, the glamorous boom-

FIG. 34. Hillside gullying originating from a miner's broken water race near Lowburn Ferry in the upper Clutha valley.

ahc

cities of the sixties were to disappear, or to continue as small villages and grow slowly again, in some cases, to the status of towns. Even today agricultural and pastoral activities are not important anywhere on the coast, and the population is heavily urban, if, that is, one may so describe the residents of such *strassendorf* types of villages along the roads near the coal mines as Hector and Granity, north of Westport.

TABLE VII

INCREASE OF POPULATION IN SOUTH ISLAND (1858-1871)

1858		*1871*	
Nelson	10,178	Nelson	22,501
		Marlborough	5,235
Canterbury	12,784	Canterbury	46,801
		Westland *	15,357
Otago	9,062	Otago	60,722
		Southland	8,769

* Politically the entity, Westland, was short-lived. In 1868 dissatisfaction with Christchurch control led to the erection of a semi-independent Westland County Council (the first of the counties); in 1873 Westland was created a province; when, however, provinces were abolished three years later (1876), Westland reverted back to county status, but without control from Christchurch. It has remained a convenient census unit. Westland provincial district must not be confused with Westland land district (which includes all of Grey County), or with Westland County (which includes none of it). Nelson provincial district and Westland provincial district were divided by the Grey River. The provincial district is the area designated for the above census returns.

As to total population gains by South Island in the feverish sixties, we must remember that the gold-seeking population came from Australia in the main, although it had been in some part a recent accretion there. To Australia or to other parts of the world a great part of it had returned by the early seventies. Yet in the period of the sixties, South Island gained more population by the "net" immigration figures alone than either net immigration or natural increase has contributed in any decade since. It was, in the main, a rough, undisciplined, poorly educated, largely male population in the prime of life. It was a population drawn from all occupations and from all over the world, but, in the nature of things, primarily from New South Wales and Victoria and from the descendants of (if not indeed from the ranks of) the freed convict exportees and the large immigration of laborers to that area in the mid eighteen-forties. The fairly large percentage of Irish names among those who stayed on the west coast is significant in this respect. They were probably without any considerable agricultural experience beyond what they had picked up in Australian employment or experience. Actual increases of population from 1858 to 1871 are shown in table VII. While some assisted immigration had continued and natural increase was rapid, this increase must be in the main attributed to the gold rushes.

THE LAST BIG TIDE OF IMMIGRATION TO SOUTH ISLAND

The decline of gold production in the seventies [74] left South Island with a vastly increased population and a very great increase in capital through the imports associated with the immigration. Condliffe [75] estimates that, in 1863 alone, the four and a half million pounds worth of exports, largely gold, was balanced by an import of seven million pounds of capital of all kinds. Still there was not enough work to engage the great surplus of laborers. Small farming as a solution was impossible because of the difficulty of getting land, which by the end of the sixties was tied up very effectively through the large scale alienation of the previous two decades, or, just as effectively, by the large pastoral leases. It would probably have been very difficult to develop it in any event, because of the lack of agricultural experience on the part of so many of the people and the fact that the residue of the gold rushes was composed, too largely, of the least successful diggers, who had no money to carry them elsewhere and therefore little to invest in farms.

By 1869, South Island was in a temporary economic slump which was to continue for a few years. The same position, more serious because of the repercussions of the Maori wars, was faced in North Island. The political and general economic background of this period has been thoroughly discussed in the chief secondary historical works already cited. When world prices rose after the Franco-Prussian War, Julius Vogel, the Treasurer and in 1873 the Premier of the Colonial government, conceived a magnificent scheme to develop New Zealand and employ the surplus labor force. The colony would borrow as much as it could and spend it on public works and further immigration; new capital would be attracted and the cumulative benefits to all would rapidly become apparent. Within a decade ten million pounds were borrowed and spent. Roads, and especially railroads, were built, mostly in South Island. The surplus population was absorbed into big working gangs, and a large inflow of assisted immigration started; over a hundred thousand came to both islands in the decade. When it is once said that even New Zealand's own historians complain that these were, in general, poorly selected, and that the competition for immigrants in Great Britain resulted in the agents taking whomever they could get, little need be added about the character of this new population. Something more as to origins and training, however, will be given below. The immigrants were, again, largely urban and unskilled, chiefly English and Irish. It is not exactly certain how many came to each island, but South Island, and Canterbury in particular, seems to have received the lion's share.

As the construction of public works tapered off toward the end of the decade, there came a further depression and a good deal of serious unemployment among the newcomers. That so much of the influx was eventually employed, chiefly in agricultural or pastoral pursuits, speaks of a very great intensification of such activity, since virtually all the land had been taken up a decade before. There was no considerable manufacturing industry to absorb the immigrants. The only industries in the colony with a total capital exceeding two hundred thousand pounds in land, buildings, machinery, and other plants, were saw-milling, gasworks, breweries, grain mills, printing establishments, and collieries.[76] One might have expected that, with an export of over sixty million pounds of wool by 1881, some considerable woolen industry might have developed in the colony, but in that year only eight hundred thousand pounds of the clip, or just over one per cent, was used locally, and the whole New Zealand woolen industry had a capital of less than £100,000.

Large numbers of men were employed in building 907 miles of railway in the colony between 1873 and 1877, but this activity rapidly declined with the building of only 701 more miles in the next ten years. We need not multiply examples. Throughout the eighties times were hard and unemployment was a serious problem; in 1880, to begin the decade, the Christchurch unemployed sent a petition to the President of the United States asking him to assist immigration thereto. The pastoral industry remained fairly stable, making up, in the beginnings of refrigerated exports of meat and dairy products, for the retreat from areas of depletion and rabbit infestation in the high country. Bonanza, large-scale wheat farming on the newly plowed tussock lands of the plains begun in Canterbury in the seventies continued, but without noticeable acceleration. In the decade as a whole there was a small net immigration gain for New Zealand, but in the five years from 1886 to 1890, there was a net emigration loss; it is thought that South Island may have barely balanced on the whole decade, so strongly had the tide of movement to North Island already set in at that time.

THE END OF THE CENTURY

With the nineties, the full effects of a new economy of farming for the trade in refrigerated meat and dairy products were felt.[77] Relatively intensive small-scale farming became distinctly profitable; no longer was it the subsistence proposition it had been, apart from the suburban milk, vegetable, and meat supply, since the beginning of settlement. Though much of the surplus population had arrived in South Island without farming experience, and had done no farming on its own since its arrival, it had, as we shall see, gone to school to the methods of local agricultural and pastoral farming on the great wheat and sheep stations. Though still with much to learn about intensive meat and butterfat production, the immigrants and their sons had learned quite a lot about sheep, about grain farming, about laying down pastures of English grass. Now they demanded land of their own to work.

By steady political pressure most of the big stations, which were by then often unprofitable in the light of new techniques, were broken up between 1885 and 1910, and the descendants of the penniless immigrants of the seventies, and of the marooned gold rushees of the sixties, became landholders on their own. There had been earlier attempts at rationalization of the land tenurial system in the interests of the landless. By a system of auction sales of pastoral leases and deferred payments for crown lands, nearly seventy-seven hundred settlers took up more than a million acres between 1877 and 1892. Various other devices, many of them described in detail by Jourdain [78] are discussed in parts III and IV of this volume. The new procedures usually made it possible for the lessee to buy, sooner or later. In any event, by 1892 the bulk of the colony's first- and second-class lands were "freeholded," and to provide more land it became necessary to purchase, by force or threat thereof, many of the large holdings for subdivision.

The general social and political repercussions of the subdivision of holdings are outside the scope of this study, but the development of intensive, small-scale farming is of central importance. With increasing prices throughout the world, the new small-farm economy was to enjoy a steadily increasing prosperity for another forty years (until the depression of the nineteen-thirties) without any fundamental changes in the land-use patterns then established. In South Island there was an increase in rural settlement, but a rather small one, in coastal Canterbury and Otago, in Southland, and to a lesser degree in the lower valleys of the Wairau, Waimea, and Motueka valleys in the north. This was the period of the most rapid development of North Island, however, to which most of the immigration of this period to New Zealand, including a very large contingent from Australia, went. There they burned off the bush, subsequently sowed English grasses on the burn, and pastured dual-purpose sheep and both beef and dairy cattle when the pastures were established. There was just a little of this in South Island, in southern Clutha county along the Catlins River, and in southwestern Wallace county along the lower Waiau River; there were, too, some generally unsuccessful imitations in northwestern Nelson and along the west coast. On the whole, South Island received but a small share of this later immigration and not enough to balance the net interisland movement in favor of North Island which began in the seventies and ran full tide between 1890 and 1910. Indeed, the rural population of South Island has increased very slowly since 1905, and there has been little expansion into new areas.

CHAPTER IV

THE CHANGING POPULATION:
ITS NUMBERS, DISTRIBUTION, AND
CHARACTER

To the themes of the natural setting and the course of the peopling of the island, one more must be added to complete the necessary background for consideration of the plant and animal invasions: a brief review of the progress of numbers of the population, its distribution through the island, its origins, its skills and occupations, and those characteristics of particular importance to agricultural and pastoral activities.

POPULATION NUMBERS

South Island's total population [1] at the most recent census of September, 1945, was about five hundred and fifty thousand, having remained almost unchanged from 1936 but representing a gain of some one hundred thousand since 1911. Since the detailed census figures are readily available in many libraries, only some rounded and approximate totals for different periods are given in table VIII. Of additional interest are the relative positions of South Island's population with respect to that of the whole country, which is shown in the second column of the same table. Although South Island has now less than one-third of the people of the country, it was the more heavily populated of the two main islands during the major period of development of land-use patterns.

The New Zealand census records the "de facto" population at some particular instant, rather than the "resident" population, as is rather common elsewhere. Most usually the census has been taken at midnight on some Sunday in March or April, although some of the earlier censuses were taken in mid-summer (December) and that of 1945 in the spring (September); midnight on a Tuesday is now preferred to Sunday. Census intervals, when first regularly established, were three years. This was later changed to five years, and while the quinquennium is still the "official" interval, exigencies of war or depression caused the cancellation of the 1916, 1931, and 1941 enumerations, and that of 1945 represented a six-month advance of date to effect an electoral redistribution before the first postwar general election. The segregation of figures for South and North Islands, of great importance to this study, has not been of interest to the government statisticians in many of their analyses, and has been effected here, where necessary, with some difficulty. The figures given in table VIII, and most subsequent tables, include all Maori, but this is a matter of little significance in South Island where it is doubtful if this group has exceeded ten thousand at any time since the beginning of the nineteenth century. In 1857 less than three thousand Maori were enumerated in South Island (including the Chatham Islands), and in 1936 only 5,197 people in South Island claimed any Maori blood (full-blood: 1,318; three-quarter: 531; one-half: 1,372; one-quarter: 1,968; unspecified: 8).

TABLE VIII

POPULATION GROWTH IN SOUTH ISLAND

Date	South Island Population	Percentage of New Zealand Population
1840	Several hundred	— (?)
1845	3,200	25% (?)
1850	8,000	28% (?)
1858	25,000	42% (?)
1870	150,000	63%
1900	375,000	50%
1945	550,000	32%

The whaling and sealing contacts and the first organized settlements had brought more than twenty-five thousand people to South Island by 1858, and very great attention has been focussed upon these pioneers. The very large influx during the period of

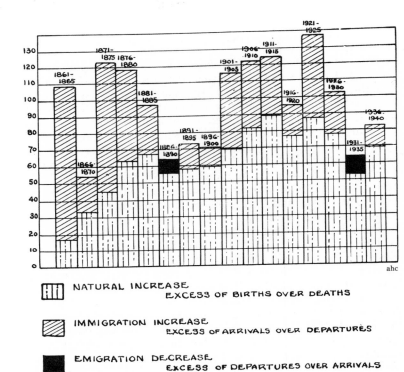

NATURAL INCREASE
EXCESS OF BIRTHS OVER DEATHS

IMMIGRATION INCREASE
EXCESS OF ARRIVALS OVER DEPARTURES

EMIGRATION DECREASE
EXCESS OF DEPARTURES OVER ARRIVALS

FIG. 35. Increase in population of all New Zealand, by quinquennia, showing proportions attributable to natural increase and excess of immigration over emigration (in thousands).

the gold rushes in the eighteen-sixties, however, contributed much more to the ultimate population, in numbers, than did either these pioneers or the immigrants of all subsequent years; the earlier the arrival of any segment of the population, of course, the greater its contribution to subsequent natural increase. The importance of the years from 1861 to 1865 is seen in table IX.

Figure 35, based on data from *Statistics of New Zealand* (for 1870) and *Statistical Report on Population and Buildings* (1940-41), emphasizes the importance of the 1861-1865 increment, as compared with those of successive quinquennia, in contributing to the blood of the subsequent population.

The proportion of South Island's population within different provincial districts at different periods is shown in figure 36.[2] The ratios changed very little between 1880 and 1940. The chief gains

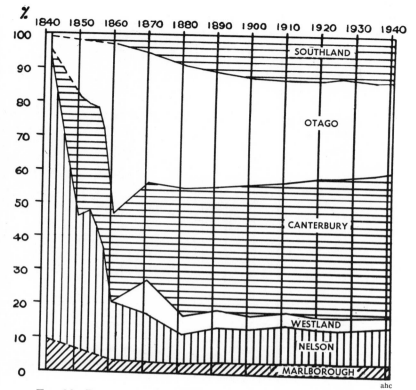

FIG. 36. Percentage of population in chief census divisions of South Island over a century.

were made by Canterbury and Southland at the expense of Otago, and were due to the intensification of fat-lamb production, dairying, and mixed farming on the two principal plains' areas.

"URBAN," "TOWN," AND "RURAL" POPULATION

The definitions of *urban* and *rural* which the New Zealand census uses are not particularly satisfactory to the purpose of understanding population distribution. The divisions: *Cities and Boroughs, Town Districts,* and *Administrative Counties* are those most generally used, and they are not based on numbers of residents; many of the boroughs, especially in one-time gold-mining areas, became little more than skeleton towns with less than five hundred population, whereas a number of centers not classified

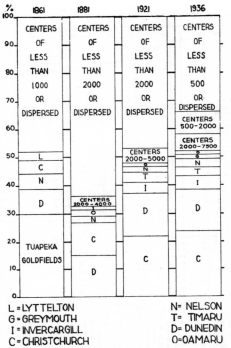

FIG. 37. Proportion of population in major centers, smaller towns, and the countryside, in four census years.

TABLE IX

POPULATION INCREASES FOR ALL OF NEW ZEALAND FROM 1855 TO 1870

	Net Immigration	Natural Increase
1855	3,937	990
1856	2,525	1,316
1857	3,042	1,532
1858	6,130	1,690
1859	8,637	1,943
1860	6,064	2,054
1861	16,222	2,332
1862	20,991	2,833
1863	35,120	3,132
1864	8,527	3,580
1865	12,309	4,733
1866	7,599	5,926
1867	4,859	6,216
1868	860	6,729
1869	3,641	6,997
1870	3,577	7,574
Total	144,040	59,577

as *Town Districts* had populations of over a thousand. In 1936, for instance, the analysis of census figures indicated the following proportions: *Cities and Boroughs:* 312,895 or 56.5 per cent; *Independent Town Districts:* 5,011 or 0.9 per cent; and *Administrative Counties* (including dependent town districts): 236,189 or 42.6 per cent. When the figures are rearranged to accord with the size of various inhabited places, regardless of administrative classification, the following preferable division suggests itself: *Urban* (over 2000): 321,072 or 57.9 per cent; *Town* (500 to 2000): 46,404 or 8.4 per cent; *Rural* (including centers with less than 500): 186,-619 or 33.7 per cent. A subjective estimate of truly dispersed population would place it at about 20 per cent of the total.

Figure 37, constructed from data in the various official statistical publications, indicates the concentration of population in major centers throughout the history of the European settlement of the island. The dominant position of Christchurch and Dunedin is particularly clear. Small towns have had a checkered history; their rate of growth has been mainly a measure of their utility as rural service stations, and has shown the same sensitive adjustment to the nature of the available transportation facilities as such towns have shown in the United States and Canada. With the extension of the railroads they increased their sizes or, at the worst, held their own; with the appearance of the automobile they declined.

Very few villages and towns in South Island were definitely planned, and where the attempt was made it often failed. Nelson, Picton, Christchurch, Lyttelton, Timaru, Port Chalmers, and Dunedin are conspicuous exceptions, but many, like Hampden (near Moeraki), exist, for all practical purposes, only on the survey maps. In the early sixties most of the towns were on or very near to the coast, except, again, the towns of Central Otago born of the gold rushes. Concentrations then began to develop inland: for timber cutting as at Oxford; at crossroads as outlined by the surveyors and therefore partly the result of a deliberate plan, as at Rakaia; at coal deposits, as at Nightcaps or Reefton; at ports; or at other places for a dozen other strictly utilitarian reasons. With the railroad building of the seventies, some came into being as great public-works camps. Some, including Greymouth, Blenheim, Kaiapoi, and Balclutha, grew up at river crossings. Along the coaching routes, towns like Ashburton, Courtenay, and Cass sprang up with the needs for accommodation houses, blacksmiths, saddlers, wheelwrights, and general merchants. Only if these had a well-settled hinterland, and were also on the ensuing railway, did they, however, persist. Cass and Courtenay, for example, are today little more than memories. Attempts at planned village settlements did occur in the seventies in Canterbury,[3] but this nostalgic trial of a reproduction of rural England quite failed. On the fringes of all the towns and villages are the homes of the farmers of surrounding acres, as is commonly found in Australia and the United States. But again, as in those countries, the farmer or grazier lives on the land he works. There are no rural villages of the European type, and except in the first two or three decades of settlement when their existence was part of a process of normal development of dispersed settlement, there have been none.

DENSITY OF POPULATION

This brief review of urban-rural contrasts, with its emphasis on the dispersed character of rural settlement, leads naturally to a consideration of population density. In a country of such varied relief and strong contrasts in natural vegetation, the very uneven distribution of population should occasion no surprise; cultural contributions to the irregularity of pattern will become apparent as we discuss the development of the agricultural and pastoral industries. As well as a dot map of such scale can show it, the accompanying map (fig. 38) shows the distribution of population at the time of the 1936 census. The crude density of population (in this case total number of persons per square mile) for the island as a whole was approximately one person per square mile in 1861, had reached five by 1881, and is approximately ten today. Crude densities for the provincial districts at different census periods, computed from the *General Reports* of the 1921, 1926, and 1936 censuses, are indicated in table X. A somewhat better indication of crude density variation is seen in figure 39, where it is shown, by counties, for the results of the most recent (1945) census. Used in conjunction with table X, this map will serve as a guide to crude density distribution for each of the years of that table. Experiments with a number of definements of the density concept, notably the density of "rural" population on "occupied" land, suggested that the crude density figures indicated the most significant characteristics of population distribution.

It is difficult to know to what degree the density of rural popu-

ahc

FIG. 38. Distribution of population in South Island (1936).

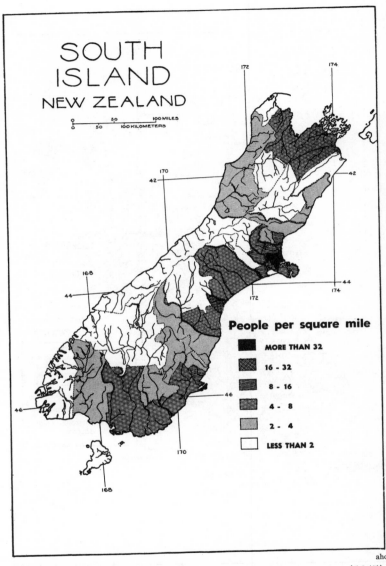

ahc

FIG. 39. Density of population in South Island by counties (1945).

lation has increased in the past fifty or sixty years. The score of years from 1885 to 1905 did see a very great increase in the number of small holders, with a reduction in size of holding, as the big estates were split up. In some parts of Canterbury in 1880, older residents report that it was not unusual to ride through hundreds of acres of tilled land without seeing a single farmstead. The plowing, sowing, reaping, and threshing were largely done on contract by gangs whose members lived in towns or villages. Whether this population should be considered as "rural" or "urban" is not at all clear. We may safely state that densities were very light in many of the inland sections of Canterbury, especially north of the Waipara and south of the Rangitata, and in Southland where big stations were still dominant. Where there were patches of close settlement in Cheviot and Waipara Counties, in 1921 for example, we must visualize virtually no dispersed small holdings even as late as 1890 when eighteen station owners, thirteen in Amuri and five in Cheviot, held some sixteen hundred thousand acres.[4] Going back still further to 1876, there were only seven small settlers, with a total of less than five hundred acres in cultivation north of the Waipara, and south of the Rangitata sixteen stations occupied four hundred and thirty-seven thousand acres.

TABLE X

CRUDE DENSITIES FOR PROVINCIAL DISTRICTS, 1871-1936

Provincial Districts	1871	1881	1901	1916	1936
Marlborough	1.3	2.6	3.3	4.0	4.5
Nelson	2.1	2.8	3.5	4.4	5.5
Westland	3.2	3.3	3.0	2.9	3.8
Canterbury	3.4	8.8	10.3	12.9	16.8
Otago	2.8	8.2	9.0	9.4	10.8
Southland		3.1	4.3	5.3	6.5

THE MIGRATORY CHARACTER OF THE POPULATION

New Zealand's population appears to be a markedly shifting one. Local tradition and sentiment are weak, and this may well be due to the fact that a large part of any local group may have been born or raised elsewhere. This is, of course, a phenomenon which goes hand in hand with the prevalent attitude toward land as a commodity or as a raw material which one buys or sells like machinery, sheep, or fertilizer. This attitude and the assumed mobility of population are important diagnostic characteristics of New Zealand life. A considerable majority of the farmers consulted in South Island had a personal project, sometimes vague but often quite specific, for trying their luck elsewhere "very soon." More often than not one could be best informed about early Westland by a dairy farmer in Southland; or about earlier days on the great sheep stations of Marlborough by a small land-holder on the Oamaru downs. It was often difficult or impossible to uncover locally a continuous record of the use of particular blocks of land.

The only statistical test of the generally accepted hypothesis of extreme mobility which could be found was a "random sampling" reported from the results of the 1921 census [5] given in table XI. It seems to indicate that if people moved at all from the district of birth, they tended to move fairly far from home. The exodus from Westland and a general movement from South Island to North Island is clear.

TABLE XI

MIGRATORY CHARACTER OF THE POPULATION

Of 100 born in:	identical with birthplace	in the vicinity of birthplace	in the same provincial district	elsewhere in South Island	in North Island
Marlborough	58	16	—	2	24
Nelson	56	10	2	8	24
Westland	36	5	8	12	39
Canterbury	58	6	8	7	21
Otago	50	5	9	13	23
Southland	49	1	1	26	23

THE LOCALITIES OF ORIGIN OF THE POPULATION

It has already been established beyond much question that the several hundred pre-1840 Europeans in South Island had come almost entirely from the Australian colonies. We have no precise figures on the proportion of the organized emigration which came to South Island from 1839 to 1850, but we do know that it was largely from the British Isles and very heavily concentrated on the London area. Marais [6] tells us that the settlers came in sixty-three ships from the following ports: Gravesend, 49; Plymouth, 5; Deal, 3; Liverpool, 1; Glasgow, 1; Greenock, 2; and Hamburg, 2. The assumption that those shipping from Gravesend came from near London, if not from the city itself, is based on the fact that intending immigrants had to pay their passage to the port of exit.[7] As is made clear in the writings of Young and Burke discussed below, those who came from the surrounding "Home" counties were from perhaps the most backward area, agriculturally and pastorally, in Great Britain.

Two ships from Hamburg, the *St. Pauli* with a hundred and forty and the *Skiold* with two hundred passengers,[8] brought the only emigrants from the European continent (with the exception of the French at Akaroa) during the period. The New Zealand Company had been seeking German immigrants with advertisements in the newspapers of German cities, perhaps sharing the opinion of the *Nelson Examiner,* which editorialized in the May 27, 1843, issue: "No emigrants are more valuable than the Germans and we hail the intended cultivation of the vine by them with unfeigned pleasure." At any rate they were warmly welcomed upon their arrival in Nelson in 1843 and 1844. By 1845, however, dissatisfied with the opportunities at Nelson, the majority had left for South Australia. Of a hundred or so remaining, a thriving settlement is later reported around east Waimea. From there they moved to the lower Moutere valley, where Pratt,[9] who had known the colony continuously since its arrival in 1843, described its prosperous condition in the mid-seventies. The occasional German names there stand out in vivid contrast with the otherwise almost uniformly British names of the Nelson settlement. Although it is hard to trace specific introductions of plants, animals, or techniques to this group, the Germans almost certainly brought in hop-growing, and their contributions may have been important in other ways, since the *St. Pauli* and the *Skiold* brought a much larger proportion of agriculturally trained immigrants than any other ships landing at Nelson.

There is some useful statistical information relating to the immigration of the fifties in *Statistics of New Zealand* for 1853-6, published in 1858. In Nelson the "net" immigration for the four years was eighteen hundred; nearly thirteen hundred came from the British Isles, 874 from British Colonies (chiefly Australia, we must suppose), and there was a net loss of 338 to non-Empire areas. For Canterbury, figures were published for 1855 only; in that year 436 immigrants arrived from the United Kingdom and 148 from other areas. For Otago, the "net" immigration for the four years was 1,380, of whom 945 came from Great Britain and Ireland, and 365 from the colonies. The net figures do not, however, indicate the great mobility of the population. In 1855, for example, total immigration was 2,796, but 1,367 individuals left the colony in the same year. In this year also there were more immigrants to both Nelson and Otago from the "colonies" (again, probably Australian) than from the mother country.

The movement back and forth across the Tasman Sea was particularly vigorous in this period, a trend for which there is much auxiliary evidence. Fitton [10] discusses some of it. With regard to the shortage of labor in New Zealand in the early fifties, at the time of the Australian gold rushes, he reports that "Almost every part of New Zealand has, during the last 12 or 18 months, suffered severely from want of [an adequate labour supply]. . . . The result . . . has been . . . the importing of labourers free of expense either from England or from the crowds of unemployed visitors attracted to the neighbouring colony of Australia." He later quotes a letter written in Melbourne in January, 1855, to the effect that upwards of two thousand had left Melbourne for New Zealand in a period of two months. Paul [11] tells of one lot of immigrants to Canterbury in the mid-fifties, which numbered 704, of whom 126 were from New South Wales and 35 from Van Diemen's Land (Tasmania). Among those from Australia, were many diggers, often recent arrivals there.

The changing situation, toward the end of the second decade and at the beginning of the third decade, of organized settlement is shown by the percentages in tables XII and XIII which were calculated from data abstracted from the *Statistics of New Zealand* for 1858 and 1861. The figures for 1861 show the effect of the year's big rush to Otago in overwhelming the original Scottish contingent there. More than one-tenth of Otago's population was of "unspecified" origin, and we may fairly assume them to have been chiefly diggers. By this slight margin Southland became, and was to remain, the most predominantly Scottish area. The nearly 10 per cent of Southland's small population of 1861 born in Australia is revealing, as is the large number born in New Zealand. Southland was largely colonized by the older settlers of Otago and other parts of New Zealand, or from Australia, rather than from Britain.[12] Crawford [13] comments on the curious mixture of Scottish settlers (some still wearing kilts) and rough Australian diggers to be seen on the streets or in the taverns of tiny Invercargill at this time.

The immigration and emigration figures for all of New Zealand

TABLE XII

BIRTHPLACES OF THE POPULATION OF THE THREE PROVINCES IN 1858

	Nelson	Canterbury	Otago
New Zealand	35.5%	21.7%	22.0%
England	45.8	60.7	19.3
Wales	0.5	0.7	0.2
Scotland	8.2	6.7	50.4
Ireland	3.3	4.6	3.0
Australian Colonies	1.9	1.1	2.2
Other British	1.3	1.5	1.2
United States	0.4	0.3	0.4
France	0.2	0.7	0.1
German states	2.6	1.0	0.3
Other and unspecified	0.3	1.0	0.9
Total	*100.0%*	*100.0%*	*100.0%*

TABLE XIII

BIRTHPLACES OF THE POPULATION OF THE FIVE PROVINCES IN 1861

	Nelson	Marl-borough	Canter-bury	Otago	South-land	New Zealand
New Zealand	41.5%	33.0%	25.3%	10.0%	23.5%	27.8%
England	41.3	43.1	53.0	27.6	22.2	36.5
Wales	0.8	0.6	0.5	0.6	—	0.5
Scotland	6.8	10.7	8.5	32.7	33.5	15.7
Ireland	2.7	5.4	6.6	11.6	6.4	8.9
Australian	1.8	2.9	1.9	2.9	9.2	2.6
Other British	1.1	1.7	1.4	0.5	1.8	1.9
United States	0.3	0.5	0.3	1.1	0.3	0.7
France	0.3	0.1	0.6	0.3	0.1	0.3
Germany	2.8	0.7	0.8	0.7	0.9	0.8
Other and unspecified	0.6	1.3	1.1	12.0	2.1	4.3
Total	*100.0%*	*100.0%*	*100.0%*	*100.0%*	*100.0%*	*100.0%*

TABLE XIV

BIRTHPLACES OF POPULATION OF ALL OF NEW ZEALAND (1881 AND 1891)

	1881	1891
New Zealand	45.7%	58.7%
England } Wales }	24.8	18.8 0.4
Scotland	10.8	8.4
Ireland	10.0	7.2
Australia	3.5	2.6
Other British	1.0	0.8
Non-British	4.2	3.1
	100.0%	100.0%

from 1862 to 1870, given in the *Statistics of New Zealand* for 1871, indicate the substantial proportion of permanent settlers from the Australian colonies in the decade of gold rushes. There was a "net" immigration in the nine years of 97.5 thousand; 62.1 thousand came from Great Britain as compared with 4.8 thousand returning, whereas against 108.1 thousand arriving from "other British" (again chiefly Australian) places, 67.1 thousand returned. There was a net loss of less than a thousand to all other sources. One may thus safely assume that 35 per cent or more of the net immigration to all of New Zealand in this period came from across the Tasman Sea. Precise figures for South Island alone are not available, but the Australian proportion was probably as large or larger there, and in any event most of the people listed were moving into, or out of, South Island at this period.

This was also the period of the greatest movement of Chinese to New Zealand, though it was never large. In 1866-1867 there were forty-two hundred Chinese in the colony, mostly in the gold fields. Many of the Chinese tended to return to their native land after they had made a small stake of a hundred pounds or so, and with subsequent rigorous legislation for Chinese exclusion, which in 1881 imposed a poll tax of ten pounds on each immigrant, their numbers remained small. In 1881 there were 5,004; by 1921 the figure had dropped to 3,266.[14] The absolute numbers of others whose cultural origins were markedly different from most of the population, were also low. The *Statistics for New Zealand* for 1867 show for that year but 2,283 of German birth, 553 of French, and 2,196 of other European (non-British) origin in New Zealand. Between January 1, 1861 and March 31, 1863, the immigration to Canterbury, which received few diggers, had been, in respect to origin: English, 1,474; Scottish, 1,084; Irish, 1,203; Welsh, 31; Channel Islanders, 31; Germans, 84; and others, 10.[15] In all, from 1857 to 1870, inclusive, the emigrants to Canterbury from Europe alone, included: English, 7,651; Irish, 3,285; Scottish, 2,830; and Germans, 224.[15] In 1869, Canterbury's emigration agent in London made special efforts to increase the numbers of Germans with, as we shall see below, little success. The Irish were to increase in proportion as greater assistance in emigration and less restriction as to type progressively ensued.

After 1871 the mobility of the population makes it more difficult to generalize further about origins for any particular locality. For the population of the colony as a whole, the percentage distribution, according to countries of birth, has been calculated in table XIV for the years 1881 [16] and 1891.[17] The new arrivals are of course progressively less important in proportional contributions to the origin of the population as a whole.

The immigration from Great Britain and northwestern Europe to New Zealand in the sixties and seventies has not been well studied, but some hints as to its character were gleaned in the course of search for other things. It was almost entirely a laboring population and no great emphasis was laid on character or skill. The proportions of "urban" and "Irish" were higher than they had been in the fifties. Wilson and Barker [18] discovered some interesting things about national origins in the population of Canterbury deriving from this heaviest period of immigration. The English formed a considerable majority in the province. They contributed most of the capitalists who were not of Scottish origin, but in terms of the main body of the people, the English were the country storekeepers, the tavern-keepers, the "bullockies," waggoners, shearers, and fencers. They provided most of the smiths and wrights and most of the plowmen for the wheat boom. Though the Scots were prominent as usual in engineering trades, the English provided most of the skilled artisans, essentially urban in background. Masons from the south of England built the stone buildings of Christchurch; leather workers and saddlers from the Midlands were in great demand; miners from Northumberland were brought out to work the Malvern coal seams. There were Scottish miners from Ayrshire too in the Canterbury coal mines, and textile workers from Galashiels started the famous Kaiapoi woolen mills.

The valleys of the Cust and the Eyre seem to have had more folk from the eastern and "Home" counties. Yorkshiremen predominated in Malvern County and gave the name Sheffield to a center which they hoped would be a great industrial nucleus. To various places in Canterbury during the late sixties especially, textile workers from Lancashire, suffering from the repercussions of the "cotton famine" of the American Civil War, emigrated and turned awkwardly to cultivating the land or tending sheep and cattle, notably at Pareora, Waimate, and in North Canterbury. The poorest type of English emigrant is illustrated by the existence until recently of a quasi-slum, known as Sod-town, on the east side of Temuka. Here a contingent from the Warwickshire sector of Birmingham settled during the period of liberally assisted immigration under the Vogel regime, and there, as in few parts of South Island, some of the squalor of the nineteenth century industrial slums of the Black Country was perpetuated.

Then too in the sixties, experienced Scottish shepherds and their trained dogs appeared in some numbers to replace or to superintend the sailors, ex-bullockies, and men of every conceivable prior employment, who had learned the management of sheep chiefly by their own mistakes. Estimates by old settlers of the proportion of men in the "high country" mustering camps of the seventies and eighties who spoke the Gaelic run well above half of the total. After the Jacobite Rebellion of 1745 the highlands of Scotland had been largely taken over by men from the Borders, both English and Scottish, for great sheep runs. The sheep lore of the borderers had been combined with the hill craft of the highlanders to create a rather uniquely suitable background for New Zealand's "high country." The steady dispossession of the highlanders from their lands was back of the wholesale migrations in the late eighteenth and through most of the nineteenth centuries. New Zealand got a relatively small but technically very important share of this migration. The highlanders achieved a virtual monopoly of shepherding, in the role of superintendence at least, in the South Island high country from the sixties until the late nineties. Many of them became managers and then runholders on their own. Their great assets, beyond their knowledge of sheep running in wild country, were their stock of collies and their ability to train the working dogs.

In Canterbury especially, the Irish (who, residents of Central Otago maintain, were in high proportion among the gold miners in the sixties and seventies) were the navvies who built the roads, bridges, and railways, forming the largest element in the roving labor gangs of the seventies. In this way they learned to be teamsters and plowmen. More than others they tended to form village agglomerations with semi-subsistence gardening. Stavely, Clandeboye, Adair, Arne, and Kerrytown were some of these, though their people have since moved out unto the land and these names are in large part today merely designations of crossroads.

There are records of a few Scandinavian arrivals in South Island in the seventies. In 1872, 117 arrived in Lyttelton, and, in 1873-1874, 120 went to Dunedin, as well as several hundred more to Canterbury, though, after 1874, only one ship brought Scandinavians to the island.[19] Some Germans, Poles, Italians, and

Canadians also participated in a short-lived experiment in bush settlement at Jackson's Bay on the west coast in 1875-1876. These people scattered soon after, and most of the Scandinavians have disappeared from South Island, being among the first to go to the opening-up of the bush lands of North Island in the eighties and nineties. A large group is still settled there in the Dannevirke area in the "seventy-mile bush." Up to May 31, 1874, 878 Danes, 223 Swedes, 559 Norwegians, and 592 Germans had been brought to all of New Zealand under the Vogel plans.[20]

The Germans, although also small in number, spread more widely and remained more generally in South Island. In December 6, 1870, the *Otago Daily Times* reported the arrival at Port Chalmers of 228 immigrants from Hamburg, which appears to be the first recorded German immigration to the island since the arrival of the *St. Pauli* and the *Skiold* in 1843. The subsequent history of this group, as related by Charlton[20] indicates that the single men and women were employed as farm laborers and domestic servants, while most of the married men were engaged in the building of the southern trunk railway, which was then pushing south from Dunedin through the Taieri plan. Later they dispersed as laborers on farms and became quickly merged with the rest of the population. There is no distinctively German area, or locality, in Otago today. In Canterbury, too, a few score of German arrivals were well dispersed, with numbers sufficient for a real identification being found only around Oxford, Waimate, Geraldine, and Marshland. At Oxford the Germans became bushmen and had a hard struggle to maintain themselves, selling a bit of timber, or cutting it for others, and laboriously breaking in this one of the few forested patches in Canterbury. These "Germans" included some Austrians and Moravians, most of whom appear to have been weavers in the old country with little aptitude for colonial life. At first they made their own sauerkraut and parsnip wine, cured their own bacon, grew (with difficulty) a little tobacco, and unsuccessfully tried to grow the vine. Today they are completely assimilated, retaining almost none of the old customs.

A very few Poles and East Prussians settled in the heavy marshland area just northeast of Christchurch city and began the task of draining and cultivating this difficult but highly productive land. In 1883 they brought out relatives and other families from the same general European area. Many of the names persist— Bolaski, Gottermeyer, Rogal, Shimanski—and are a very striking contrast in Christchurch to the nearly uniformly British names of the people. Eventually these folk turned to market gardening, specializing in onions, and it is for their superb onion crops that they are famous today.

There are several ways of throwing some light on the problem of locality of origin of the people through an examination of the census returns. Since there has been little immigration since 1921, we should use no later figures. The first column of table XV shows the percentages of the population enumerated at that time who were born in the several source areas (the basic data is from the *General Report* of the 1921 census). The one-fourth of the population which was not born in New Zealand originated chiefly in the British Isles, especially England. Going back a generation to the fathers of those enumerated in 1921 (column 2) we get a somewhat clearer picture of origins, although nearly one-half of these fathers were born in the country. The most useful percentages are shown in column 3, which gives the proportionate distribution of origin of such fathers of the enumerated population in 1921 as were not, themselves, born in New Zealand. Of these, nearly one-half came from England, one-fifth from Scotland, 15 per cent from Ireland and 9 per cent from Australia.

TABLE XV

BIRTHPLACES OF THE POPULATION OF ALL OF NEW ZEALAND (1921)

	(1) Birthplace of all people enumerated	(2) Birthplace of fathers of column 1	(3) Birthplaces of those fathers born outside of New Zealand
New Zealand	74.4%	44.2%	
England	12.3	26.4	47.2%
Wales	0.2	0.5	0.9
Scotland	4.2	11.4	20.5
Ireland	2.8	8.5	15.2
Australia	3.9	4.9	8.8
Other British	0.6	0.7	1.3
Non-British	1.6	3.4	6.1
	100.0%	100.0%	100.0%

We are still left, however with the large group of fathers born in New Zealand about whose origins table XV is unrevealing. Table XVI is helpful in this regard, in that it indicates distribution of origin in different age groups (data again from the *General Report* of the 1921 census). The older the group the more likely will its origin be of significance in determining the source of the born-in-the-country group (table XV). Actually only 14 per cent of New Zealanders, sixty or more years of age in 1921, had been born in the country. More had been born in Scotland (17½ per cent) and Ireland (15½ per cent), and these countries together were nearly as important as England (40 per cent). Almost two-fifths as many of the folk sixty years or more in age had been born in Australia as had been born in New Zealand.

TABLE XVI

BIRTHPLACES OF THE POPULATION OF ALL NEW ZEALAND BY AGE GROUPS

Place of birth	60 or more	AGE GROUPS					
		50-59	40-49	30-39	20-29	10-19	0-9
New Zealand .	14.0%	46.1%	62.1%	71.0%	79.9%	91.1%	97.1%
England	40.0	26.4	19.2	13.7	9.0	4.6	1.3
Wales	0.7	0.4	0.3	0.3	0.2	0.1	—
Scotland	17.6	8.6	6.0	4.4	2.8	1.5	0.3
Ireland	15.6	7.3	3.5	2.1	1.3	0.3	0.1
Australia	5.7	6.9	5.9	6.1	4.7	1.7	0.9
Other British .	1.3	0.8	0.5	0.6	0.7	0.4	0.2
China	0.5	0.4	0.3	0.3	0.4	0.1	—
"Germany" ..	1.0	0.5	0.3	0.1	—	—	—
Other Foreign.	3.3	2.3	1.6	1.3	1.0	0.2	0.1
At sea, etc. ..	0.3	0.3	0.3	0.1	—	—	—
	100.0%	100.0%	100.0%	100.0%	100.0%	100.0%	100.0%

Perhaps the best single measure of the relative importance of various sources of "effective" immigration (that is, those who stayed, survived, and procreated) at different periods will be found in consideration of the "foreign"-born group at any period for which a two-way breakdown showing time of arrival and area of origin can be made. Table XVII shows this breakdown for 301,760 persons (out of a total of 312,630 persons of non-local birth) for whom the necessary data was available from the *General Report* of the 1921 census. Obviously interpretations of these figures without further data as to marital state, "effective fertility" (in terms of surviving children), and so forth, must be qualitative rather than quantitative. Yet it seems clear that, for New Zealand as a whole, Scotland and Ireland made almost as effective a contribution, taking them together, as did England, and the contribution of population of Australian birth was proportionately very significant. In the seventies the Irish contingent supplied nearly one-fifth of the effective immigrants. After 1882, and especially with the heavy migration of Australians to North Island's bushlands between 1892 and 1911, the force of any such readings is lost, because the major tide of immigration flowed to North Island.

TABLE XVII

BIRTHPLACES OF SURVIVING IMMIGRANTS * TO ALL OF NEW ZEALAND FROM 1872 TO 1921 (BY PERIODS)

Place of birth	Before 1872 (31,231)	1872-1881 (54,849)	1882-1891 (29,901)	1892-1901 (27,322)	1902-11 (77,427)	1912-21 (81,030)
England	41.0%	50.1%	48.5%	36.1%	47.0%	54.6%
Wales	0.6	.7	1.0	.7	.8	1.0
Scotland	23.4	16.6	18.4	11.7	15.6	16.1
Ireland	14.1	18.9	17.4	9.9	6.7	6.2
Australia	13.5	5.3	7.2	31.4	22.6	13.2
Other British ...	2.6	1.1	1.7	1.8	1.8	3.3
China	0.3	0.5	0.6	1.1	0.8	1.7
Germany	1.0	1.5	0.9	0.7	0.4	0.1
Other Foreign ..	2.2	4.6	3.9	6.2	4.3	3.8
At sea, etc.	1.3	.7	.4	.4	—	—
	100.0%	100.0%	100.0%	100.0%	100.0%	100.0%

* 312,630 people of non-New Zealand birth who were alive in New Zealand in 1921, whose birthplace was specified, and who arrived in the country in the indicated periods.

THE SKILLS AND OCCUPATIONS OF THE PEOPLE

There is no more important consideration for this study of the population than that of the skills which the people possessed upon their arrival, or the speed with which they learned them. It was these people, with whatever skills they had, who introduced the exotic plants and animals to the country. Most of the immigrants were imported for agricultural or pastoral work, and every attempt must have been made not only to obtain the genuine article in Europe, but, unless he possessed some other skill more useful to the new settlement, to list an immigrant as an agricultural laborer, shepherd, or whatever, if he knew one end of a plow or a sheep from the other.

In its first issue, March 12, 1842, the *Nelson Examiner* listed as follows all 217 of the immigrants receiving free passage to that date according to occupations declared by preference upon arrival:

146 agricultural laborers; 9 sawyers; 4 watermen; 17 carpenters; 1 wheelwright; 3 blacksmiths; 3 shoemakers; 2 tailors; 2 slaters; 4 bricklayers; 2 bakers; 4 brickmakers; 3 masons; 2 butchers; 1 lime-burner; 4 gardeners; 2 millwrights; 2 compositors; 1 farrier; 1 brazier; 1 machine fitter; 1 plumber; 1 flax-dresser.

This list suggests a very satisfactory group in some respects, although, for the Nelson settlement as planned, even the two-thirds listed as agricultural laborers is rather low. On April 9 of that year the paper classified some 59 off a ship newly arrived. Of these there were but 23 farm laborers, farm servants, or gardeners, the rest being:

2 sempstresses; 1 dressmaker; 11 carpenters and joiners; 5 blacksmiths; 2 bakers; 2 masons; 1 millwright; 2 shoemakers; 3 sawyers; 5 bricklayers; 2 brickmakers.

Another seven men who arrived on the same ship were unclassified. These two examples are hardly representative, in that they show relatively high proportions of agricultural skill; other lists incline to more artisans or undifferentiated laborers. Similar lists appear in advertisements or editorial columns of the Canterbury and Otago papers.

By 1854 one might have supposed that agriculture or the new pastoral excitement would have more strongly influenced the declared occupations of some 1,310 men as listed in the *Canterbury Gazette* for July 1:

Gentlemen, stockowners and farmers, 389; merchants or mariners, 130; mechanics, 227; laborers and servants, 564.

It would be interesting to know how many men had promoted themselves at least one class since their arrival. The first immigrant ship to South Canterbury, the *Strathallan,* arrived there on January 14, 1859. There were 235 passengers, including 90 male adults and 63 female adults. Of the males, 84 were listed as follows: [21]

25 farm laborers; 20 general laborers; 1 ploughman; 5 gardeners; 12 shepherds; 2 blacksmiths; 1 engineer; 1 bricklayer; 8 carpenters; 1 joiner; 3 sawyers; 1 millwright; 1 shoemaker; 1 bookbinder; 1 tailor; 1 painter.

Among the single women, 11 were listed:

7 domestic servants; 1 dressmaker; 1 laundress; 1 nurse; 1 shop-keeper.

It is difficult to believe that these represent a careful selection of men for an agricultural and pastoral beginning on the untouched tussock of the plains and downs of South Canterbury.

The *Statistics of New Zealand* for 1858 and 1861 provide a useful breakdown of occupations by provincial districts (tables XVIII and XIX). Data for both years are included because of the digger influx of the latter year, and the absolute figures are changed to percentages.

TABLE XVIII

Occupations of the People in 1858

	Nelson	Canterbury	Otago
Agricultural and pastoral	8.3%	8.4%	9.9%
Mechanics and artificers	6.0	7.5	5.9
Trade, commerce and manufacturing	2.7	2.6	1.7
Laborers	7.6	7.7	7.9
Professional	1.5	1.6	1.1
Miscellaneous (including domestics)	7.4	6.5	7.6
No occupation (including women and children)	66.5	65.7	65.9
	100.0%	100.0%	100.0%

TABLE XIX

Occupations of the People in 1861

	Marlborough	Nelson	Canterbury	Otago	Southland	New Zealand
No occupation	57.6%	75.9%	64.2%	32.6%	60.8%	57.8%
Trade, commerce and manufacturing	3.2	2.3	3.2	3.4	2.7	3.3
Agricultural and pastoral	13.2	6.6	8.8	5.8	10.2	7.5
Mechanics and artificers	5.2	4.8	5.5	6.0	5.8	5.8
Mining	—	2.4	0.1	39.9	1.0	11.3
Clerical, medical, legal	0.7	0.4	0.5	0.2	0.6	0.5
Teachers, surveyors, etc.	2.0	1.0	0.8	0.5	0.9	1.0
Laborers	12.0	3.3	8.2	4.8	5.7	5.7
Domestics	4.1	0.6	5.6	1.7	5.2	2.8
Miscellaneous	2.0	2.7	3.1	5.1	7.1	4.3
	100.0%	100.0%	100.0%	100.0%	100.0%	100.0%

Though most of the laborers and domestics were, no doubt, closely connected with agriculture, the proportion of employed people given as engaged in agricultural and pastoral pursuits is, for these years, remarkably low. If, as seems probable, many of those engaged in plant and animal husbandry reported to the census their pre-immigration trade or profession rather than the one in which they were currently engaged, we have an even more striking indication of the relative absence of agricultural and pastoral background in the population. There is perhaps more reason to suppose that of even the small number listed in the "agricultural and pastoral" class many were but newly turned to such pursuits.

Of a mass of 15,029 statute adults who were assisted in passage to Canterbury between 1855 and 1870, there were roughly seventy-five hundred men and four thousand single women. These represented, according to professed occupations shown in table XX,[22] the best-qualified group of immigrants on record.

TABLE XX
OCCUPATIONAL CLASSIFICATION OF CANTERBURY IMMIGRANTS (1855-1870)

Men	Women
2,411 farm laborers	2,497 general servants
1,046 ordinary laborers	285 dairy women
405 ploughmen	195 needle women
369 shepherds	123 cooks, etc.
452 carpenters	
138 blacksmiths, etc.	

(other categories had no particular relation to the needs of time)

In addition to such immigrants of the fifties and the sixties, there were the diggers whom it would be virtually hopeless to classify as to skills. Then came the assisted immigrants of the seventies. For these the agents in England received a capitation bonus, and the press and historians unanimously consider that they were much below the grade of immigrants arriving in the fifties and sixties. Their prevailing urban, often urban-slum, background is stressed by those who have studied their origins.

Employing data from the report of the census of 1881,[23] in that year the proportions of the population employed in agricultural and pastoral activities for the different provincial districts were (total population given in parentheses): Marlborough (9,219) 15.3 per cent; Nelson (26,273) 10.2 per cent; Westland (15,010) 3.0 per cent; Canterbury (112,178) 11.5 per cent; and Otago–Southland (133,342) 10.9 per cent. In Nelson and Westland the mining population (respectively 12.5 per cent and 23.7 per cent) greatly exceeded that engaged in farming.

It is difficult to ascertain trends in such proportions, because it is impossible to compare so much of the data in early and later censuses. Nevertheless the situation in 1921, as shown in table XXI, is instructive.[24] Table XXI includes, of course, all of the population. A breakdown for the male population engaged in primary production in the island (51,741 of the 62,503 listed) shows some interesting regional contrasts (table XXII).

TABLE XXI

Occupations of the People of South Island (1921)

	Numbers	Percentages
Primary Production	62,503	13.09%
Industrial	45,712	9.57
Transport and Communication	19,501	4.08
Commerce and Finance	29,047	6.08
Public Administration and Professional ..	18,023	3.77
Domestic and Personal Service	15,858	3.32
Other Occupations	21,285	4.46
Dependents	265,729	55.63
	477,658	100.0%

TABLE XXII

Proportions of Employed Male Population in the Different Primary Industries by Provincial Districts (1921)

	Marl- borough	Nelson	Westland	Canter- bury	Otago	Southland
Agricultural farming ..	20.8%	9.3%	0.8%	44.1%	25.5%	16.4%
Sheep farming	42.8	26.0	4.5	25.2	31.5	19.2
Dairy farming	18.8	24.8	31.6	18.3	26.3	36.9
Mixed and undifferen- tiated farming	11.6	3.1	5.3	11.0	6.3	13.6
Total—agricultural and pastoral	94.0	63.2	42.2	98.6	89.6	86.1
Bush Sawmilling	6.0	9.2	50.7	.6	3.1	9.5
Coal Mining	—	27.6	7.1	.8	7.3	4.4
Total—primary industries	100.0%	100.0%	100.0%	100.0%	100.0%	100.0%
Total male employed population in pri- mary pursuits	2,952	7,509	1,499	18,674	11,823	9,284

Although the proportions of those engaged in agricultural and pastoral occupations tended to increase in the earlier years, these

have steadily decreased during the last half century, a fact well
enough illustrated in table XXIII by a comparison of the occupations of breadwinners in the years 1896 and 1926.[25]

It is clear that an effort was made to obtain immigrants with
agricultural or pastoral skills. We may eliminate the yeoman
farmer (the prosperous land-owning peasant, if you like) because
there were so few in Great Britain in this period following upon
the enclosures, and so little reason for them to emigrate in any
event. The religious or political persecutions which prompted so
many of this class to leave the continent in the same period did
not occur in Great Britain. Politically and socially the farmer of
independent means was on the right side of the fence in the old
country. Yet, despite the efforts, Fuller wrote of the immigrants
in 1859:

A larger proportion of labourers from the rural classes is most desired
in a young colony, but labourers from the population of towns generally
predominate.[26]

TABLE XXIII

OCCUPATIONS OF BREADWINNERS, ALL OF NEW ZEALAND (1896 AND 1926)

	1896	1926
Primary Production	36.0%	24.0%
Industrial	22.0	22.6
Transport and Communication	5.8	9.9
Commerce and Finance	11.6	14.2
Public Administration and Professional	6.2	9.8
Domestic and Personal Service	9.8	7.5
Others	8.6	12.0
	100.0%	100.0%

Agricultural laborers, gardeners, etc., represented one-fourth
to one-third of the immigrants in the earlier period, but there are
good reasons to suppose that many of their skills were of little
use in the new land. It has already been stressed that most of the
ships from Great Britain sailed from the big ports, and a great part
of them from near London, in the earliest period. Few of the big
ports were near the good agricultural regions of Great Britain
and, as the emigrants had to pay their way to the ports, we have
further assumed that those actually from the country were, in
general, from the most backward areas.

GENERAL CHARACTERISTICS OF THE POPULATION

The prevailing poverty of the immigrants has been inferred from the general circumstances of the immigration. Beaglehole places them a class above paupers as a whole:

The colonists of New Zealand came mainly from that class of the Respectable Poor, as distinct from the mere proletarian on the one hand and the thoroughly successful artisan on the other.[27]

Although evidence that paupers were excluded is not convincing, the speed with which most of the newcomers improved their positions was truly remarkable. There was every incentive for the laborer to advance his circumstance and, in the new country, he had some opportunity for doing so. With his new independence he started to exert steady pressure for political changes to his own advantage. John Robert Godley, for some time the moving spirit of the Canterbury settlement wrote to England as early as 1851:

These people come out from England in no wise radical or bitter against authority. After a short apprenticeship of colonial agitation, however, they get bitter, abusive, disloyal, democratic, in short, colonial. This process has made the Wellington and Nelson people Chartists in about eight years; how long will it take to chartise Canterbury?[28]

It was to be some time before the laborers were able to get land for themselves on any considerable scale, or to make their political influence felt, but, in the meantime, they made steady progress economically as they learned the new husbandry techniques, or were able to employ their own artisan skills. Paul[29] describes the steps by which a laborer was able to become independent in the Canterbury of the fifties, and in a later chapter (p. 309) of this volume, the process will be discussed further.

It was from the small proportion of agricultural laborers (but more largely from the capitalists), the Australian immigrants, the dribbles of peoples from Germany and Scandinavia, settlers remaining from the pre-1840 period, and above all from invention and adaptation of wide variety on the spot, that South Island derived its husbandry techniques. Perhaps the English influence was paramount over that from any other source area; if any locality has second or prior place it is New South Wales. The point to be made is that the sources were extremely varied. That a high type of agricultural and pastoral skill was developed is indicated in the degree to which a rather small proportion of the population exercising such skills provided the principal support for the island's economy. It may be that the renowned efficiency of production of butterfat, wool, and meat in New Zealand is in part derived from the fact that the supply of labor skilled in such activities was always small, and that the labor force as a whole preferred, or was trained for, other occupations. It is indeed arguable, though the argument is not conclusive, that the absence of high skill in the new population was ultimately advantageous.

The importance of the lines of cultural inheritance stretching across the Tasman Sea from the earliest contacts to the end of the nineteenth century have been repeatedly emphasized. Especially in the sealing and whaling era and in the first twenty years of organized settlement was the import of capital (in terms of sheep), and skill to use that particular kind of capital on rough grass ranges, derived from the Australian colonies. While we may assume that most of the assisted immigration of the late sixties and the seventies learned its husbandry skill after arrival, we must also assume that a considerable body of varied and valuable experience relative to land use came in with the diggers, even though a majority of the flotsam of the rushes left in New Zealand may have been the least successful of the alluvial miners. Almost certainly to them must we attribute the introduction of water races for stock and irrigation. We shall find that the large-scale, increasingly mechanized, bonanza wheat farming of the seventies and the eighties had its antecedents not in Great Britain, but in America and New South Wales. In large gangs on these farms, as well as in the railroad construction camps, great numbers of the unskilled immigrants went to work, and there, more often than not, they were to learn techniques of plowing, sowing, reaping, and harvesting adapted to South Island conditions.

It was not until the perfection of marine refrigeration and the beginnings of shipments of frozen meat and dairy produce direct to England that more typically English farming methods could be applied extensively to these lands. When they were applied, however, they were always modified by the inherited equipment of animals and plants introduced by the early regime, as well as by the natural physical equipment of the area (often modified by this regime over half a century), and by its peoples' rapidly established habits of thought and action.

There is in South Island today a lack of any solid rural tradition, of any peasant-like feeling of love for the land and the countryside. I think this is partly to be explained by the degree to which urban people became agriculturists or pastoralists overnight. In the realm of pure conjecture, it is this writer's belief that the migration of a yeoman-farmer class to South Island would have resulted in an entirely different and much more conservational attitude toward the land by its people. It is a matter of regret that greater efforts were not made to leaven the group by the introduction of larger numbers of just such a peasant class from northwestern continental Europe. To those of such origin, who migrated in large numbers to North America in the same century, we can trace the beginnings of some of the most satisfactory land-use practices and attitudes in that continent. People who look on land as a commodity, as a means of earning a living which, while different from a factory or a commercial occupation, is yet of the same kind as these, seem not to develop a strong resistance to practices leading to mutilation of the area within which they live. As we shall show, the people of South Island live today in a large degree by the agricultural and pastoral production of the country. It is a sad observation arising from the examination of the genesis of that production, that it is not associated with any strongly established love of the land itself.

III

THE INVADING ANIMALS

CHAPTER V

THE HEARTH AREA

With some understanding of the people who settled South Island, and of the conditions of the countryside to which they came, we can turn to a discussion of the plants, animals, and skills in husbandry which they brought with them. The circumstances of arrival, acclimation, territorial penetration, and historical change of individual elements or complexes of elements associated with the agricultural and pastoral economy, are important considerations in such a discussion. Hardly less interesting or significant are the characteristics of the hearth areas.

The plants, animals, and associated skills came more often from the British Isles, ultimately if not immediately, than from any other area, although the limitations of this generalization, especially in terms of an immediate source area in the Australian continent, must be repeatedly emphasized. From within the British Isles, it is from England that New Zealand received its major agricultural inheritance. Little of whatever agricultural skill Scotland or Ireland could claim reached New Zealand, although the progress which Scotland had made in the management of rough, hill-country sheep stations was of much importance in these distant Pacific islands. The general agricultural and pastoral situation in England at the time of the major movement of people halfway round the world to New Zealand deserves, therefore, our first attention.

There are many excellent studies which describe the principal features of the various agricultural and pastoral revolutions occurring in England from the time of the Tudors until 1850. Ernle [1] and East [2] are the most reliable general writers, and from Arthur Young [3] comes some excellent first-hand information. Of the agricultural changes in the late eighteenth century Ernle comments:

The divorce of the peasantry from the soil, and the extinction of commoners, open-field farmers, and eventually of small free-holders, were the heavy price which the nation ultimately paid for the supply of bread and meat to its manufacturing population. [4]

The sixteenth century saw the enclosure movement begin in earnest in England with a considerable displacement of grain fields by sheep runs. Gradually the old open-field system gave way to more and more enclosed farms, although the final and most extensive development of the enclosure movement occurred only in the first half of the nineteenth century. Enclosures gave an opportunity for "high" (better or more scientific) farming, with the use of grass-root-grain rotations and the abandonment of fallow, although advantage was not always taken of the opportunity. New manures and new ways of applying the old, new care in the breeding of animals, in seed selection, and in methods of tillage were known and practiced by a considerable body of the best farmers. The work of Jethro Tull, Robert Bakewell, "Turnip" Townshend, Coke of Norfolk, and others of Arthur Young's important predecessors and associates, had made known what could be done. The best farming practices in England between 1820 and 1860 included, except for a knowledge of the use of many new machines and many new strains of plants, most of the best practices in use in the early twentieth century, if not indeed until the present time.

The best English agricultural and pastoral practice was not, however, typical of the English countryside, and it was unusual in most parts of Scotland, Ireland, and Wales. Moreover, in 1837 most of the progress made between 1790 and 1812 had been lost. There had been a large-scale abandonment of difficult land. East's remark that "the human geography of southern Britain in the eighteenth century had more in common with that of earlier centuries than of the years to come" [5] can be applied to agricultural and pastoral husbandry in general for forty years into the following century. Turnips and clovers were still not in general use, and Coke's four-course Norfolk rotation had not spread beyond the neighboring counties of Essex and Suffolk. The only other counties in a satisfactory condition of agricultural practice were Hertfordshire and Leicestershire. Even drilling of grain and horse-hoeing of turnips had not become general a century after Jethro Tull's publication of his *Horse-Hoeing Husbandry* in 1773.

Machinery was still used only to a very limited extent in tillage and was yet largely in a stage of what Ernle has called "agricultural heirlooms." Typical were the huge, cumbrous, wooden cart-plows, slowly drawn by some half-dozen oxen or horses and with as many as three or four men and boys in attendance. Many early and widely reported machines appeared only on the fields of the few good farmers; their general use often had to await reintroduction as American innovations. Not only was sowing chiefly broadcast, but the grain crops were still, in the main, reaped and threshed by primitive hand methods. Only a few large threshing machines, worked by water power, horses, or, less commonly, by steam, traveled the country doing contract work. Bell's reaper, invented in 1826, although widely discussed, was not accepted in England for thirty or forty years, not much earlier, in fact, than it was accepted in Canterbury, New Zealand.

There were, perhaps, more advances in livestock husbandry than in agriculture, but cattle were still largely housed in drafty sheds in the winter, and sheep still had to be bred for long legs and agility to keep from getting themselves mired on the "roads" and paths. Fattened animals often were driven long distances to market and the consequent loss of weight reduced the incentive for more careful husbandry. These, then, were some of the characteristics of farming in England at the time of the earliest settlement of New Zealand and of the heavy early migrations to the Australian colonies, whence came many of New Zealand's techniques of land husbandry. The agriculture of lowland Scotland was little better, of Ireland incredibly worse.

As for the farmers themselves, few of those who actually owned and managed land in Britain seem to have migrated to the Southwest Pacific, partly as a result of the diminution in numbers of this class, which, according to Ernle,[6] was most rapid between the years 1813 and 1835. Certainly by 1835 the agricultural depression had been fatal to most of the remaining small free-holders, whether they were gentry or what may have remained of yeoman farmers or peasant proprietors in the nineteenth century.[7] It was generally true, as it is probably true of all considerable emigration movements, that most of the emigrants to the Australian colonies who had any knowledge of land husbandry were of the class of agricultural laborers. In England, in the early nineteenth century, these people were wretchedly poor, and as a group extremely conservative if not indeed openly rebellious toward innovations on the part of their masters.[8] The enclosures had led to the creation of a landless and unattached mass of agricultural labor; the new industrial agglomerations had attracted much of this labor to their slums, perhaps that part with the greatest initiative. The trebling of prices during the Napoleonic wars had not been counterbalanced by the bare doubling of wages; and the Poor Laws tended only to make a desperate social situation somewhat worse. For these and undoubtedly other reasons, no one disputes the material and cultural poverty of the majority of agricultural laborers in Great Britain in the early nineteenth century. Arthur Young describes the situation (and he was a proponent of enclosures as a necessary prerequisite to "high farming"):

Go to an ale-house kitchen of an old enclosed country, and there you will see the origin of poverty and the poor-rates. [For whom are they to be sober?] For whom are they to save? (Such are the questions.) For the parish? If I am diligent, shall I have leave to build a new cottage? If I am sober, shall I have land for a cow? If I am frugal, shall I have half an acre of potatoes? You offer no motives; you have nothing but a parish officer and a work house. Bring me another pot.[9]

This background of the agricultural and pastoral development of New Zealand is of great importance to various of the characteristics which that development displayed.

While in England agricultural laborers were experiencing such material and cultural poverty, in New Zealand settlement had begun with the establishment of whaling stations on the Sounds and the Fiords. A century later a British visitor, R. O. Stapledon, the distinguished grassland expert from Aberystwyth, made a comparison of the use of land in Great Britain with that in New Zealand; his report[10] reflects the often clearer perspective of the visitor. Young's description of French agriculture is the most instructive of all his writings, and there are few shrewder observers of the English countryside in the seventeenth and eighteenth centuries than Archenholz and Kalm. Stapledon's comparative statistics for New Zealand as a whole, and England and Wales taken together, are summarized in table XXIV as an introduction to this present attempt to reconstruct the history of a century of change in the use of land in one of New Zealand's two chief islands.

TABLE XXIV

COMPARISON OF LAND USE IN NEW ZEALAND WITH ENGLAND AND WALES IN THE MID-1920's [11]

England and Wales	New Zealand
Total area: 37,138,000 acres (excluding water)	Total area: 65,400,000 acres (including water)
Total area devoted to livestock and farming, including hill grazing: 30,775,000 acres	Total occupied area (including 10,-000,000 acres of virgin forest, bush, mountain tops, river beds, glaciers, littoral sands, fern and scrub lands): 43,600,000 acres
	Total utilized area: 33,300,000 acres

Percentage Utilization of These Last Two Areas in Each Region

England and Wales		New Zealand	
Permanent grass	49.0%	Pastures on plowed land	15%
Temporary grass	8.4%	Pastures on surface sown land.	31%
Mountain and heath grazing .	16.2%	Natural pastures	48%
Total grass and grazing	73.6%	Total grass and grazing	94%
Supplementary and forage crops	11.7%	Supplementary and forage crops	4%
Total area to stock feed	85.3%	Total area to stock feed	98%
All other crops	14.7%	All other crops	2%
	100.0%		100%

England and Wales	New Zealand	
15,984,400	Number of sheep	24,547,955
6,163,300	Number of cattle	3,503,744

Relative stock units (of cattle and sheep only, and letting 7 sheep = 1 cattle beast) *

100   71

* The validity of this equation is discussed on page 169.

Although, as will develop, the percentages for South Island are often significantly different from those for New Zealand as a whole, Stapledon's comparison is very useful. It emphasizes the greater importance of "high" farming and of supplementary forage crops in England, an area of less benign climate and enormously greater consumer population. At the same time it stresses similarities in terms of pre-eminent devotion of land to grass, and of a preoccupation in both areas with sheep and cattle husbandry as the major purposes of land use. In the twentieth century the New Zealand farmer's market has been, apart from the small share attributable to the needs of his own people, chiefly England itself. In a world of easy communications, both British and New Zealand farmers have coincidental access to new ideas, methods, and inventions. The more settled parts of the New Zealand countryside have some striking similarities to the landscape of parts of rural England. To an important degree, today, the same breeds of animals graze the same English grasses, by the same methods of management, and produce wool, meat, or butterfat for the same market in both countries.

The husbandry methods, now so similar, have developed along lines which were often markedly divergent. The beginnings of New Zealand agriculture corresponded more to the general, rather than the highest, level of British agriculture a century ago. New Zealand has made important contributions to British practice in methods of husbandry, and has received, in turn, techniques therefrom. Nevertheless, much of the similarity of land use today must be attributed to the continued, direct importations of men, animals, and ideas from what we must, in all fairness, term the hearthland.

Up to this point, the traditional point of view as to cultural origins in New Zealand is substantiated—to this degree New Zealand *is* the "Britain of the South." Unfortunately, however, the traditionalists have neglected to consider the very important differences beneath the superficial similarity, an understanding of which is necessary to obtain a clear picture. And it is especially with these differences and their origins that this book is concerned. Some of these differences are climatic; despite many similarities in temperature and rainfall regimes, for example, there is little need of roofed winter shelter for animals in New Zealand, even at latitudes as high as those of Southland (46 to 47 degrees). Other marked differences are associated with sharp contrast in land forms and in native vegetation, large areas of which persist in South Island, albeit often in altered form. Again, the products of New Zealand farms have to be prepared for a distant market; for meat and dairy produce this means a refrigerated journey halfway around the world. There are many other differences of importance, some obvious and some subtler than these, which can be explained only by an examination of the historical development.

CHAPTER VI

SHEEP

Although it has been more convenient in the discussion of the people of New Zealand to consider first the historical course of events and then numbers, distribution, and types, in the following discussion it may be more helpful to reverse the procedure and give first consideration to the more nearly contemporary numbers, distributions, and types of the individual husbandry complexes associated with particular items.

Of all the introductions to South Island by the occupying European culture, there has been none of greater economic importance than that of sheep. Buchanan, a thoroughly competent observer in a fairly recent period, who has made a study [1] of the pastoral industries of New Zealand in respect to what might be termed their contemporary economic–geographic connotations, has devoted four out of a dozen maps to sheep. [2] His statistics, based largely on the 1925-1929 quinquennium, and his conclusions are very useful, but to provide additional rather than repetitive evidence, it is necessary to go beyond the scope of his inquiry and include data for the 1930-1939 decade, and, especially, the 1940-1941 [3] season. There have been other contributive studies, notably some chapters of Belshaw, [4] and an attempt has been made here to evaluate the observations and evidence of the written and spoken opinion of academic students and government officers and of the farmers themselves. In connection with this latter source of information, Arthur Young in 1770 made an observation which is pertinent in spirit at least: "I was forced," he wrote, "to make more than one honest farmer half-drunk before I could gain sober, unprejudiced intelligence!" [5]

The overwhelming importance of wool and mutton or lamb in South Island today can be readily seen by the proportion of the occupied area devoted directly to grazing or raising stock food. Of South Island's total area of 37,528,960 acres,[6] approximately 63.6 per cent could be termed "occupied area" in April, 1941. A breakdown of the land use of this area is given in table XXV.

TABLE XXV

Use of Occupied Area of South Island (April 1941) [7]

(1) Occupied area .... 23,862,575 acres

(2) Occupied but unimproved area .... 17,243,525 acres, or 72% of (1)

Of the occupied but unimproved area:
   (a) Tussock and native grasses .... 12,633,405 acres, or 73% of (2)
   (b) Fern, scrub and second growth 1,587,362 acres, or 9% of (2)
   (c) Standing native bush .... 1,347,297 acres, or 9% of (2)
   (d) Barren and unproductive .... 1,649,203 acres, or 10% of (2)

(3) Occupied and Improved area ..... 6,618,960 acres, or 28% of (1)

Of the occupied and improved area:
   (a) Grasses, clovers and lucernes .. 5,428,823 acres, or 82% of (3)
   (b) Green fodder (excluding grains,
      pulse and roots) .... 517,859 acres, or 8% of (3)
   (c) Grain and pulse crops including
      those fed off .... 598,306 acres, or 9% of (3)

Taking (2 a), (3 a), and (3 b), together (which does not include, it will be noted, the grazing contributions of (2 b) and (3 c)) there were 18,580,087 acres, or 78 per cent of all of the occupied area and over 50 per cent of the area of the island, devoted directly to grazing or the raising of stock food. Even the 3 per cent of the island which was in arable that year had half its production devoted to the food for stock.

It is difficult to determine the average number of sheep for any given year because of the slaughter of so many lambs at an early age; the number of sheep shorn in a year, although certainly below the true figure, often gives a better picture than the number of sheep in existence at the end of the fiscal year (April 30). From May 1, 1940, to April 30, 1941, there were 12,205,032 sheep shorn in South Island.[8] At the latter date there were 594,481 cattle in the Island, a drop of some twenty thousand since the 1925-

1929 period. Using Fawcett [9] as authority, we may equate one cattle beast to seven sheep in terms of grazing units (ignoring the numerically unimportant pigs and horses). On this basis, sheep represented 74.5 per cent of total "sheep grazing units." With most of the occupied land used for grazing and supplementary fodder, and most of this going to feed sheep, it is clear that the best short, descriptive characterization of South Island today is "sheep-country."

The general economy of the island depends upon the export of the products of pastoral farming as a means to import manufactured and semi-manufactured goods; it is interesting to note that in consequence of this circumstance, New Zealand had in 1936 the lowest customs tariff in the world.[10] Between 1920 and 1936, pastoral produce for New Zealand as a whole comprised between 91.1 and 94.2 per cent of the total value of all merchandise exports [11] (fifty-three million pounds ° of a total of fifty-seven million pounds in the seventeen years). Total pastoral production appears not greatly in excess of the export figures, as can be seen by an examination of data from the *Official Yearbook* for 1938 (table XXVI).[12] Again, between 1928 and 1937 New Zealand's annual wool production varied between 252.5 and 304.3 millions of pounds; local mills, in the same period, used only from 5.5 to 7.8 millions of pounds of wool.

TABLE XXVI

RELATIVE PRODUCTION AND EXPORT OF LEADING PASTORAL PRODUCTS
(ALL OF NEW ZEALAND)

	Production	Export
Creamery butter	3,322,699 cwt. (*1935-6*)	2,796,145 cwt. (*calendar year 1936*)
Cheese	1,769,984 cwt. (*1935-6*)	1,658,206 cwt. (*calendar year 1936*)
Sheep and lambs slaughtered	12,015,895 carcasses (*calendar year 1936*)	10,175,595 carcasses (*calendar year 1936*)
Beef	2,764,655 cwt. (*1936-7*)	712,987 cwt. (*1936-7*)
Pork	851,500 cwt. (*1936-7*)	570,686 cwt. (*1936-7*)

Another interesting aspect of this question is that of a total value of production given for New Zealand as £114.2 millions

° In all of these citations, pound refers to the New Zealand pound.

for 1935-1936, pastoral and dairying industries (with the contributions from poultry and bees which are relatively unimportant), together with subsequent processing of the products (for example, in butter and cheese factories and freezing works), contributed £63.3 millions. Manufacturing other than this processing (which added £6.9 millions of value) [13] was £23.2 millions. Minor items included (in millions): agricultural cash crops £9.2, mining £4.0, forest industries £3.0, and fisheries £0.4; building and miscellaneous gave a total of £11.1.[13] These are, of course, figures for all of New Zealand. The proportions of these production figures for South Island cannot be directly inferred but, for 1937, the relative proportions of sheep, cattle, and sheep grazing units for the two islands are given as shown in table XXVII.[14] Although South Island had but 30 per cent of the total grazing units of New Zealand, 76 per cent of these units concerned sheep, thus again emphasizing the pre-eminence of sheep in its economy.

TABLE XXVII

SHEEP, CATTLE, AND SHEEP-GRAZING UNITS (1937)

	South Island	North Island
Sheep shorn	14,140,122	17,165,696
Cattle	628,855	3,760,246
Sheep grazing units	18,542,107	43,487,418
Sheep percentage of s.g.u.'s	76%	39%

In order to interpret more clearly the distribution of these sheep within the island, we may well survey the distribution of types of land use in the different land districts. The figures (table XXVIII) make clear what might be inferred from the distribution of natural vegetation, relief, and land forms, namely that Canterbury, Otago, and Southland not only contain over 70 per cent of the area of the island, but a still greater proportion of that total area which had grazing possibilities. The northwestern bush country is thinly occupied and, as table XXVIII indicates, comparatively little of the occupied area of Nelson and Westland is in a condition to graze sheep and cattle. "Standing native bush," "fern, scrub, and second growth," or "barren and unproductive," are the designations which apply to most of the occupied land of these districts. Even Marlborough has very much larger proportions of its occupied land in these categories than do the three major southern land districts. The high degree of areal occupation of most of the southeastern counties, in which the percentage of improved land is not great away from the coast, is a reflection of widespread occupance of the tussock grasslands, though the feed available thereon is now often very scanty. Although the "high country" is almost certainly the area most completely devoted to sheep, the major concentrations are on the southeastern plains and downs. North and west of the heavy line drawn on the map (fig. 40) there are less than two hundred thousand of the more than twelve million animals on the island.

TABLE XXVIII

DISTRIBUTION OF LAND USE BY LAND DISTRICTS [15]

	Marl-borough	Nelson	Westland	Canter-bury	Otago	Southland
(1) Total area (in millions of acres)...	2.8	4.4	3.8	9.7	9.6	7.1
(2) Occupied area (in millions of acres)	2.3	1.2	1.0	8.1	8.0	3.3
Percentage Distribution						
(3) Area occupied but unimproved (per cent of (2))....	82%	71%	85%	66%	80%	57%
(4) Area in tussock and native grasses (per cent of (3))	61	28	13	84	83	71
(5) Area of improved land (per cent of (2))	18	29	15	34	20	43
(6) Area in grasses, clovers, and lucerne ° (per cent of (5))	90	85	96	75	85	89
(7) Area in green fodder excluding grains and pulse fed off (per cent of (5))	2	2	.005	9	8	10
(8) Total area in grazing and fodder crops (per cent of (2))	66	46	25	84	85	83

° Including that area sown with grain and pulse crops at the same time.

No dot maps showing different distinctive breeds can be made, as the breed data are not available for divisions smaller than land districts. Figure 41, however, does show something of relative distribution. The large number of pure Merinos and Corriedales,

ahc

Fig. 40. Distribution of sheep in South Island (April 1941).

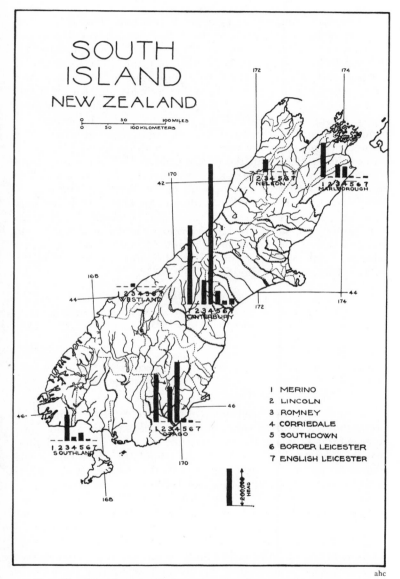

ahc

FIG. 41. Distribution of distinctive breeds of sheep by land districts in South Island (April 1941).

which average somewhere near one-half Merino blood, is an indication of the significance of the native tussock grasslands, the dry climate, and the rough terrain on which the agile Merinos do so well. Professor C. P. McMeekan of Canterbury Agricultural College, certainly one of the most careful students of South Island sheep, speaking in terms of breeding animals and future plans, is of the opinion, however, that the Rommey Marsh, dominant in North Island and Southland, is gaining increasing importance in Canterbury and Marlborough as well. The more intensively the Canterbury plains are farmed, the higher the percentage of Rommeys is likely to be. But the persistence of the Merino itself, and by inheritance in the Corriedales and half-breds, is a remarkable trend in the historical development of the industry. The map of breed distribution (fig. 41), it should be noted, includes only those sheep of a recognizable breed. The numbers of half-breds (probably, also, some one-half Merino in blood as a rule), and of crossbreds (containing little if any Merino blood), together with the totals of all sheep, for the different land districts at the end of April, 1941, is shown in table XXIX.

TABLE XXIX

HALF-BREDS, CROSSBREDS, AND TOTAL NUMBER OF SHEEP
(SOUTH ISLAND, 1941)

	Marl-borough	Nelson	Westland	Canter-bury	Otago	Southland
			(in thousands)			
Half-bred	417	88	1	1,000	520	25
Cross-bred ...	430	299	61	2,626	2,591	2,779
Total sheep...	1,183	464	87	3,100	3,939	3,006

Generally, the half-bred sheep of Otago, Canterbury, and Marlborough are a result of putting a long-wool ram to a Merino ewe. A crossbred is generally any mixture of non-Merino, and most usually long-wool, blood. In North Island this definition is all-inclusive, but apparently in South Island crossbreds may include both three-quarter-breds (one-fourth Merino) and even quarter-breds (three-fourths Merino), although the latter might, more logically, be included with the half-breds. There is no distinction in either of these cases as to whether the ram or ewe has the greater proportion of Merino blood. Only one successful attempt to fix a breed of half-breds (the Corriedale which is discussed below) has been made, and the demand for Merino ewes in the breeding of half-breds justifies some of the concentration upon

Merino sheep which persists in the high country. In fat-lamb production, the lamb is less and less frequently bred to be more than one-fourth Merino. Southdown, Rommey, or Lincoln rams may be used on half-breds or Corriedale ewes or even on long-wool strains. South Island maintains flocks of Southdowns, for example, chiefly for a supply of breeding rams.

This brief description of localization of types of sheep begs the question of what the methods of sheep farming and other auxiliary phenomena, such as the sizes of holdings, may be, and how these vary over the island. The information on which this interpretation is based was gathered principally from visits to numerous farms of all types. Although many of the interviews primarily sought data about the past, most farmers prefer to begin any such discussion with a detailed analysis of the farm as it is today. The conclusions have been discussed with agricultural specialists and checked against the researches of other students.[16]

Inasmuch as arable farming, for the creation of permanent and semipermanent pastures, and for the growing of supplementary forage and a few cash crops, is discussed in later chapters, we may be brief here. The high country of Marlborough, Canterbury, and Otago, that is, the mountain basins, mountain slopes, and foothills which carry native tussock, is mainly divided into large sheep stations, more often than not leased from the government, on which Merinos or half-breds (especially Corriedales) are run. On the downs country some arable, chiefly in rotation with semipermanent leys * of English grasses, begins to appear, carrying capacity is greater, and half-breds become almost universal. On the plains where pastures are better and supplementary food more plentiful, half-bred ewes are used principally in combination with non-Merino rams. However, in Southland, coastal Otago, the Waimea-Motueka plains of Nelson, and the limited sheep-raising areas of Westland, the sheep-blood is almost all long-wool and, as in North Island, is showing an increasing run toward the Rommey Marsh. To a small extent on the foothills and downs and to a large extent on the plains, rotational cropping is carried on; that is, there are few really permanent pastures, although most of the land may be in grass each year. Unless and until irrigation is much

---

* This distinctly English expression for a sown pasture is a dialectical variant of "lea," and is commonly used in New Zealand. I believe its wider use might be advantageous, as there is no neat convenient synonym.

more widely introduced to prevent the grasses running out, this is likely to continue.

It is a singular fact that there is no fixed or traditional, or even roughly similar, system of rotational management of paddocks (fields) in vogue on various farms. Even on the same farm, farmers seem to continually vary their practices. New cash crops, grasses, and grazing systems, as well as new types of rams or ewes, are forever being tried out. As a result, South Island sheep farming successfully defies most attempts at subclassification. The high-country stations which run pure Merino sheep on natural tussock grasslands, would seem, at first glance, to be a clear type. Yet of these there are some stations which sell only wool and manage to take care of their flocks in winter, when the native pastures are nonproductive, by one of several devices. If the station manager is fortunate enough to have a balance of summer and winter country there is no problem; if not, he may be able to grow his own supplementary feed, as is done by irrigation in the basins of Central Otago or on limited flats by the water's edge in the lake country. On other high-country stations where there is a deficiency of winter feed, managers make a practice of selling surplus ewes to stations on the foothills, down-lands, or high plains, where they are bred to long-wool rams to produce half-breds. Still other high-country stations themselves run half-breds (or Corriedales) and are able thus to sell surplus wethers as well as ewes; in this case the wethers are fattened for slaughter as mutton after being kept for a longer or shorter time as wool-producers. Again a high-country station owner may board out some of his flock for the winter to lower neighboring stations which make a specialty of such winter work.

Sheep managers in the "middle country" zones, besides being on the "taking" or "boarding" end of the high-country economy, also produce surplus half-bred ewes for the low-plains stations where they are bred by non-Merino rams for the production of fat lambs and surplus half-bred wethers, which are fattened for slaughter there or on farms of the lower plains. These intermediate stations are less dependent on wool than are those of the high country, but their wool-check is still, usually, their major single source of income. On the lowest plains, the fattening of sheep and lambs is perhaps the most important sheep-husbandry aspect of farming, but this is intricately interwoven with cash-crop production and even, as we shall see, with dairy farming as well.

Three general types of the sheep business, that is, wool production, breeding for replacement, and meat production, have been described; it needs only to be added that every possible gradation between, and mixture of, these types occurs. Some attempt to rationalize these types into regions is given in figure 42, but it can only be an approximation.

The size of flocks and the size of holdings naturally become progressively smaller in the steady gradation from high, natural-tussock, dry-sheep country to the low, intensively managed, English-grass, fat-lamb areas. Amuri, Tawera, and Lake Counties are typical of the highest "high country," with the average size of holding well over four thousand acres; Tuapeka, Waimate, Oxford, and Waipara represent the intermediate group, with holdings averaging from five hundred to a thousand acres; Levels and Rangiora Counties typify the areas of most intensive land utilization for sheep production, on small holdings of a hundred to two hundred and fifty acres. The small size of holdings in counties suburban to Christchurch is more immediately a reflection of dairy, truck, and even poultry farming than of intensive sheep-farming, though small sheep-running farms are found there, too.

TABLE XXX

PERCENTAGE OF NUMBERS OF FLOCKS, IN DIFFERENT-SIZE CLASSES,
FOR EACH OF THE LAND DISTRICTS (1941)

Number of Sheep in Flock	Marl-borough (per cent)	Nelson (per cent)	Westland (per cent)	Canter-bury (per cent)	Otago (per cent)	Southland (per cent)
1-200	26.5	50.0	58.0	22.4	24.7	25.3
201-500	23.3	29.7	29.7	29.4	22.4	23.6
501-1000	20.1	14.4	9.3	24.3	23.3	27.4
1001-2500	21.1	5.3	3.0	18.1	22.0	20.5
2501-5000	6.1	0.4	—	4.2	5.8	2.3
5001-7500	1.9	0.2	—	0.9	1.0	0.5
7501-10,000 ...	0.5	—	—	0.3	0.5	0.2
10,001-20,000 ..	0.4	—	—	0.3	0.2	0.2
Over 20,000 ...	0.1	—	—	0.1	0.1	—
	100.0	100.0	100.0	100.0	100.0	100.0

Figures for the distribution of sizes of flocks and of absolute sizes of land holdings are available only for land districts. But because there is considerable localization significance, even within such large areal units, percentage distributions [17] of flocks and holdings are given in tables XXX and XXXI. These distributions show a nice gradation in the types of country available for sheep

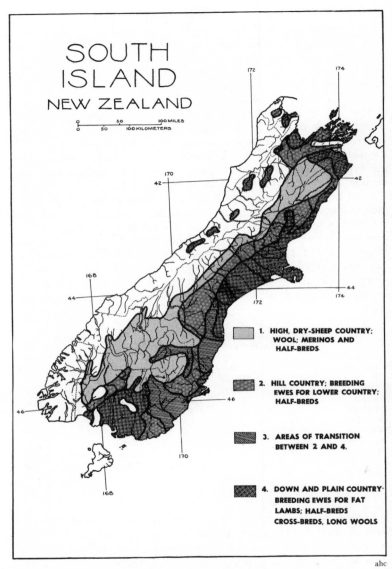

SOUTH
ISLAND
NEW ZEALAND

1. HIGH, DRY-SHEEP COUNTRY;
   WOOL; MERINOS AND
   HALF-BREDS

2. HILL COUNTRY; BREEDING
   EWES FOR LOWER COUNTRY;
   HALF-BREDS

3. AREAS OF TRANSITION
   BETWEEN 2 AND 4.

4. DOWN AND PLAIN COUNTRY·
   BREEDING EWES FOR FAT
   LAMBS; HALF-BREDS
   CROSS-BREDS, LONG WOOLS

ahc

FIG. 42. Regional distribution of types of sheep farming in South Island.

management on different scales. There are no opportunities for running large flocks in Nelson and Westland. Six of the eleven flocks in South Island which number over twenty thousand head are in Canterbury. The only surprising feature of this distribution is the relatively large proportion of large holdings in Westland. There, it must be remembered, there is a small percentage of utilization of the area held, so that large areas may carry relatively small flocks of sheep or herds of cattle. The high percentage of holdings under forty acres in size in Nelson is understandable in terms of its horticultural emphasis. In Canterbury, the same feature is, in part at least, a reflection of the great number of semi-suburban dairying and truck farms in the Christchurch area. Overall, there is an indication of fairly intensive husbandry on the lower plains.

TABLE XXXI

PERCENTAGE OF NUMBERS OF HOLDINGS IN DIFFERENT SIZE CLASSES, FOR EACH OF THE LAND DISTRICTS

Number of acres in holding	Marlborough (per cent)	Nelson (per cent)	Westland (per cent)	Canterbury (per cent)	Otago (per cent)	Southland (per cent)
Under 40	31	35	22	37	28	22
40-150	17	26	20	19	20	21
150-320	13	14	23	16	17	28
320-640	12	11	18	14	14	17
640-2000	17	12	12	10	11	9
2000-5000	6	2	2	2	5	2
Over 5000	4	–	3	2	5	1
	100	100	100	100	100	100

HISTORICAL DEVELOPMENT OF THE SHEEP INDUSTRY

On his second voyage Cook picked up two rams and four ewes at the Cape of Good Hope, but they suffered severely from scurvy on the voyage and only one ewe and one ram survived by the time the *Resolution* reached New Zealand. After carefully nursing the remaining two back to health, Cook had them put ashore on the Queen Charlotte Sound area, May 20, 1773. Then, on the morning of the twenty-third, Cook relates, "the ewe and the ram, I had with so much trouble brought to this place, were both found dead; occasioned, as was supposed, by eating some poisonous plant. Thus my hopes of stocking this country with a breed of sheep, were blasted in a moment." [18]

Of his last visit to South Island, in May 1777, Cook remarked, "On my present arrival at this place, I fully intended to have left not only goats and hogs, but sheep, and a young bull, with two heifers, if I could have found either a chief powerful enough to protect and keep them, or a place where there might be a probability of their being concealed from those who would ignorantly attempt to destroy them. But neither the one nor the other presented itself to me." [19] He did leave goats and pigs, as he had done before, rightly supposing that these animals had a better chance of surviving.

How many sheep may have been brought in by sealers, whalers, and casual traders in succeeding years we cannot know. There is nowhere any reference to any considerable number, though early importations to North Auckland are known. Bell, whose settlement on Mana Island in 1834 was noticed above, had ten head of cattle and 102 sheep with him. We know, too, that goats, pigs, and "other livestock," possibly including sheep, were kept by the whaling settlers at Port Underwood in the late thirties. [20] Presumably sheep may figure in the "cattle" known to have been sent by Jones to his stations on the southern coasts in 1838 and 1840, for as late as the mid-nineteenth century the generic denomination "cattle" was used to include all domestic animals, and unless "horned-cattle" are specified, we may indeed be dealing with horses, sheep, swine, or goats. Before British sovereignty was declared in 1840, some nine of the Company's ships, with 1,079 passengers, had arrived at Port Nicholson from English and Scottish ports, and in 1840, eighteen vessels had arrived there from Sydney. Though there is no available record of livestock on the ships from Britain, some of the animals carried on the ships for purposes of meat and milk may have been still alive when the ships reached New Zealand. McNab [21] reports that seven of the Sydney ships brought thirteen hundred sheep as well as 128 passengers, two hundred cattle, and sixteen horses. It was in 1840, too, that a shipment of New Zealand wool to Hobart Town was highly praised, but this was, presumably, from the Bay of Islands area or from Mana Island from which small quantities of wool had been exported since 1835. [22]

The Wakefield-planned settlements of the New Zealand Company did not, of course, include the idea of extensive sheep farms producing a single staple for export. The staple-export colonies of the days of the cod and the beaver, of sugar, spices and tobacco, dyewoods and indigo, gold and silver, were no longer considered a profitable investment by English capitalists in the early nineteenth century unless a fairly dense and sedentary, or at least submissive, native population was present to supply labor (especially after the official ban on the slave trade). Yet, as the early settlements ran into continued difficulties from lack of land easily adapted to agriculture, and the slow return on capital thus invested became evident, it was perhaps inevitable that the running of sheep should have superseded the original plans for using the land. New South Wales and Victoria are just within the range of distance in which it was possible or profitable to transport considerable numbers of sheep. Had it been necessary for sheep to be brought from as far away as England or the Americas, the relatively high mortalities, experienced even on the twelve-hundred-mile voyage across the Tasman Sea, might have made such importation unprofitable and given the whole history of land use in New Zealand another orientation. On South Island's eastern slopes, with large areas of natural grassland and a climate almost as equable in temperature regime as that of Australia, and with a much more consistently adequate rainfall,[23] loss of flocks from droughts seemed unlikely. No native predatory animals such as the Australian dingo existed, and losses from attacks of Kea parrots, wild dogs, or wild pigs were only a minor nuisance. The Australian colonies had their capitalists ready to move in with their flocks, or had sheep to sell to English capitalists willing to gamble on their ability to adapt Australian techniques. Large sheep-runs had, of course, grown increasingly common in England in the three centuries preceding 1840, especially with the progress of enclosures, and they had spread over the highlands of Scotland as well. Yet the methods of management were not applicable to South Island conditions. All the capital equipment of hedges or fences, buildings, communication routes, and markets for meat as well as wool, accumulated through centuries, were lacking; the very sheep themselves were of a breed little known or used at home. It is, thus, to the Australian colonies that the roots of South Island's dominant productive industry must be traced.

This point deserves emphasis. The historians of New Zealand have exhibited a strong tendency toward Little-Englandism on the one hand, or environmental-*cum*-economic determinism on the other, in tracing cultural origins. The indebtedness of cultural land-use habits in South Island to its accidental proximity to

Australia and to the accident of prior experiments there in the running of Merino sheep is, perhaps, as important as the accident of government from London, of the existence of an English textile industry able to absorb its wool, and of a population predominantly English in character. South Island has proved eminently suited by nature to the raising of sheep, but large parts of it are equally suitable to the growing of many agricultural cash crops, including varieties of trees. Had the Japanese Empire anticipated its recent abortive expansion by a century and stretched to include New Zealand, one can imagine it proving highly suitable to a wide variety of other uses. The prevalent view of natural predestination of sheep to South Island is one of the principal obstacles to sound historical research in New Zealand; it deserves to be ranked with the common New Zealand cult of ancestor-worship, which traces virtually all of the blood-lines of the present population to hand-picked selections from the best of all classes in England and Scotland.

The origin of the Merino breed on which this development was based is not clear. It was known in Spain from the twelfth and thirteenth centuries and may be a Moorish importation there. The breed was at home in the arid climates of both the hills and valleys of the Iberian interior and was involved in the seasonal transhumance between the two. Eventually four varieties were to become widely known: The Escurial (or Escorial), the Paular, the Negretti, and the Infantado. The Negretti blood was dominant in the nineteenth-century Merino breeding activity.* The Merino, in general, is a small, wiry individual with a body conformation not unlike that of a mountain goat. Although it is not derived from any of the short-wool † breeds of England, it is much more akin

---

* The heavily wrinkled Negretti and the small, much tighter-skinned Escurial were the ancestors of most of the Merino sheep now so widely scattered about the world. Exported to Saxony, France, England, and to the United States in the late eighteenth and early nineteenth centuries (an earlier ban against exportation from Spain, aimed at maintaining a Spanish monopoly on fine wools, having been circumvented in 1765), by 1820 Merino studs existed in virtually all the major sheep-raising areas of the time. The Rambouillet and Saxon seem to have been largely Escurials, while the English studs were mainly, if not entirely, Negretti.

† At the beginning of the nineteenth century the short-wools were far the most numerous in Britain; and they probably represented the earliest, perhaps the autochthonous, sheep there, for they were traditionally and by their particular qualities the sheep of the open-field farmer. They were the breeds formed by centuries of far-traveling, close feeding on scanty pasturage, and a starvation allowance of hay in winter. Examples of valuable strains later selected from this type are the Ryelands of Herefordshire, the Dorsets, the black-faced Wiltshires,

to these than to the larger, heavier, coarse-fibered long-wools, in its shortness and fineness of wool and its ability to survive on slim feed. Earp [25] said that at that time (the early fifties) "Almost all of the sheep in New Zealand have been imported from New South Wales and are of the pure Merino breed." He further remarked that Merinos had already been crossed, in some instances, with English long- and short-wools (notably Leicesters and Southdowns), and that the Southdown-Merino cross was spoken of highly as giving a better carcass without materially affecting the wool.[*]

The story of the establishment of the Merino breed in Australia is best told in G. A. Brown [26] and E. W. Cox.[27] The first sheep of any kind in New South Wales arrived with Governor Phillip in 1788, and some of these, at least, were taken aboard at the Cape of Good Hope.[28] For several years after 1788, other sheep were brought in not only from the Cape but from Calcutta as well. Those from the Cape were of the Hottentot variety, a breed about which little information seems available. The Indian sheep are described as small, thin, mostly black or dark grey in color, and carrying a harsh, spare, and wiry fleece.

After many experiments with such stock, the first Merinos were imported from the Cape of Good Hope in 1797. They were divided among existing flocks and generally diluted with other blood, though one lone flock was bred pure and improved by careful selection for the best wools. This flock was of the Escurial strain and, with some of its animals and some of the Negretti strain imported from the stud of George II direct to New South Wales (they luckily survived), a new flock was started by the "father" of the Australian sheep industry, Captain John Macarthur. The next year, Captain Macarthur imported some ewes (breed unrecorded but probably long-wool) from Ireland. Crosses produced

---

and the Sussex Southdowns. The long-wools are generally much better represented in South Island's present sheep population, including the Cotswolds, the Lincolns, the Leicesters, and the Romney Marsh sheep of Kent. While the short-wools were of every imaginable type, the long wools were more uniform, taller, heavier in carcass and fleece, with straight, long wool, and they were almost universally polled, white-faced and white-legged.[24]

[*] This cross, tried again in subsequent years, did not yield a sufficiently sturdy offspring for the climate and terrain of South Island. Several farmers and breeders recalled for this writer instances of such experiments. Merino-short-wool crosses have never been important there, except in the production of fat-lambs. Rarely is a Southdown-Merino cross allowed to reach maturity, and, in any event, Southdowns are now almost always bred to half-breds.

sheep with a curious hair and wool mixture in the pelt. Macarthur's second station, Camden, gave the name "Camden Merinos" to the Macarthur type of Negretti-Escurial cross. The so-called "Tasmanian Merino" was slightly different from the "Camden," especially in terms of more Escurial blood. Another flock-owner imported, in turn, rams from Rambouillet in France and from the Elector of Saxony's flocks, Escurial blood in the main.

The high European reputation of Merino wool seems to have been the principal reason for these introductions to Australia. Spanish wools had long been of major importance in the manufacture of the finest English woolens. None of the English breeds was then as directly specialized on wool production or grew as valuable a fleece. Since the New South Wales grazier was likely, as his flocks grew, to have less and less market for his meat, and since the Australian wools had to be sent halfway around the world to England, every attempt to produce the greatest value per unit of weight and bulk had to be made. Under English conditions of management, with much handling, the rather wild, temperamental Merino suffered somewhat in comparison with more docile breeds. But on the free and fenceless ranges of New South Wales this handicap was removed, and there, in the dry, hard grasses, the warmer, drier climate, and the rough ranges, the Merino was, for the first time in its wanderings from Spain, environmentally again at home. E. W. Cox, at the beginning of his chapter on the establishment of the Merino in New South Wales, has this to say: "It would seem that Providence had kept this great gift for the young continent—young in so far as habitation by white man is concerned—and it began to prepare for the bestowal of this gift some thirty years before the recipient was ready to receive it, for the work done in Saxony and other countries must certainly have helped Australia to a great extent." [29]

James Atkinson, himself a pioneer Australian grazier, published in 1826 *An Account of the State of Agriculture and Grazing in New South Wales* in which he made the following statement about the Merino:

From [the] time [of the introduction of the Merino breed], the improvement has been every year more considerable; and within the last few years, a great number of Merino and Saxon sheep have been imported by different individuals; the price of the rams has fallen in consequence, and they are now within the reach of the poorest breeders; the progress of the improvement will therefore be much more rapid than heretofore, and it may be safely anticipated, that in twenty years more, nearly the whole sheep stock of the colony will approach the perfection of the Spanish breed. The greatest facilities are presented for the attainment of this object; the climate dry, and free from noxious damps and fogs; the soil, more especially in the interior, sound and firm, covered with an abundance of nutritive grass and herbage; the country also open and clear, admitting the free circulation of the air; all combine to render the country peculiarly adapted to the constitution of the animal.

The early Merino individuals imported to South Island were, however, from all accounts caricatures of the present Merino high-country sheep of South Island, bare in the points and very short in the staple. Yet some of the earliest recorded yields of up to four pounds of wool per animal were already an improvement over the average of two and a half pounds from New South Wales. These figures are from the Nelson-Wairau area in which the first development began.[30] The first years' issues of the *Nelson Examiner* make it clear that a number of sheep and cattle were imported very early and run by land-holders or interlopers squatting on unsold sections in the fern, scrub, or scrub-brush areas. By 1844 there were nearly five thousand sheep in Nelson,[31] and the rapid increase in numbers thereafter has been commented on above.[32] There was a rapid penetration of the Wairau-Awatere via Tophouse, via the Kaituna-Maungatapau route, or by way of Port Underwood, until most of the suitable land was occupied by the early fifties.

Almost the first thing done in all the tussock areas was to set fire to them and to repeat the process each year in late autumn or winter. The January 23, 1847, issue of the *Nelson Examiner* quotes a traveler's report that all the plain between Grovetown (just north of Blenheim) and the sea had been fired. The purpose was twofold. A good deal of spiny *Discaria* and other wool-tearing or wool-dirtying shrubs were thus destroyed and the work of shepherds made easier. Perhaps more important was the fact that the hard, mature tussock could not be eaten by the sheep and, if burning was not resorted to, these animals were limited to the feed in the sub-stratum of inter-tussock vegetation.[33] After the area was burned, however, the new growth of tussock gave good feed while young and tender, and continued to do so when kept well pruned by the sheep. The long-term effects of this rapidly established general practice will be considered below.

In the meantime, sheep had been introduced along the south-eastern coasts before either the Otago or the Canterbury settlement was formally established. The Deans' initial consignment of livestock in 1843 included forty-three sheep.[34] They continually added to their flocks, importing directly from New South Wales where prices were low. Rhodes had established a station at Purau across Lyttelton Harbor opposite the future site of Lyttelton, and in 1844, had there a mob of four hundred sheep.[35] More sheep must have been imported,* for William Deans wrote [36] on November 25, 1845, that the Purau station would have fifteen hundred ewes lambing that season, and that it expected to clip four thousand pounds of wool for which one shilling a pound had been offered.

In the Australian depression of the early and middle forties, the price of sheep in New South Wales had been reduced to as little as 2s. to 2s.6d. per head. By 1847, prices had recovered somewhat, especially with the increased exports of the by-products (skins and tallow), but wethers brought only 5s. to 6s. each. These low prices were of tremendous assistance in the establishment of the Merino-squatter pastoral complex in South Island, and on better pastures, with more consistent rainfall, the sheep were more productive. Though the wool from New Zealand continued to sell at a disadvantage of a penny or two per pound, the yield of wool was definitely greater, which more than offset the price differential, as was clearly demonstrated by the Deans' experience.† In fact, sheep were thought to be worth one-half more in New Zealand than in New South Wales.

The price paid for sheep in New South Wales was not, however, their value per head landed in New Zealand, for normally up to 50 per cent of the cargo was lost on the voyage or shortly after

---

* These sheep were of varying origin. While mainly Australian (probably "Camden Merinos"), he did import also from the Sturgeon Flock at Gray's Hall in England—descendants of the Royal Negrettis of George II—some from the Escurial flock of the King of Württemberg, and six rams and five ewes from the Rambouillet flocks of M. Gilbert, near Boulogne.

† The average yield of wool in New South Wales had increased from about one and one-half pounds per sheep in 1820 (though Macarthur's first flocks were giving two pounds) to roughly two and one-half pounds in the 1840's. Meanwhile prices, which had been upwards of 2s.6d. per pound for good fleeces in the twenties, declined rapidly to well below a shilling in 1840, rose to 11½d. in 1844, and 15d. in 1846, only to fall again to 10½d. in 1849.[37] Meanwhile the Deans had clipped 130 pounds of wool from twenty-eight sheep (over four and one-half pounds) and received 10d. per pound.[36]

landing. In 1847, for example, the Deans purchased six hundred sheep in Sydney which cost, over-all (and the 554 survivors landed at Port Cooper) £507. Subsequent losses in lambing, through storms, etc., resulted in only 430 of the original six hundred being added to the working flock. From various examples of this kind the cost of a live two-toothed ewe * landed in South Island and surviving the landing, may be estimated to have been between twenty and thirty shillings.

In 1848 the Deans lambed 480 animals; in the shearing, these sheep averaged 3½ pounds, the rams 6½ pounds—with one ram giving 7½ pounds—of fine, carefully washed wool. In 1849, 568 lambs represented a lambing average among the bred ewes of 125 per cent, and the young sheep averaged 4¾ pounds of wool of good quality. Assuming a price of one shilling, they expected the wool to bring from five hundred to six hundred pounds clear of all expenses.[38] Given a fair lambing percentage, and a yield of four pounds of wool a year, this still left a wide margin of profit for the new industry.

The Deans were learning, by hard experience, the lessons also being learned in the same decade further north. The Merinos did badly in the heavy, wet country around Riccarton and that stretching between Lake Ellesmere and the Ashley river along the coast. From the want of stones in the area, their hooves grew too rapidly, and many were lost by rolling on their backs and not being able to rise. Consequently, the first Canterbury "high-country" type of run was started by the Deans in the Alpine foot-hill area, which noses out onto the plains between the Waimakariri and Selwyn Rivers. It was easier, too, to keep different flocks, or selected groups within the flocks, separated on the hills in pre-fencing days.

This first experiment on, and success with, Merinos on the high country in this area occurred while the Deans were also making experiments with English grasses to prepare for the butchering and dairy needs of the expected settlement on the plains. That the Deans realized the mutual suitability of tussock and Merino may be gathered from a portion of their *Report on Conditions on the Plains in Reply to Captain Thomas:* "Beyond a very few South Down rams to improve the quality of the mutton of colonial sheep, we would not advise that any rams should be imported, as

---

* At one year of age a sheep has two teeth in the front of its lower jaw, at two years four, at three years six, and at four years the full complement of eight—an easy way to determine ages of young sheep.

fine-wooled sheep can be got from New South Wales superior to any in England." [39]

The Southern settlements, too, had imported Australian sheep in considerable numbers in the forties. In 1843, William Deans reported [40] a thousand sheep at "Wikowiti." * Shortland,[41] actually on the spot in 1844, reported 150 sheep from Mana Island at Orere, near Onekakara. Monro, in one of his series of articles in the *Nelson Examiner* (July 20, 1844, *et seq.*), reported that Jones had two thousand sheep at his Waikouaiti farm. It was from these stations that the nursery stock for the new Otago settlement was obtained.

Inevitably the Australian importations brought with them the "scab" † then so prevalent in New South Wales. It appeared in a severe form in Nelson in the late forties and, in 1849, the Governor-in-Council for the Province of New Munster issued the first scab ordinance pertaining to South Island. Though the disease was difficult to control in the earliest days, it did not reach its peak here until the late fifties. Sheep men, anxious to establish some vested right in a grazing license by act of occupancy, were only too glad to turn any animal that could walk out to the claims they had staked on the tussock hills, either to strengthen their claims or, later, to meet ordinances requiring minimum stocking. The spread of scab was aided by the continual migration of flocks to new runs, the lack of official supervision, fences, or even, in many cases, adequate shepherding.‡ The Deans reported a serious outbreak in 1848 which they cured in four months by a "thorough dressing." [43] Fortunately foot-rot and catarrh were as yet unknown.[44]

As we have seen, the fifties saw the pattern of expansion by

---

* Presumably Waikouaiti.

† The "scab" was a skin irritation caused by a mite, *Psoroptis communis*, which seriously affected the general condition of the animals as well as their fleeces. The affliction had first appeared in New South Wales in the thirties, arriving from England, the Cape, or India; it remained a problem there for many decades. The most sensational report, given by different authors, was of one infected herd driven through Victoria in 1862. It was represented to have infected, in all, a total of three hundred thousand sheep. Of these two-thirds were cured by dipping, sixty thousand died from the dip, and forty thousand from the scab.[42]

‡ The absence of fences meant, inevitably, the escape of sheep into relatively inaccessible mountain areas. Through the whole century, and until today, South Island has had many small herds of wild sheep, which are shot, like the wild goats and deer, for sport and as vermin.

the "squatocracy," set in the northern reaches of the tussock
grasslands in the forties, repeated in Canterbury and Otago (including Southland), and extended to the borders of the alpine
shingle screes of the former, or the lower limits of either *Nothofagus* bush or alpine herb fields of the latter. It may be stressed
again that the customary characterization of the failure of the
planned compact agricultural settlements, in terms of unsuitability
of the habitat for agriculture with the limited capital available,
is not a sufficient explanation. It is of course true that much of the
best agricultural land in coastal Canterbury and Southland, in
the lower-Taieri–lower-Clutha area of Otago, in the Waimea–
Moutere–Motueka area of Nelson, and in the lower Wairau required much difficult drainage to bring it into peak agricultural
production. But there was, by evidence of the great mobs of sheep
bought in New South Wales, plenty of capital available. The
choice was one of alternative employment of that capital. True,
the prices charged for land in the "blocks," from one to three
pounds per acre, was high, but whether it was too high cannot be
categorically stated; other possibilities for investment must have
proved too attractive, even had the price been much lower, as long
as large areas could be leased outside the "blocks" at a rather
nominal fee.*

This is especially evident in the case of Canterbury. Australian
Merinos could be imported, or acclimatized mobs from the Marlborough area driven in, at reasonable prices; the most expensive
lessons of modification of Australian techniques to South Island
conditions had been learned in the northern part of the island.
Not until the country was blocked out to its limits by pastoral
runs was any real advance in agriculture made. And this was not
because agriculture or a fairly intensive dairying industry would
not pay. On Banks Peninsula, and around Christchurch, Nelson,
and Dunedin, it had proved and continued to be profitable, with
exports even to New South Wales.† We must simply conclude
that sheep raising was more profitable, and our best evidence is
found in the rush of English capitalists to join the Australian
squatters in the game. The acceptance of the best of competing

---

* Fuller [45] argued that the advantage over agriculture of running sheep in the
back country was chiefly the cost of transport of the finished product. A ton of
grain might sell for ten pounds, which perhaps would meet the combined cost
of production and transport. Yet a ton of wool, worth at least a hundred pounds,
could easily absorb the cost of draying.

† See table VI, p. 116.

alternatives does not imply the lack of possibility of, or even a considerable degree of attractiveness in, others; the entrepreneurs loved not wheat the less, but sheep the more.

The dependence of Canterbury on beginnings in the northeast cannot be stated too strongly. By 1850, Weld alone had eleven thousand sheep at Flaxbourne, and in 1851 there were a quarter of a million sheep in New Zealand, mainly around Cook Strait (chiefly in the Wairarapa valley east of Port Nicholson, and the Wairau-Awatere area), occupying almost certainly over a million acres. Thomson's [46] figures for the sheep population for 1851 are given in table XXXII. In 1855, some forty-nine pastoralists in the Wairau-Awatere (out of a total population of 627 souls) were running a quarter of a million sheep on half a million acres.[47]

TABLE XXXII
SHEEP POPULATION (1851)

Auckland	11,075
Wellington	64,009
Taranaki (New Plymouth)	2,700
North Island	*77,784*
Nelson	92,014
Canterbury	28,416
Otago	34,829
South Island	*155,259*
Total for New Zealand	*233,043*

Before this great reservoir of sheep could be effectively tapped for Canterbury, some routes by land to the south had to be found. Even if the area had not lacked easily accessible harbors, the driving of sheep to the north coast, the loading, the sea trip to Banks Peninsula, and the unloading and driving over the Port Hills probably would have been a more expensive proposition than importing from Sydney. The first overland journey was made in 1850 by a Captain Mitchell and companions via the Wai-hopai river, past the headwaters of the Awatere to the Acheron, east (that is, upstream) for some distances along the Clarence, and then across a divide into the Hanmer plain (fig. 43). Subsequently, after many mistakes, the route was rediscovered. Then in 1851-1852 an adventurous squatter named Lee found a better stock route via the Awatere, over Barefell pass, down the Acheron

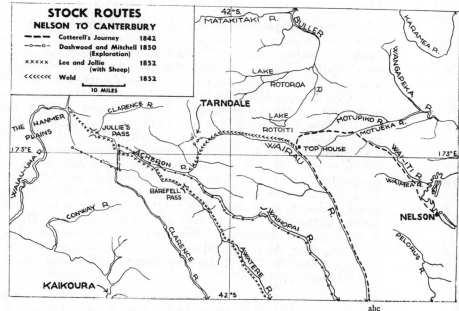

STOCK ROUTES
NELSON TO CANTERBURY
- - -   Cotterell's Journey   1842
-o—o-   Dashwood and Mitchell 1850
        (Exploration)
xxxxx   Lee and Jollie   1852
        (with Sheep)
<<<<<< Weld   1852

10 MILES

Fig. 43. Stock routes—Nelson to Canterbury.

to the junction of the Clarence, and then south to the Hanmer basin. The pass between the Clarence–Acheron valley and that of the Hanmer–Waiau-uha, was named after Jollie, a companion of Lee, with whom he drove sheep over this route in 1852. Paul [48] gives a transcript of Lee's account of this journey. Though they had to burn vigorously to clear scrubby growths in the ravines in order to get through, he reported enthusiastically on the grazing possibilities of the back country. On April 10, 1852, the *Lyttelton Times* reported their arrival in the Waiau-uha with eighteen hundred sheep, sustaining a loss of only 3 per cent on the way, and this chiefly from strays and from drownings while fording the rivers. This became at once the chief stock route to Canterbury. In 1853, several parties drove at least five thousand sheep over it; in 1854, single flocks of as large as four thousand were taking it; and in 1855, at least twelve thousand sheep were driven through Barefell pass alone.

The favorable position of Nelson, and the improvement of stock prices there with the opening of the route, led the *Nelson Examiner* to editorialize: "To Mr. Lee .... we are under the deepest obligation." [49] From the port of Nelson, however, this route was long and difficult; up the Wai-iti, over to the upper Motueka, across to the upper Motupiko, down the Wairau, up the Waihopai or Awatere and across Barefell pass to the upper Acheron, to the Clarence, and over Jollie's pass to the Hanmer basin. Weld, the Flaxbourne pioneer, discovered a much easier way: from Top House, close to the course of the upper Wairau, through the relatively level country of Tarndale to the upper Acheron, and thence by Lee's route. The overland journey from Nelson to Canterbury was cut to six days. The route crossed all the main rivers so near to their sources that, in late summer at least, the fording of the rivers was of comparatively little moment. There were, however, considerable obstacles to the construction of a dray-road along the route, and no road of any kind has been put through to this day.* Weld also commented that the whole route was excellent for stock:

As a general rule, the sides of the mountains, the lower hills, and the valleys, are covered with grass; the black birch [probably one of the *Nothofagus* species] is found along the Clarence and Wairau to a level of about 3,000 feet (as nearly as I can estimate) above the sea, the manuka at a slightly less elevation. [50]

Fitton [51] writing of the same period, says: "An uninterrupted series of sheep and cattle grazing stations has, for some time, occupied the whole available country between Nelson and Canterbury." At any rate, thus were a great part of the sheep to Canter-

* The present shortest land routes from Canterbury to Nelson are: (1) From Hanmer basin across the Lewis pass to Reefton, down the Inangahua stream to the Buller, up the Buller to Murchison (or from Lewis pass by the Maruia and Matakitaki valleys to Murchison), up the Buller to Glenhope and by the Motupiko and Wai-iti valleys to Nelson, or (2) from the downs of Cheviot county through to the sea by the mouth of the Conway and thence up the coast to Flaxbourne. Both of these routes have probably involved heavier engineering costs than would the interior one, but they do serve areas of heavier population which is a considerable advantage. The coastal route involved cutting ledges into, or tunnels through, a great many headlands which abut the sea in cliffs. The railway along the coast which was in process of construction for over sixty years, has only recently been completed; yet, by watching the tides, Weld was able to make his way along this route, though it was impractical for any large numbers of sheep. Until the Lewis pass road went through (1940), the only alternative was via Arthur's Pass to the Grey, up that valley and over a saddle to Reefton.

bury supplied until the seventies, when Canterbury became self-sufficient.*

If the first requirement was the stock, the second was the land on which to run it. A good many of the details of the fulfillment of this need have been discussed in chapter III. While considerable quantities of land were sold at prices ranging from three pounds in the Canterbury block down to the ten shillings and five shillings per acre prices for which land outside the blocks was sold (following Grey's "cheap land" ordinance of 1853), most of the early development was based on leaseholds outside of the blocks, generally for fourteen years, under the Crown Land's Ordinance of 1851 (which implemented provisions of the Imperial Government's Australian Land Sales Act of 1852). Many of the sales helped to confirm control of the leaseholds; in any event, the squatters were temporarily as sure of their lands as if they were indeed freeholders, because of certain clauses in leases defining pre-emptive rights. By application, leaseholders were allowed to purchase certain areas on their runs before any other purchaser could buy, which meant that the designated areas need not be purchased until an official challenge was issued. Provisions varied, but a leaseholder generally had pre-emptive rights to so many acres for his homestead, for each shepherd's hut, for so many chains of fencing or acres of cultivation, or for a variety of other improvements. Apart from pre-emptive rights, the run-holder was free to buy any other acreages he chose. By pre-emption, or other purchase, the squatters quickly gained control about watering places, any patches of bush, patches of river terraces, or valley bottoms with any possibility of being tilled—in fact, of all those bits of land without which no sheep-grazing run could be worked (fig. 44). Though the leaseholds were usually put up to auction at the expiry of the fourteen-year or other period, it would have been ruinous, in most cases, for others to bid in on them.†

---

* Andersen [52] quotes customs records on the importation of sheep to Canterbury as follows:

	1866	1871
By sea	1,137	1,445
From Nelson	17,948	26,030
From Otago	7,947	12,664

† When a run-holder was financially shaky, this could be done, however, as without his lease, the grazier might be forced to sell his leasehold as well. If he had resources, he could allow another bidder to win, and then dicker with him for some arrangement by which the two essential parts of the run could be worked together.

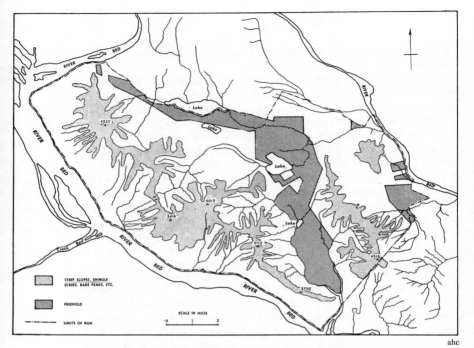

ahc

FIG. 44. Typical layout of a Canterbury high-country run. *Lighter shading:* steep slopes, shingle screes, and bare peaks; *heavier shading:* most productive areas (including all the arable), which were freeholded.

This process, called "spotting," or "picking the eyes out of the country," or "peacocking," * was chiefly responsible for the tight control which the squatters maintained over government-owned lands. Another device, in use a little later in Canterbury, depended on a regulation of the Provincial Council preventing any purchase of sections less than twenty acres in area without going to auction. By "grid-ironing" his purchases of land to leave alternate, isolated patches slightly under twenty acres in size unbought, the squatter could be assured that nobody could cut in on land, without his notice, for which he had to pay only slightly more than half of the purchase price.

An idea of the approximate scale of the blocking out in Canterbury is given on the map for South Canterbury in 1863 (fig. 45).[53] Andersen[54] gives the figures (table XXXIII) for a series

* An Australian term indicating that the devices were probably trans-Tasman in origin.

of South Canterbury runs in the fifties. In 1857, according to Andersen, there were 95,900 sheep on 791,000 acres, and the heaviest stocking was at the rate of one sheep to five acres. In 1859 the Mackenzie country had one run with 1,500 sheep; in 1860 there were eight runs with 17,500 sheep in the basin. By 1866 all of South Canterbury had fifty stations with 629,443 sheep and fourteen farms with 23,691 sheep. In 1875 these had increased to 65 stations with 1,148,080 sheep and 113 farms with 95,454 sheep. The comparative figures for Central and North Canter-

FIG. 45. Division of South Canterbury in the 1860's into large sheep runs.

ahc

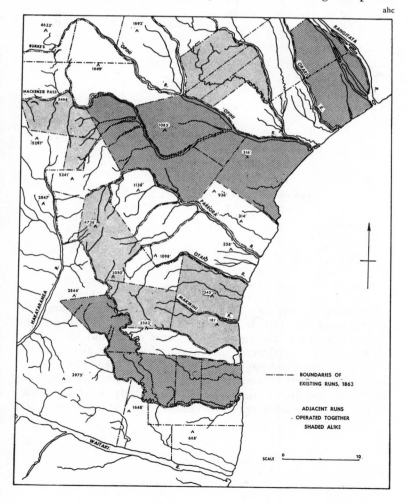

bury at this time are given in table XXXIV. The peak number of sheep in this area (that is, between the Rangitata and the Waitaki rivers) was reached with two million sheep about the end of the century.

TABLE XXXIII

SIZE OF SOUTH CANTERBURY RUNS IN THE 1850's

Acres (in thousands)	Number of Sheep (in thousands)			
	1854	1855	1856	1857
150	13.2	24.0	23.0	30.0
30	2.0	4.0	5.5	6.0
60	2.8	7.0	5.1	8.0
25	1.4	2.1	2.5	1.8
66	3.0	4.0	6.0	8.0
60	.8	1.5	2.2	2.6
20			2.5	3.0
40	4.1	2.5	4.4	5.0
25			2.5	3.0
30	1.0	2.3	3.5	4.0
40		2.0	3.5	4.7
60			1.1	2.7
60			4.0	6.0
20			1.2	2.4
40		1.4	1.8	2.0
25			1.9	2.4
40			3.0	4.3

TABLE XXXIV

NUMBER OF STATIONS, FARMS, AND SHEEP
(CENTRAL AND NORTH CANTERBURY)

Number of	1866	1875
Stations	122	119
Sheep	1,006,352	1,359,667
Number of		
Farms	169	811
Sheep	75,660	352,649

In Central Canterbury, Paul [55] indicates somewhat smaller sizes of runs from the start. In 1854-1855 there were 142 runs in the Canterbury block, averaging 9,650 acres each, and there were 53, averaging 29,500 acres, outside of the block; also, outside, 1,310,300 acres were applied for and 250,000 acres gazetted. As the higher country or areas more distant from Christchurch were taken, the sizes increased, as in South Canterbury. In 1855 licenses for two stations on the upper Rangitata were requested at 57,500 acres apiece.[56] An expectable expansion of size from the centers outward is evident in these figures.

Though the above picture is largely based on Canterbury evidence, much the same patterns were followed in Otago. By the mid-fifties, sheep men were investigating the basins of the Maniototo, Ida, Manuherikia, and upper Clutha, as well as the tall-tussock plains of Southland. Hocken [57] states that, in 1856: "Of what was called the Southern Country, extending between the Mataura and Jacob's River, and inland to the mountain ranges, little was known beyond that it was the abode of a few whalers, and that there were some good harbours, notably the Bluff, which must be of vast service in developing the capabilities of the province." In 1857, the first runs were taken up on the Manuherikia.[58] In 1860, the last frontier had been reached: two diligent explorers, Rees and Von Tunzelmann, had claimed land around Lake Wakatipu. Getting sheep into that country was, at first, a severe problem. Von Tunzelmann went in from the south, but Rees had an epic drive across the wild and little known hills from the east coast.[59]

One of the most difficult problems in the pastoral advance was lack of accurate surveys of the area. Thomson's surveys of Central Otago barely kept ahead of the settlers, and the same story was true to the north. So carelessly were the boundaries of the runs established that one of the settlers stated in 1856: "There will be a mighty pother one of these days about these runs and their boundaries, when the country becomes fully stocked. How are we to tell the boundary line with no single thing to mark it, and no possibility of artificial fencing?" [60] Actually the problem of fencing was solved by the later introduction of barbed wire, but this did not solve the vexing survey problem.

Given land and sheep, we are concerned to know how the runs were managed and how the general techniques of sheep farming developed.[61] In selecting the run, it was necessary to explore for unattached country, though by the early sixties there was little of this left. The exploration, as indeed most of the traveling in the tussock country, was made on horseback, generally on great, rugged, but agile hacks, bred and trained for rough country in one of the Australian colonies. Often when the run was hopefully staked out and even before official application was made, it received its first all-over burning. If the license was granted, plans for the purchase of sheep and preparation for their reception went on together. The run-holder tried to become established before the sheep arrived, to hire his "shepherds" (most usually men who knew little about sheep) and other hands for the station. For a small run of five thousand acres, the owner would need at least one shepherd, a cook (often called the "hut keeper"), a "bullocky" (bullock driver), and two spare hands for rough carpentry and general work.* A half a dozen good bullocks, a couple of saddle horses, and a flock of from one thousand to five thousand ewes would be minimum requirements. Well before the sheep were driven in, building materials, tools, and food (chiefly flour, sugar, and tea) were loaded on the great, high-wheeled drays and laboriously hauled over the plains and hills and through the fords of the streams and rivers. A few yards of post-and-rail fences on embankments † were constructed for the necessary sheep-drafting during dipping, shearing, or lambing. The first buildings erected were usually of cob, and almost always with a door wide enough to pass a wool-bale, so that any one building could be used as a temporary wool store. If the tussock had not been burned, this was also now done, often as much to "knock" the horse-wounding *Discaria* and *Aciphylla* individuals, as to promote better feed. The run-holder and his men lived on tea and "damper" (pan-bread) almost exclusively, with what game, either birds or wild pigs, might fall to their guns. When the sheep came in, wether-mutton became the third corner of the tea-damper-meat triangle on which a whole generation of sheep squatters lived. An eye-witness said of the life:

Long wearisome rides and walks in search of truant cattle and sheep, *bivouacs* night after night on the damp cold ground, mutton, damper, and tea (and that colonial tea!) at breakfast, dinner and supper, day after day, week after week, and month after month; wanderings in trackless "deserts," with a choice of passing the night on some bleak mountain top or wading through an unexplored swamp; and after all this labour finding that perhaps his flock are infected, and that no small amount of money as well as toil must be expended before he can

* In the fifties these were often sailors, who, while unused to animals and the back country, were in demand as jacks-of-all-trades because of the trained deftness of their hands.

† Post-and-rail fences, little known in England but not uncommon in the backwoods communities of early America, may have been a contribution of early American whalers. More frequently, because of scarcity of timber, fences of sod and wattle were used.

profit at all:—these are the real experiences of a settler's early days in a young pastoral country.[62]

The records of many early stations, however, indicate that the venture was profitable, if arduous. As soon as possible, more permanent buildings were constructed, including a proper wool shed, more elaborate drafting races near it, gardens, fences, horse and ram paddocks, permanent washing places (important only in the early days), and dipping vats or trenches to combat scab.

Apart from the cost of leasing the land, expenses for a small station of five thousand acres, starting with a thousand ewes, came to about three thousand pounds over the first three years.[63] Under the land regulations in force in Canterbury up until 1862, for runs of from one thousand to five thousand acres, the yearly rental was twopence per acre for the first thousand acres, and a penny for each additional acre. Thus, for a run of five thousand acres the land charge was a pound a year, an almost negligible item of expense. About half the expense of the first few years was the initial cost of sheep. As many of the run-holders could not afford to stock their land to more than a fraction of capacity, and as there was plenty of capital available in the colony, a system of putting out sheep "on terms" grew up. Samuel Butler, who went to Canterbury in 1860, describes this system in his classic description of life on an early sheep station.[64] He could buy a thousand ewes for £1,250 and put them out to a squatter. He would receive 2s.6d. a head per annum in lieu of wool, and 40 per cent of the annual increase; male and female equally, would be credited to his account at the rate of 2s.6d. a head in each subsequent year. At the end of the agreement, sheep of proportionate increased age were to be returned without any allowance for loss by deaths. Mortality did occur, and sometimes in a severe winter involved great losses, but these losses were absorbed, under this agreement, by the man in whose care the sheep were placed. Suppose, for example, a squatter started with a thousand ewes in January (midsummer) 1860. Ignoring rams kept for breeding, the numbers of sheep, through the year 1867, might have developed as shown in table XXXV.

Of the 5,164 sheep returned, a thousand ewes would be eight years old and close to the end of their productive life, another eight hundred would be six or seven years old and would bring very little at a sale; possibly thirty-six hundred sheep would be in good shape (counting weaned lambs as such). If sheep had dropped from 25s. to an average of 10s. a head in value, this would still be £1,800 worth of sheep as against £1,250 spent at the beginning. In the meantime, wool money would have brought in a total of over two thousand pounds in increasing yearly amounts. As the practice flourished it was apparently profitable to the graziers as well. It is given here in some detail to help explain the extraordinary rapidity with which tussock lands were stocked with sheep. The table also indicates how rapidly, with even a fair mortality experience and lambing average, the flocks increased when there was little demand for meat.

TABLE XXXV

HYPOTHETICAL INCREASE FROM A BASIC FLOCK OF 1000 EWES IN A SEVEN-YEAR PERIOD

January	Ewes	Ewe Lambs	Wether Lambs	Ewe Hoggets	Wether Hoggets	Wethers	Total
1860	1000						1000
1861	1000	200	200				1400
1862	1000	200	200	200	200		1800
1863	1200	240	240	200	200	200	2280
1864	1400	280	280	240	240	400	2840
1865	1640	328	328	280	280	640	3496
1866	1920	384	384	328	328	920	4264
1867	2248	450	450	384	384	1248	5164

The problem of finding laborers was often severe. There were few trained shepherds, still fewer with trained dogs. Whoever did the shepherding was, in the early sixties, given a hut of his own, his tea, flour, salt, sugar, and the right to kill wethers for meat. In addition his money wage was from thirty-five to forty-five pounds a year. Laborers were often given higher cash wages without being so liberally "found." All the authorities agree that, with the competitive magnet of the gold fields, at first Victorian and then local, the hired hands were an extremely motley collection, and almost universally lacking in knowledge of sheep. The ability of the Merino to live well, grow valuable wool, and increase in spite of ignorant or inexpert handling, together with the cheapness of land, seems to have been the basis for the successful advance of pastoralism. And of course, with a seeding in of a few Australian sheep managers, or hands with experience there, and of a few old country sheep men and farmers or farm laborers, the new and unskilled had many tutors. The major skills to be learned were: to get to know the differences in pastures that sheep might be moved around in order to maintain some evenness of pruning of the grass; to train and manage dogs in the field so that the sheep could be mustered rapidly when need arose; to operate as a rule-of-thumb veterinarian for curing minor ills, for aiding with lambing, and for tailing and castration of young lambs; to track and find sheep caught by snow or bad weather; to shear the sheep and prepare the wool; to dip sheep for scab prevention; and to pare away hooves attacked by foot-rot. These things were somehow learned, and by precept, trial and error, and invention, a large highly skilled sheep-tending labor force was available within a period of twenty-five years.

One of the factors of technique which compelled shepherds virtually to live with their sheep, and hence to get to know them better, was the lack of fencing, until barbed wire was later introduced. In 1855 only 12,260 acres were fenced in Canterbury, mostly with expensive ditch-and-bank, topped with post-and-rail; it was not until 1856 that the first plain galvanized wire was advertised for sale in the *Lyttelton Times*. As this was often as thick as a man's little finger it was expensive and brutal stuff to work with; for the open tussock country it was nearly useless. In 1860 there was still little else but this heavy No. 4 wire, rolled in 224-pound coils, and in short lengths which required the frequent tying of knots. Slowly, more easily manipulated wire came in greater quantities into the market. By 1863 a fencing ordinance in Canterbury required the erection of fences between runs, where one party to the boundary so desired, at mutual expense.

The sheep imported continued to be largely Australian and Tasmanian Merinos, but the island quickly became virtually self-sufficient in its Merino sheep. Even in the fifties, however, managers experimented with a variety of English long-wooled and short-wooled breeds. As early as 1852 [65] twenty rams with mixed Merino, Southdown, and Leicester (presumably English Leicester) blood were offered for sale. Perry [66] says that considerable numbers of rams of English Leicester, Lincoln, and Romney Marsh breeds were introduced into Auckland and Wellington, but there is reason to doubt that there were really very many. Perhaps sentiment or tradition, as much as practical considerations, induced one Murray of Taieri to import Border Leicesters for the New Zealand and Australasian Land Company in 1859. Although there were few sheep but Merinos, it is, however, important that experiments with other breeds began early.

The rapid increases in numbers of sheep in the fifties and sixties occurred despite continued difficulty with scab. This disease was accentuated by rapid movement of sheep, and often little relieved by official regulation and concern; indeed official controls of all kinds rested lightly on the pioneer community. In 1850 only three flocks in the Wairau were clear of scab.[67] Slowly official inspection was made compulsory at ports of entry from Nelson to Bluff.[68] References in the *Lyttelton Times* show that Canterbury was well aware of the danger, but steady importation from the north and the driving of new mobs over existing stations made it hard to control. Dipping was the standard remedy (fig. 46). Tobacco was the essential ingredient of the dips and this made them expensive; moreover the procuring of iron tanks to heat water, and of fuel for the fires, was never easy.* As early as 1858, however, the Canterbury Council enacted a stringent ordinance relating to scab control, with extremely heavy fines for violation, and it was reasonably well enforced.† The incidence of scab decreased steadily from Nelson south, and was never a problem south of the Rangitata.

The end product of this economy, so heavily dependent upon sheep, was the single staple wool. Once a year each of the sheep was shorn. This was done roughly, at first, by inexperienced hands using poor equipment, and at almost any time of the year. The reason for the variability of season (shearing is best done in early to middle spring) was that shearing involved the mustering in from the run of all the sheep, a large and expensive job; advantage was taken of this congregation to draft out any sheep to be sold. If it were more convenient to have such drafting-out done later in the season, the shearing might be left over. Again, shearing needed extra hands and, gradually, it came to be done more

---

* A correspondent of the *Lyttelton Times* in 1854 wrote that, from his own experience, a concoction of fifty pounds of salt, six pounds of sulfur, one-half pound of saltpeter and ten pounds of tobacco to fifty gallons of water was a good remedy. The ingredients varied, but this may be taken as representative. This mixture, it was claimed, would cure any sheep if dipped twice at intervals of three weeks.

† Not only was the landing of scabby sheep intended to be vigorously punished, but every owner of infected animals was liable to a fine of from one to five shillings per head, had to report the diseased condition of his sheep to adjoining owners within forty-eight hours, and to an inspector within a week, under threat of a fifty-pound fine. All scabby sheep had to be branded and kept a half mile from run boundaries, if unherded. Two justices could order scabby sheep constantly herded by day and guarded by night. (*Canterbury Ordinances*, 1858).

Collection of the Canterbury Museum.

FIG. 46. Dipping sheep in Canterbury in the eighties, primarily as a protection against "scab."

and more by large gangs who did little else, moving from station to station; the shearing consequently had to take place when a gang of shearers could be booked in.

Fortunately the shearing method prevalent in most of England until after this time, and initially practiced in New Zealand, was rapidly superseded. The old technique involved the tying of the sheep's legs, laying it on a stool, and clipping more or less at random. A new technique of sitting the sheep up, opening the neck and belly, and then running up the back, so as to keep the fleece as much as possible in one piece, had been developed in Northumberland and the Border counties at the beginning of the nineteenth century. It was introduced early to Australia where its labor-saving advantages gave it great value, and thence it moved to New Zealand.[69] As indicated above, the wool was washed, generally on the sheep at first, to save weight in transport. This required a pit, perhaps bricked in, some twenty feet by ten feet, and, in the most elaborate cases, a boiler to warm the water. Soap and ammonia were added to the water in which the sheep were soaked, after which they were driven into a nearby stream to be rinsed off. When the sheep were dry, they were shorn, and the wool packed (initially without much sorting) into the huge five-foot-six-inch woolsacks by tramping and tamping with a wooden spade, or later by screw presses which were introduced in the late sixties. Then the bales were loaded on the big drays, with teams of a dozen or more oxen, hitched tandem in pairs, to haul them the rough journey of often as much as a hundred miles to the nearest port. In 1860 Canterbury thus raised and shipped 2,842,470 pounds of wool, and Otago's 717,075 pounds brought in a revenue of £47,805.[70] The first wool ship to go direct from Dunedin to London, instead of via Sydney or Melbourne, sailed in 1858;[71] the first ship direct from Lyttelton left in the following year.[72]

Since the sheep runs had occupied all the available country between Cook and Foveaux straits (as well as a little grassy country in the middle valley of the Grey on the west coast)[73] by the end of the sixties, and as the bush-burning technique by which sheep were later to push slightly into the forested areas of Nelson, Westland, and western Southland had not yet been developed, the sheep industry had to settle down in the late sixties, the seventies, and eighties to improvement of its exploitation of lands already held. The gold rushes probably hindered rather than helped the industry. While the rushes were on, labor was lost to the diggings; when a lull ensued, the available labor was too often in complete ignorance of methods of sheep husbandry. New demands for wether mutton from the diggings allowed a little profit on surplus stock, but prices of all necessities went up, greatly increasing expenses, while the price of wool, governed by the London market, was indifferent to purely local developments. It is true, nevertheless, that wool prices, along with the prices of most commodities, did advance in world markets in the fifties, following the flow of gold from the Pacific borderlands.

In central Otago there was the further uncertainty for the squatter as to when a tent town might spring up on his choicest piece of agricultural river flat. There were, however, some compensating improvements, especially in the roads built to take supplies into the gold fields, which greatly simplified the problems of getting the wool cut. Each province saw the establishment of local road boards, and, though bullock drays and saddle-horses were to remain important media of transportation for many decades, coaches began to appear to facilitate business and social travel and to relieve the isolation of the back country stations. The peripheral nature of settlement might suggest the possibility of greater use of small boats, and some use of them was made in North Canterbury, North Otago, and western Southland. Lack of good harbors and a prevailing storminess of the sea, however, maintained the importance of inland travel.

General techniques changed little in the seventies except in terms of greater efficiency. Increased use of fencing meant that mustering became more seasonal as it gradually became the prerogative of certain gangs who operated from farm to farm like the shearers. A big station would have huts scattered over the hills (fig. 47). Moving with their "swag" * on horseback, the musterers are reported to have looked like an old-time army train. The packer-cook would serve a meal in the morning, break camp, lead the string of horses loaded with swags to the next hut, unload and have dinner ready when the musterers made their night's rendezvous. These professional musterers were drawn from the ranks of the best shepherds and were heavily dependent on their dogs. The two chief types of dog included the "header" to "pull" or

* An Australasian term for the kit of any itinerant worker or tramp; therefore the names "swagger" and "swagman."

Fig. 47. Shepherd's hut on Banks Peninsula. In such huts in the high country, shepherds spent much of their lives. The meanest shack has its fireplace.

ahc

bring the sheep back, and the "hunt-away," a noisier animal concerned with driving. As long as the wilder Merino blood was dominant (as it was through most of the nineteenth century), there were almost as many headers as hunt-aways, but today, with an increasingly heavy proportion of the more docile English breeds, the ratio of the latter to the former reaches as high as four to one. The Scottish shepherds had brought with them their own "collies," and working dogs are still so called, but they must not be thought of as belonging to any particular stable breed. They were not of a particular breed even in the highlands of Scotland, and in New Zealand they have interbred with a number of other types, including some which have no reputation for sheep work. Generalizing broadly, they may be said to be fairly small, about the size of a springer spaniel, sharp-nosed, and with a rather heavy coat of thick dark hair, usually black. Although in recent years there is evidence of an increasing uniformity of type, the sheep dog was, and is, a mongrel; the emphasis was, and is, on training, not on breeding. No more likely origin for the superstition regarding superior intelligence in mongrels could be found; there is no more thrilling sight to be seen in New Zealand today than sheep dog trials, or even sheep dogs at normal work. Some dogs did go wild and, like the wild pigs, did prey on stray young sheep, but the problem was never serious. It would be hard to over-emphasize the important role the dogs played in establishing and maintaining the sheep industry on the higher, more mountainous country.

Storms and floods harassed the sheep owners at all times. Big snows in the winter were especially a source of worry in the high country, sometimes extending down to the plains, and "snow-raking" became necessary.* Burdon,[74] in his excellent collection of reminiscences about the high country, quotes many examples of severe storms. Canterbury lost heavily in lambs in July and August of 1870, which testifies not only to the snow but to a haphazard system of flock management in which the breeding season was not carefully controlled to prevent lambs appearing in midwinter. In the frequent eulogies of New Zealand's climate it is not emphasized that in South Island's higher country, from Nelson to

---

* "Snow-raking," that is, the hunting out of sheep caught by snow and the trampling down of a path by which they could escape, gave rise to one of the typical hazing stunts for a "new-chum," or tenderfoot, who would invariably be sent out to find the "snow-rake."

ahc

Fig. 48. A modern, medium-sized wool-shed in the middle Awatere valley (only a part of the drafting races is shown).

Southland, there are more or less severe losses of sheep from snow in one year out of five.

After improving with the general price rise of the fifties, the price of wool fell rather steadily from 1860 until 1895. The 1860 average was 16d. per pound; this fell to 11d. in 1870 and, while a slight rise occurred in the early seventies, it again fell steadily until 1895, when it went below 6d. Only increasing efficiency or alternative sources of revenue enabled the graziers to continue. Examples of improved techniques included better built and designed sheds (fig. 48), swing-gate drafting (thought to have originated, or been independently invented, in New Zealand), the screw press, and mechanical clippers.

New changes were in preparation for the sheep industry on the downs and plains, though little new was to appear up-country. A small market for aged and surplus sheep first appeared in boiling-down works for tallow; no longer need these be driven over a cliff into the sea or perhaps into an inland ravine (whence the place-name of Glencoe stream in Canterbury). Australian experiments in preserving meat for shipment overseas following 1858 [75] had no parallel in New Zealand. But the sixties did see, twenty years before the introduction of refrigeration, the beginnings of more and more experiment with English sheep on better pastures (newly sown English grasses), in an attempt to maximize the wool return per acre. Not only was there greater profit in running long-wools on land quite unsuitable to Merinos,* but much of this land, which had been put to a steady succession of grain crops, showed, by declining yields, that it would be more profitably returned to grass. Moreover, even on the higher country some men believed that a larger wool check would result by crossing the Merino with long-wools and running the progeny on much of the same country. The principle was that greater yields per sheep might more than offset lessened prices per pound for the lower-count wool. Above all, within the limits described in chapter I of this volume, there were considerable local variations in climate and terrain, and almost any of the old-country breeds did well in one place or another.

By the beginnings of the seventies, and paralleling the greatest agricultural spurt, a few of most of the major English breeds, both long-wools and short-wools, were dotted over South Island in small experimental studs. The experiments which were to result in the Corriedale breed were begun between 1866 and 1868. As yet, with no market for any quantity of meat, the agricultural lands were often more profitably employed in producing cash crops than wool. The small but growing butchers' demands, however, did pay for some of the experiments, the depleted wheat lands sown to English grasses provided the land, and the English sheep, in a more benign climate, almost universally showed an improvement over their homeland reputation (fig. 49). When re-

---

* E. G. Studholme, son of one of the pioneers of Waimate County, recalled in conversation that in 1866 on their station, which included much flat land below the Hunter's Hills in the area now tributary to the town of Waimate, no less than sixteen thousand Merinos were down with foot-rot in one season, and that three months were spent by all hands "foot-rotting" (paring away the diseased parts of the hooves).

ahc

FIG. 49. English sheep grazing English grasses in the shade of English oaks at Te Waimate, South Canterbury.

frigeration provided a market for mutton, two decades of experimentation had initiated the means by which the demand was to be met.

The severe effect of repeated burnings, and later of overstocking and rabbit infestation, began to appear in the declining numbers of sheep carried in the hills and mountain slopes in the late seventies and early eighties. Arguments for and against burning have raged through the high sheep country, as hot as the fires themselves, for nearly seventy-five years. Upon one fact nearly all are agreed. As early as the late eighties, for certain, runs of a given acreage in many places could no longer carry as many sheep (of the same Merino breed) as they had done formerly. Most residents (though there are some doughty dissenters) who have known the hills over a long period, say that the tussocks are much smaller individually, that they are much less densely distributed per unit area, and that the sub-tussock stratum of vegetation has been greatly impoverished as to the quantity and the species more nourishing and palatable to sheep. Cumberland [76] has reviewed much of this evidence; and much may be understood from firsthand observation. From a check of the earliest descriptions (for example, those of the surveyor Thomson who made some of the first trips through central Otago, and letters and diaries of early residents of the Marlborough and the Canterbury high country), it seems undoubtedly true that a fairly serious vegetation depletion has been general, and that it reaches far beyond the central Otago hills which L. Cockayne called "man-made deserts." Soil erosion is not yet serious, but Cumberland [77] reported that "accelerated wind and frost erosion is now rife, especially on the Dunstan range and adjacent river flats (Central Otago), in the Ahuriri-Waitaki valleys (North Otago), and in inland Marlborough."

The problem of the seriously depleted tussock cover has not been overlooked, but it has not benefited from any effective action to solve it. Although it was difficult (in 1942 at least) to find examples to photograph, those examples did clearly expose an erosion problem and did as clearly indicate the necessity for quick and effective action before conditions further deteriorated. Cumberland's arguments, carefully documented with field evidence, should make the government acutely aware of their problem. Others, too, have written from time to time on the subject, including Clark,[78] Zotov,[79] and Cockayne.[80] In 1939, the report of a Committee of Inquiry [81] appointed by the government was published; and in 1941, the Soil Conservation and Control Act was effected. The operation of this Act, however, should not be left to engineers who have too often been more concerned with shifting shingle in the lower courses of the rivers than in controlling the destruction of vegetation in the catchment basins. Above all, there is need for competent forest and grassland ecologists to conduct more thorough investigation and research. The existence of reduced carrying capacity and seriously depleted tussock cover are serious and disturbing facts.

The causes of this erosion are, on the whole, a combination of burning, over-stocking, and rabbit infestation. Which may be the most important is still uncertain. In Central Otago, in an experiment on one station, some areas were fenced (or so it was intended) from both rabbits and sheep; the sheep have been kept out, but the rabbits, as evidenced by plentiful droppings, have been persistent visitors. Yet within the fence a formerly badly depleted area, which admittedly has been protected from burning as well, has made a remarkable recovery. In the high country of Canterbury are depleted areas which have never seen many rabbits, but they have been continually burned and probably overstocked. Rabbits, then, apparently are not the sole culprits. In most of Otago and Marlborough, all three factors have been at play. The grazier says that he has to burn to get a spring "bite" for his sheep, that without burning the tussock is useless as feed, that if he does not burn, his neighbor will, and in the process his sheep may be burned to death in a grass fire spreading over his land in a hot summer month. These truths he holds to be self-evident justification for burning, and he says, correctly, that the effect of burning alone has never been satisfactorily isolated from the effects of other causes. As to overstocking, this is, he claims, often a matter over which he has no control. Dozens of high country tussock sheep men today are, and have been through most of their experience, in debt to banks or loan companies. These companies insist, so the graziers say, upon maximum contemporary stocking, regardless of its ultimate effects. The government supervision of its leased lands, today more and more meticulous, was often perfunctory in the past. A ranking of importance among the causes we may never strike, but here is a clear case of serious habitat mutilation by man and by two animals he intentionally introduced, one, the rabbit, be it said, to his intense sorrow (see pp. 259-72).

In the late seventies, as wool prices declined, sheep men, noting that their wild-grass ranges were carrying fewer sheep, might have anticipated a steady decline in the numbers of sheep and in the importance of the industry. The increased local demand for mutton was insignificant with flocks totaling millions. Boiling down * was only a stop-gap expedient. Except for agriculture, for which much of the sheep land was never to be suitable, there was not much pressure to divide up the big estates for the increasing population. In 1880 South Island was still dominantly a land of big sheep-runs, with the region's income still heavily dependent on the Merino wool check. By 1886 South Island flocks had

---

* One grazier of eighty thousand sheep in Marlborough put sixteen thousand through the tallow-works in one year.[82]

reached a figure of nearly ten million, at which level they were to hover for another forty years.*

Then, in 1882, refrigerated shipments of meat began to move from South Island to England and were going strong by the late eighties. There is no need here to describe the technical and general economic repercussions of this development; Condliffe,[84] especially has discussed this in detail. The individual sheep at once became a far more profitable investment. Though total numbers of sheep were not to change greatly in South Island, the emphasis of sheep farming on all but the highest country was considerably altered. With careful breeding and fattening, a sheep was worth perhaps three times what a single animal had been worth before. More and more, heavier animals with bigger frames and thicker, longer wool took the place of the pure Merinos. Intensive sheep farming, usually combined with agriculture, became the dominant motif of land use over all parts of the island where English grasses could be induced to grow or where supplemental feed crops could be produced. The possibilities of making a good living, on a little land, with sheep as a major end of the husbandry, led to an irresistible demand for the break-up of the large estates on plain-and-down country, whether freehold or leasehold. By a system of compulsory repurchase and graduated taxation, this was effected. The first of the great sheep stations, Flaxbourne in coastal Marlborough, was also one of the first to be subdivided; dozens of others followed.

South Canterbury, that is, south of the Rangitata River, is a good exemplary area and has been used before. After first being blocked out in big sheep runs (fig. 45), gradually more and more of the good country was purchased through the sixties and the seventies until, as in the rest of the island, most of the land possible for intensive mixed farming had been made freehold by 1878. The

---

* Total number of sheep for South Island (in thousands): [83]

1861	1871	1884	1898	1921	1941
2,760	7,830	9,207	9,809	10,511	13,780

Distribution of sheep in the provincial districts (in thousands): [83]

	Marl-borough	Nelson	Westland	Canter-bury	Otago	South-land
1861	369	181	—877—		620	74
1898	850	896	28	4,073	—3,961—	
1941	1183	464	87	5,100	3,939	3,006

rate at which the number of smaller holdings increased in the next thirteen years is shown by table XXXVI.[85]

TABLE XXXVI

INCREASE IN HOLDINGS IN SOUTH CANTERBURY (1878-1891)

Size of Holdings	1878	Number of Holdings		
		1881	1886	1891
1-10 acres	190	303	442	560
10-50 acres	241	330	422	486
50-100 acres	172	194	196	211
100-200 acres	230	245	252	283
200-320 acres	112	158	149	173
320-640 acres	107	150	175	196
640-1000 acres	50	39	55	40
Over 1000 acres	85	108	125	135

The methods by which men of limited means obtained small holdings, usually from the government, included: sale on deferred payments, perpetual leases, twenty-one-year leases on small grazing runs, village homestead settlements, occupation with right of purchase, leases in perpetuity, and other devices.[86] All of these were not enough to satisfy the land hunger on the basis of remaining Crown land alone. As a result, twenty-seven estates of over a thousand acres (the largest, Waikakahi, had nearly fifty-three thousand acres) and sixteen smaller estates were bought up in South Canterbury between 1894 and 1914 and let out again in sizes of allotments as small as was consistent with making a fair living on the different classes of land.

By 1900, throughout the island, the "cocky" * was getting his few acres to farm. It is interesting that his desire to own his land led in turn to various purchase arrangements being made, and that the land, so laboriously regained to the Crown, was once again rapidly alienated. Condliffe,[87] who discusses this problem in detail, feels that this was a mistake which led to further land speculation and the possibility of further aggregation, though he points out this latter had not yet been evident at the end of the nineteen-twenties. At any rate, it is evident that, between 1885 and the end of the century, with a new bias taking hold of the South Island sheep industry, there was a rapid division of land which could be intensively farmed with sheep into smaller allot-

* The small farmer, called "cockatoo," from the Australian terminology which signified to the squatter a bothersome, self-invited, declassé invader of his territory.

ments in Southland's plains, to a small extent in coastal areas near the mouths of the Wairau and Awatere, and along the shores of Tasman Bay. Some of the newly divided holdings were employed for dairying, but to a far smaller degree than was the case in the North Island.

Two of the most important changes that took place technically were in the type of sheep and in the type of fodder which they converted into mutton and wool. The introduction of long-wool breeds, and of short-wool mutton types, was rapidly accelerated. It could not be done overnight, however, and certain basic factors maintained the importance of Merino blood. The high-country managers had to continue to run Merinos for obvious environmental reasons, as many of them continue to do today. Until pastures were improved in the lower country (of progressively less intense relief), it did not pay to run sheep which would not make the most economical possible use of the native grasses. Again, the lower country depended on the higher for surplus breeding ewes which, to suit the country on which they were raised, had to be of at least half-Merino blood. In fact, at first, the practice of putting either long-wool or short-wool English rams to Merino ewes to produce a mutton animal was the principal change. The short-wools (principally Southdowns) gave an earlier maturing lamb, but until the demand for lamb, as distinct from mutton, became important, this was not of much significance. Moreover, the cross between Merinos and long-wools gave in its half-bred progeny a more efficient animal for the production of wool, in terms of income per acre, than any other type except on the highest and the lowest land (that is, the wettest and heaviest). Finally, it should be said that, as the tussock deteriorated, there were ever larger areas in which the Merino was a more profitable animal than any other. The point is moot, but some of the most progressive high-country graziers believe that, with relatively light grazing, it is more profitable even today to run Merinos over their former territory which has been invaded by half-breds. Just as it is often more profitable to run scrubs, or specially adapted beef-cattle crosses, on low-nutrition country rather than purebred Herefords or Polled Angus, so the Merinos may maintain or even advance their territorial sway as rabbits and cultural practices continue to diminish the nutritive assets of native pastures on the half-bred country.

The newer types of feed, especially the English grasses and

the *Brassicas*, are discussed in chapter XIII. As to the newer sheep, there has been a degree of regional specialization, the end result of which is seen in the map (fig. 41) which shows the proportions of distinctive breeds by land districts. Otago's first important non-Merino introductions were Border Leicesters; Canterbury's, their English "cousins." ° The first of the standard half-breds were by Leicesters out of Merinos, solely, as noted above, for maximizing the efficiency of wool production. Sheep of both the Lincoln and Romney Marsh breeds were present early, however, and with the demand for mutton, were of greater value as the long-wool part of the cross. The Lincoln † proved rather narrowly specialized to the needs of the heaviest and wettest land. With the increase of dairying, it could not meet the competition of butter-fat production in such areas as Springs County, parts of Southland County and the satellite counties of Christchurch, and is now unimportant. The Romney Marsh,‡ on the other hand, has shown remarkable adaptability, possibly through more careful local selection, to a wide variety of conditions in both islands of New Zealand and has steadily advanced to become the leading one of the old English breeds. The Romneys have a higher lambing percentage, in terms of twin births particularly, than any other South Island breed; the ewes are also the best mothers.

Not long after shipments of refrigerated meat got under way, South Island found itself in sharp competition with Argentina

° The English Leicester has some claim to be considered the first of the local British breeds to be carefully improved and fixed. Unlike the short-wooled "heath" sheep of southern England, the ancestors of the Down breeds, which are possibly autocthonous,[88] the progenitors of the long-wool breeds, including especially the Lincolns and Romney Marshes, are probably of Flemish origin. It was Bakewell who took this breed from the country around about his Leicestershire farm and began its systematic improvement in 1755. Twelve years later it was being established in Northumberland and in the Border country. There it was interbred with hardier local breeds and a new type developed, very similar in points to the original Leicester but hardier in cold and wet country, and less subject to foot-rot and scald on heavier land. The new breed became gradually fixed and known as the Border Leicester. Its relative disadvantages were in its later maturity and slightly lighter fleece. Later, as the Leicesters were displaced by the Romneys as the leading progenitors of long-wool blood, it was in Canterbury that the heaviest concentrations of both Border and English Leicesters were to remain, though in about the same very small proportion to total sheep numbers in all three of the southern land districts.

† A native of the Lincolnshire fens where it developed slowly, probably since its supposed introduction by the Romans, until improved with Leicester blood in the eighteenth century.

‡ The Romney Marsh originated on the reclaimed marsh lands of coastal Kent, from Sandgate to Rye.

and Cape Colony in the production of frozen mutton for the London market, and successful experiments in the specialty production of fat lambs were begun. It developed that most of the existing breeds and crosses were slow in maturing. As the Down breeds had a reputation for quick development, different ones were tried, the Southdown emerging as the most satisfactory. A hardy, close-cropping, short-wool, able to get along well on higher and drier country, it seemed ideally suited to Canterbury's plains. It was found, however, that the ewes were poor mothers, that its lambing average was below that of other breeds, and that its short coarse wool brought very low prices. Hence its use was restricted to the siring of lambs from half-bred ewes. This specialized use has meant that there are almost as many registered stud Southdowns as flock sheep of that breed in South Island (whereas in other breeds the studs form a very small proportion of the total) and that there are usually nearly twice as many rams as breeding ewes maintained,* a circumstance completely unparalleled among the other breeds on South Island.

The half-breds dominate the flocks of South Island today. It is true that these are still being produced in considerable numbers each year, chiefly by Romneys out of Merinos, yet the majority of them are interbred among themselves, and the half-breds are almost achieving the status of a distinct breed. This is prevented only by the continual introduction of new first-cross blood with the consequent occurrence of throwbacks of Merino or long-wool type in most consternating fashion. Attempts to inbreed half-breds and fix a distinct new breed which would be a South Island product, especially designed for South Island's habitat qualities, were made very early. The beginnings of the most successful experiments occurred on the Corriedale station of North Otago in 1874, long before the refrigeration revolution, specifically to obtain the most profitable wool-producer. These involved Lincoln rams; other experiments used Leicesters, or more generally, Romneys. Regardless of the specific long-wool ancestors, the inbred flocks came to be known as the "Corriedale type" (later, and only gradually, "breed"). The breeders finally formed an association which allowed any flock, continuously inbred for fifteen years

* Palates vary, but the writer is prepared to strongly support the thesis that there is no tastier lamb grown than that got by the Southdowns out of the half-breds, fattened off their mothers in South Island's excellent climate. The Merino quarter of blood gives a tangy, gamey sweetness to the meat.

from stud Merino and stud long-wool bases, to be registered as Corriedales. Eight such registered stud flocks existed in 1905; 105 in 1923, and the number has continued to increase. It will probably be many years before complete standardization of show points and interchange of rams bring as great a uniformity of type as with other breeds. Nevertheless, the present evenness of type makes it easy for an amateur to distinguish a Corriedale from an ordinary half-bred flock before shearing: each animal with an extremely heavy, all-over covering of wool, even down the legs to the hooves and over the face like an English sheepdog, each still retaining the indefinable but unmistakable "look" of the Merino. Economically it is truly the all-purpose sheep, with its heavy yield of next-to-Merino quality wool, with a good market for surplus fattened-off ewe-mutton, with its high lambing percentages, with its suitability to all but the wettest and roughest country, and with its basic contribution to the fat-lamb trade. It will lose out to Romneys in South Island only as pastures are greatly improved; how rapidly no one can guess.*

New techniques such as automatic (lately electric) shearing clippers and automotive transport have assisted the sheep industry, but they have in no way radically changed it. By 1900 the variety of forms of husbandry between the highest and lowest country was well established; all the present markets, and most of the present competitors with sheep in the use of the land, were in existence. Except in the mountains, sheep were then, as they are today, the chief end of husbandry in a mixed-farming enterprise. As the relative emphasis on sheep or cash crops varies so radically from year to year and place to place among individual farmers, little more in the way of generalization can be made. Some varied types of farms which carry sheep are described, as they function at present, in the appendix (pp. 389-93).

---

* Corriedale stud stock has been sold all over the world, and some of the largest, so-called, Corriedale flocks are in Australia, Argentina, Chile (the Magellanes or Punta Arenas or Tierra del Fuego area), and South Africa. Though they have been imported into the United States in large numbers, perhaps the greatest function of the breed here is found in the use of Corriedale rams on Merino (often locally called Rambouillet) ewes to produce an improved class of quarter-breds, in the dry country at least. Its adaptability is evidenced by its successful acclimatization in areas as diverse as the Kenya plateau and Tierra del Fuego.

SOUTH
ISLAND
NEW ZEALAND

ONE DOT REPRESENTS
1000 HEAD OF CATTLE

ahc

FIG. 50. Distribution of cattle in South Island (1941).

CHAPTER VII

CATTLE

Cattle on South Island in 1941 were outnumbered by sheep twenty to one, but assuming that one head of cattle is equivalent to seven sheep in feed consumed, nearly one-fourth of the grazing in the island in that year could be attributed to cattle. The distribution of these cattle, and the areal variations in emphasis on dairying are indicated in figures 50 and 51.[1] The maps are based on data for counties; table XXXVII [1] was prepared to provide a brief summary of the same information by land districts, and to give some indication of the relative emphasis on cattle or sheep in the six districts. Figure 50 indicates, at a casual glance, a remarkable similarity in the pattern of distribution of cattle as compared with the distribution of sheep shown in figure 40. This is true chiefly because intensive cattle husbandry competes with intensive sheep farming in most of the areas of good land; indeed both cattle and sheep are often of importance on the same farm. On the lower plains, and especially in the coastal areas of Marlborough, Canterbury, Otago, and Southland, there are few "sheep" or "cattle" areas which largely exclude the alternative animal. On the west coast, however, where sheep are relatively unimportant, cattle husbandry is dominant; the cattle percentage of total grazing (on the seven-to-one ratio) being over fifty for Westland, Grey, Inangahua, Murchison, and Buller Counties. A high proportion of cattle in areas suburban to Christchurch and Dunedin is easily explained in terms of farms supplying liquid milk to the

219

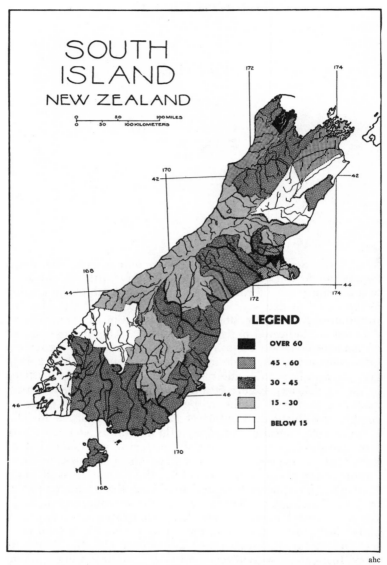

ahc

Fɪɢ. 51. Distribution of dairy cows in milk per one hundred cattle
(1941).

cities, and of holding paddocks for fattening or slaughtering beef animals. Other areas, including Rangiora, Springs, and Akaroa Counties, where more than half of the "grazing units" are cattle, indicate special environmental suitability in the case of the heavy, wet lands of the first two counties, and, chiefly, a debt to the course of historical development in the case of the last. We find, expectably, few cattle and a very markedly low proportion of cattle to sheep in the high, dry country.

TABLE XXXVII

Distribution of Cattle and Dairy Cows in South Island by Land Districts (1941)

Land District	Total cattle	Total cattle per 1000 occupied acres	Dairy cows in milk per 100 cattle	Total cattle per 100 sheep shorn
Marlborough	42,110	18.5	31.0	4.1
Nelson	71,934	60.0	43.5	18.3
Westland	44,398	43.7	27.6	61.2
Canterbury	170,195	21.0	38.0	3.7
Otago	113,167	14.1	35.3	3.3
Southland	152,677	46.8	38.5	5.8

The distribution of dairy cows, indicated in the *Dairy Cows per 100 Total Cattle* county ratios of figure 51, shows some more marked specializations. The dairy cows are clearly concentrated on the lowest and best land or near the cities. Since the number of dairy cows in milk in any season would be between 70 and 75 per cent of total cattle on the average,[2] if the cattle were all used for dairy purposes, it is apparent that the number of cattle raised for beef purposes is everywhere considerable. The non-surburban counties which show the greatest specialization of their cattle industry toward dairying are: Buller, that is, the wet coastal strip north of Westport; Takaka, in the lower valley of the river of the same name on Golden Bay; Marlborough, just below Blenheim in the Wairau valley; Kowai, Eyre, Springs, and Ellesmere Counties in the heavy, wet, coastal lands of Canterbury; and Geraldine County, which has similarly much very heavy land between the lower courses of the Rangitata and Opihi rivers. The concentration of interest in beef production for such cattle as there are in Amuri, Cheviot, and Awatere Counties, for example, which lack land suitable for dairying, is to be expected; these areas have few cattle in any event. The fairly considerable number of beef cattle in Westland, Grey, Inangahua, Sounds, Wallace, and Clutha

Counties needs some comment. These counties were once fairly heavily bushed; their rainfall is great enough to make second-growth, especially of bracken fern, a distinct problem. Sheep cannot combat this second growth and, consequently, beef cattle alone, or beef cattle used in conjunction with sheep, are introduced to utilize the feed. In North Island, where this problem of second growth is paramount in the sheep industry, large numbers of beef cattle are kept as "fern-crushers" * primarily to help keep pastures in shape for the sheep. This is true to a degree of Sounds, Clutha, and Wallace Counties; on the west coast, however, the emphasis is mainly on the production of beef itself.

TABLE XXXVIII

PERCENTAGES OF CATTLE TYPES IN EACH SOUTH ISLAND
LAND DISTRICT, 1918

	Nelson	Marlborough	Westland	Canterbury	Otago	Southland	South Island
Jersey	21.5%	14.4%	11.7%	7.6%	3.5%	1.1%	7.0%
Friesian * ..	5.5	5.4	4.6	6.0	5.0	7.1	5.9
Ayrshire ...	5.7	2.9	2.8	1.6	8.3	5.9	4.7
Shorthorn ..	58.1	64.5	48.8	75.9	67.6	60.8	66.1
Hereford ...	3.3	8.0	26.1	6.5	10.7	18.7	11.6
Other dairy.	3.0	2.9	3.5	1.2	2.0	4.3	2.6
Other beef..	2.9	1.9	2.5	1.2	2.9	2.1	2.1
Total	100.0%	100.0%	100.0%	100.0%	100.0%	100.0%	100.0%

* That is, Holstein-Frisian.

It is almost impossible to get precise figures on distributions of cattle breeds for South Island. An impression of predominance of Jerseys among the present dairy cattle, and of white-faced Herefords in the beef breeds, is certainly gained in travel about the island at present. In 1918, however, a detailed census of breeds was taken, the results of which are given for the different land districts in the *New Zealand Official Year Book* for 1918. Table XXXVIII shows the percentages of the major types in each land district for that year (purebred cattle, small in number, are included with animals listed as of their distinctive breed). This distribution of cattle types may be referred to the percentage of the total cattle in each land district which is shown in table XXXIX.[4]

* While the cattle eat the young fronds more readily than do sheep, the crushing action of the bovine hooves is thought to be the most effective agency in destroying the fern.[3]

TABLE XXXIX

	1918 (of 570,882 head)	1940 (of 594,481 head)
Nelson	9.4%	12.1%
Marlborough	6.2	7.1
Westland	6.4	7.5
Canterbury	30.7	28.8
Otago	21.5	18.9
Southland	25.8	25.6
Total	*100.0%*	*100.0%*

This heavy predominance of the Shorthorn existed for good historical reasons, as well as for its general suitability as a dual-purpose farm animal. Without knowledge of the historical development, however, we might have expected a very much higher proportion of specialized beef or dairying breeds in 1918; and, though the figures are not available, it is probable that the proportions of Jerseys and Herefords in South Island have sharply advanced in the past twenty-five years at the expense of the Shorthorns. One cannot trust one's own haphazard observations; Herefords, Angus, Jerseys, and Holstein-Friesians are much more striking to the eye than Ayrshires or Shorthorns as seen in pastures by the roadside. Even the few Red Devons create an impression far greater than their numbers warrant. Nevertheless, a great many farmers and government officials assured this writer that the trend toward Jerseys for dairying, and to Hereford and Angus types for beef, at the expense of the dual-purpose animals, is a marked one in South Island, as the successive figures for all of New Zealand show it to be for the Dominion. Table XL [5] shows the changes between 1918 and 1928 in the proportion of types for New Zealand as a whole.

The importance of Shorthorn blood is still evident in the mixed breed or herd cattle used for both meat and beef purposes. It is likely to persist, not only through the inertia of existing numbers, but also because a type which is not too specialized is often the most suitable animal for general beef and dairy needs, particularly if the concentrated attention and special feeds that highly specialized breeds need cannot always be provided. The dairying Shorthorn and the beef Shorthorn are simply selections during the past fifty years from a single type of general-purpose animal. The Shorthorn does not produce beef as good as that of the Polled Angus or Hereford, nor is it as efficient a butterfat factory as the Channel Island or Holstein-Friesian breeds. But it did survive for many decades on indifferent pastures, supplying not only milk and beef but, often of the first importance, the brawny steers which pulled the plows and the wool-drays. The Ayrshire, somewhat similar to the Shorthorn, and its equivalent in function in Scotland, was introduced on a fairly large scale into the parts of the Island settled most largely by Scots, and this breed still persists in recognizable importance south of the Waitaki river.

TABLE XL

PERCENTAGES OF CATTLE TYPES IN NEW ZEALAND

	1918	1928
Jersey	12.7%	39.5%
Friesian	7.1	7.4
Ayrshire	1.8	1.6
Milking Shorthorn	} 58.0	13.7
Beef Shorthorn		13.0
Hereford	10.2	13.3
Angus	5.1	11.0
Other Dairy	2.3	.2
Other Beef	1.7	.3
Unspecified	1.1	
Total	*100.0%*	*100.0%*

The Shorthorn became the first important cattle breed for basically the same reason as did the Merino among the sheep. Most of the cattle came to New Zealand from New South Wales, and there a specialization on Durham, Yorkshire, or Teeswater cattle, gradually known simply as short-horns, was evident as early as the eighteen-twenties. Writing in 1826, Atkinson, who has been quoted above in connection with the introduction of Merinos to New South Wales, made this observation:

The smaller breeds of British cattle, such as the North Devon, South Wales, and Galloway Scot, would all answer extremely well, and pro-duce more beef and more milk than the Hereford, Sussex, or large Yorkshire breeds; but perhaps, some animals of these latter kinds, especially the Yorkshire, would be very desirable for the purpose of crossing the present race of colonial cattle, the majority of which may be described as large-boned, thick-skinned, large head and horns, coarse neck, heavy forequarters, deficient hind-quarters and very bad milking stock; the short-horn Yorkshire are the reverse of all this: by judicious crossing with these, a breed might perhaps be obtained with a lighter forequarter, more meat upon the best joints, and better adapted for dairy purposes; at the same time not too tender, or requiring better keep than the country, in its natural state, is able to supply.

This statement is of interest, not only because Atkinson's advice was followed so widely, but because it describes so well the type of pre-Bakewell cattle which were still most common in Great Britain in the early nineteenth century. In light of the fact that the Yorkshire cattle were known rather as workers and milkers than as beef animals,° the following statement by Atkinson in 1844, in the second part of his work, is of a good deal of interest:

The horned cattle of the colony were derived from various countries, England, Cape of Good Hope, India and other places; and were bred with little discrimination, they were necessarily of a very mixed description. About fourteen years ago, Mr. Macqueen introduced the superior Durham, or shorthorn breed of cattle . . . which has become a favorite horned stock of the colony. Many herds may now be seen which, although of greatly superior numbers, equal in excellence any found in England. . . . At present the preference shown by the butchers for the Durham is a strong inducement to the cultivation of that breed.

In a long monograph on the beef Shorthorn in Australia, Ellis reports his painstaking research into the early history of the breed in New South Wales and England. Writing of the work of the Colling brothers of Yorkshire, who applied Bakewell's method of inbreeding and selection to their local breed of cattle, he says: "By the year 1825, both in the colony of New South Wales and in the cattle world of Britain, the shorthorn era had definitely arrived." [7] One is tempted to remark that it had barely arrived in 1825, for whether in response to Atkinson's urgings or other-

---

° The cattle of Britain were divided, in the eighteenth century, into three general types; Middle-horns, prevailing in the south and west of England, in Wales and in Scotland; Long-horns in the northwest of England and the Midlands; and Short-horns in the northeast, especially Yorkshire and Durham. The Middle-horns included the Devons, Herefords (not yet bred with white-faces), Ayrshires, Galloways, and Anguses; the Long-horns included no breed now commonly known in the new worlds. The cattle of the northeast were famous for their size and milking qualities—pre-eminent qualities in a day when, to quote Ernle: "The pail and the plough set the standard; the butcher was ignored." The more distant origin of the Shorthorn is not at all clear. Before it moved to the banks of the Tees it was known as the Holderness breed. Ernle goes on to suggest that it was probably of more recent foreign origin than many of the other breeds, or had, at least probably, some blood of Dutch origin. [6]

wise, the first known introduction of purebred Durham cattle, the results of the Collings' work, had occurred only in 1824. The importer was one Macqueen, who at the same time took to New South Wales a flock of fine Saxon sheep, some valuable Highland dogs, and some thoroughbred stallions. In a memorial to the Secretary of State, dated August 10, 1838, Macqueen said his herd was "allowed to be the progenitor of the finest breeds of horned cattle in New South Wales." Other importations, however, appear to have then followed in rapid succession. In volume II of the *New South Wales Herd Book, 1876*, it is stated that the Australian Agricultural Company's purebred Durham, or Shorthorn, herd was commenced in 1825 with the importation of a bull and three heifers. And again, the chief agent of the Australian Agricultural Company reported on his return to England in 1830:

> The improved breed of Durhams succeeds exceedingly well in the colony and should, therefore, be sought after. Where they cannot be obtained pure, repeated crosses by good Durham bulls, and half-bred bulls in the absence of the latter, with the best selected colonial bred cows, will produce a very desirable result both as to flesh and to milk.[8]

So much for the situation in the land of immediate origin of South Island's cattle. We have to picture there a variety of breeds, but with more and more emphasis on the strong, long-legged, shorthorned cattle of northwestern England. Philpott [9] states that there is no certain record of importation of cattle south of the Auckland peninsula until Bell's importation of ten head (with his 102 sheep) to Mana Island in 1833, unless the "animals" left by Captain Raven at Dusky in 1792 [10] included cattle. McNab,[11] however, thinks it incredible that there should not have been cattle in earlier whaling stations along the coasts of the island. Yet though horses were introduced to Preservation in 1835 to pull up the whale boats or even parts of the whales onto the beach, the earliest certain introduction of cattle to the same station did not occur until fifteen head were landed in 1838.[12] In evidence by Jones and Weller to the legislative council of New South Wales, July 6, 1839,[13] Jones deposed that he had "sent cattle to his stations recently." Sometime in 1839 or 1840 he did send cattle to his new agricultural settlement at Waikouaiti. Eighteen thirty-nine was also the year of the reported, though not authenticated, arrival of cattle at Port Underwood for the Wairau.[14] An earlier introduction to the Sounds area by whalers or the Maori is probable, for Wakefield [15] claims that he saw wild cattle on the hills at the entrance to Pelorus Sound in 1839, "the descendants of some given to the Kapiti natives a few years before by a Sydney merchant in payment for a cargo of flax." Just how they might have crossed Cook Strait is not clear.

Fifty cattle, including two bulls, were introduced to Akaroa Harbour in 1839.[16] Rhodes, the importer, states that they were from Macqueen's herd at Hunter River in New South Wales and were "nearly pure Durham." * It is probable that the eight-year-old pure Durham bull offered for sale in the *Nelson Examiner* of March 8, 1845, as an animal "bred in the colony" must have come, assuming the claims of the advertiser to have been correct, from Auckland peninsula.

Although the cattle industry of Nelson was initially little more progressive than the rest of that settlement's early enterprises, there are continual references to the import of cattle from New South Wales after 1840 in the early issues of the *Nelson Examiner*. Gradually some cattle appeared here and there, especially on a few large stations, but with an odd one on the subsistence "squatting plots" of the laborers as well. Pratt,[18] who was one of the earliest Nelson settlers, indicates that the obtaining of beasts by the poor would not have been easy; working bullocks cost thirty pounds each and cows, fifty pounds. The advertisements in the *Examiner* for 1842 and 1843 often offered kegs of Irish butter (by report this was often so heavily salted as to be virtually inedible) and a good deal of preserved beef however, indicating that cattle were none too plentiful.

The German settlers off the *St. Pauli* were among the first of the small holders to have cattle, and Fox wrote to Colonel Wakefield in 1844 that among the few farms started in the lower Waimea that year, one man had four "milch-kine" and some heifers, others had bullock teams, and still another was making a cheese a day and sixty pounds of butter a week, and was supplying Nelson with beef.[19] In this same year, Duppa was running two hundred head of cattle with his seven hundred sheep further up the Wai-iti valley.[20]

---

* The biographer of the Rhodes family, a grandniece of W. B. Rhodes, has a slightly different report of this, quite possibly based on better evidence than Rhodes' later memory. She states that there were thirty to forty head of breeding cattle, bought from a herd descended from that of Macqueen. At any rate, there was a considerable herd imported then and they *were* nearly pure Durham.[17]

Even such scraps of evidence indicate a fairly steady stream of cattle, for all three usual purposes, into the area. With the opening of the Wairau, the flow increased. Between November 25, 1847, and July 22, 1848, 569 head were landed in Nelson.[21] In 1848, a dairy was started near "The Beaver" (that is, Blenheim) and the owner wrote that his cattle were "disgustingly fat," and that, as far as the Nelson area was concerned, "the cattle in the Waimea are fast dying of starvation, it is so overstocked." [22] This is almost certainly a gross exaggeration, but it suggests considerable numbers. In the tussock of the Wairau-Awatere area the cattle did thrive, and it is a legitimate speculation that, had cattle produced an easily shipped commodity like wool for the world market, the invasion of the open grassland might have been made by Durhams instead of Merinos.[*] As the Durham is the only breed mentioned in any of the early writing, and as most of the cattle seem to have, indeed must have, come from Australian areas, we can assume that a large part of such cattle as were not scrubs were indeed the short-horned animals.

The French settlers at Akaroa had brought no cattle with them, and were unable to pay the prices demanded by Rhodes for his relatively highly bred animals, though his cattle were pastured at Flea Bay, one of the few open grassy spots on the peninsula, only a few miles from Akaroa township. The six hundred francs asked for a cow, and the nine hundred to twelve hundred francs for a draft animal, were well beyond their purses.[23] The director for the Nanto-Bordelaise Company did manage to import for the settlement a bull, a dozen cows, and a pony from Sydney, but the cattle were too precious to kill and a little beef was bought from the Rhodes herd as well as some butter, at two to three shillings a pound, from the Pigeon Bay settlers after 1843.[24] After this latter date, settlements appeared at Purau, Island Bay, McIntosh Bay, and in many other of the peninsula's inlets besides Pigeon Bay, in each case chiefly dependent upon cattle. Rhodes held a disposal sale of his Flea Bay stock in 1845, helping to equip the new settlers. To get their purchases from Akaroa Harbor to Pigeon Bay, a fifteen-mile track had to be cut over the hills through heavy bush, an undertaking which took eight men three weeks,

---

[*] The speculation is not without point. There is little to choose between cattle and sheep, as to suitability of habitat, over all but the highest and roughest mountain country of South Island. Market demand, prices, and transportation techniques, rather than nature, seem to have influenced the choice here.

or so at least is the tradition among descendants of the Hay family. There were, also, later in the decade, fifty head of cattle at Rhodes' station at Purau—possibly new imports.

Perhaps the Deans, at Riccarton, contributed more than the others to the beginnings of the cattle industry in the Port Cooper plains region. It is worth recalling that the first cattle on the plains were the oxen which, by inference, must have pulled the plows used in the abortive agricultural attempt by McKinnon and others at Riccarton in 1840. The Deans built a large shed with ten double stalls for milking almost immediately after their arrival, and set about importing cattle as well as sheep from New South Wales. Again the low prices of stock there helped them tremendously; while Rhodes had paid sixteen pounds for an animal in 1839, John Deans was able to purchase heifers at two pounds and steers at thirty shillings.[25] These were descended from Macqueen's cattle in New South Wales [26] and were hence, presumably, Durham in type. They had intended to ship eighty head in May of 1843. Whether this intention was fulfilled or not, in January of 1844 they had one bull, fourteen bullocks and forty-one heifers alive and thriving. One of the brothers, who returned with the cattle, wrote:

I had a very long and rough passage with the cattle, and lost a good many about the time of landing, but considering the length of the passage we cannot complain much of our luck. . . . We will have more cows this year than we will be able to milk, but we intend to select about twenty of the best milkers and make cheese and butter, and fatten pigs with the whey and buttermilk, for all of which we should be able to get a ready market among the surveyors and any shipping that may come into the harbour. We will just allow the other cows to suckle their calves. I reckon calves worth as many pounds here as shillings at home.[27]

In 1845, the Deans brought two laborers from the plains of Ayrshire and established them in a dairying enterprise in the area at the head of the bay [28] now known as Gebbie's Flat (fig. 52), Gebbie being the surname of one of these men. This was a more convenient situation for supplying ships and producing for the Wellington and Australian markets. That South Island was able to compete successfully in the New South Wales cheese market from the first must have been largely due to better conditions for grazing. In the 1845-1846 season these new dairymen made three thousand pounds of cheese and twenty-one hundred pounds

James Tocker

FIG. 52. Dairy cow in glade in the Governor's Bay area near Gebbie's Flat, in a remnant of the original forest of Banks Peninsula.

of butter between them.[29] These must have been good, for a favorable reputation was then established in New South Wales for "Port Cooper" cheeses, and a demand for dairy products from Banks Peninsula was to continue strong in the Australian colonies for many decades. It is indicative of the methods by which farm laborers could become independent fairly rapidly in South Island from the beginning of European settlement that, by January of 1847, these men who had held "bowens" * of cattle from the

---

* A "bower," pronounced *boo-er,* in lowland Scots dialect, is one who manages, or rents for a share of the profits, the dairy stock of a farm with the pasture on which to run it; an odd special quirk of meaning to this old, generic Teutonic word. The Deans' use of the word "bowen" [30] in this connection, if it is not a typographical error, is unusual, but I assume it to be derived from the same source.

Deans and shared profits with them, had managed to become owners of five cows, a heifer, and a calf.[31]

By 1846 the Deans' cattle had increased to a hundred and thirty head; in that year and the following, they found a new market for fat cattle, which could not otherwise have been disposed of, in the feeding of troops brought to Wellington to quell a current Maori uprising.[*] This early trade in beef, with more demands expected from the projected Canterbury settlement, led the Deans to think of the butcher rather than the pail for the first time. Heretofore they had concentrated on Durhams of good milking quality, but John Deans wrote in August of 1848:

> Our present stock of cattle are good enough to look at and good milkers, but they are nothing like some of the breeds at home for the butchers, they grow fast enough and fat enough, but the beef is coarse in the grain and generally gets dry after being in the salt some time.[32]

By the time the advance group of surveyors for the Canterbury settlement arrived, the Deans had a good stock of cattle and good pastures on which to fatten them. By burning and grubbing up tussocks and flax, plowing, cropping, and then sowing English grasses and lucerne (alfalfa), they had a high carrying capacity on the improved paddocks. The steers sold for about thirteen to fourteen pounds each; this was a good price, as lean animals (despite a sharp rise in prices since the early part of the decade) could be purchased in New South Wales for half that sum. In 1850 they imported from that colony eight Durham bulls and 162 heifers; all the bulls and 148 of the heifers survived the journey and landing.[33] In the Deans' report of conditions on the Canterbury Plains, they especially recommended the importation of purebred Durham bulls from England to improve the stock from New South Wales, and showed both nostalgia and common sense in recommending the import of Galloways from their Scottish hearth area to improve the beef strains. At this point the Deans' story becomes but a small chapter in that of the Canterbury settlement. It should be clear, however, what a large measure of experience they were able to contribute to its beginnings.

After 1840 there were rapid developments from the earlier beginnings south of Banks Peninsula. In 1844 Tuckett [34] recorded

---

[*] Of thirty such shipped in 1847, four head were lost on the trip to Port Nicholson, often a very stormy one; but on arrival the prime animals, running nine hundred pounds each, fetched £22 10s. apiece.

cattle at many points, notably at Moeraki, at Waikouaiti (where the original herd had increased to two hundred head) and at the mouth of the Aparima (Riverton). The first two ships of the Otago Association brought no cattle, but bought their basic stock of breeding cattle from Waikouaiti,[35] another example of the debt of the "organized" settlements to their precursors. The prices of cattle produce quoted in the first issue of the *Otago News* (Dec. 13, 1848) were reasonable enough: beef brought 6d. to 7d. per pound, cheese 1s. to 1s. 6d., butter (fresh) 1s. 8d., butter (salt) 1s., and milk 4d. per quart. Stock itself was quoted at £12 10s. for cows and £30 to £40 a pair for working bullocks. The *Otago Witness* for Nov. 10, 1849, gave a figure of 357 cattle and 18 working bullocks for the Otago block proper as of March 31 of that year. On April 6, 1850, the same paper reported that these had increased to 921 head, indicating heavy new importations during the year.

While interest continued to be chiefly centered on sheep in South Island in the fifties, the demand for agricultural and dairy products, which arose with the gold discoveries at Bathurst in 1851 and the subsequent rush to the Port Phillip (Melbourne) hinterland, insured that the rapid, early progress in cattle husbandry would be continued. Not only did cattle supply more milk, butter, cheese, and beef than the infant colony could consume, but also the power for the plows, the wool drays, and general traction needs, such as the towing of boats up the lower reaches of the Avon, Wairau, and Taieri rivers. And, as Australian prices sky-rocketed in the fifties, the cattle needs of the island were more and more supplied from the increase of existing flocks. For example, when Duppa disposed of his holdings in the Wai-iti in 1852,[36] five hundred to six hundred head of what were claimed to be purebred Durhams were dispersed. In August, 1855,[37] there were four hundred cattle in the Wairau alone.°

Methods of handling dairy products were crude. There was no cooling or other special care of the milk. Locally the products were chiefly bartered with merchants for household necessities, and spoilage was not a general problem. The "Port Cooper cheeses" and butter which were shipped to Melbourne and Syd-

---

° Fitton quotes from a contemporary letter: "There is a considerable number of settlers in the Wairau plains who are occupied in sheep and cattle grazing, some few having dairy farms, making cheese and butter which they salt down and send to Wellington or Nelson."[38]

ney, however, required more care. The cheeses were packed in hogsheads or boxes heavily insulated with oat hulls. Butter was packed in crocks or tubs, in brine alone or heavily salted. Banks Peninsula used some American equipment (especially churns) brought by at least one United States vessel which traded up and down the coast in this decade.[39]

By 1857 there were eighteen dairies on that peninsula alone, each producing an average of four tons of cheese annually.[40] The chief drawback there was the difficulty of communication, both from bayhead to bayhead and from the peninsula to the plain. Other dairies operated on the plains and a considerable annual surplus of cheese and butter was exported each year from Canterbury. In the first eleven months of 1855, Canterbury exported over three tons of butter to the rest of New Zealand, and over two tons to Australia; of cheese, respectively, nearly twenty-two tons and more than twelve tons. Dairy produce formed some 10 per cent of the exports in value.[41]

The increase in the numbers of cattle in the different provinces in the decade from 1851 to 1861 is shown in table XLI.[42]

TABLE XLI

NUMBERS OF CATTLE (1851, 1855, AND 1861)

	1851	1855	1861
Nelson	} 5,838	13,893	11,100
Marlborough			8,479
Canterbury	2,043	15,355	33,576
Otago	} 3,161	15,600	34,544
Southland			9,139

That Otago maintained a lead over Canterbury in numbers of cattle after quickly surpassing Nelson, while falling rapidly behind in sheep, was probably attributable to climatic more than cultural factors. The higher rainfall areas of the south, less suitable for Merino sheep, were better adapted to the Durham cattle. Yet Otago did not show a surplus production of dairy products as did Canterbury, and no dairy products whatever were included in the list of products exported in 1854 from Otago.[43] The localization lists given by the *Otago Provincial Gazette* for 1855 show that nearly half of the total cattle were in the northernmost and southernmost districts of Otago, about one-fourth centering on each of the Waikouaiti-Moeraki and Balclutha areas. Waikouaiti was thus maintaining its early lead as a cattle center.

Fuller [44] makes some good observations as to why cattle stations in the tussock lands competed unfavorably with sheep stations. No returns could be expected from the butcher under three years from the start; labor requirements for dairying were much heavier than for wool growing; generally a much longer time ensued before anything above expenses could be made. The techniques of starting a cattle station on the tussock are described by Fuller, Paul, and others, and much additional material is available in various letters and diaries.[45] Very briefly, the process was as follows:

A mob of from fifty to some hundreds of heifers, with a few bulls, was needed to begin with. A stockyard was built with a row of stout milking "bails" along one side in which to securely tie the wild range cows before milking. Then followed the breaking in of heifers * for milking; the careful selection of and breeding from best milkers; the never-ceasing herding of the cattle which involved skill in the use of the Australian stockwhip; and the attempts, often futile, to regulate breeding and hence calving periods.

Such stations persisted in the competition with sheep farms and agriculture only as they became founded on English grasses and combined the production of dairy products and beef with that of cash crops and wool. Dairying on the free ranges was short-lived except in Westland where such farms were started somewhat later in clearings in the bush and persisted into the new century.[46]

Oxen were important to the sheep industry for all of the draying necessary to bring in supplies. The techniques used in driving oxen were derived from Australia and, possibly, partially thence from the Cape or England.[47] Burdon describes the technique of harnessing as follows:

The drays were built with a pole joined to the axle, and on to this pole the first two bullocks were yoked. The yokes were pieces of wood about 3 ft. 6 ins. long, slotted so as to fit on the top of the bullock's neck. A piece of U-shaped iron fitted under the bullock's neck and up through holes in the yoke, where it was fixed by a key. The polers' yoke had a ring in the middle, fixed by means of two pins to the end of the pole. All the bullocks except polers pulled by means of chains fastened to the centre of their yokes, the first chain being fastened to the end of the pole.[48]

* The use of the term heifer beyond the period of first calving is still frequent in New Zealand; it was nearly universal in the early literature.

The pull was effected by chains fastened to the centers of the yokes of the teams and thence to the pole (or tongue) of the dray, except in the case of the "polers," the team nearest the dray, whose yoke was fastened to the tongue itself. The oxen exerted their pull against the yokes fitted to the backs of their necks. The more efficient head-yoking was rarely, if ever, employed, another reflection of the small influence of continental European tradition in the country.

The "bullocky" (bullock driver) became a specialist who controlled his team with a long Australian raw-hide stockwhip, riding or walking beside them. On occasion, as many as sixteen or eighteen bullocks would be attached to a single dray. Thus, in traversing a river bed or swamp, enough of them would hold their footing to balance those which were swept off their feet or bogged. Shorthorns, with their great bony frames, were universally considered the best animals for the purpose; indeed the early preference for the Durham breed is laid by many older settlers to its superiority under the yoke. Polled animals slipped their yokes so easily as to be almost useless, giving rise, perhaps, to the superstition that the size of horn was a measure of strength and intelligence. Yet none of the longer-horned breeds ever displaced the Shorthorns in draft work to a noticeable degree, and selection in favor of long-horns must have remained within the breed. Actually longer-horned breeds were rarely available in any event. Bullocks were, of course, slow, but absolutely irreplaceable in the trackless wilderness of the back country. Not only could they outpull horses by as much as two to one, but they could pull up much steeper grades, especially on the cut banks of rivers, and between the different terrace levels so sharply characteristic of the upper courses of most of South Island's rivers (fig. 9).

In the period of the gold rushes, all of the contributions of the cattle industry—beef, brawn, and butterfat—were in steady local demand. Importations of cattle from Australia, which declined in the late fifties, spurted anew,[49] and butter disappeared, at least temporarily, from the export lists. The import of Irish butter in some quantity also suggests a strong market. In 1864, various prices quoted in the *Otago Daily Times* were 1s. 11d. per pound for fresh butter, 1s. 4½d. for cheese, 1s. 3½d. for salt butter, and 6½d. per quart for milk. The heaviest demand was, apparently, for dairy products, and the hardy Ayrshires, established in Otago partly by Scottish sentiment, increased rather rapidly in the southern provinces.

Ayrshires were not available in Australia to the degree that Durhams had been, and in the sixties what was to become a steadily increasing flow of imports of breeding stock from Britain began; the new steamships greatly reduced losses by shortening of the voyage. The use of cows as ship's dairies became universal, displacing the goats which had been so common in the thirties, forties, and fifties. Channel breeds were in most demand for this purpose; they took up less room and were then, as they are today, the most efficient producers of butterfat from a given quantity of concentrated feed. These were, preferably, sold after the voyage, as one trip was reckoned to be all an animal could stand. The date of 1862 for the introduction of Jerseys to New Zealand is given by Philpott; [50] the same authority gives 1864 for the appearance of the first Holsteins, or Friesians as they are more generally called in South Island. These two premier milk-producing breeds increased rapidly in North Island; in South Island they diluted the basic Shorthorn and Ayrshire stock only very slowly. It is worth noting, however, that the first important experiments in the local breeding of Jerseys took place in South Island. [51]

It was the husbandry of the dairy cow, rather than that of other animals or any plants, which lifted the penniless laboring immigrant in Canterbury to the status of a yeoman farmer. This was especially true of the Ellesmere-Springs and Rangiora districts. [52] There is no farm economy more demanding of constant attention that that of a dairy; moreover, this area of heavy land involved tedious months of clearing "flax" and digging drainage ditches before good English grass leys could succeed. By bitter experience the small holder had to learn to know his animals, his soils, and his grasses. It is small wonder then that the Christchurch area became the nursery region of the herds of many breeds for the whole Dominion.

The attempt to find animals adapted to special local environmental conditions is perhaps another reason why there was early experimentation with specialized animal breeds well in advance of refrigeration. The market that refrigeration gave was, however, needed for any great expansion of the cattle industry which was in competition with sheep and cash crops for the land. There was little else in the way of obstacles to advancement. No buildings but crude milking shelters were needed; diseases, except for isolated outbreaks of pleuro-pneumonia, were virtually unknown. The cattle industry advanced to meet the demands of the greatly increased population brought by the gold rushes, and then leveled off again toward the end of the sixties.

In the seventies, the agricultural expansion slightly increased the demand for draft animals at first, but horses were more and more coming into favor, as the work of initial breaking and clearing tapered off, as roads appeared, and as bridges sprang up across the rivers. The appearance of the railroads reduced much of the wool-draying. It was the new flood of immigrant population with its demand for dairy produce that again encouraged the expansion of the industry. Though of little moment at the time, the first New Zealand co-operative dairy factory for cheese production was begun at Springfield at Otago in 1871; [53] this factory also began butter "milling," that is, the collecting of butter from their suppliers as it came from the churn, and processing and packing it.

The subsequent history of the cattle industry in New Zealand is related in some detail by Condliffe,[54] Buchanan,[54] and Philpott[54] among many writers. The relevant, important facts may be quickly summarized here, and the initial developments even more quickly reviewed. With refrigerated shipments of dairy produce beginning in the eighties, and with the introduction of the technique of starting English grasses on the ashes of the burned forests in North Island, the South Island was soon left far behind in importance as a cattle center. Especially because of the practice of using beef animals to "crush" the fern ahead of the sheep, North Island maintained its lead in beef as well as dairy animals. The dairying of South Island continued to be on the areas of the best land, where it competed with the production of mutton and lamb. The Wairau delta, Rangiora County, Springs County, the bayheads of Banks Peninsula, and the plains of the Taieri, Tokomairiro, and the lower Clutha, are examples of such regions. But the greatest dairying area was to be in Southland's plains, especially in the valleys of the Mataura, Oreti, and Aparima Rivers. Once the technique of heavy liming was adopted to establish good rye-grass pastures in this area of high precipitation, dairying faced stiff competition only from sheep; cash crops, except for oats and grass seed, were not nearly as important as in Otago, Canterbury, and Marlborough.[55]

The areas which are the most exclusive realm of cattle in South

ahc

FIG. 53. Original rain forest, an established pasture, and reversion of pasture to second-growth brush in Clutha County, southern Otago.

Island do not, however, comprise the best land. These are, rather, some reclaimed from the bush in southwestern Clutha County (fig. 53), in southwestern Wallace County, and in the counties of Westland, Grey, Buller, Takaka, and Sounds. Of some twenty possible steps in the conversion of virgin bush to English grass with or without the use of the plow,* only a few have been accomplished in most of these areas. The great difficulty of checking second-growth (especially the exotic nuisances like blackberry in Westland, and gorse or broom nearly everywhere) is a definite

* Philpott [56] gives this exhaustive list from the long experience of this process in North Island: 1. virgin forest; 2. felling and burning (mostly burning); 3. sowing with coarse, cheap, and often weedy English and Australian grasses; 4. cutting brush; 5. stumping and logging; 6. first subdivision; 7. plowing and re-grassing; 8. cropping with green, root, and clover crops; 9. early manuring and top-dressing with crushed bones and bone-dust; 10. draining swamp areas; 11. introducing better dairy stock; 12. introducing better grasses; 13. introducing better top-dressing; 14. discontinuance of supplementary crops and plowing; 15. more subdivision; 16. heavier top-dressing; 17. more stock improvement; 18. use of ensilage; 19. intensive subdivision; 20. rotational grazing.

brake to further advance. Moreover, since summers are cooler and shorter and hence dairying somewhat less profitable than in North Island, the conversion of the bush has often involved too great a financial risk to take. There is a much greater winter check to pasture growth in Southland than in Taranaki, for example, and the lactation period in the cattle is definitely shorter. If pastures can be maintained on the west coast, however, they are usually most productive (fig. 54).

In summary, we may review a few of the most important contributions which cattle husbandry made to the extension and consolidation of settlement on South Island. Cattle provided an important dietary supplement, especially in dairy produce rather than beef; they allowed the economic utilization of much poorly drained or "bush" country not suitable to Merino sheep and not easily made available to agriculture; they provided a meat supply which transported itself to the gold fields (together with surplus sheep); and above all, they contributed the traction power without which most of the early sheep-runs could not have brought out their wool, nor the agriculturists have broken their land. As the importance of oxen for draft work declined, the position of

FIG. 54. High-production pastures near Seddonville in Buller County on the west coast; a rare and remarkable conquest of the subtropical rain forest in an area of heavy and persistent rainfall.

ahc

cattle, except for dairying on the best land and the running of beef types on some of the roughest, became less important. Yet the existence in New South Wales, in quantity, of an all-purpose type of cattle with a recognizable degree of Durham blood, which throve on the tussock and bush clearings of the early decades of the European penetration of South Island, is one of the most important facts to remember in assessing the contributions of invading flora and fauna to the development of patterns and techniques of land use in the area. One cannot speculate too largely on the possible direction of that development if the Merinos and Durhams of New South Wales had not been so readily available; but it must, almost certainly, have been a far different direction. The colonies of New South Wales, Victoria, and Van Diemen's Land (Tasmania) contributed not only the basic animals, but also a remarkably steady market for the beginnings of South Island's dairy industry. As late as 1885, 98½ per cent of the butter exported from New Zealand went to these three areas.[57] The cattle industry today is concentrating more and more on types of cattle imported directly from Europe, using techniques originating in North America and Europe rather than in Australia (though many of the inventions and developments have been autochthonous), and it looks almost entirely to a European market. These facts should not, however, obscure the contributions which the Australian colonies made to its beginnings.

CHAPTER VIII

THE MINOR DOMESTICATED ANIMALS

HORSES

H orses, pigs, and goats preceded cattle and sheep to the shores of South Island, yet today none of these domestic animals is really important in the area. Of the three, horses are probably of greatest significance, in spite of the competition of internal combustion motors, though their numbers have declined sharply since the peak years from 1905 to 1915.* For New Zealand as a whole, the number of horses had risen from 187,382 in 1886, to 404,284 in 1911, only to fall again to 253,052 in 1941.[2] The increase between 1896 and 1911 was most rapid in North Island; the decrease since 1911 has been approximately even over all parts of the Dominion. The relative numbers in the different land districts in 1941 (table XLII)[3] showed nothing unexpected in view of the distribution of population, sheep, and cattle already cited. Had a cultural group of Mediterranean origin been responsible for the colonization of the country, we should have expected the introduction of more donkeys and mules; on January 31, 1937, there were but 218 donkeys and mules in all of New Zealand.

* Fleming[1] shows how this has worked in Ashburton, Canterbury's principal sheep and agricultural county. In 1916-17 there were thirteen thousand horses and eleven thousand tractors; in 1933-4 there were ten thousand horses and 458 agricultural tractors. The Agricultural and Pastoral Statistics for 1940-41 give corresponding figures of 6,500 and 959.

Initially, with oxen handling the heavy traction requirements, horses were needed only for saddle transportation and for working the sheep and cattle runs. As roads opened up, however, and when the most difficult land-breaking and stumping had been accomplished by the oxen, horses came into increasing demand. By the time of the Canterbury wheat boom of the eighties, especially after stock water races began to scar the high, dry interfluves on the plains, the horse had become indispensable to agricultural production.

TABLE XLII

NUMBER OF HORSES BY LAND DISTRICTS

	1937	1941
Marlborough	5,843	5,437
Nelson	5,530	4,507
Westland	2,073	1,714
Canterbury	50,986	40,256
Otago	29,753	25,330
Southland	24,170	22,603

The breakdown into types for 1918 was given in the *Official Year Book* for that year, and is the last available for land districts (table XLIII). Breed differentiation seems to have had no significance in the horse population comparable with that in the case of sheep and cattle. We have no good clues as to the special breeds of horses most common in Australia in the earliest years. Because they were, in the main, used as saddle horses, it may be presumed that they were much lighter than any of the heavy cart-horse breeds. Through the seventeenth and eighteenth centuries, horse breeding had been in a great state of flux in England, and the admixture of blood had been so great * that horses imported to Australia from England would probably have been as variable in

* In England the Midlands were noted for a large black horse which Bakewell used to cross with Zealand mares to create a better working type. Suffolk was famed for the Suffolk Punch, a very compact horse of about fifteen hands and very useful for draft purposes. By 1834 Burke was able to write that "There are three distinctive breeds of horses peculiarly appropriate to farm-work in England—the Lincoln, the Cleveland, and the Suffolk." The first was the Bakewell—improved black cart-horse; the Cleveland was a somewhat lighter, bay-colored animal; while the lightest of the three, the Suffolk, was more usually a chestnut shade. Of the Scottish horses, only the Clydesdale, almost the only heavy type used on Scottish farms, was well known. Extremely variable in color, it was almost as big as the Lincoln and was definitely stronger and more docile, but it was less active than the Clevelands or Suffolks.[4]

type as the perhaps more numerous importations from India and the Cape.

TABLE XLIII

TYPES OF HORSES BY LAND DISTRICTS (1918)

	Thoroughbred	Draft	Harness & Saddle	Total
Nelson	60	3,678	4,262	8,076
Marlborough	77	3,417	3,690	7,328
Westland	46	791	1,868	2,769
Canterbury	886	43,199	21,430	66,582
Otago	485	25,097	12,707	38,753
Southland	306	21,431	8,138	30,169

We know nothing of breed or type of the forty-three horses Captain Bruce is said to have landed at Preservation Inlet in 1835.[5] It is likely that Jones introduced horses with his first cattle to Waikouaiti, and that Rhodes did likewise at Akaroa. Certainly they were imported in the first year of settlement at Nelson. The Deans brought in three mares with their first stock and reported, in the same year, some forty to fifty mares at Waikouaiti.[6] They even recommended horses ("Clydes," Clevelands, or Suffolk Punches) in preference to oxen for plowing in their report to Captain Thomas in 1849.[7] On April 6, 1850, the *Otago Witness* reported only forty-five horses in Otago; Canterbury had only fifty head by the end of 1851. By 1855, however, there were 1,504 horses in Nelson, 1,189 in Canterbury, and 650 in Otago. In 1861, Nelson had 2,360 horses; Marlborough, 1,519; Canterbury, 6,049; Otago, 4,790; and Southland, 812—a total of 15,520 animals.[8] By 1881, there were approximately a hundred sixty thousand horses in all of New Zealand, more than half of which were on South Island, we may safely assume, because of its greater population and more mature development. The rapid increase in the twenty-year period was associated with the contemporaneous agricultural advance.

The relative scarcity of animals kept prices high in the fifties. Cart horses were advertised for fifty pounds in the *Nelson Examiner* for August 8, 1855. This was, currently, the yearly cash wage of an agricultural worker. A bitter complaint was made by one observer as to the quality of horses for which such prices were charged:

In vain are well bred stallions imported into the colony from time to time if mares continue to be (as in a majority of cases I fear they are) the refuse of Australian studs, thrown in, probably for nothing, as make-weights to complete a cargo.[9]

This same observer, however, mentioned the importation of an Arabian stallion from England and twelve well-bred mares from New South Wales. He recommended importation from Van Diemen's Land, which had a good name for horses; like the Deans, he preferred Clydesdales, and he also mentions the Suffolk Punch as a good type for Canterbury.

The early demand, however, was for hacks, not draft animals, and not until the late seventies did these latter become more important than saddle beasts in the advertisements in the newspapers. Perhaps through sentiment Otago had concentrated on breeding Clydesdales and, for some such reason, Otago became the breeding center for draft horses, which is, probably, why Clydesdale blood is thought to be the most important among that of heavy breed lines in present draft-horse stock. As early as 1888, Bradshaw [10] speaks of Clydesdales as if there were no considerable number of other breeds. Horsemen tell me that, currently, it is impossible to distinguish breed lines in the lighter horses, but that in the draft animals Clydesdale blood, with some admixture of Cleveland and Suffolk, is obviously dominant. Percherons and Belgians seem never to have entered the island in any numbers. In some ways the high-country hack, a solid, tough, and yet nimble animal suitable for the mustering of sheep or cattle on the rough hills and mountains, has become almost a distinct breed in itself in New Zealand; it is, however, far too variable yet to properly be ranked as such.

Horses were indispensable to the management of sheep from the first and are still virtually so to the present systems of sheep husbandry on all but the lowest country. It will be some years before they are completely replaced in traction requirements in agriculture. Horse-racing, by far the dominant spectator recreation in New Zealand, fosters a large thoroughbred breeding industry. Yet, with all this, the horse has never been a primary domestic animal in the sense of being a focus of interest and a foundation of major patterns or techniques in the use of the land. It deserves to be ranked with the pig, as a minor animal, rather than with sheep or cattle, even with regard to the earliest period; it is certainly of little importance today.

PIGS

The functional place of the pig in South Island's present land-use economy [11] is variable and difficult to determine or characterize. Sources of pig feed are both large and well-distributed, including the by-products of dairying (skim milk, buttermilk, and whey), agriculture, and food-processing industries, as well as pasture and domestic slops. Yet these are rarely used effectively [12] and the numbers of pigs in late years (table XLIV) [13] have barely exceeded those of horses (some five hundred more for the island in 1941).

That the pig population is low for an area with considerable emphasis on dairying is clearly indicated in the statistics; [14] only one county (Springs) had more pigs than dairy cows in 1941. The ratio of "pigs per hundred dairy cattle" was 43.3 for all of New Zealand; although this rose to 64.8 for Canterbury as a whole, the major dairying region of Southland had the remarkably low ratio of 17.4. Canterbury is, of course, the leading agricultural area of the South Island (indeed of all of New Zealand) and has a large local surplus production of low-grade potatoes, grains, and other roots to supplement the dairy by-products in pig feeding which Southland lacks. There is, however, one other significant contributing influence in this contrast and that is the generally greater emphasis on cheese production in the south of the island.* Cheese production provides only whey, much less valuable than skim milk and buttermilk, both of which are available from the butter-making process. Moreover, the skim milk is available on the farm, whereas the whey has to be carted home from the cheese factory; though this is often true of buttermilk, as well, it has a greater protein content per unit bulk. The shift of emphasis as between cheese and butter, largely a matter of government policy and dictated by needs in Britain, has un-

* The relative proportions of cheese and butter forwarded for export from the different land districts of South Island from April 1, 1936 to March 31, 1937 were: [15]

	Butter (tons)	Cheese (tons)
Nelson	2,253	—
Marlborough	724	713
Westland	890	13
Canterbury	2,462	1,833
Otago-Southland	1,781	13,619

doubtedly contributed to the disorganization of the swine industry.

TABLE XLIV

NUMBER OF PIGS BY LAND DISTRICT

	1937	1941
Marlborough	8,007	6,594
Nelson	19,156	19,660
Westland	6,758	6,090
Canterbury	49,216	41,913
Otago	20,663	15,961
Southland	14,649	10,257
	118,449	*100,475*

There are many explanations from an economic point of view for the failure to use the existing pig feeds more effectively. Except in Canterbury, the dairy by-products are generally produced where there is little hope of supplementary agricultural by-products being available without the payment of rather high transportation costs. This is especially true of Southland, where very large quantities of both whey and buttermilk are wasted each year. Again, there is little grazing available to pigs, with an intensive husbandry of sheep or cattle dominating most farms. The marketing of pork has been given only slight attention; pork products are not well prepared for market in comparison with Canadian, American, and Danish practice. Neglect of attention to profitable feeding regimes, to adequate housing, and to the timing of farrowing with the temporary existence of certain pig-feed surpluses, are all evident.°

All of these things are, however, in the opinion of this writer, fundamentally bound up with a cultural attitude toward pigs and pig-raising which derives from a dislike for, or lack of interest in, the pig as a domestic animal. To make a good living the New Zealand farmer has not had to bother with pigs; mutton and beef have been plentiful enough and cheap enough, so that this more efficient meat producer has not been in demand from the butchers. "Why," at least a dozen representative farmers asked me, in so

---

° Slowly, the example of a few successful pig farmers and the intensive educational program in pig husbandry which the Department of Agriculture has been promoting for some years may take effect. I did hear a few farmers beginning to repeat and accept as established agricultural doctrine that time devoted to pigs might be more profitably so spent than on other animals or crops. But, generally, pig husbandry is rather thoroughly ignored as a directive of land use.

ahc

FIG. 55. A pighouse and pasture on the west coast near Westport illustrate the characteristic indifference of New Zealand farmers toward the husbandry of swine.

many words, "should I bother with the dirty beasts?" Perhaps a sow with a yearly brood to give some home-cured ham and bacon and to act as household scavengers may be kept; anything more is generally considered a nuisance (fig. 55).

Through the first half century of settlement, pigs were by far the largest and numerically the most important of the island's "wild" animals. These are referred to in tourist brochures as "Captain Cookers," although one does not hear them so described by the people of the island. Though much reduced in numbers, wild pigs can still be shot in all the less accessible parts of the mountain country. The name "Captain Cooker" may well be justified. The Polynesian Maori had failed to establish pigs in New Zealand; perhaps the animals had not survived the long voyage by canoe. Indeed, as indicated above, dogs and rats were the only animals which the Maori did successfully introduce.[16]

The visits of Cook's second and third expeditions to South

Island led to several introductions of pigs as well as poultry. On June 2, 1773, Furneaux released a boar and two sows in Queen Charlotte Sound, "so that we have reason to hope this country will, in time, be stocked with these animals, if they are not destroyed by the natives before they become wild; for afterwards they will be in no danger." [17] After a visit to other Polynesian Islands, late in the same year, Cook introduced pigs and poultry to North Island which were, presuming from the length of time the expedition had been away from the nearest other source at the Cape of Good Hope, from those islands. If later visitors to North Island supposed the pigs there to have been pre-European Maori importations because of similarity to those in Tahiti, the defect in their reasoning is thus explained.

When Cook visited Queen Charlotte Sound in October of 1774, he "went to the place where I left the hogs and fowls; but saw no vestiges of them, nor of any body having been there since. . . . As we were coming away Mr. Forster thought he heard the squeaking of a pig in the woods . . . probably they may have been those I left with them when last here." Later in the month, one of his party saw a large black boar on Long Island in the Sound, and Cook remarked: "I thought it might be one of those which Captain Furneaux left behind, and had been brought over to this isle by those who had it in keeping. Since they did not destroy those hogs when first in their possession, we cannot suppose they will do it now, so that there is little fear but that this country will, in time, be stocked with these animals, both in a wild and domestic state." On November 8 he put two pigs, a boar and a sow, on shore "so that it is hardly possible all the methods I have taken to stock this country with these animals should fail." [18]

Again, on the visit to Queen Charlotte Sound on the third voyage, he left another pair of pigs, though he had learned that of "the animals which Captain Furneaux sent on shore here . . . I was now told were all dead; but I could get no intelligence about the fate of those I had left in West Bay, and in Cannibal Cove, when I was here in the course of my last voyage." He goes on to point out, however, that "I have, at different times, left in New Zealand not less than ten or a dozen hogs, besides those put on shore by Captain Furneaux. It will be a little extraordinary, therefore, if this race should not increase and be preserved here, either in a wild, or in a domestic state, or in both." [19]

Lieutenant Governor King of New South Wales made presents

of pigs from the Norfolk Island colony to North Island Maori in 1793 when he returned the kidnapped flax-dressers, but of these Captain Bamford, of the *Fancy*, later reported all but one dead; no signs that any of the Cook introductions survived in domestication are reported from this area.[20] It is, however, most likely that, in both islands, animals escaped into the bush and survived. The climate was relatively benign; the feed, most particularly the succulent roots of the ubiquitous bracken fern (*Pteridium esculentum*), was lush. Whether the Cook importations survived or not, however, there were many others from 1792 onward, from which the wild pigs everywhere encountered by the earliest settlers might have been descended. Captain Raven, who left the first sealing gang at Dusky in 1792, reported on his return a year later that the "animals" he had left had fed well on what the Fiordland bush provided, and had been prolific in reproduction. As this is difficult country for sheep or goats because of the very great and continuous rainfall, and one suspects that larger animals would have been specifically mentioned, it is a fair guess that these were pigs.[21] Though there are few introductions recorded, the presence of pigs was reported by visitors from the eighteen-twenties onward.[22]

In 1831 the London brig, *Tula*, found pigs on Cornwallis Island.[23] A vessel visiting Cook Strait in 1831, the *Argo*, took back to Sydney as part of her cargo: fifty-five tons of flax, ten tons of potatoes, two sacks of wheat, thirty jars of pickled oysters, and thirty pigs, though the precise point of origin of the individual items cannot be traced.[24] Captain Jay of the American ship, the *Mary Mitchell*, kept a most precise log during his stay in Cloudy Bay in 1836.[25] He reported that pigs had achieved a very important place in the economy of the Maori in that area. In one of their huts he observed: "4 sows, 2 with litters of pigs, 2 boars. . . ." Similar reports of pigs both domesticated and wild, and in all stages in between, are reported by Dieffenbach,[26] Wakefield,[27] and Crawford.[28] McNab[29] reports many other ships than the *Argo* returning from South Island to New South Wales with pork as part of their cargo. The Pakeha-Maori * around Cloudy Bay often spent the off-season from whaling cultivating potatoes, shooting pigs, or collecting either commodity among the Maori villages to barter with visiting traders and whalers.[30]

* Europeans were the "Pakeha" in Maori speech. Other Europeans referred to their fellows who "went native" as "Pakeha-Maori."

It must be clear, from the fragmentary nature of the evidence, that we cannot hope to make any sensible guess as to the numbers or general distribution of wild, half-wild, or tame (rather than domesticated) porkers on South Island in 1840. They are reported from the Marlborough Sounds area, on Banks Peninsula,° in the extreme north of Westland,† and on the southeastern coasts. Both Tuckett and Monro [33] commented, in 1844, on the numbers of pigs between Banks Peninsula and Fiordland. Shortland [34] reported that in buying a whale boat in 1843 the Maori paid seven hundred baskets of potatoes and 41 pigs,‡ and also recorded that the country back of the present city of Dunedin was "thick with pigs." Hocken [35] reports that in 1845, two runaway sailors made a good living at their camp, on the banks of the stream where Dunedin was to be established, by hunting pigs and selling them to the whalers at Otago Heads. There are observations of pigs scavenging the offal around the try-works at nearly all the shore-whaling stations.

Wild pigs do not seem to have been as frequent in the Nelson district. In his landings in Tasman Bay in 1827, D'Urville [36] comments on their infrequency—indeed on their complete absence about Astrolabe Inlet. John Deans,[37] writing from Nelson in 1842, observed "the pigs are all extirpated hereabouts long ago," although there is good reason to doubt the verity of this observation. Dieffenbach,[38] however, described Motuara Island in Queen Charlotte Sound as being "overrun" with pigs in 1839, and both Shortland and E. J. Wakefield, of Colonel Wakefield's advance party on the *Tory*, commented on the frequency of pigs in the Port Underwood area as well as through Queen Charlotte Sound. Domesticated pigs, as distinct from the tame pigs of the Maori and the whalers, seem to have been introduced to this area first. Fox wrote in 1843 [39] that there was a fair stocking of pigs in the few little patches then being cultivated as subsistence farms in the Waimea and Wai-iti valleys.¶

° An observer reported the hills of Banks Peninsula "thick with pigs" in the early forties.[31]

† J. D. Peart [32] reports Capt. H. G. Moore as finding many wild pigs around Tasman Bay about this time.

‡ The baskets averaged about thirty-five pounds each. Shortland suggests "very moderate" figures of 6d. per basket for the potatoes and 12s. each for the pigs, making the whale-boat cost just over forty pounds.

¶ Pratt [40] recorded that American pickled pork was imported in some quantity at this period, which does not suggest a local surplus of pigs.

It was in 1843 that the Deans introduced two pregnant sows with their first stock to Riccarton.[41] In January 1844, the two pigs had increased to nineteen, and the comment appears that the pigs "require no food besides what they can gather, unless they have young ones."[42] By 1849, however, it appears that the Deans were beginning to treat their pigs on a tame, rather than a domesticated basis. With some thirty pigs about the place, only one or two were kept in a shelter for fattening; others were confined by ditch-and-bank fencing. But plenty of fat wild pigs nearby, easily shot and often making superior pork to their own, reduced the incentive for careful pig husbandry. We must assume that similar experiences were the lot of other settlers, and that carelessness in looking after pigs became the rule; for industry applied to it became needless effort when pig-shooting, the only early game-sport available for anything larger than birds, was both widely popular and productive of large bags. We must also assume that many pigs may have escaped through this very carelessness to introduce new blood among the large numbers of wild animals.

The necessary differentiation between tame and domesticated animals makes the early statistics of pig numbers not only unreliable but also, in a real sense, rather absurd. An early census in Otago[43] recorded 132 swine in the block, surely a gross underestimate of the total of wild, tame, and domesticated pigs in that area. We must allow, of course, for the effectiveness of earlier hunting, and some indication of this is given by the price of a shilling a pound which was fetched by pork brought to Dunedin from Waikouaiti in the first year.[44] So, in Southland, but 242 swine were reported for 1847.[45] For the second decade of settlement, the number of pigs in New Zealand for the different Provincial Districts are listed in table XLV.[46] Yet Burdon,[47] who carefully read the Tripp letters and diaries, says that, on the two high-country runs of Tripp and Acland alone, more than five thousand wild pigs were killed in the first five years of occupancy (1856-1861). Hochstetter describes the situation with regard to pigs in New Zealand in general, and in Nelson in particular *circa* 1860:

Cattle and swine run wild in various districts of the islands, and it is astonishing to what numbers the wild pigs are multiplying. They find an excellent and everywhere plentiful food in the fern-roots, which formerly served the Maoris as a chief article of food. They retire shyly from the immediate vicinity of the settlements, because the settlers hunt them down energetically; but they congregate in the yet uninhabited valley in [an] enormous number. The Wangapeka valley in the Province of Nelson I saw for miles up and down literally ploughed up by thousands of wild pigs. They are nearly all black. Their extermination is sometimes contracted for by experienced hunters, and it is a fact that three men in 20 months, upon an area of 250,000 acres killed not less than 25,000 of them; they moreover pledged themselves to kill 15,000 more. Where the wild pigs are very numerous, they do a great deal of damage to sheep breeding.° [48]

TABLE XLV

Total Pigs for the Years 1851, 1855, and 1861

	1851	1855	1861
Nelson	} 2,609	4,814	2,985
Marlborough			1,452
Canterbury	1,255	4,996	9,586
Otago	} 2,371	1,556	2,218
Southland			585

There is little doubt that, by the seventies, wild pork had greatly diminished in supply, as the high-country stations were better patrolled, and prospectors for gold had pushed into the farthest valleys, living as much as possible off the country. Yet one must believe the almost unanimous testimony of shepherds, deer-cullers, and sporting hunters, that pigs continue to exist in thousands today in the hills and mountains of the back country. Persistent shooting, the ever-increasing destruction of the bush, and their incidental consumption of rabbit-poison, just barely serve to keep the animals under control. Opinion is conflicting as to the damage they do to the forests. Certainly they establish runways in the lowest forest stratum and root about a great deal in the litter, but they do not browse and ring-bark as do the more certainly destructive deer.

There is general agreement that South Island's domesticated pigs today are most largely Berkshire in blood, and that, for the rest, the Tamworth and Yorkshire strains are most important. It is not clear why this should be, except that all are very popular

° In the first German edition of Hochstetter, he ascribes this Bunyanesque tale to Van Haast. Neither Hochstetter nor Van Haast was careless in his observations, but one cannot help feeling that they were both taken in on this occasion. Nevertheless this story suggests that the figures of pigs in Nelson in table XLV referred only to those in sties on farms, and thus bear no relation whatever to the size of the pig population as a whole.

English breeds through the world of agriculture which has any cultural roots in the British Isles. As to the wild pigs, M. J. Scott, a thoroughly informed expert on New Zealand's swine, feels confident that Berkshire blood is prominent in most of the wild pigs now shot, though Yorkshire and Tamworth characteristics can also often be seen. Dieffenbach [49] described the New Zealand wild pigs as "a peculiar breed with short heads and compact bodies," a conformation which might well have been inherited from introductions of native pigs from other Polynesian islands by Cook and others. Thomson [50] quotes a contemporary observer that pigs shot in 1854 had long, pointed snouts and long legs, and were nondescript in color. Hochstetter's report on the black wild pigs of Nelson, quoted above, suggests the black Berkshires, or, alternatively, the Polynesian strains. Other observers have fancied some Hampshire blood in the wild stock of Canterbury. There are several references to the importation of Berkshires in the earliest days, but no reference to other types. For example, Saunders states that in 1845 he imported to Nelson from England "the large and small breed of Berkshire pigs, which soon superseded the coarse, unthrifty, native bristle growers that had spread so widely over New Zealand." [51] What these may have been, it is impossible to discover. Apparently we can make no clear statement about types among the wild pigs.

TABLE XLVI

TYPES OF PIGS BY LAND DISTRICTS (1918)

	Pure Berkshire	Pure Yorkshire	Other Purebred	Crossbred	Total
Nelson	1,740	243	183	7,442	9,608
Marlborough ...	2,000	312	187	4,288	6,787
Westland	867	114	120	2,106	3,207
Canterbury	14,544	551	489	22,397	37,981
Otago	1,746	1,603	140	11,042	14,531
Southland	1,531	1,439	207	8,088	11,265

In 1899 the *New Zealand Official Year Book* described the Berkshire as by far the favorite domesticated pig of New Zealand; it added that both the large and small breeds of white Yorkshires were to be met with, but were not so generally approved as the black pigs, and that the use of red Tamworths to cross with the blacks for bacon production was prevalent. The distribution of types among the different land districts in 1918 is shown in table XLVI.[52] By the time the type, or breed, ceased to be recorded by the census in 1928, a marked change was evident in New Zealand as a whole (table XLVII).[53] These figures may, however, represent simply a decline in registry of litters of pure Berkshires. If there was a definite increase in Tamworths and Large Whites at the expense of the Berkshires, it must have been chiefly following a government-sponsored effort to produce hams and bacon better suited to the British market. There is today a general use of boars of these breeds on sows of crossbred, but dominantly Berkshire, type.

TABLE XLVII

Types of Pigs (Per Cent of Total for All New Zealand)

	Pure Berkshire	Pure Yorkshire	Other Purebred	Crossbred
1918	26%	3%	2%	69%
1921	24	2	2	72
1924	24	2	1	73
1927	14	1	3	82

In conclusion, we may make the observation that in its domestic swine, and to an indeterminate but probably large degree in its wild pigs, South Island may recognize a fourth distinct, dominant, hearth area for its exotic animals. To the Iberian mountains, the North Yorkshire or Durham vales, and the shores of the Firth of Clyde, must now be added the middle Thames valley. Cultural initiative and tradition and chance space-relationships thus work with habitat quality and the status of techniques to establish in new lands new combinations of characteristics drawn from the old. We may also observe that pig husbandry has never been a popular or areally important directive of land use in the island. South Islanders were granted a large and satisfactory supply of wild pork in the early days by virtue of the rapid increase of wild pigs in the first half of the century in the unpenetrated interior. When this supply diminished, or became less easily available, pig husbandry seems to have been regarded as an unpleasant occupation in comparison with the raising of sheep, cattle, or agricultural crops. The *Official Year Book* for 1899 makes the observation that "pigs require no better attention than a good grass paddock, with a liberal supply of roots, and a little un-threshed pea-haulm [whole stalk of the field-pea plant] for a few weeks before killing, with plenty of water and shelter from the sun during the warmest summer months." However, the South Island farmer preferred to reserve the good grass paddocks for his sheep and cattle, and, to be profitable under any other regime, pigs needed a great deal more attention than is implied here, especially if the pork was to compete in the British market with that from Denmark. Generally, the South Islander still refuses stubbornly to give them that attention. One cannot escape the impression that pig-keeping is generally considered a dirty and unpleasant, if not indeed degrading, occupation.*

GOATS

Another invader, as early as the pig in its arrival, and fully as hardy, was the goat. Its relative unimportance today as a domestic animal demands some comment here. There is no certainty whatever as to how many goats there may be in the island at present; it is only known that wild animals in the hills and mountains far outnumber those on farms which may be listed by the Dominion Statistician. There were 9,055 domestic goats in 1891; there was no further report of enumeration until 1916, when 17,601 were listed for all of New Zealand.[55] The 17,730 of 1918 were divided between 5,931 angora goats and 11,799 others. Numbers then showed a fairly steady and rapid increase until 1930, when 39,127 were listed. This is the last report on goats by any census agency. Where those enumerated may have been located, or to what degree these figures include the large wild goat population of South Island, is not clear. In a fairly thorough coverage of the chief agricultural and pastoral districts of South Island by this writer, not more than a hundred goats all told were seen, and these were used mainly for special purposes of milk supply near the large urban centers.

On Cook's visit to Queen Charlotte Sound on the second voyage in 1773, he landed a pair of goats on the shores of the sound and turned them loose.[56] These had been brought from the Cape of Good Hope. Another pair were given to a chief in the area in 1777.[57] There is no clue as to the probability of the survival of this last pair, though Cook was fairly certain that the first pair had died or been killed between the second and third voyages.

---

* This is brought out rather strikingly by J. R. Fleming [54] in his survey of the farms of Ashburton County. For the period 1915-1935 there were, on the average, some eight hundred thousand sheep shorn, and some twenty thousand cattle compared with only eight to nine thousand pigs. Scarcely a farm had more than the customary two or three scavenging sows.

Whether there were further introductions before the eighteen-thirties we do not know; they were, however, then introduced to the whaling settlements. Tuckett [58] found goats in 1843 with the settlers at Tautuku Bay; he also reported drinking goats' milk at Onekakara. Of the goats around Port Underwood, Dieffenbach [59] said that they "thrive better than cattle, to the introduction of which the almost total want of grass is a most serious objection." Crawford [60] also commented on the presence of goats in the Port Underwood area in the early forties. There is hearsay tradition that the hills of Banks Peninsula in the forties had many goats roaming wild upon them,[61] but it is surprising to find no direct evidence of goats in the French settlement at Akaroa.

TABLE XLVIII
GOATS, 1851 AND 1858

	1851	1858
Nelson	5,842	3,820
Canterbury	356	724
Otago	582	343

In censuses of stock in Otago for 1849 and 1850,[62] fifty and 159 goats, respectively, were recorded. What their function was is obscure; perhaps they represented ships' dairies rather unceremoniously dumped in the settlement. At any rate, as milk producers, they were cheaper to buy, and much easier to care for, than were cattle at the same period. The Barker letters [63] state that good "milch goats" were purchasable for ten shillings apiece in Lyttelton in 1850. That most of the goats of the island were in the north, however, is clear from official statistics quoted by Thomson (table XLVIII).[64] For some unexplained reason the decline evident in the number of goats everywhere, and especially in Nelson, continued until 1861, but had increased again by 1886 (table XLIX).[65]

TABLE XLIX
GOATS, 1861 AND 1886

	1861	1886
Nelson	419	1,660
Marlborough	1,099	641
Westland	—	1,778
Canterbury	625	536
Otago	156	1,356
Southland	9	8

There is very little more to go on than these bare figures; almost nothing has been written about goats in all the varied sources consulted. It is certain that domestic goats are of negligible importance today. Yet on the upper levels of the high country are thousands of wild goats which constitute a serious menace to the native vegetation, undoubtedly contributing both to a lower capacity for carrying sheep and to an acceleration of soil erosion in such areas.

Authoritative information about these goats is not easy to obtain; that herein comes mainly from conversations with members of the staff of deer-cullers maintained by the Department of Internal Affairs, or from the annual reports of that department. The goats appear to be in greatest numbers on the flanks of the northern mountain complex in Nelson and Marlborough, but they are found here and there throughout the mountain areas to the south. Goats seem to prefer drier and more open country than do the deer.

That wild goats are more numerous in the northern mountains may be, in part, a reflection of the greater numbers of domestic goats reported in Nelson as compared with the more southern districts in the earliest days. In the fifties Fitton [66] reported that "a few goats also have, like the pigs, escaped from owners and bred in the mountainous districts." They have been deliberately released on a number of occasions, so this writer was told by old settlers, to combat two aggressive species of bramble, the exotic blackberry (*Rubus fructicosus*) * in the rainier west coast areas, and the native lawyer vine (*R. australis*) in the drier sheep country. The officials of the State Forest Service report that goats were at one time (the date has been forgotten) so colonized in a state forest area at Hari Hari, south of Ross in Westland.

Only recently have they come to be considered as a pest hardly less serious than the rabbits or deer. The first systematic attempt to control their numbers was made in the 1931-1932 season in connection with a deer-destruction drive in Marlborough; the *Annual Report* of the Department of Internal Affairs for the 1934-1935 season intimated that goats were relatively unimportant, and only a few were killed in the 1936-1937 season in the central area of the main Alpine divide. Not until 1937-1938, however, was a systematic drive undertaken which was specifically aimed at goats,

* Rather like *R. frondosus,* the high-bush blackberry of the northeastern United States.

and a total of 16,480 was then killed in the area marked B alone
(fig. 59). While the deer drives were being undertaken in the
area, the bag of goats was small, but another special goat drive
in the same area in 1940-1941 netted 15,035 animals.[67] Considering the difficulties of stalking and shooting goats, and the ease
with which they can slip through a "net" of hunters in a deer-
destruction party, it seems fair to assume that there are no less
than fifty thousand wild goats on South Island today. Most men
in the high country suggest local figures which would give a far
greater total. There is little compensation to the region for what
damage they do; perhaps a few skins may be sold, but nothing
more.

Breeds of goats do not seem to be recognized in the domesticated animals, apart from the Angoras, and there is little indication of breed or type in the wild animals. The colors of these
latter are extremely variable; though pure white, pure black, and
various all-over shades of khaki are sometimes shot, the prevailing
skins are most usually of mixed patches of black and white, or
black and tan. The white and tan combination is not common.

So much for the goats, except for the Tahr (or Thar, *Capra
jemlaica*), a Himalayan wild goat which is more conveniently discussed along with deer and chamois. The goat has been one of
the least noticed, and was long believed to be one of the least
important, introductions into South Island. To all with a consciousness of the collective destructive power of deer and wild
goats together, however, they appear today in the rôle of a very
undesirable intruder. As with the pigs, they found no natural
enemy, plenty of food and a satisfactory climate, and have been
able to spread rapidly; their only hazard, until organized destructive drives began, was the rifle of the high-country shepherd. And
he, in turn, was not likely to waste ammunition on such a difficult
quarry and target while plenty of deer could be found. Moreover,
the incentive to shoot the animals was low; a man would be very
hungry indeed to stoop to "goat mutton" while venison or even
Merino flesh could be had.

CHAPTER IX

THE ANIMAL PESTS

THE RABBIT

The rabbit has become one of the most familiar and most notorious occupants of the South Island landscape. It is now of some importance among the minor contributors to New Zealand's export trade, as indeed it has been for more than half a century. Small exports of rabbit skins began in the early seventies. Andersen [1] quotes what appears to be one of the first reports of the industry, a newspaper advertisement offering twenty thousand rabbit skins at twopence a skin in 1872. In 1873 some thirty-three thousand skins were exported; by 1878 the annual export had increased to nearly three million skins, and by 1881 to eight and a half million. The value in that year was nearly eighty-five thousand pounds, a revenue of approximately twopence-halfpenny a skin. For New Zealand as a whole, rabbit skins were the seventh in value of items of export in 1881, being exceeded only by (in order of decreasing importance) wool, gold, wheat, Kauri gum, oats, and tallow. [2] Among considerable items of export of less value than rabbit skins were barley, timber of all kinds, sheepskins, leather, and preserved meats. True, the skins formed less than 2 per cent of the value of exports, but wool contributed 49 per cent, gold 16 per cent, and wheat 12 per cent for that year. [2] The southern parts of South Island contributed the major portion of the skins, a fact obvious from a consideration of the graph (fig.

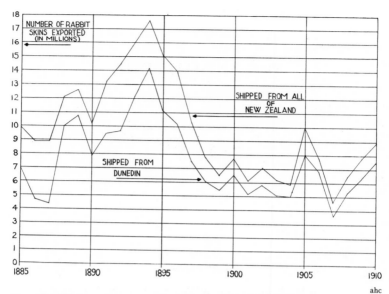

ahc

Fig. 56. Fluctuations in rabbit-skin exports from 1885 to 1910, illustrating both the fluctuations in number of rabbits (apparently a natural phenomenon unrelated to the effectiveness of extermination efforts) and the concentration of the pests in southern South Island.

56) which shows the total number of rabbit skins exported from New Zealand from 1885 to 1910, together with number of skins exported from Dunedin. Equally conclusive are data which show that virtually all frozen carcasses of rabbits and hares exported from New Zealand were shipped from Invercargill and Dunedin between 1900 and 1910.

After 1907 the annual export figures for rabbit skins were never to fall below four million, though they did drop to just under five million skins in 1917. In 1925, a new high of nearly twenty million skins was reached, and after a decline, another peak of nearly seventeen million skins was reached in 1936; in 1944, nearly fourteen million skins were exported. Between World Wars I and II, over a quarter of a billion skins were exported from South Island with no noticeable long-term trend toward diminution of the supply. With prices (in 1944) at approximately tenpence per skin, there was a very profitable living for hundreds of full-time or part-time rabbiters who reaped this annual harvest. How many rabbits a yearly take of twelve and a half million skins represents, cannot be easily estimated. Some optimists believe that half of the existing rabbits are caught, shot, or poisoned each year. Others believe that there may be upwards of one hundred million rabbits in New Zealand, on the average, at any given time. Most of these, from past and present evidence of the origin of the skins, are certainly in South Island, chiefly in Otago, Southland, and Marlborough. Most of Canterbury is relatively free from them, although hares may often be seen in the high-country tussock areas. The excessive rainfall of the west coast seems to discourage them across the Alpine divide.

There is a small part of public opinion which believes that the income from rabbit skins more than balances any harm that rabbits do to the region. As with the question of burning the tussock, it is difficult to isolate the effect of the rabbits except where their burrowing on steep hillsides has led to under-running and serious acceleration of soil erosion. But even in such cases it is impossible to determine how seriously the rabbits contribute to this regional mutilation, because nearly everywhere that rabbits are obviously active, burning and overgrazing have had some effect too. It can be taken as certain that the rabbits have contributed a good deal to the sorry pictures of soil erosion and vegetation deterioration shown in figures 57 and 58. How much they cost the country each year in terms of competition with sheep for grazing, even ignoring the charge of depletion of potentially permanent resources which may be leveled against them, is likewise impossible to determine on any simple accounting basis. Assuming there to be only fifty million rabbits in New Zealand at any time, and making a further assumption that twenty rabbits consume as much vitamin-rich herbage as would one half-bred sheep, we might hazard the speculation that they displace two and a half million sheep. In output of wool alone, two and a half million crossbred sheep would bring in much more income than even the seventeen million rabbit skins exported in 1936. These figures are admittedly hypothetical, but they are based on estimates from graziers, as well as scientists concerned with both sheep and grasslands, and are, on the whole, conservative. If we add to the charge against the rabbit what he may have contributed to permanent resource depletion, it is almost certain that New Zealand, and especially

ahc

Fɪɢ. 57. Man-made desert in Central Otago. Ragged weathering of the up-ended blocks of schist give a saw-edge profile to the Raggedy Range in the background. In between the rocks a tussock grassland of moderate density flourished a century ago. Today the denuded ground is mantled with little but scattered clumps of scabweed (*Raoulia lutescens*). Everywhere are rabbit droppings, and old rabbit burrows puncture the slopes. Here European man allowed sheep, rabbits, and fire to wreak their combined devastation, which resulted in the creation of one of the world's most desolate deserts.

South Island, has suffered rather heavily from the introduction of the animal to the country.

The high price of rabbit skins might be supposed to lead to permanent reductions in numbers, but either the elimination of the rabbit is too difficult a problem, or the New Zealanders have partially learned, and misapplied, a lesson in conservation. Whales, seals, forests, and more latterly, soils and grasslands have been, successively, rather mercilessly destroyed or mutilated; the rabbit is, in contrast, rather conservatively "farmed" over large areas. That this is against the interests of any run-holder who owns his land would seem to be obvious, and indeed, where run-

ahc

Fig. 58. A hillside which has become a gigantic rabbit warren, four miles north of Alexandra in the Manuherikia valley. Destruction of vegetation and loss of soil by gullying are obvious corollaries of rabbit infestation.

holders, even on leasehold property, do their own rabbiting or supervise it strictly, the pest is kept well under control. But if more or less permanent rabbiters are employed, under loose supervision if any, the advantages of putting the production of skins on a sustained-yield basis have been too obvious to be ignored. To take only one example: rabbiting in South Island is almost entirely a winter occupation. It is true that the summer skins are unsalable, but any policy of extermination of the pest must follow a year-round drive. Yet too many run-holders complain that they cannot afford to pay rabbiters, but rather let out, and in some cases of badly infested runs even auction off, rabbiting rights. Naturally a rabbiter who has bought a concession will operate it only when it is profitable to do so. The practice of having the same men do the rabbiting year after year on the same run is a vicious one, and it is said that many high-country run-holders who lease their land from the government, and whose stock is encumbered by heavy loans, have taken to rabbit-farming themselves to realize some ready cash.

That this is not a simple question of the virtues of lease-hold versus free-hold is evident from the fact that many runs which are technically free-hold are so deeply encumbered with mortgages as to leave the owner little freedom of action. Indeed, many complain that the land and mortgage companies force them to so overstock their runs that the rabbits make only an incidental contribution to deterioration. The suggestion has been made, and it appears sound, that if sheep were taken off the most badly infested runs and these were left alone for some years, the tussock vegetation would win a straight battle with the rabbits. The political and economic questions involved, however, make this an unlikely probability, despite the fact that most of the area is leasehold. The Department of Lands and Survey, which controls the land leased from the Crown, has taken over one of the largest, and worst infested runs * in the upper Awatere valley in Marlborough and is experimenting with the running of cattle instead of sheep. The theory is that the cattle will not graze closely enough to expose the crowns of the tussocks to the lepine incisors. While this may work out, it is difficult to visualize its extension, unless there is, permanently, a greater demand and a higher price for frozen beef which must compete in European markets with the chilled beef from Argentina and South Africa.

This may be a discursive introduction to the rabbit problem, but it should give more point to a discussion of its origin. The beginnings of the rabbit plague on South Island parallel, of course, its much more widely advertised development in Australia. There the rabbits have been since the beginning of European settlement; they were included in the first return of livestock dated May 1, 1788; [3] three of the five reported belonged to Governor Phillip, so they had evidently arrived with the first fleet. Cunningham [4] has the following note on the rabbit in New South Wales written in 1827:

Rabbits are bred about the houses, but as yet we have no wild ones in enclosures, although there is a good scope of sandy country on the sea-coast, between Port Jackson and Botany Bay, fit for little else than goat pasture and rabbit warrens, in which way it may be profitably made use of, while at present it yields absolutely nothing.

* Where goats as well as rabbits had to be counted as vermin.

In the first fifty years there are references only to what are, clearly, hutch rabbits. In 1844, however, wild rabbits are described on an island off the coast of New South Wales,[5] and in 1846 a very illuminating paragraph appeared in the *Port Phillip Patriot* for June 26:

... numerous rabbits, which have from time immemorial escaped from the hutches and clutches of the vendors in the market place, have taken refuge under the police office and have increased rapidly. They appear to thrive well in the locality they have chosen.

Suttor [6] states that it was not until the late fifties, when a mania for acclimatization had arisen in the community, that the rash experiment was made of introducing to Australia the true wild rabbit, an animal which, even in the damp climate of England, could hardly be kept within proper bounds without an annual and wholesale massacre. It was on Christmas Day, 1859, according to Suttor, that the clipper *Lightning* arrived at Port Phillip with twenty-four wild rabbits, and he says that, if these were not the first of their kind, it was certainly within three years of this date that the rabbit menace was beginning to be recognized. He quotes *The Argus*, a local paper of the time: "The game at Barwon Park is reported to be thriving well; as for the rabbits, they are becoming a pest." New South Wales was not to be outdone by Victoria. The *Sydney Morning Herald* of December 3, 1860 has this statement: "Those who recollect an English rabbit warren and know how large a part it contributes to the provision market will be glad to hear that an attempt is now being made to introduce the wild rabbit on the estate of Mr. Holt at Cook's River." Holt imported sixty rabbits and named the property "The Warren." By 1865 the rabbits had increased to several thousands.[7]

The destructiveness of the rabbit pest in successive decades in Australia has become notorious. Stead [8] is but one of many writers to describe its history on that continent. It has not, however, been generally realized outside of New Zealand that a close parallel to this development took place contemporaneously in South Island. The introduction of the rabbit cannot be considered, of course, apart from that of many dozens of exotic birds, fish, and terrestrial game, which was enthusiastically undertaken by individuals and organized groups. Thomson has the following very neat interpretation of this culturally promoted invasion of animal life which often became a pest:

The early settlers of New Zealand found themselves in a land which, as far as regards climate and natural conditions, seemed to them to reproduce many of the best features of the homeland from which they came. They thought with affection and with the glamour of youthful remembrance of the lakes and rivers, the woods and fields, the hills and the dells of that homeland. They recalled the sport which was forbidden to all but a favoured few, but which they had often longed to share in—the game preserves, the deer on the mountains or in the parks, the grouse on the heather-clad hills, the pheasants in the copses and plantations, the hares and partridges in the stubbles and turnip fields, the rabbits in the hedgerows and sandy warrens, and the salmon of forbidden price in the rivers—and there rose up before their vision a land where all these desirable things might be found and enjoyed.[9]

The landed class wanted the familiar sporting animals, and the far more numerous members of the underprivileged classes, especially those who had lived for a generation in the relative freedom of pioneer life, were even more avid to enjoy the sport and food available to their fathers only at a poacher's risks. Indeed many of the transportees had been sent to New South Wales as the price of a dinner of roast venison or rabbit stew. A wide variety of game, and freedom to take it at will, regardless of social and economic position—these symbolized for them (as could little else) a new freedom from galling class discriminations.

Acclimatization societies were rapidly established, that of Canterbury dating from 1864.[10] They introduced dozens of varieties of birds; salmon and trout ova, which were hatched and the fry released; rabbits and hares; deer, moose, and wapiti; thar and chamois; wallaby and opossum. There were a great many more; the gray Norway rat was a frequent but unintentional import; stoats and weasels were later introduced in an attempt to check rabbits, but they proved more interested in the dwindling numbers of the native flightless birds.* The history and significance of all of these introductions cannot be reviewed, but

---

* Burdon [11] reminds us of the introduction of the Mongoose to Jamaica for the purpose of exterminating the rats, a purpose which it accomplished only with the destruction of a large part of the other small terra- and avi-fauna of the island as well. In South Island the stoats and weasels, along with domestic cats, which were also released to war on the rabbits, played especial havoc with the weka. In 1884, sixty-seven weasels and stoats were imported and released by the government and large numbers of ferrets (Burdon believes upwards of seventy-five thousand) were bred and released on the island. Ironically and tragically enough, the weka, which thus became all but extinct, was one of the few effective, indigenous enemies of the rabbit.

that of rabbits, and of the deer and like large animals, is of enough importance to invite discussion.

The date of the first introduction of rabbits to South Island is no better established than that of many other "firsts," and is, in terms of a precise year, equally unimportant. Even if none had been brought directly from England, the close associations with New South Wales and Victoria offered every opportunity for their importation from the earliest days of settlement. As early as 1844, Tuckett [12] reported rabbits thick on the islands just north of Tautuku Bay on the southeastern coast; with the assistance of a beagle, six were caught alive during his visit. Hares were shipped to Akaroa in 1850 along with deer, partridge, and pheasants from England, but only the pheasants were landed alive. [13]

A good deal has been made of a pair of silver-grey rabbits liberated in Marlborough in 1859, [14] but no particular items need such emphasis when the introductions which followed this (if indeed it was the first) were so continuous and widespread. For example, the *Otago Daily Times* for October 12, 1863, reported the landing of a goldfinch, a blackbird, a hare, and half a dozen rabbits for the local acclimatization society. The Annual Report of the Canterbury Acclimatisation Society for 1866 states that "an enclosure has been set aside for the silver-grey rabbits presented by Sir George Gray, which have thriven well and increased to a great extent and have been distributed to members far and near." In July, 1867, the *Southland News* reported the successful acclimatization of rabbits in that province.* From whatever sources they came, they soon found homes in the gorse hedges, the river banks, and the stony hillsides. Slowly gathering momentum, the rabbit tide spread inland, its advance becoming increasingly rapid in the seventies. The major centers of dispersal seem to have been in Marlborough and Southland.

Perhaps the earliest awareness of the possible menace of the rabbit to the welfare of the region appeared in a note in the *Otago Daily Times* in March, 1869. In less than fifteen years it was estimated that a million acres had been damaged in Marlborough. [16] It was in the tussock country, beyond the limits of agriculture that the rodents flourished. And it was from Southland that the main threat to the sheep country developed. [17] Up the hills and plains of Southland the rabbits swarmed, along the shores of Lake Wakatipu on the west, and into South Otago by

* Thomson [15] gives a long list of reported introductions in addition to these.

the Pomahaka valley on the east. By these two routes they soon colonized most of the country south of Waitaki.* By 1876, one run in Central Otago, where in 1873 hardly a rabbit was to be seen, employed sixteen men and a hundred and twenty dogs in an attempt to keep them down; even the killing of thirty-six thousand in one year seemed to have little effect upon them. On another run, fifty thousand were killed in a year, but the weekly expense of twenty-seven pounds was ruining the run-holder.

Every possible defense was employed, but most of the rabbits were destroyed by shooting, trapping, and poisoning. For a while poisoning was stopped because of its destructive effect upon the hawks, major enemies of the rabbits. The Colonial government was quick to move; the Rabbit Nuisance Act of 1876 was closely modeled on a similar Tasmanian Act of 1871. Under its provisions any given area might be declared a rabbit district if a petition to that end, signed by ten or more land-holders within the area, were received, provided only that there was no counter-petition with a greater number of authorized signatures. When established, such a board elected three or five trustees with the power to levy a halfpenny per acre for expenses. Each such board could send exterminators into the lands of any unco-operative constituents. The boards had a very limited effectiveness, however, since, apart from the districts in which boards did not operate, there were large areas of river and mountain wasteland, or untouched government reserves, in which the rabbits could find adequate refuge. An unco-operative run-holder, or group of such, could endanger to the point of nullification the efforts of neighboring boards. The Act was changed in 1882 to provide government inspectors in place of trustees, and again in 1883 to provide power to rate the land-holders up to a penny a head for sheep and fivepence per head for cattle; the government also undertook to provide a pound-for-pound subsidy up to a limit of ten thousand pounds. This act also provided for the erection of rabbit fences across private land without compensation to the owners.

In the eighties Canterbury was being threatened from the north and from the south, and advantage was taken of the new law to erect two long rabbit fences on the Australian style.†

---

* By tradition, probably correct, rabbits were sometimes carried across the rivers by shepherds and gold-seekers, before the menace was generally realized.

† Stead [18] discusses the futility and enormous cost (exceeding four hundred thousand pounds) of these fences in Australia.

In the north, rabbits were pouring into the Amuri from Marlborough, and the Hurunui rabbit fence was built, running inland from the coast for fifty miles. In the south, by 1887, rabbits had crossed the Waitaki. Toward the mountains they had divided into two "armies," after passing between Lakes Hawea and Ohau. One deployed eastward on the arid plains of the Waitaki and along both banks of the Ahuriri. The other moved around the northern shores of Ohau, crossed the Hopkins and Dobson Rivers, and threatened to cross the Tasman River. Against this threat, an eighty-mile fence was erected from the Waitaki, opposite Kurow, up the Hakataramea valley, then to the west, through Gray's Hills to the banks of the Tekapo River. Another section defended the gap between this river and Lake Pukaki in the Mackenzie Country. From the head of the lake a further extension ran up the Tasman Valley and into the highest Alpine areas.

Fences had proved quite inadequate in Australia, and greater roughness of terrain created even more serious problems in the construction of barriers in South Island. Deeply sunk in the ground though the fences were, the rabbits tunneled under them on rough hillsides; flood-gates across the streams were forever getting out of order; slides of rock, and even of snow, frequently damaged the fences; and where they crossed lowlands, the underground meshes tended to rust away rapidly.

Yet, there is some evidence that the southern fence did pay. In 1889, runs north of the fence found their leases in demand well above the upset rental established for the auctions, while south of the fence many leases did not receive a bid. Today local opinion is that country to the north of the fence (long since in disrepair and largely removed) is better ground. Newspaper opinion of the time, however, was fairly unanimous that the fences had failed.

Since the nineties, control of rabbits through rabbit boards has continued, but the fight has fallen more and more into the hands of the individual run-holder. Where possible, whole runs, and in exceptional cases subdivisions of runs, have been rabbit-fenced. Though the rabbits were never a plague in the agricultural country proper, agricultural holdings have had to be heavily fenced against the pests in central Otago and Southland, and in parts of coastal Otago, South Canterbury, North Canterbury, and Marlborough.

The fencing problem is a serious one. The recommended standard is 42-inch netting, 1¼-inch mesh of 17-gauge, grade A, wire. The life of such fencing in Australia varies from three years on the wetter country (rusting below the ground) to upwards of forty years in the driest areas.[19] A similar variability in effective life is reported in South Island as between the heavy precipitation area of Southland and the Central Otago "desert." Besides the actual durability of wire and posts, effectiveness is decreased in many cases by lack of care in construction or upkeep. Many expensive fences have been installed only to have their effect nullified by an improperly constructed gate, or by the arrangement of corner braces so that rabbits might be able to climb the fence by an easy runway.

Once a property is adequately fenced, and the fence kept in repair, the destruction of rabbits can be accomplished in many ways. Stoats, weasels, cats, and dogs are not effective in themselves; the suggested introduction of rabbit diseases has never been undertaken, because of the uncertainty of their possible spread to domestic dogs or poultry. Dogs, men, and guns represent a fairly effective but now much too expensive triumvirate. Digging out, similarly, is too high in cost. The use of poisonous gases (notably calcium cyanide dust, which indicates all the openings in a warren, allowing these to be sealed up) promises well, but has been little tried in New Zealand, although some use has been made of carbon monoxide from the exhaust of gasoline engines. Trapping is essentially a rabbit farmer's expedient, its major use being to obtain rabbits for the freezing works, and it contributes little to rabbit extermination. The principal, and most effective, method of killing rabbits in South Island is by poisoning, whether for extermination or for obtaining skins; the two are, of course, not mutually exclusive. Both phosphorous and arsenic have been used, but strychnine is now the most common poison. The almost universal custom is to turn a shallow fresh furrow with a plow for variable distances on different parts of the run, and in this furrow to strew bits of poisoned carrot. The rabbits are attracted by the odor of freshly turned earth. In 1941, in walking along one such furrow half an hour after the poison had been set out, the writer found two dozen dead rabbits in the space of a quarter of a mile.

Fences, with poisoning, will serve to check and even eliminate rabbits on any particular run. There are, however, rabbit warrens through the roadsides, hills, and river beds to such a degree that there seems little hope of eliminating these centers of pestilence. The spread of gorse, and the extension of its former range by manuka (and similar bush types), has steadily increased the territory of safe rabbit refuge.

The continued existence of rabbits in large numbers is sufficiently evident from the figures of annual exports of rabbit skins. They persist especially where the most serious soil erosion and vegetation deterioration has taken place, notably in Central Otago and Marlborough. A considerable abandonment of holdings has taken place in these areas, and a share of the blame for the abandonment must fall to the rabbit. Yet in itself, the spelling of the country from sheep grazing and the cessation of annual burning may also help to reduce the rabbit pest and allow the natural tussock cover to be rejuvenated. Ultimately the rabbit may be thanked for drawing attention to a degree of regional resource deterioration for which it is only partly responsible. To prevent the ultimate destruction of all economic utility of the high tussock country, all of the factors which are contributing to this waste will have to be attacked together.

It is difficult to distinguish definite varieties of wild rabbits. The skin colors, according to the exporters, run well over 90 per cent of the silver-grey tone which is distinctive of the European wild rabbit. A few blacks, whites, and reds, even an occasional piebald, are taken, and may bring higher prices; the origin of these variations is obscure. It is reasonable to trace most of the present rabbit population to descent from English silver-grey warren-rabbits released for sporting purposes. Other colors may represent mutations or inheritance from crossing with escaped hutch-rabbits of varied origin which have gone wild. The hare has been rather unimportant in South Island, though there have been many introductions since 1867. The chief center of the hare population seems to be South Canterbury and, at different times, a considerable number of frozen hare carcasses have been shipped to England, chiefly from Timaru. In their peak years they were exported in the following numbers: 10,744 in 1910; 11,418 in 1911; and 7,240 in 1912.[20] This trade had died down and the number of hares is thought to be decreasing.

The story of the introduction and spread of rabbits, forms one of the most disheartening chapters in the history of South Island. Heedlessly, and yet under the strong cultural compunction to taste freely of long-forbidden fruits, South Islanders scattered rabbits through their back country. Whether they will ever be free of this scourge it is impossible even to hazard a guess.

THE INTRODUCED GRAZING AND BROWSING GAME ANIMALS OF SOUTH ISLAND

Occasionally some stray sheep and cattle have joined the pigs, goats, and rabbits which live in a truly feral state throughout the more inaccessible mountain and forest country of the island. Of much greater importance than these, however, are the thousands of deer, chamois, and thar which roam the mountains of Stewart Island and the Alpine axis from Preservation Inlet to the Wairau Valley. They have altered the character of the vegetation associations profoundly by intensive and selective browsing, contributing to the acceleration of erosion and run-off and, hence, to difficulties in controlling the lower courses of the rivers on the plains. They consume a great deal of feed which could be utilized by sheep and cattle and have, at times, done considerable damage to crops. The number of sportsmen who enjoy the shooting which they provide is small, and these have never, in themselves, begun to cope with the natural increase, let alone the "capital stock," of the herds. The only other contribution of the deer to community weal is in terms of the export of a very few skins annually.

The eight areas of infestation a decade ago are indicated on the map (fig. 59) by the letters A,B,C,D,E,F,G, and H. By far the most serious contemporary menace is the Red deer (*Cervus elephas*) commonly found in areas A,B,C,F, and H. Fallow deer (*Mazama dama*) are found in small numbers toward the southwest of area C and in area G. Virginia deer (*Cervus virginianus*) are found in small numbers in region C, to the southwest of Mount Aspiring, and around the shores of H (Stewart Island). Wapiti (*Cervus canadensis*) are confined to a most inaccessible area (region D) where they are still increasing in the absence of any natural enemies, but where they appear to be none too healthy. The moose (*Alces americana*) are confined to the lower valleys of region E, and are still fewer in number. The thar, or tahr (*Capra jemlaicus* or *Hemitragus jemlaicus*), a beardless wild goat imported from the Himalayas, keeps almost entirely to the highest alpine glaciated regions around Mount Cook, just south-center of the T-C area. The farthest north that one has been shot was in the upper Rangitata Valley. The chamois (*Rupicapra*

ahc

FIG. 59. Areas in South Island infested by large exotic game animals.

tragus or *R. rupicapra*) from the highest mountains of southern Europe, the only antelope introduced, also keeps to great elevations. The thar and chamois were released simultaneously in the Mount Cook area, but the latter is now generally met with at lower elevations and very much further north than the former. Individual chamois have been shot in the Lewis Pass area at the northern tip of the T-C area shown on the map. Until 1942 no other kinds of deer, such as the sambar (*C. aristotelis*), Japanese (*C. sika*), Black-tailed, and South American, all of which have been introduced into North Island at one time or another, had been reported in South Island.

It is as difficult to estimate numbers as was the case with rabbits, wild pigs, or wild goats. Some indication can be gained, however, from the numbers killed by organized destruction parties sent out each year in the period 1932-1941 to kill the largest possible numbers of these animals, including, of course, wild goats, pigs, sheep, or cattle. The reports are difficult to analyze because individual areas were culled in different years; the personnel employed has varied in numbers and in skill, and the areas attacked offer diverse opportunities for success. Previous to the season of 1932-1933,* the figures of destruction are not very well localized. In 1929-1930 a tail bonus was paid on 16,423 deer for all of South Island. In 1930-1931, 20,870 animals were killed, including 263 on Stewart Island (F), and 8,988 in region C. In 1931-1932 the official deer-killing parties destroyed eleven thousand deer over all of South Island, almost all in region B, and, in addition, the tail bonus on 17,958 deer was paid to private hunters and unofficial parties. For succeeding years the results have been tabulated in table L.[21]

After the 1931-1932 season, the tail bonus was discontinued; it was thought that a growing market for deer skins provided sufficient stimulus to private parties. Consequently, the figures in table L are far from complete as estimates of numbers destroyed. For example, the Department of Internal Affairs, which directed the drives, estimated that over a hundred thousand deer were destroyed in the four seasons from 1930 to 1934, most of them in

---

* All the seasons in which culling occurred include parts of two years, the season extending through the summer from October to May. Some of the figures given for one season will, however, refer to deer killed in the previous season, as the fiscal year ends on March 31, and many deer are shot after this date in most deer-drives.

South Island. Large but indeterminate numbers have been killed, in addition to those listed in the table, in succeeding years. For example, though the total number of animals destroyed in the three seasons from 1938 to 1941 by the Department's men, was under ninety thousand, the most authoritative estimates obtainable from official and private sources suggested that at least another fifty thousand, perhaps as many as a hundred thousand, were killed in that year.

TABLE L

ANIMALS DESTROYED BY OFFICIAL DEER-CULLING PARTIES OF THE DEPARTMENT OF INTERNAL AFFAIRS

| | Red Deer | | | Wapiti | Red Deer | | Tahr | Chamois |
SEASON	A *	B	C	D	F	H		T-C
1932-33	...	...	6,357a	...	...	...	...	...
1933-34	...	4,009	4,891b	...	...	...	...	...
1934-35	...	1,064	1,317	6	4,815	...	...	...
1935-36	...	896	18,249	...	...	...	...	6
1936-37	...	26,424c	....	...	...	...	2,765	2,875
1937-38	...	1,159	...	101d	8,299	406e	...	96
1938-39	...	...	18,065	59	2,268c	356e	906	1,497
1939-40	3,454	20,813	6,701	...	...	399e	63	892
1940-41	941c	8,233	11,825	...	3,306	426	195	403

a Over five thousand of these killed in South Westland.
b Includes a few chamois.
c Includes a few deer from region C.
d Includes one Red deer.
e Includes a few Virginia deer.

* Letters refer to regions so designated on the map (fig. 59).

Officials believe that deer are now being destroyed at a rate which exceeds their natural increase in the periodic visits of cullers to the different areas. From a careful examination of the above figures, and an analysis of notes of conversations with deer-cullers and regular residents of deer-infested areas, a very conservative estimate of the numbers of animals in the different areas in 1942 is shown in table LI. This gives a minimum total, excluding goats, of just under a hundred thousand animals,* 90 per cent

* An estimate of three hundred thousand deer for all of New Zealand in 1922, with most of them on South Island, was made by A. N. Perham of the Forestry Department in a lengthy report (*Appendix to Journals, House of Representatives, 1922, paper C-3A*). He was making such an ardent plea for action against the deer menace as he then saw it (and which he discussed with many examples and photographs), and he had so little evidence of total numbers on which to go, that his estimates must be treated with great reserve. Certainly, had they been correct, and did we accept the 25 per cent average annual increase in numbers which he hypothesized, we should have expected that many more deer would have been accounted for in the drives of the 1931-1941 decade.

or more of which are almost certainly Red deer. As this is the first "census" attempted on any basis beyond mere guesswork, it will meet with sharp disagreement in many quarters; few, however, will consider the numbers to be too high. If these hundred thousand large animals are added to fifty thousand wild goats, upwards of ten thousand wild pigs, together with a few wallabies, wild cattle, and wild sheep, we must visualize a great army of nibblers, browsers, and tramplers in the mountains and forests of the island.

TABLE LI

ESTIMATED NUMBER OF DEER IN SOUTH ISLAND, 1942

Region	Number	Kind of Animal
A	7,500	Red deer
B	35,000	Red deer °
C	35,000	Chiefly Red deer
D	500	Wapiti
E	100(?)	Moose
F	12,000	Red deer
G	750	Fallow deer
H	2,000	Red and Virginia deer
T-C	5,000	Thar and chamois

° Plus a large number of wild goats, perhaps as many as the deer.

The strong demand for the establishment of game animals in New Zealand by all social classes among the settlers resulted, as has been indicated, in the formation of very active acclimatization societies. Importations were continued up until just before World War I by the government, which hoped to attract tourists to the Southern Alps by creating on their slopes and in their valleys one of the great game regions of the world. Without imputing to the men responsible a nearly impossible prescience, we cannot blame them simply because of the sorry event of their activities. But because the result has been a considerable deterioration of the area, we must try to understand the manner of the invasion and penetration.

At least three importations of Red deer were made in the fifties: Felix Wakefield landed a stag at Nelson in 1851, another stag was liberated near Nelson in 1854,° and the Deans brought a

° Thomson [22] gives these examples, as well as any later ones not otherwise credited. Attributing elementary common sense to the importers, we may assume the prior or contemporaneous release of some hinds. That this is not an absolutely tight inference, however, may be gathered from the story that in one shipment of English birds the males were released in one body some hundred or two miles

fawn to Riccarton in 1853.[23] If these were the only importations they would not have constituted a very prolific foundation for the present herds. However, in 1861 Lord Petre sent a stag and two hinds from his park in Essex to Nelson,[24] and most of the vast herds of region A are thought to be descended from these three, although some of these were established in the Lillburn valley, region C, in 1900.

The Otago Acclimatisation Society introduced fifteen Red deer to Otago in 1871. The *Otago Daily Times* carried an item in the issue of January 30, 1871, reporting the arrival of six Red and two Axis deer at Dunedin. Whether these were part of the same consignment, is a question. The fifteen deer were, however, established in two lots near Palmerston, on the lower Shag River, and east of Lake Hawea in the Lindis Pass area. The former group spread over the Horse Range for a time, but, perhaps being too accessible to hunters, it ultimately dwindled there to a very few individuals. The Lake Hawea herd, descended from Red deer imported from Scotland, increased more rapidly than did those in Nelson, and became the ancestors of most of the present deer in region C. The Tourist Department later released English Red deer near Lake Wakatipu in 1903 and at Dusky Sound in 1909. The first Red deer on Stewart Island were released at Paterson Inlet in 1901. Canterbury, which received only an occasional straggler from the principal areas of Nelson and west-central Otago, finally, through its acclimatization society, received nine Red deer which were released in the Rakaia Gorge. In 1901, the Southland Acclimatisation Society freed three stags and ten hinds, imported from Victoria, at Lake Manapouri west of the Waiau, strengthening the introductions of the previous year from Nelson to Lillburn. Besides the three deer landed at Dusky in 1909, the only animals released on the west coast appear to have been seven or eight fawns from Victoria, which were liberated at Mount Tuhua in Westland in 1903.

There were thus enough importations of Red deer, of which we have record, to account for the present herds; there may have been many others. The other species were not landed in such numbers, nor did they flourish as well. The first Fallow deer were landed in Nelson from England in 1864, but their ultimate fate is

from the area of liberation of the females on the assumption that the sexes were of different species. For this tale there is no documentary record, but it is firmly entrenched in the developing folklore of the island.

unknown. Between 1867 and 1871 fifteen animals were released on the Blue Mountains near Tapanui, and from these are descended the present considerable herd of Fallow deer in that area. Some imported by the Canterbury Society to the Culverden Estate in 1871 appear to have died out.

Seven Axis deer were introduced to Goodwood in Otago in 1867, but all seem to have been killed by the settlers because of the damage they did. Doubtless the same fate overtook the two which the *Otago Times* reported in 1871, for none have been killed or even seen in several decades. The Wapiti (Elk), a present from Theodore Roosevelt, were first released in George Sound, to the south of Milford Sound, in 1905. The few hundred remaining have spread to Bligh Sound, Caswell Sound, and even to Lake Te Anau. Occasional animals found east of Te Anau are presumed to have swum the lake. The moose have done rather poorly, possibly because of the absence of a cold winter and of suitable food. There have been no reports of descendants of the four animals released near Hokitika in 1901, but recent deer-stalking parties have found ample evidence in droppings of descendants of the ten released at Dusky ten years later. There is no reliable evidence, however, that a moose has ever actually been seen since the animals were first released.

Six Tahr were released near the Hermitage, Mount Cook, in 1904; in 1913, three more were liberated near the Franz Joseph Glacier. Though Julius Von Haast agitated for the release of chamois in the eighties, it was not until 1907 that eight animals, a gift of the Emperor of Austria, were liberated on Mount Cook. In 1913 two more were released in the same area.

The habits of different species of invading deer have been discussed by Hardcastle.[25] He claimed that in New Zealand the hinds * calve at two years, being mature enough to take a stag at eighteen months, whereas in Europe they rarely calved until nearly three years of age, taking a stag for the first time at twenty-eight months. These observations, if true, suggest an added reason for the remarkable expansion in numbers of the herds. The lack of natural enemies undoubtedly contributed greatly to

---

* By tradition the term "stag" and "hind" are reserved for Red Deer; the designation "buck" and "doe," originally applied to the male and female of Fallow Deer, have been borrowed for a wide variety of other species and are also used for antelope and even rabbits. For animals heavier than deer, such as wapiti, moose, and bison, the use of "bull" and "cow" is more common.

the rapid increase in numbers, though this may also have caused a decline in the quality of the deer. Other hints as to the habits of the animals may be gathered from the hunters and deer cullers. These reports inform us that the Red Deer are more or less nocturnal in habit: they feed in the late afternoon, night, and early morning, and take a siesta in the middle of the day. Their diet, reconstructed from an analysis of stomach contents, consists of grass, bushes, young tree bark, shoots, and leaves; when they are overcrowded, as sometimes happens in a particular mountain valley, they may become as nearly omnivorous, vegetatively speaking, as the goats. By some perverse mischievousness they often tear up and off, or otherwise destroy, much more than they consume. Perham [26] estimated that a single deer consumes as much as three sheep; four, as much as three head of cattle.* Of course a deer may depend for most of its fodder upon items which would be largely ignored by sheep or cattle.

Generally the deer tend to move to the high tops and the associated alpine meadows and herb fields in the late summer and autumn. They enter the bush again as the snows descend in early winter, and may work through it and out into the lower border of the forest by late winter or early spring, when their threat to cultivation on the isolated flats of the high country becomes most acute. In the summer they gradually climb the slopes again until autumn brings them out of the upper fringe of the forest. This annual routine seems to be followed by the deer of regions C, F, and G at least. In the south of region B, however, in the Canterbury high country, the relative absence of forests results in a few deer living in the tussock areas the year round. They will seek daytime shelter in brush-filled gullies, and tend to concentrate on the warmer faces in winter. Generally, in all areas, the deer seem to stay closely attached to certain herd nuclei, and each herd seems to have a favored home grounds until overcrowding forces the departure of small groups to form new colonies. This is taken advantage of by the killing parties which concentrate their efforts on the "home areas."

The Fallow Deer are much more difficult to hunt; it is fortunate that they do not seem as well suited to the environment, or at least so their relatively low rate of increase as compared

---

* The carefully calculated ratio of seven sheep to one cattle beast was not worked out until somewhat later; and it may not be true in the forests or on the forest margin. Perham's estimates in general are, however, dubious.

with Red deer would indicate. They rarely appear on the open tops, keeping to the deep bush where they are not easy to find, though they become more frequent visitors to the flats in winter, and hence, in their limited area, are more destructive to agriculture. It is not uncommon in some parts to see a rabbit fence extended upward (with much larger mesh wire, or even cord netting) by means of long poles, to prevent the agile deer from leaping in and out of such cultivated patches. The Wapiti, because of their greater size, do greater per capita, per acre, damage to the heavy bush in which they prefer to spend most of their time. Fortunately their present habitat is isolated fairly well from agricultural or pastoral lands; moreover, it seems too wet for them * and the carcasses examined after shooting show evidences of respiratory diseases. The moose, though very little is known of them, appear to keep to quite low elevations, and there is no evidence that they have succeeded in crossing the Fiordland watershed at any point.

The chief damage attributed to the deer is that of the profound alteration which is occurring in the character of the forests, especially toward their higher borders. Much of this damage is not immediately apparent, because the upper tiers of the forest have remained largely unharmed. But the deer are preventing the growth of seedlings, as they clear away, by browsing or trampling, the lowest tier, and the age distribution among the members of the constituent species of the forest is becoming more and more heavily weighted toward late maturity. The continued activity of the herds, even in their present numbers, and kept well in check as they are, must lead eventually to important changes in the present associations. Not only do they regularly attack *Nothofagus* seedlings when other food is low, which is perhaps the greatest damage they effect, but they also regularly eat such individuals as broadleaf (*Griselmia* species), the native gums (*Panax* species), ribbonwood (*Gaya lyallii; Coprosma* species), the pepper tree (*Drimys colorata*), Tutu (*Coriaria* species), and many others, depending upon how hungry they are. As the forest floor is trampled and cleaned out, and this seedling nursery as well as the seedlings themselves destroyed, the utility of the

* Parts of the area in which they live experience a precipitation of well over two hundred inches a year, and in this as in its temperature regime, the climate shows little similarity to the hearthland of the Wapiti (that is, the American Elk) in North America.

forests as protectors of the water-shed and reservoirs for run-off must be greatly diminished.

Among additional disturbing evidence from the deer-culling parties is the fact that, with exhaustion of more and more palatable species, the deer are, each year, attacking species of plants not previously touched. And to all the trampling, eating, and careless tearing of the vegetation must be added the serious effects of antler rubbing. Some of the worst-mutilated areas are in South Westland and around Lake Manapouri where, over stretches of hundreds of acres, only adult trees remain, while the forest floor in some of the wintering areas is trampled like a stockyard.

Above the tree-line the damage is not so discernible and probably not so serious, but the mountaineering enthusiasts who have given us reports on these areas suggest that shingle slides may be increasing in area, and that the herb fields are decreasing in size and variety of plant population. Occasionally, where deer may have been caught in a sheltered hollow above the tree-line and been forced to winter hemmed in by snow drifts, very thorough destruction is reported. At these elevations in the T-C zone, or further north in region B where wild goats are also active, it cannot be said categorically which animal does which specific damage; some better estimates might be made by careful examination of droppings, but this does not appear to have been done.

The attack of deer on high-country agricultural flats has been mentioned, and it is perhaps less serious today than it once was. A more threatening activity of the deer, in the West Southland pioneering area, is trampling and grazing in areas where grasses have been freshly sown on new bush-burn. The first attempt is the only real hope of getting the grass to take; if it fails, the bush quickly reverts to useless second growth until a second burn can be made, often many years later.

Continuous agitation concerning the deer menace began as early as 1912, but did not result in legislative reaction until the passage of *The Animals Protection and Game Act* in the 1921-1922 session. The methods of dealing with the menace have varied widely. At first, protected seasons were removed from one after another of the species, and bounties on tails began to be paid. In 1929, the State Forest Service, the local acclimatization societies, and the officers in the National Parks were authorized to destroy deer, and attempts to find a larger market for deer skins were made. It was not, however, until after a conference of interested private parties was held with government representatives in Christchurch in 1931 that all protection was removed from deer, chamois, and tahr, and that the payment of the tail bonus was extended to all parts of South Island. Just previously it was realized that sporadic shooting parties might be increasing the problem by scattering the deer, and organized deer hunts, using the combing or drive methods, were employed. By the time of the outbreak of World War II in 1939 a very efficient permanent organization had been established and many huts built and tracks cut in the chief deer regions. After 1939, however, the bulk of the experienced personnel was siphoned off to the armed forces, and a new start has only recently been made.

IV

THE INVADING PLANTS

CHAPTER X

THE PLACE OF PLANT HUSBANDRY

The landscape of South Island is liberally sprinkled with plants of wide variety, which have been introduced since Cook's first visit in 1770. Many plants were introduced intentionally, either as fundamental elements of the agricultural or pastoral complexes or for non-utilitarian motives of sentiment and nostalgia. Not a few were fortuitous invaders, and many of these have become truly noxious weeds, although others, imported by design, have also become nuisances in the new land. An introductory glance at the contemporary scene will underline the importance of a discussion of the origins and spread of the new plants.

In emphasizing the dominant position of sheep husbandry in the island, some indication was given of the small proportion of the total land area devoted to exotic plants in the early nineteen-forties. Table LII [1] shows the small part of the *total land,* and the larger but still relatively small portion of the *occupied land,* which may be termed *improved land,* or land which is chiefly arable. Table LIII [1] shows the percentage of this improved land devoted to each of five groups of exotic plants, and that the major portion of the area of improved land is devoted to grasses, clovers, and exotic trees.

The degree of mixing of different types of land use on individual farms makes it impossible to distinguish clearly between agricultural and pastoral areas. A number of maps of types of farming regions were attempted, and each proved to be as misleading in one respect as its fellows were in others. It is true that there is no difficulty in classifying certain extreme types, such as the purely wool farm in the high, rough mountain country, or the purely dairy farm (not common in South Island) on heavy, wet coastal areas. There are, too, some farms where virtually all of the cash income is obtained from the sale of fruits, tobacco, or other cash crops. The difficulty is that the extremes are, again with the exception of the mountain wool farms, characteristic of no considerable continuous areas and of no very large number of farms. The gradation from one type of farm to another is rarely sharp and frequently all but imperceptible. A number of specific farms on which cattle or sheep figure more or less prominently are described in the appendix (pp. 389-95), and the wide range of economic enterprise, which is so typical of South Island's farms, is evident among them. The Census officials and the officers of the Department of Agriculture have made many attempts at classification. For example, in the schedule of the 1926 census, farms were classified as "agricultural," "sheep," "dairying," "mixed," "fruit," and "market gardens." Among the several dozen classified farms in all parts of the island which were selected at random and visited during the preparation of this study, not more than five or six were found which fitted neatly into one pigeon-hole or another. More frequently an individual farmer in the course of a year might run through three or four or even the full gamut of all six occupations on his own farm.

TABLE LII

RELATIONSHIP OF IMPROVED LAND TO TOTAL AND OCCUPIED AREAS (1941)

Land District	Per cent of total area	Per cent of occupied area
Marlborough	15%	18%
Nelson	8	29
Westland	4	15
Canterbury	28	34
Otago	17	20
Southland	20	43

Since there appears to be no statistical basis upon which any more refined classification, with proportionate weighting, can be based, an attempt has been made to describe five farming types which are believed to come at nodal or terminal points of the range. The following classification was considered as useful as any available by a number of competent agricultural observers to whom it was presented.

1. *Horticultural type* (farms range from five to a hundred acres): This exemplifies an intensive form of plant husbandry, usually on the best land, but often existing close to large cities or in spots of particular climatic advantage with little regard to special qualities of soil. Besides those on the urban fringes, farms approximating this extreme occur most frequently on the seaward edge of Nelson's Waimea plain, in the lower Wairau-Awatere valleys, in coastal South Canterbury, and on some of the irrigable terraces of Central Otago and the middle Waitaki valley. Nelson also has tobacco and hops, and South Canterbury's examples are perhaps chiefly potato farms, but trucking and orcharding occur throughout.

2. *Dairying type* (representative farm: about seventy-five acres): This is also an intensive type of husbandry, confining itself in general to good land, as does the first. Some rough, non-arable land is included, but the dairying areas are generally on flats and, with the exception of the Murchison and Inangahua basins, at fairly low elevations. In its relatively "pure" form, it occupies no very continuous areas, to the exclusion of gradation types, except on the west coast. The growth of hay and roots for additional feed, and, more recently, of increasing quantities of grain to supplement whey and buttermilk as pig feed, leads this type by gradual transition into one or another of the mixed farming types. Even more common perhaps is the joint production of fat lambs and butterfat.

3. *Intensive mixed farming type:* Within very broad and indeterminate limits, here would fall most of the farms involved in the production of fat lambs and of the field cash crops, principally potatoes, wheat, and grass seeds. Here, too, is found the most intensive cultivation of *Brassicas* and a concern for high-production pastures of English grasses which rivals that of type 2. Two special "nodes" within the range of this group might perhaps be designated as sub-types: (a) cash crop, and (b) fat-lamb production.

(a) *Cash crop* (farm area extremely variable): About one-third of each farm is in grass, which is used to pasture sheep, lambs, cattle, pigs, and/or horses. Some of the fields may be cut for hay, others may be allowed to ripen for threshing the grass seed. The rest of the farm would include, in longer or shorter rotations with grass, a wide variety of roots or grains, with emphasis placed on wheat, peas, potatoes, or some such crop for the off-the-farm sale. It is a common type in the lower Wairau-Awatere plain, in the medium-to-heavy lands of the Canterbury plain, in the alternating plains and downs of the South Canterbury-Hakataramea-North Otago area, and in the Taieri-Toko-mairiro basins.

(b) *Fat-lamb production* (representative farm: a hundred and seventy-five acres): About two-thirds of each farm is in grass and *Brassicas* (members of the cabbage-turnip family) for supplemental feeding. Interspersed with cash-crop farms throughout most of the moderately heavy land of the island, it becomes the almost exclusive representative of the general intensive mixed-farming type in Southland, where climatic factors limit the production of cash grain crops. It need hardly be re-emphasized, however, that a farmer who obtains almost his total income from the sale of fat lambs and wool, or from one (or even a small group of) cash crops is a rarity in this group.

4. *The store-sheep type* (representative farm: four hundred acres): Farms of this type are described in the appendix, pp. 389-95. It may be well to emphasize here that many of these, especially on the upper plains of Canterbury, grow considerable quantities of roots and grains and should in reality be called less intensive mixed farms.

5. *The high-country wool type* (farms from a thousand acres up; farms ten thousand acres and over not uncommon): This type is also described in the appendix, pp. 389-95. Even these specialized enterprises usually have some arable for winter feeding, as well as a domestic kitchen garden.

We are interested here, however, primarily in *kinds* of production from a wide variety of types of farms, rather than from special categories of farms which are to any real degree mutually exclusive in their products.

TABLE LIII

PROPORTIONS OF AREA OF IMPROVED LAND (BY LAND DISTRICTS), DEVOTED TO DIFFERENT GROUPS OF EXOTIC PLANTS (1941)

	M	N	W	C	O	S
Grasses, clovers, and lucerne.....	89%	85%	96%	73%	84%	86%
Green fodder and roots, excluding grains and pulse fed off	2	2	1	9	8	9
Exotic conifers and broadleafs	1	9	2	2	1	—
Orchards, hop-fields, market gardens, fallow, land in farmyards, etc.	1	2	1	1	1	1
Grain and pulse, including crops fed off	7	2	—	15	6	4

M—Marlborough; N—Nelson; W—Westland; C—Canterbury; O—Otago; S—Southland.

Table LIV [2] indicates the statistical position of agriculture in the total value of production for the whole Dominion.

THE PLACE OF PLANT HUSBANDRY

289

TABLE LIV

PROPORTIONATE VALUE OF PRODUCTION *

	1900-01	1910-11	1920-21	1930-31	1939-40
Agricultural	12.1%	7.5%	8.9%	9.1%	7.1%
Pastoral	36.1	38.5	30.3	25.6	26.9
Dairying, poultry and bees	10.6	13.8	26.3	22.7	25.1
Mining	8.6	8.6	3.1	3.7	3.5
Fisheries	0.3	0.3	0.4	0.5	0.4
Forestry	6.0	5.2	4.6	3.0	3.1
Factories	16.0	15.2	18.7	23.9	23.4
Building and miscellaneous	10.3	10.9	7.7	11.5	10.5
Total	100.0%	100.0%	100.0%	100.0%	100.0%
Total value in millions of New Zealand pounds	33.9	53.4	99.5	97.2	142.8

* These figures are for all New Zealand. There is nowhere a division of the figures for the two islands.

The value of production given for "agricultural," "pastoral," and "dairying, poultry, and bees" includes all subsequent processing. The value of agricultural production as defined by the statisticians has not been greater than 10 per cent of that of total production in the last thirty-five years, and had declined in 1942 to approximately 7 per cent of the whole. If the superstructure of additional processing and the expenses of the farmer are both neglected, the Dominion statistician offers another indication of the relative importance of agriculture, this time in terms of gross farming income (table LV).[3] The total value of agricultural production (table LV) includes an estimate of that part which was not sold but used again in production, and therefore classified in one of the other categories, so that the figures as given are fairly comparable. Only one more example need be cited in evidence of the relative position of agriculture in New Zealand farming: while 70 to 80 per cent of the remainder of farm production is exported, only 10 to 12 per cent of that attributed to agricultural production leaves the country.[4] While this results in the relative insignificance of the direct contributions of agricultural production to the country's international trade, agriculture thereby assumes a somewhat larger relative importance to the internal economy.

Agriculture, most narrowly construed, is thus relatively unimportant areally and as a source of income to New Zealand farming as a whole. It is certainly more important in South Island farming, though to exactly what degree is not clear. Perhaps 15 to 20 per cent of the total value of production, and between a quarter and a third of gross farming income on South Island farms, could be called agricultural in origin. It must not be forgotten, however, that most of the production of animal products is from improved pastures, and that these pastures in South Island are most largely made by plowing and the sowing of English grasses. Few of the so-called "permanent" pastures remain down for more than ten years, most for no more than five or six years, and a goodly proportion of the grasses are in two- or three-year temporary leys. In this sense the rôle of exotic plants in the intensive production of pastoral and dairy products is an indispensable one, and the introduction and spread of the English grasses of little less importance than that of the animals which they nourish. Indeed the introduction of the grasses and clovers everywhere followed, or went hand in hand with, the cultivation of grains and roots.

TABLE LV

GROSS FARMING INCOME

Type of production	Income (in millions of £ N. Z).	
	1930-31	1939-40
Agricultural	£ 7.3 (11.4%)	£ 9.4 (12.8%)
Pastoral	£31.4 (48.9%)	£32.3 (43.9%)
Dairy, poultry and bees	£25.5 (39.7%)	£31.9 (43.3%)
Total	£64.2 (100%)	£73.6 (100%)

Relief and soils are the major environmental factors which may turn land use toward arable in South Island. Thus land is plowed (more or less frequently) for grasslands, feed crops, or cash crops, on most of the plains and downs country (fig. 60). Exceptions are principally due to climatic factors, as in the rain-shadow regions of the intermont basins east of the Alps, where insufficient irrigation water is available, and in the cool, wet climate of much of the Southland plain, which tends to make for lessened production of grain and longer periods for the grass leys. High rainfall severely limits arable on the discontinuous and narrow alluvial terraces of Westland or on the inconsiderable areas of level land adjoining them. Where breaking has been attempted there, the poor *pakihi* soils and militant second growth, especially of the noxious, ubiquitous blackberry, have proved severe limiting handicaps. Elsewhere, the chief natural influence

Fig. 60. A field of peas in Marlborough (grown for seed export to Great Britain) which illustrates how effectively even low hills cut off the area which can be plowed.

on the density of plowed land is that of relative roughness of surface. Nelson, for example, has very little land suitable for the plow; Canterbury, in contrast, on its great stretch of gravelly plains, has much. In Marlborough, Otago, and Southland the arable is always on country of easy relief.

Previous to 1840, potatoes were the only crop of any significance. Within twenty years of the beginning of organized settlement, wheat had become of much greater importance, and by 1880 it was the supreme crop of the south and was produced in a quantity comparable to that of most of the succeeding sixty years. As settlement became more dense and the markets for mutton and butterfat overseas were opened through use of new technical inventions, the *Brassicas* and a wide variety of exotic grasses and other herbage plants were sown on more and more land. Had circumstances of soil and climate similar to those in much of North Island obtained, the sowing of the grasses might have meant the virtual disappearance of the plow. In South Island, however, on much of the land where agricultural farming had been established, the soils were much more porous, and the rainfall lower and less reliable; as a result, the pastures tended to run out fairly quickly. Moreover, the cooler winter demanded more supplementary feeding as pasture growth was severely checked, and this need was met in large part by the growing of quantities of the *Brassicas*. The growth of wheat, roots, and green feed fitted well into the regime of rotational grassland farming with its constant renewal of pastures, which was established as the dominant pattern for South Island's mixed agricultural and pastoral farming fifty years ago, and which is essentially the dominant pattern today. It is true that new herbage strains and varieties, and new techniques such as irrigation in areas of twenty-five to forty inches of rainfall, are being tried to extend the area and life of the "permanent" pastures. It is also difficult to extrapolate the trend of the past half-century for another fifty years with any confidence. But since the climatic regime virtually assures the necessity for supplementary feed in winter over most of South Island, we may expect to have a continuance of the same general type of farming practice for many years to come. This is especially true if South Island's emphasis on the production of wool and fat lambs continues. A more purely dairying economy, such as that of North Island's lower country, is better suited to meet an off-season slack in pasture growth without supplementary feed, because many cows can be dried off at that time. For many other reasons already discussed, we may not expect South Island to move much further in relative emphasis on dairying.

CHAPTER XI

POTATOES

Potatoes were introduced to the island no later than 1773, when Tannen, master of the *Adventure,* planted them at Motuara on Queen Charlotte Sound. Cook remarked in his journal for May 29, 1773, that "the turnips, carrots and parsnips . . . together with the potatoes, will be of more use to them than all the other articles we had planted. It was easy to give them an idea of these roots by comparing them with such they knew [that is the kumara or sweet potato]." [1] On the same visit to Cook Strait, Cook had "set some men to work to make a garden on Long Island, which I planted with garden seeds, roots, etc." [2] Upon the expedition's return to the Sound more than a year later, Cook in his journal for October 22, 1774, described the gardens on Motuara as "almost in a state of nature, having been wholly neglected by the inhabitants. Nevertheless, many articles were in a flourishing condition, and showed how well they liked the soil in which they were planted." [3] Forster [4] is authority for the statement that potatoes were planted at five different places on the Sound and that the Maori were carefully instructed in their husbandry. On the third expedition, Cook's journal for May 15, 1777,[5] reported the gardens in a bad state, but that the potatoes still survived.

This writer has seen documentary evidence of potatoes in the area for the next forty-three years. Bellinghausen's Russian expedition on the *Mirny* and the *Wostok* touched at Queen Charlotte Sound in 1820. Wild cabbages, thought to have spread from the gardens established by the Cook expeditions, were gathered; and potatoes were in use, though they were so scarce and precious that they could not be bought.[6]

In the eighteen-thirties, however, potatoes had become much more plentiful. Dieffenbach [7] has several references to potatoes in use among the Maori and the Pakeha-Maori (the "squaw-men" of early New Zealand) who lived with the natives during the off-season for whaling, that is, the summer. Dieffenbach [8] states that "provisions were plentiful, and we were enabled to lay in a large stock of potatoes and pigs at a very moderate price." Jerningham Wakefield, who was with Dieffenbach on the *Tory's* visit in 1839, confirmed the abundance of potatoes in several references.[9] In early reports there is, of course, a certain amount of confusion inevitable in the use of the word "potato" as a generic term. It may often have included as well that much earlier exotic, the Maori kumara or common sweet potato (*Ipomea batatas*). Yet we can make some reasonable assumptions. The much easier culture, and the much greater food production per acre of the white potato (*Solanum tuberosum*), as well as its greatly superior storage qualities, would certainly have tended to cause it to displace the kumara as a basic food crop in all parts of the island. Even mild and sunny Nelson had been much too cool for optimum conditions of growth of the kumara.

McNab has abundant evidence [10] that long before the *Mirny's* visit to Queen Charlotte Sound the cultivation of the potato had become widespread on the southern shores. In the *Sydney Gazette* for September 4, 1813, Williams, who had visited the region of the Bluff and the lower Oreti, reported that the natives had "a field of considerably more than a hundred acres." That the natives were making the fullest use of the potato was indicated by a description of "one well-cultivated bed, filled with rising crops of various ages, some of which were ready for digging while others had been but newly planted." One can readily imagine the ease with which these and other potato plots from Preservation Inlet to Banks Peninsula, subsequently reported, may have been initiated by seed supplied from provisions of the dozens of ships visiting the coast. Alternatively, or additionally, Maori from North Island, coming south for the whaling and sealing or on war parties, may well have introduced the plant and its culture if the first attempts made by Cook did prove abortive. The potato had been well established in North Island in competition with kumara shortly after the turn of the century. A decision among alternative possibilities of origin need not be attempted here. What is important is that by the eighteen-thirties potatoes were being widely grown from Blind Bay [11] to Foveaux Strait, and indeed a surplus for export to New South Wales was available. The abundance of local supplies of such a basic food was of great importance to the prosperity of the whaling stations.

The potato was, of course, cultivated by the earliest Europeans as well as by the Maori. The first truly agricultural settler in South Island seems to have been one Thomas who, in 1838, started "Cherry Farm" at Matanaka, two miles up the Waikouaiti river from its source. He had made slow progress in cultivation with his grub-hooks and spades when Jones bought his claim to the land with other "purchases" prior to that of the agricultural settlement he initiated at Waikouaiti in 1840. By 1844 there were about one hundred Europeans farming there, and at that time it was by far the most progressive settlement in South Island.*

The information about the southern shores in the early forties discussed above included the reports of Captain Mein Smith, who made his trip in 1842; of Shortland's trip of 1843-1844; of Tuckett, Monro, and Selwyn, all of whom visited the area in 1844. Tuckett referred to considerable cultivation by the European whalers at Moeraki, of which potato culture was almost certainly the central feature. Shortland reported that Mr. Hughes of Onekakara grew plenty of potatoes along with his other crops. South of Waikouaiti the next settlement described by the visitors was at Otago Heads, where some twenty Europeans, besides many Maori, lived, mostly with enclosures of gardens around their huts. Tuckett rhapsodized over their potatoes: "I have not seen elsewhere in New Zealand such fine potatoes; supposing that I saw only a picked sample, they excelled all other picked samples." [13] Shortland describes how the Maori met one of the greatest threats to successful potato production—the depredations of that other, equally ubiquitous exotic, the pig. [14] After the potatoes were sown, the pigs were taken well into the interior and left to range at will until the potatoes were

---

* The colony which Jones then established was a pioneering contemporary of that miserable group established by the Nanto-Bordelaise Cie. at Akaroa. Jones' original farmers were thirty-two Welsh folk from New South Wales, according to his records, but these did not remain and when reports came in 1842, 1843 and 1844 of the flourishing condition of the Waikouaiti farmlands (Smith, Shortland, Tuckett, Monro, Selwyn, etc.), the personnel was largely of new blood drawn from New South Wales whose names strongly suggest Irish origins. [12]

dug, when as many pigs as were required were caught and brought back. Apart from the porcine menace, general conditions, notably the cool, wet climate, were favorable to potatoes on the southern shores, and visitors found them to be the standard "crop" in all the auxiliary cultivations of the whaling stations.

At Banks Peninsula, Hay describes early Maori potato culture as if it might have preceded his own father's settlement at Pigeon Bay in 1843.[15] We have no direct evidence of pre-1840 cultivation of the tubers in this area however, though they proved an invaluable subsistence crop to the early French settlers at Akaroa. Arriving too late in 1840 to prepare land for wheat, Captain Lavaud reported the progress of the first six weeks on October 15. After a good deal of trouble in removing ferns and deep roots, the settlers sowed potatoes.[16] Later de Belligny applied his training obtained at the *Jardin des Plantes* in Paris and established French Farm across the bay from Akaroa, where he could experiment with potatoes and other vegetables. In 1841 Lavaud reported that each settler was cultivating a fifth of the two and one-half acres that had been on the average allotted, and that potatoes, with cabbages, broad-beans, and salad plants, had survived the raw and violent southwest winds.[17] In 1842 Captain Mein Smith, surveyor-general of the New Zealand Company, reported that the settlers seemed to be chiefly dependent on their vegetable gardens, which he described as doing well.[18] De Belligny had not, and did not, however, succeed in making much headway with vines, fruits, and tobacco—specialty crops which, if successful, might have provided an export surplus and have raised the economy of the little settlement above the level of a hand-to-mouth subsistence.*

On the northern shores of the island, potatoes and a variety of other vegetables had long been in cultivation; it is not impossible that the Maori had continued their husbandry without interruption from the time of Cook's first plantings. We have seen that potatoes were plentiful in the Port Underwood whaling

---

* That many vines and fruit trees eventually were established is evident from those remaining today in the gardens of early homesteads, a number of examples of which were seen by this writer around the Akaroa area. Horticulture was, however, faced with competition from dairying, sheep and cattle raising, and the harvesting of cocksfoot on the peninsula; an orchard industry which the marine climate and the combination of volcanic and loessal soils might well have nurtured never took root. The French settlers either adopted the patterns of land use established by later comers, or left.

haven when the New Zealand Company's *Tory* visited the area in 1839. Yet even the well-established potato had to be imported into Nelson in 1842 to help the settlers over the first winter on Blind Bay.[19] The cultivation of the potato did, however, provide a very useful first crop on the land dearly won for agriculture from the roots of thickly growing *Pteridium* and *Phormium* individuals. Pratt describes the early laborious spadework (literal as well as figurative) in the settlement.[20] Potatoes provided a high-yielding cash crop easily integrated with the process of preparing the land for grains or grass. A file to keep an edge on the spades was as much a part of the basic equipment of these pioneers as it ever was for axes in a lumbering community.

One of the chief difficulties was that the local seed, supplied by Maori from the Port Underwood area, seemed to have deteriorated. There is more than one hint that the Maori conducted in inverse selection for seed, eating or selling the best tubers and keeping only the smallest, which seems odd in view of their long experience with kumara-growing. New seed from England and New South Wales soon improved the yields, however. On May 30, 1844, the *Nelson Examiner* reported crops, grown from seed imported from Van Diemen's Land, which yielded one-third to two-thirds more than those from the native tubers. It is possible, of course, that the poor quality of native seed was due to unfavorable climatic conditions. Today the potato growers of South Island north of mid-Canterbury depend almost entirely on seed from South Canterbury, Otago, or Southland, a situation analagous to the concentration of North American production of seed potatoes in the Maine-New Brunswick-Prince Edward Island area. At any rate, potatoes were of basic importance to the embryo rural economy described by Fox in his report of a trip through the area southwest of Nelson township in 1844.[21]

The Deans, at Riccarton, grew enough potatoes in their early years to more than supply their own needs. They had one and a half acres in 1843-1844 and two and a half acres in 1844-1845. In 1845 they harvested thirty tons from the two and a half acres, but were able to dispose of only half of the crop.[22] Initially they experienced some difficulty with frost in the lower ground. They planted the potatoes from early August until late November, manured the ground with what animal droppings they could save, and obtained yields of seven to twenty tons per acre. They always had new potatoes by Christmas time, and new potatoes have remained a traditional Christmas delicacy in South Island. Not until the Canterbury settlers appeared in 1850 did potatoes constitute a main crop on the farm, and then only because of shrewd Caledonian eyes looking toward the probable bull market in basic foodstuffs when the new population arrived. In 1851 the Deans sold fifty tons of potatoes to the settlers in addition to supplying their own needs and storing seed for the thirty acres to be sowed in the 1851-1852 season. That particular field of potatoes represented 6 per cent of the five hundred acres in crop in the whole settlement that year. To dig the potatoes, they employed twenty men for three weeks: seventeen or eighteen Maori and two or three Europeans. The employment of casual labor for the harvesting of a big cash crop noted still earlier than this in Nelson, which was to become a standard pattern in the management of agricultural labor, was thus established very early. The Maori, however, because of their very small numbers in South Island, contributed little labor to either the agricultural or pastoral beginnings. The shortage of labor in the fifties undoubtedly did much to keep potato acreage down, since potato culture demanded a heavy supply of labor at the peak period of agricultural work. Still potatoes ranked third in acreage in Canterbury of crops listed in the *Canterbury Provincial Gazette* for July 1, 1854 (table LVI). In the first eleven months of 1855 (*see* table VI, p. 116) potato exports from Canterbury totaled 854¼ tons and were worth £6,834. This was second only to wool (£21,837 16s.) among exports that totaled £40,037 15s. 1d. during the period.

TABLE LVI

CANTERBURY CROPS (1854)

	Acres		*Acres*
Wheat	807	Barley	287
Oats	802	Gardens and Orchards	227
Potatoes	364	Maize	1
Artificial grasses	289	Other	143

Total: 2920 acres

In the earliest years at Otago, potato culture was important in preparing the cut-down and burnt-over bushland for grain. In contemporary statistics for Otago, exclusive of the Waikouaiti area, given by the *Otago Daily Times* for April 6, 1850, potatoes headed all other crops in acreage (table LVII). By the 1854-1855 season the rôle of the potato as a pioneer in helping to prepare the land for grains was much less important areally as more and more land was made available for wheat and oats. The *Otago Witness* for August 23, 1856, quoted detailed locality figures of acreages in different land use for all parts of the Otago settlement. Only in the area of the township of Dunedin were potatoes the most important crop listed. The breakdown for the settled portion of Otago Province (a narrow coastal strip of settlement from the Clutha to the Shag Rivers) is shown in table LVIII. The total area in crops was about thirty-six hundred acres, and nearly two thousand acres more were fenced though uncultivated. In exports, too, Otago potatoes were less important relatively than those from Canterbury. In 1854, of a total export from Otago valued at £8,376, wool contributed £5,893, oats £1,785, and potatoes only £270.[23] The comparative acreages in crops for the three provinces for 1856 are shown in table LIX.[24]

TABLE LVII
OTAGO CROPS (1850) °

	Acres		Acres
Potatoes	92½	Wheat	20¾
Gardens	49	Grass	19½
Oats	27¾	Barley	10¼

Total: 219¾ acres

° Exclusive of Waikouaiti area.

TABLE LVIII
OTAGO CROPS (1856)°

	Acres		Acres
Wheat	1,363	Potatoes	424
Artificial grass	1,314	Gardens	88
Fallow	997	Turnips	45
Oats	687	Barley	4

Other crops ...... 32 acres

° Settled portion only.

Having served its pioneering purpose, the potato thus dropped rapidly into the minor, but indispensable, agricultural rôle which it has played until the present time. Comparative figures for acreage of potatoes in 1890-1891 and 1940-1941 are shown in table LX.[25] Total acreage and yield have both declined considerably in the past fifty years as potatoes have disappeared as an export crop, particularly as restrictions on imports of New Zealand potatoes to Australia have been raised. With the lowest acreage in potatoes since 1892, 1940-1941 was, however, a somewhat unusual year. South Island had over twenty-five thousand acres in potatoes in a few individual years between 1900 and 1915.

TABLE LIX

Comparative Provincial Acreages in Crops (1856)

	Nelson	Canterbury	Otago
Wheat	3,832	4,028	1,930
Barley	1,176	360	21
Oats	1,334	919	805
Maize	28	2	—
Potatoes	826	654	355
Sown grass	5,042	1,384	1,718
Gardens and orchards	708	393	117
Other crops	924	267	76
Total acres cultivated	*13,870*	*8,007*	*5,022*

TABLE LX

Potato-Growing in the Different Provincial Districts in 1890-91 and Land Districts in 1940-41

	M	N	W	C	O	S	Totals
Acreage:							
1890-91	1,221	1,108	272	9,532	6,629		18,762
1940-41	186	462	16	8,739	1,376	867	11,646
Yield (tons):							
1890-91	7,914	5,265	1,431	65,158	33,860		113,628
1940-41	1,153	2,206	88	46,630	9,210	5,763	65,050
Yield per acre (tons):							
1890-91	6.5	4.8	5.3	6.8	5.1		6.1
1940-41	6.2	4.8	5.5	5.3	6.7	6.7	5.6

M = Marlborough; N = Nelson; W = Westland; C = Canterbury; O = Otago; S = Southland.

Coastal Canterbury from Rangiora County to the mouth of Waitaki River is by far the most important potato-growing area in the South Island, and indeed in all of New Zealand (table LXI [26] and fig. 61). In 1929-1930, of 23,214 acres grown in all of New Zealand, the Canterbury land district produced 14,606 acres. In 1940-1941 this area grew over 50 per cent of all of the country's potatoes. Though rather more potatoes are grown north of the Rakaia than to the south, the most distinctive area of potato

FIG. 61. Distribution of potato acreage in South Island (1940-1941).

culture is around Waimate, south of the mouth of the river. Little evidence of outside cultural influence can be seen in local practice which owes a very great deal to local initiative. Though potato culture is often of a very primitive spade-and-hoe type elsewhere, it is rather highly mechanized there, and some unique labor-saving devices for planting, digging, and sorting have originated in the area.

TABLE LXI

DISTRIBUTION OF POTATO-GROWING ACREAGES WITHIN CANTERBURY 1929-30 AND 1940-41

	1929-30 (acres)	1940-41 (acres)	1929-30 (tons per acre)
Rangiora	1,696	360	4.8
Waimari	1,503	886	5.1
Paparua	1,883	1,123	5.7
Eyre	1,099	465	5.6
Haswell	491	158	5.6
Springs	463	351	5.5
Ellesmere	1,798	859	5.7
Ashburton	912	883	5.2
Geraldine	465	353	5.6
Levels	943	429	4.8
Waimate	1,666	1,668	6.8
Other counties	1,687	1,204	4.7
Total Canterbury	14,606	8,739	5.6
Total New Zealand	23,214	16,998	

Over 70 per cent of the acreage of potatoes in New Zealand and over 80 per cent of the yield were associated (1941) with six principal varieties. Forty per cent of the area, representing 35 per cent of the yield, is planted in Auckland Short-top. The other leaders, in order of importance, were: Dakota, Arran Chief, Inverness Favorite, King Edward VII, Gamekeeper, and Northern Star.[27] Records of varieties have been kept only since 1936, and there is no certainty as to when different ones were introduced or what the areal importance of different kinds may have been in the past. The opinions of New Zealanders are simply too varied to be reconciled, and there is no useful early documentary evidence other than Hilgendorf's [28] listing of Arran Chief and Up-to-date as the chief varieties in Canterbury in the nineteen-twenties.

CHAPTER XII

WHEAT

The statistics for total acreages in the three leading grain crops for three representative periods are shown in table LXII.[1] Wheat displaced potatoes as the principal cash crop and leading supplier of dietary starch in the early fifties, and it has maintained its place without challenge until the present. This remains true despite the much greater acreage devoted to oats since the eighties. All but a few hundred acres of the wheat are threshed each year, whereas in the 1890-1891 season only some three-quarters of the oats were threshed,[2] and by 1940-1941 this proportion was reduced to one-quarter.[3] The decline in oat acreage in the past fifty-year period has been entirely in terms of oats threshed for grain. While this area decreased from 292,788 acres to 70,371 acres, the area sown to oats and used for chaff, hay, ensilage, and feeding-off increased from 93,456 acres to 216,809 acres. At present wheat is produced for the home market alone and, indeed, does not meet even this demand. The production of oats as grain declined especially with the decrease in the number and use of horses. However, the need for supplementary feed for the steadily increasing sheep and cattle population has meant that there has been, as compared with wheat, a less rapid decline in acreage devoted to oats. The barley acreage has always been small, and the bulk of it has been threshed and sold for brewing-malt purposes; increase in acreage has mainly been a reflection of increasing consumption of malt beverages manufactured in New Zealand. In

1940-1941, only 5,483 acres of barley were used for supplementary feed in all of South Island. The only other grain or pulse crop of any areal significance in South Island has been peas. The growth of these, chiefly for the United Kingdom seed market, has been a fairly recent development and was accelerated particularly during both world wars.

TABLE LXII

ACREAGES OF WHEAT, OATS, AND BARLEY BY PROVINCIAL DISTRICTS IN 1860-61 AND 1890-91, AND BY LAND DISTRICTS IN 1940-41

	M	N	W	C	O	S	Total for South Island
				1860-61			
Wheat ..	494	4,396	–	12,802	4,929	140	22,761
Oats ...	341	1,860	–	4,540	4,518	443	11,702
Barley ...	125	1,126	–	1,490	166	23	2,930
				1890-91			
Wheat ...	7,179	8,891	–	279,150	84,895		380,115
Oats	6,066	11,530	395	154,776	213,567		386,334
Barley ...	2,420	4,048	–	10,361	3,960		20,789
				1940-41			
Wheat ..	9,219	938	3	192,094	29,103	8,206	239,563
Oats	8,770	4,520	300	177,702	52,583	43,305	287,180
Barley ...	3,686	1,284	4	21,256	7,075	682	33,987

M = Marlborough; N = Nelson; W = Westland; C = Canterbury; O = Otago; S = Southland.

The grain and pulse crops of New Zealand, with the exception of the very small area in maize, have been heavily concentrated in South Island and especially in the Canterbury plains (fig. 62) since the sixties.[4] As with potatoes, there always is considerable inter-island movement of the threshed grains even though there is an over-all national deficit in production to meet the country's consumption needs. Thus, South Island has always been a grain exporter and maintains that rôle today, although the import and export figures for the country as a whole conceal this fact. For example, in 1940-1941 Canterbury alone harvested 82 per cent and Canterbury and Otago together harvested 94 per cent of the area in wheat for threshing in the whole of New Zealand. Of the total acreage in oats in New Zealand, 94 per cent was in South Island; 58 per cent of this total was in Canterbury, and 31 per cent in Otago and Southland. Of oats threshed for grain, the island accounted for 98 per cent of the country's total. Similarly, 83 per

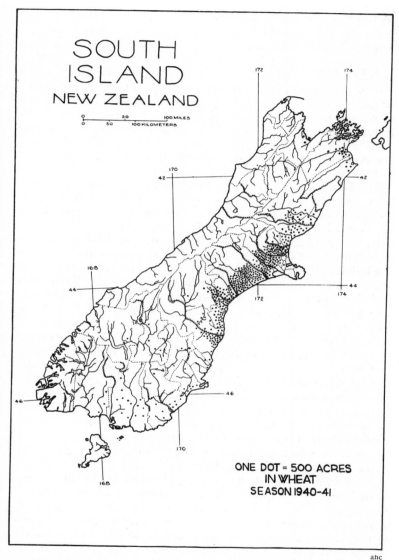

ahc

FIG. 62. Distribution of wheat acreage in South Island (1940-1941).

cent of the total barley acreage and 95 per cent of the small national area (roughly thirty-five thousand acres) in field peas were
in South Island. It has not been possible to determine the precise
proportions of South Island's grain cash crops which are exported
to North Island, but grain and grain products, along with coal
and lumber, constitute very important exports from the South
Island to the North Island. A statistical breakdown for inter-
island commodity exchanges should reveal the rank of South
Island in per capita exports of agricultural cash crops as a relatively high one. This is a circumstance which virtually all outside
observers and most local students of economic and agricultural
history rather consistently forget or ignore.

The introduction of wheat and the spread of patterns and practices associated with its production has been chosen to illustrate
one phase of the island's historical geography. Grain production
on a considerable scale for export (if only to North Island) has
been and remains a very important feature of land use in the
area. This point is stressed in order to emphasize the fact that
the following paragraphs represent not just the satisfaction of an
antiquarian's curiosity, but an attempt to understand the genesis
and development of an important feature of present land use.
The question of the advisability of continuing to produce the
largest part of home consumption needs of wheat, for example, is
in New Zealand a hotly debated one. Many of the present leading
areas in wheat production, notably the plains of Ashburton County
in Canterbury, are being supplied with irrigation water under
rapidly developing schemes of "humid-climate" irrigation. The
non-wheat-growing areas suggest that the tariff protection af-
forded wheat is, since many of the rotation wheat lands may now
be profitably converted to permanent pastures, an undue burden
for the buyers of bread and flour to carry. But whatever the future
has in store, wheat production is at present of great significance
in the pastoral-agricultural patterns of the island.

As one would expect, the immigrant eaters of wheaten bread
started to grow the grain at the very beginning of agriculture in
the organized settlements in the island. Initially the choice of
wheats to be grown must have been haphazard. English and Scottish wheats would certainly be readily available, but so would
wheats from the Australian colonies, whose origins may be traced
to many other wheat-growing areas of the world. The early literature, and a great deal of inquiry, supplies little definite informa-

tion about particular varieties. Wheat of some kind may have been left in New Zealand by de Surville as early as 1769 [5] and had come into fairly common use among the Maori in the Auckland Peninsula after Marsden established his farm at the Bay of Islands in 1814. It does not appear to have entered Maori cultivation in South Island, however, as it did in the north. If Cook planted wheat in Queen Charlotte Sound in 1773 or 1777, it seems to have disappeared without trace. Bell quite likely had wheat growing at Mana Island in the thirties, but of that we cannot be sure. The visitors to the southern shores between 1842 and 1844 did report a certain amount of "corn" (presumably wheat) growing at different stations. Tuckett specifically mentioned a "poor crop of smutty wheat" at Waikouaiti but reported it doing better to the south at Palmer's Station on the coast between the Tautuke and Tapuke Rivers and also at Aparima and Tuturau. Shortland confirmed some of these observations and mentioned that Mr. Hughes at Onekakara had several acres of wheat, a large barn, and a threshing floor, and that Hughes ground his own flour in a hand-mill. Selwyn was apparently better impressed with the Waikouaiti venture than was Tuckett; he mentions several fields of "corn," including one of fifty acres.[6]

Meanwhile the struggling group at Nelson was endeavoring to supply as much of its own bread flour as possible, and wheat found a place with potatoes, generally following them in rotation, on the little agricultural plots scattered over the lands of "flax" and fern. The fern-covered land was easier to clear but generally less fertile than that in *Phormium* and raupo, once the latter was cleared and drained. The *Nelson Examiner* for May 30, 1844, quoted yields from fern-land, in the second year of agricultural production at Nelson, as: wheat, 23 bushels; barley, 18 bushels; and oats, 15 bushels. Definite figures for the heavier land are not given, but the yields were said to be "considerably higher." Wheat production was to remain the most important purely agricultural activity on Nelson's limited arable until the turn of the century. Only in the last forty years has the rare endowment of sunshine enjoyed by the southern shores of Tasman Bay been utilized in the production of more profitable crops, such as tobacco and various fruits, which could not succeed as well elsewhere.

Canterbury was the latest starter in this agricultural race but, with such favorable natural conditions, it made much more rapid progress than the north or south. The first grain grown may have been was that on the later site of Riccarton in 1840 (*see* p. 62). Dr. Monro had not thought highly of the area for wheat; in respect to the "agricultural capabilities" of the Port Cooper plains, he comments: "the soil is a light and easily worked loam, well suited I should imagine for potatoes, oats, barley, turnips, and similar crops—hardly stiff enough for wheat." [7] There was and is considerable truth in this casual observation, but the more closed the economy, the less important the physical optima in comparison with immediate cultural demands in determining local uses of land. Such economies as those of the Deans brothers' farm between 1843 and 1849 are certainly not very open ones. The Deans had a few acres in wheat for their own needs each year, and in the 1844-1845 season they reported sixty to seventy bushels per acre from land previously used for potatoes. It is interesting that the growth of wheat and potatoes, while serving subsistence needs, seems to have figured most largely in the eyes of the Deans as a good preparation of the ground for English grasses, rather than as an end in itself. The wheat was sown in May, as a rule, and harvested in January or February—a calendar of production not dissimilar from the norm of present practice. They estimated that the plain as a whole would be little more difficult to break up than old pastures "at home," and that wheat might be sowed directly on the new breaking. [8]

The planned settlements which began in Otago in 1848 and in Canterbury in 1850, grew steadily increasing quantities of wheat both as subsistence crops and for sale to the settlements in other parts of New Zealand and in Australia. By 1855, for example, Canterbury had grown a sufficient surplus to export 3,688 bushels in the first eleven months of that year (2,829 bushels to other parts of New Zealand and 859 bushels to Melbourne) to a total value of £2,212 16s. Some flour (27½ tons) was exported also in the same period. [9] There seem to have been few attempts until the late sixties, however, to orient the programs of individual holdings toward wheat-growing as the only, or even as a very dominant, end of farm production. In the fifties, wheat was definitely as much a part of mixed-farming practice as it is today. There were, of course, few sheep on the small farms and somewhat less of exotic grassland than at present, but grassland pastures, though of rather short life, appeared in rotation with wheat and other crops from the first.

Acreages of plowed land expanded slowly, as the first capitalists to acquire large blocks of freehold leased most of their holdings to graziers. Occasionally small agricultural plots appeared where laboring men (by far the most numerous part of the population) managed to acquire bits of land. The process was not easy. In Nelson they squatted on unsold company sections and eventually obtained title, in some cases with little more expenditure. In Canterbury, however, the workingman had to spend some years as a shepherd, "bullocky," or other hand around sheep or cattle farms, and to save some of the fifty to seventy-five pounds a year (above keep) which was the going wage; the temptations of the nearest "pub" must have eaten into many such hoards. Alternatively, a man might rent an acre or two near one of the "towns" (agricultural villages) of Nelson, Christchurch, or Dunedin, have his plowing done in exchange for his labor, sell that labor otherwise on the market when he could, and work on his land during slack periods.[10] If very frugal and industrious he might eventually buy a few acres. As his condition improved, his original sod hut *might* be replaced by a frame cottage, and his ditch-and-bank fences *might* blossom with gorse or be surmounted by a post-and-rail superstructure. Land prices of three pounds an acre in Canterbury, to begin with, and prices little lower than that in Otago, were serious hindrances to the development of a cotter class south of Nelson; there the cheaper land and the opportunities for squatting had encouraged it. One must suppose that, by reducing the available supply of labor, the development of such a class would have worked against the interest of the squatters and other large land-holders, and one could hardly expect the latter to have abetted it. The shortage of labor with the emigration of men to the Victorian gold fields in the early fifties did raise wages, but it is debatable whether this greatly improved the opportunities of the land-seeking laborers.

A great deal of the early agricultural land was broken by the spade, both because of the nature of the land first used, and the unsuitability of much of the heavy English and Scottish agricultural machinery first introduced. It was not possible to apply many techniques of the old country directly to the new land, and not a great many of the newcomers had had agricultural backgrounds at home. Canterbury and Otago had less fern-land than Nelson, but both had a good many swampy areas in which *Phormium* was a prominent member of the plant association (notably in the Taieri basin and the region skirting the landward side of

Banks Peninsula). It was on the land where the "flax" was grading out into tussock that the most satisfactory first beginnings were made. Some of this could be plowed out of grass by short plows drawn by eight bullocks, but more generally it was necessary to attack it with axe, spade, and grub-hook where the tough roots of the *Phormium* were too thick. Thirty to forty shillings an acre were paid in Canterbury for such clearing, after which a four-ox plow at thirty shillings an acre would suffice for the actual plowing.[11] Land bought for three pounds an acre thus rapidly became land costing six pounds an acre before it had borne its first crop. The additional practice of letting the land lie fallow for a year after the first plowing in order to sweeten it, further delayed return on the investment and, in April of the autumn of its first sowing to wheat, it was recommended that it be cross-plowed, sown, rolled, and harrowed. The less well endowed, financially, usually took a crop of potatoes as a cash or subsistence crop during the first year.

Labor-saving machinery, where it was possible to employ it, was always in demand, because of the chronic shortage of labor. Very strong teams and strong plows were necessary in the initial stages. The *Lyttelton Times* for July 18, 1857, reported a plowing match in Christchurch which featured seven-horse and eight-bullock teams. Bullocks were preferred for breaking the worst land on account of the "flax," "toitoi," and "tutu" roots, and for these the heavy wooden plow was used. The cast-in-one-piece English iron plow was found to break too frequently, even for the purpose of second plowing on heavy land or for the easier all-tussock country; and the Scottish plow, with a separate cast share fitted to a bar of wrought iron, was in demand. The "swing" plow very rapidly replaced the old-fashioned, heavy-wheeled traditional English implement. The swing-plow was wheelless, and the success of its use depended entirely upon the skill of the plowman who had to be a thorough horseman or "bullocky" as well as a competent mechanic. In place of the two to four men traditional with an English plowing team, the plowman worked alone and, his hands full with the manipulation of the implement, had to guide his team by voice. An improvement over both the spade and the old labor-devouring implement, it was however only one step removed from either. It had been in use in North America for some time, but had not long been introduced to Great Britain before the earliest colonists for New Zealand had left. Indeed, it may well have arrived in South Island from New South Wales, where it seems to have been in use for some years previous to 1840. This single furrow plow and a simple tine harrow completed the list of heavy farm machinery in general use through the first decade, unless such local improvisations as large rollers made from available logs should be included.[12]

After the first breaking was done, one or two horses, or at most a pair of oxen, were sufficient for the work. Many a tale is told of makeshift teams in the early years, of cows hitched with riding horses, of horse-collars used upside down on oxen, and so forth. The seed was broadcast by hand after the first narrow furrows had been plowed, leaving good lodging troughs for the grain. The grain dish or bag was suspended from the neck of the sower, the twenty to thirty pounds of seed making a heavy load to carry over rough ground. The sower might manage to sow from ten feet to fifteen feet on each side of his line of march. After the sowing, the ground was harrowed several times, cross-ways and angle-ways, after which nothing more was done until the grain was ready to cut, unless perhaps one of the log-roller packers was used. In the early years there appears to have been no feeding-off of the late autumn and early winter growth of grain as is now often practised.

In the seventies came the double-furrow steel plow and beam-suspension, with a big wheel on the rear and two small ones in front, to regulate the depth and width of the furrow. With these plows the big teams, reminiscent of the first days of breaking, returned, and the way was opened for the large-scale plowing of the great *Poa* and *Festuca* tussock areas of the Canterbury plains and of the *Danthonia* tussock regions of Southland. Wheat-raising was the short-term objective, but often the landowners were using a few wheat crops to pay for the expenses of breaking preparatory to laying down as much of the land as possible in grass for as long a time as this would hold. Not until the late eighties did steam engines appear to compete with the horse teams; the internal combustion tractor pulling a big gang-plow is mainly a development since World War I.

The bottleneck in the expansion of wheat production was not, however, to be found in methods of plowing, nor was it to be found for long in seeding operations. Early in the sixties seed drills appeared and, especially after the double-furrow plows came into use in the seventies, these all but replaced broadcast sowing in

New Zealand and Australia, as they had done in North America and on the best farms of Great Britain. Probably nothing hastened the introduction of drills more than the earlier importation of sparrows, which increased with rabbit-like fecundity. Sparrows constituted one of the more unfortunate evidences in the new landscape of the pioneer's nostalgia for things past. Some machinery for broadcast sowing made its way to the island, but before it had any chance to establish itself the drills had made it obsolete.

The real difficulty lay in the very primitive methods of harvesting and threshing. The first crops in South Island were harvested, as were crops of wheat in Roman times, with sickles. Scythes, however, soon fitted with rakes or cradles, quickly replaced them. A man known as a "raker" usually followed the cutter, and a third, the "binder" (in South Island more generally called a "tier"), followed the second. The second and third individuals of the train were occasionally women. Grain itself was used for tieing, and the later prejudices against the use of the combined harvester-thresher machines (usually called "headers" rather than "combines" in Australasia) can, in part at least, be traced to the resultant early necessity for cutting the grain on the green side. The use of the header, of course, requires the grain to be nearly dead ripe. The first reaping machines, English or Australian copies of McCormick's invention, appeared in the fifties. By the late sixties they were being made on the island, notably by the Atlas Foundry at Timaru in 1868.[13] The *Otago Daily Times* of March 1, 1869, also reports reaping machines being made by Reid and Gray of Oamaru. They were relatively simple. The first model known in Canterbury was a Burgess and Key, with reciprocating knives run from the "bull-wheel," much after the fashion of the modern hay mower. They cut narrow swaths and carried two men, a raker as well as driver. The former had to see that the grain fell evenly onto the platform or table behind the knife, and had to rake off when he judged a sheaf lot was cut. He either rode the machine or walked behind; the tiers had to do their best to keep up. The machine was drawn, at first, by two horses; but with the addition of an extra horse, one driver, one raker, and five tiers could manage some ten acres a day. Reels were added to hold the grain against the knife and lay it evenly on the platform. In 1870 a side-delivery machine appeared which automatically swept the table in sheaf lots, thus saving one man's work and relieving the tiers from the necessity of having to keep up with the reaper in order to prevent the horses treading out the freshly cut grain. The "tilter," which accomplished the same purpose by periodically tipping the table was, perhaps, more generally used in Canterbury; sometimes an extra man was carried to tilt the table by hand. Both of these machines increased the cutting power of one reaper to some twelve acres a day, and much better records even than this were set by working the horses in shifts and oiling the reaper while the horses were being changed.[14] By 1871 over eight hundred [15] and by 1876 over a thousand [16] such machines were in use in Canterbury. With subsequent improvements, Wallace [17] reported that on the Acton estate at Rakaia in 1889, records of the cutting of three hundred acres of wheat in one day, by fifteen binders with teams of horses being alternated every three hours, had been established.

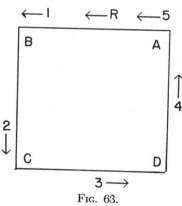

Fig. 63.

The bottleneck was thus being shortened, but hardly widened, for the binding continued to follow the early Babylonian pattern. In the seventies, ever larger acreages were going into wheat in Canterbury; and the labor problem, now much less acute for the operations of plowing, cultivating, seeding, and reaping, became focused on binding. Evans [18] described this system in use for a four-sided field (see diagram, fig. 63). The reaper R starts from corner A going toward corner B, a tier following him. The reaper of course makes much greater speed than the tier. As the reaper rounds corner B, a second tier begins, and in like manner at corners C and D a third and a fourth. As the reaper starts from corner A again, a fifth tier begins; as the reaper rounds corner B, the first tier should be ready to start on the second side. These five tiers were supposed to keep up with the machine; the diagram (fig. 63) shows the position of the tiers, numbered from one to five, shortly after the second round has begun. Though tiers were often the most expert and the highest paid craftsmen on the farm, no method was worked out by which more than five could be used with one reaper. The reaper had to wait on the speed of these five tiers for if, under the system of side-delivery reapers, the grain were allowed to stay on the ground, a strong wind (such as one of Canterbury's famed Nor'westers) could possibly intervene to blow the grain into unmanageable tangles or even over into the next farm.

In 1874 the wire-binder with slotted canvas rollers, not unlike those of contemporary machines, was introduced.[19] Cutting a seven-foot swath, and with the other additional burdens on the "bull-wheel" drive, more and more horses were needed. The wire was always a nuisance; it not only caused trouble in binding, but it also got into the threshing machines and into the chaff and straw which was fed to the stock. It required extra men at threshing to cut the wire with pliers, and of course the wire was expensive. Though the wire binders made headway (the contemporary press records the introduction of considerable numbers from the United States), they were soon replaced by the twine binders with the Appleby knotter which first appeared in South Island in 1880.[19] At first the imported two-ply sisal, or manila, twine was too thick for the knotter, and an annoying proportion of untied sheaves was the result. Experiments were then made with New Zealand's own hemp (*Phormium tenax*), and one James Maddren developed a single-ply twine from it which had sufficient strength to stand the strain of the knotter. New Zealanders claim that the single-ply idea, and even a little of the *Phormium* twine itself, was exported to the United States, and that this was the genesis of the general adoption of single-ply twine in this country. It has not been possible to check the originality of Mr. Maddren's idea or the validity of the New Zealand claim to this major technical contribution to American grain farming. At any rate, with the twine binder, the tiers were released for stooking (that is, shocking), and the last great difficulty in speedy mechanical harvesting was overcome. An interesting cultural inheritance was the practice of using the narrow, unstable, six-sheaf English

Karl Kippenberger

FIG. 64. Wheat in stook (shock), South Canterbury.

"church" stook, which involved much labor in re-stooking after the frequent, violent autumn winds; despite similarities to North American climatic conditions at harvest time, the stout round buttressed stook was not used for many decades (figs. 64 and 65).

The bottleneck was now shortened to the threshing operation, but this meant that it was widened as well. The British method of stacking and then threshing at leisure during the winter, in order to space out labor requirements, was followed everywhere. Initially, of course, no other method was possible. Before the sixties much, if not most, of South Island's wheat was threshed with flails. Peg-drum threshers (revolving drums in concave, stationary cradles of slats) were, however, introduced before the end of the fifties. Worked at first by hand (the Deans and a few other enterprising souls attached them to waterwheels, adapting the wheels later to grind flour), they threw the straw and some of the chaff out of one end; the grain and the rest of the chaff falling between the slats. Usually a winnowing machine, worked by hand,

Karl Kippenberger

FIG. 65. Downs country, originally exploited by large-scale sheep farming on the native tussock grasses, was later plowed for wheat growing—also on an extensive scale—as indicated in this old photograph. Today much of this type of country is in rotational grassland farming in which sheep are again the most important element.

was attached. An industrious crew might manage up to two hundred bushels a day. Then horse gears were attached and the size of the machine increased; a six-horse plant involved a machine perhaps three to four feet wide, nine feet long, and five feet six inches tall. Ten men would be needed, employed as follows: one man forking grain from the stack, one man forking grain into the machine, one man driving the horses, two men shaking out threshed straw and forking it into a pile, two men raking grain and chaff from a tarpaulin laid under the machine, and three men on the winnowing machine (one feeding, one turning, and one bagging). The machines were stationary and difficult to move.

The next step came with the introduction of the steam engine in the mid-sixties and with it the "combine," a machine which combed, threshed, winnowed, and bagged in one self-contained series of operations. The combine was able to thresh over five hundred bushels a day and by the mid-seventies it had completely displaced the old peg-drum mill. In the eighties, outputs of one thousand bushels a day were reached, and the cost of threshing had been reduced to sixpence a bushel.[20] When the air-blast for removing straw, and other improvements, were added by the early nineties, up to two thousand bushels a day could be handled by one mill. These heavy, wooden, "English" mills, which were to be the chief means of threshing in South Island until the nineteen-twenties, were rather difficult to move about. This problem was solved by the use of a steam traction engine, which not only hauled the mill but also ran it by transferring the engine's power to its belt wheel. The great cost of this elaborate apparatus took threshing out of the hands of all but the largest farmers, and it became the special domain of the threshing contractor and his gang. These gangs moved about the country from farm to farm in the same manner as did shearing or harvesting gangs.

Recent changes in implements in New Zealand grain farming have generally followed those commonly observed in the United States, Canada, and Australia. South Island had largely ceased to import the heavy and awkward (however reliable and durable) English implements, and has depended more on the lighter, cheaper, American types of machines, with modifications developed in both Australia and New Zealand to suit local conditions. Three-furrow plows, ballbearings, internal combustion tractors, tractor-binders and header-harvesters made their appearances and were more or less widely accepted. The reluctance with which New Zealanders turned to the header-harvester, however, which was introduced into Australia in 1897,[21] was partly the result of the same heavy-handed tradition which has made New Zealand's farmers refuse, until very recently, to thresh from the stook, and partly the result of much more limited areas of flat land in fields of wheat. By 1939, however, nearly 40 per cent of all wheat in Canterbury and Otago was header-harvested. This trend has been accelerated by the introduction of small "all-crop" harvesters for the smaller farms, which will handle anything from grass seeds to field peas. The header-harvester has had an interesting effect in greatly reducing the areas sown to certain wheats (such as Hunter's) which shell out too badly. These wheats were by 1942, chiefly restricted to two special areas: (a) Downs country where irregular ripening makes the header-harvester unsuitable; and (b) dairying country where threshed wheat straw has a special value.

The Wheat Research Institute in Christchurch has shown that heading reduces harvest costs from 40 to 50 per cent under any other method, and that wheat so harvested gives as good a flour in milling as can be obtained.

Many other aspects of changing techniques associated with the wheat industry might be cited.* One technique, however, has changed little, namely, bag-handling. The small gauge of the railroads (three feet six inches), the small quantities produced per farm (in 1936 only six farms in all South Island had more than four hundred acres in wheat), and the variety of produce handled by any railroad station—all these factors have militated against the development of elevators and loose-grain box cars. As grain exports have dwindled and disappeared, such methods of handling grain in bulk may never be needed. But there was a period, in the days of the great Canterbury wheat boom of the eighties, when the railroads could not begin to cope with the harvest traffic. On occasion, farmers had to wait four to five weeks for "railway waggons." [23] At Rakaia and Pleasant Point, as many as thirty teams at one time would be banked up at a loading platform, just as teams bank up at elevators during threshing time in the wheat country of North America. The continuance of bag-handling, however, has probably some analogy to the handling of wool bales and may have been sustained partly through cultural inertia. It is a practice which has tended to keep costs high and which has contributed directly to the distribution of weed seeds through both islands as bags move back and forth on successive tours of duty. [24]

The social organization of wheat production was no less interesting or significant in the development of land-use patterns than the changing techniques of husbandry. The "bonanza" period of wheat production was the twenty years from 1875 to 1895. The Canterbury lowland was the principal location for large wheat-producing units. Owners of large flocks on the tussock plains and downs soon learned that by putting the greatest acreages possible into wheat, a double purpose could be accomplished. The net

---

* It might perhaps have been emphasized before that the introduction of new implements and techniques was publicized, and good farming methods encouraged, by the early formation of Agricultural and Pastoral Societies in South Island from Nelson to Southland. Though the latter district was the last in which organized agriculture began, yet, by July of 1862, the first agricultural show and plowing match was held at Invercargill; and, in October, 1867, the Southland Agricultural and Pastoral Society was formed. It was the last of such provincial societies to be organized except that in Westland. [22]

profits from the exceptional yields of the virgin grassland soils for the first two or three years were much greater per acre than the yield of wool. Then, when the wheat yield declined to a profit position more nearly on a parity with wool, the erstwhile fields of wheat could be sown to English grasses, producing, for a few years at least, much better pasture than the original tussock provided. Much more labor was required for wheat production, but this was gradually made available from the heavy immigration of laborers during the seventies.

TABLE LXIII

ACREAGE OF SOME NEW ZEALAND ESTATES MANAGED BY THE
NEW ZEALAND AND AUSTRALIAN LAND COMPANY

	Freehold (acres)	Leasehold (acres)
Acton (near Rakaia)	15,162	2,520
The Levels (near Timaru)	60,233	11,605
Pareora (South of Timaru)	17,413	
Hakataramea (on river of that name)	24,327	70,300
Ardgowan (near Oamaru)	4,480	
Totara (near Oamaru)	10,613	158
Moeraki (near Hampden)	6,666	49,355
Clydevale (near Balclutha)	36,496	7,115
Kawarau (near Lake Wakatipu)	454	206,910
Edendale (South of Gore)	54,214	872
Sundry small properties	4,119	
Total	234,177	348,835

Some of the estates on this potential wheat land included, free-hold and lease-hold taken together, twenty to thirty thousand acres.[25] Sometimes they were owned by large companies such as the New Zealand and Australian Land Company; in addition to their many big estates in Australia, this company ran some of the largest wheat and sheep farms in New Zealand (table LXIII).[26] Many of the famous estates, however, were individual enterprises, such as Cameron's *Springfield* station, Grigg's *Longbeach*, and Studholme's *Te Waimate*. Cameron pioneered with the water races which made the agriculture of the higher plains possible. By 1880, he had forty miles of water races on his run alone.[27] In 1894, his peak year of grain-growing, he had fifty-five hundred acres under wheat and twelve hundred under oats, and once he had thirty-five reaping machines working at one time—and he ran between twenty-five thousand and thirty thousand sheep a year as well.[28] Grigg's *Longbeach* station, also in Ashburton County, had four thousand to six thousand acres in crop annually. Up to three hundred hands were employed at the height of the harvest, and the village of the station hands formed a township of its own.[29] In contrast, Cameron largely depended on temporary help, the numbers varying with the season. During the depression of the early eighties, with so many men "on the swag" (that is, on the road), the station became a sort of "hoboes' home." Wheat production is, of course, not conducive to steady year-round employment, but Cameron kept large numbers of men busy in the off-season helping with the sheep, clearing water races, trimming hedges, repairing wire fences, and picking stones. Stones were always a serious problem on the higher plains, and even down towards the sea where the rivers had recently occupied beds as they swept back and forth on their lower courses.

The bulk of the wheat was produced, however, on a smaller scale. Sometimes the large landholders let or sublet their land to small holders,[30] or had the cultivation done by contract. In either case, the stipulation was often made that English grasses were to be sown after the first, second, or some definitely named successive crop, was harvested. By the time the fat-sheep industry was established, hundreds of thousands of acres had thus had their first sowing of English grasses. On too many of the large leasehold estates on the lighter plains country, however, a rotation of wheat with fallow on alternate years, with an occasional skipping of the year of fallow, was used, and a good deal of the land was "mined out" to the extent that it would not support the more nutritious, but more demanding, of the exotic grasses and clovers to which it was later sown.

Contract cropping turned out to be an excellent school for the rather large number of immigrants who were unfamiliar with farming, or who came from English agricultural communities where Arthur Young's preachments were still, nearly a century later, regarded as somewhat radical. It also helped them to acquire sufficient capital to become small lease-holders, if not owners, of land. A great many of the older generation of farmers interviewed in 1941 and 1942 were the sons or grandsons of mechanics, factory workers, clerks, or shepherds who had learned the techniques of arable farming in this way. The forms of contracting varied. Sometimes a single man contracted for the labor of himself or, perhaps, of his team as well. He might go further and supply all of his own equipment and seed. Larger contractors agreed to supply labor and provide for other needs in large quantities for all parts of the farm work, or different large contractors might specialize in one or more of the following: plowing, sowing, harvesting, or threshing. Sometimes, as the demand for surplus feed developed, one of the contractors might lease the land to grow turnips between harvest and sowing. This practice, if at all extensive, must have been hard on the land.

An early phase of land tenure for grain-sowing was the lease of land, for money rental, from the Crown or from private owners. It is generally believed in South Island that this practice, also developed for small sheep-runs and continued into the mixed-farming period, was responsible for the introduction of husbandry methods which had no relation to the maintenance of productivity. In an attempt to check the carelessness of lessees and contractors a method of share-cropping, hitherto used only slightly in Otago, was introduced into Canterbury's wheat country. At Studholme's *Te Waimate* station, for example, the share-cropper gave his labor and implements, perhaps horses as well; the owner gave the seed and the land. The harvest was shared differently according to the contributions of each party and according to the yield, a fifty-fifty basis being a common one. By the end of the eighties, this practice had superseded most other lease or contractual arrangements almost everywhere wheat was grown in both Canterbury and Otago.[31] Contracting was steadily undermined with the subdivision of holdings and the spread of mixed arable and pastoral farming; the last refuges of the contractors were the plowing camps, which had also been the first form in which contracting had appeared in the sixties.* Early in the new century competition of steam engines had practically eliminated the camps, and they did not survive the introduction of kerosene and gasoline tractors.

It was principally the early wheat production which paid for two important technical developments that were to prove of tremendous importance in the later mixed farming economy. These were, in chronological order, the drainage of lands too wet for farming, and the provision of water for domestic and animal

* The life of the men in the plowing camps, as indeed in virtually all the contracting camps, was not easy. The size of the camps varied, the last plowing camps, with eight to twenty men and five to eight teams, being relatively small. They lived in tents or in traveling "whares" on wheels (caravans). Their food was based on the alimentary triumvirate on which rural South Island had largely depended for half a century: mutton, "damper," and tea.

supply on areas where the water table was too far below the surface. The latter need was felt particularly on the crests of the great coalescing gravel fans which formed the Canterbury plain, but was also a problem on some interfluves of the downs country. On much of the coastal land which geomorphological processes had very recently reclaimed from the sea—the Taieri plains, the land behind the coastal dune-ridge from the Waitaki to the Waipara, the lower reaches of the rivers of Nelson, Marlborough, and Southland—not only was the water level ordinarily too near the surface, but floods were frequent as well. These swampy regions were, however, among the first used for agriculture, because of their considerable fertility and their nearness to the coast and the first centers of settlement. After the clearing of the roots of the "flax" and the "tutu," drainage ditches had to be dug. The swampy area was discontinuous, with some of the higher, well-drained gravel ridges extending to the coast (as at Wakanui), but many of the wet lands were of considerable extent. The Eyre-Mandeville swamp north of the Waimakariri covered some fifty thousand acres.[31] Around Lake Ellesmere and inland from Banks Peninsula, across the virtual bog on which Christchurch was built, the wet lands were quickly crisscrossed with large main drains and small ones tributary to them. These feeder drains would last for years if they were floored with thick layers of sand covered in turn with silt. The techniques of drainage were partly initiated by men with some engineering experience, and partly by farmers with previous knowledge of reclamation of wet lands in England. Extensive inquiry failed to uncover any direct transference of techniques from the Lincolnshire fen country. The probability of such cultural connection is high, however, and further search may well uncover some such relationships.

Clearing was not usually tackled until after the drains were made. Enough has already been said of the techniques of clearing. The cost was reduced by the sale of *Phormium* leaves to temporary "flax" mills, which sprang up in the fifties and continued operations until the last of the swamps was reclaimed nearly fifty years later. In the seventies, for example, there were seven "flax" mills operating around Rangiora. The occasional buried logs which were found in the swamps offered but little compensating revenue for the extra labor involved in removing them, and where they were at all dense, costs of clearing mounted to fifty or sixty pounds per acre. At Woodend, for example, four years' work was required before the land could be tilled by a spring-plow. Nor were the problems solved with the end of plowing by the bullock teams. In Canterbury the "Nor'wester" tended to lift the dried peat in clouds, and considerable further expense in planting shelter belts had to be met. Such initial expenses could be quickly amortized only by very intensive cultivation.[31]

Where individual landowners had made heavy investments over considerable areas they quickly subdivided the land for lease or sale. The Bridge estate near Southbridge and Rhodes' swamp, now known as Marshland, were thus treated. In this latter area, now the suburban market gardening region upon which Christchurch is expanding to the northeast, a contingent of Poles and East Prussians, brought out under the Vogel scheme in the seventies, settled to engage in dairying and intensive gardening. Later they brought out relatives; one is somewhat startled to find among the names of long-established and most respected agricultural settlers of the Christchurch area those of Bolaski, Rogal, Gottermeyer, and Shimanski. Initially they leased the land in ten- to twenty-acre lots for ten-year periods at thirty shillings an acre; later, however, many of them purchased it for thirty pounds an acre upwards. Carrots and general garden vegetables were their early specialties (the carrot crop bringing high prices for special horse feed in Christchurch), but· onions later became, and remained, the featured crop of the Marshland area.

Problems varied locally. Around the shores of Lake Ellesmere it was difficult to plan permanent works because of the fluctuation of the level of the lake, which covered thirty-eight thousand acres at mean sea level, but extended over as much as fifty-nine thousand acres at high water when the outlet to the sea through the barrier beach became blocked. The lake was once the drainage outlet for both the Rakaia and Waimakariri Rivers, as well as for all the intervening territory; it is, presumably, the remnant of a great inlet of the sea (in which Banks Peninsula was a prominent island) which has been filled in with the erosional detritus of these two drainage systems. Today Ellesmere receives the drainage from about three hundred square miles of hill and mountain country as well as nearly five hundred square miles of plain. The Maori used to cut the bar and drain the lake periodically to obtain the great harvest of eels then left exposed on the flats.[32] Since 1868 the European settlers have attempted to keep a breach in the bar permanently open; strong southerly winds pile up great quantities of shingle however, and the constant long-shore drift from the southwest has made necessary almost continuous work to this end. At present the opening is maintained by drag-lines.

To the south of Ellesmere, between the lower reaches of the Rakaia and Ashburton Rivers, was a particularly difficult *Phormium* and raupo swamp. By 1882, however, some hundred and fifty miles of open drains had been dug, and it was taken over in that year by an energetic farmer with means, one John Grigg. On this, the famous *Longbeach* station, he built his own brick and tile works, and for many years laid an average of sixty miles of drain each year. The first use of this land, as noted above, was for wheat production, but it quickly became a mixed farming area in which dairy products and fat-lambs rivaled wheat. Pastures are much more nearly permanent in this heavy land than at higher elevations on the plains. Similar drainage histories can be reconstructed, from newspaper files and the often second-hand memories of the older farmers, for several other areas, such as the lower part of the Waimea plain of Nelson, and especially for the distributary region near the mouth of the Wairau in Marlborough. It was on such land that most of South Island's grain was grown in the sixties and early seventies.

By the early seventies, much of the high-country tussock land near the rivers was plowed. But, at any distance from the rivers, there was no drinking water available for the draft animals which were essential to cultivation. The lack of water was of special significance where the intention was to cash in on the virgin fertility by harvesting a few wheat crops only as an antecedent to laying the land down in English grasses. This in turn would allow more intensive sheep husbandry with the object of increasing the per-acre yield of wool. One of the first solutions attempted was the digging of wells, but a water level which often rested more than two hundred feet below the surface proved in general to be an obstacle economically, if not technically, insuperable at the time. Only very large stations well supplied with capital, like that of the New Zealand and Australian Land Company's *Acton*, could afford the expense. Where the water level was within a hundred feet of the surface, many diggers from the west coast, at a loose end in the seventies when the opportunities for individual success in the gold fields became limited, found employment in well-digging for different stations, especially in the Hinds district. In such wells water was raised in canvas bags by horse-windlass.* Another technique, tried in dozens of places in Canterbury from the Rangitata to Rangiora County, was that of hauling water from the rivers to large storage tanks. Particularly capacious ones were built at Burnham and Rolleston, just southwest of Christchurch, for township supply. This proved very expensive, however, and the cost became prohibitive at any considerable distance from the rivers.[33]

The solution finally adopted, which replaced the others and which represents the most important technical development in the whole history of agriculture *per se* in Canterbury, if not in the whole island, was the building of water races. Led off by weirs at upper levels of the rivers, water was distributed over the plains in shallow, narrow channels, so that it was plentifully available, first for the agricultural draft animals and then for the sheep and cattle which fed on the exotic pastures which succeeded the wheat fields. Water races are exactly similar in principle to irrigation ditches worked by gravity, except for the smaller scale on which they are constructed; the stock-watering channels were rarely more than two feet wide and eighteen inches deep. One is tempted to marvel at the slowness with which the idea caught on. The building of water races to supply water in the force necessary to wash out the impacted auriferous gravels had been developed with a high degree of skill in Otago and on the west coast during the sixties. Yet the large comprehensive systems of Canterbury were not planned until the late seventies nor inaugurated until the following decade.

It has not been possible to determine which of the many claims in Otago made for different "firsts" in the use of mining water races for irrigation of gardens and orchards, as well as for domestic supply, deserves the palm. Lacking authentic details, the strongest tradition favors a Frenchman named Ferrand.[34] There are many contemporary descriptions of such irrigation in different parts of Central Otago.[35] It was from these slender beginnings that Otago was to develop its small but important irrigated, stone-fruit orchards, and that irrigated pastures were to appear at many places along the Clutha River or its tributaries. References in the *Otago Daily Times* throughout 1862 make it clear that there were

* The analogies to the interfluve areas of the United States Great Plains, and the similar problems of water supply when the agriculturists attempted to take over grazing lands, will be obvious. The most successful American solution, the steel windmill, however, was not available at this earlier period in South Island.

many hydraulic water races in use in that year. Pyke, presumably drawing on the same sources, confirms this activity.[36] In 1863 the first small water races for watering stock appeared in Canterbury at Winchmere or Wakanui, just north of the mouth of the Ashburton River.[37] No genetic connection between these and the mining races has appeared in the evidence. The great publicity about the Otago gold fields which was current in Canterbury in 1862 and 1863, notably through news stories in nearly every issue of the *Lyttelton Times*, as well as the certainty that large numbers of people went back and forth between Canterbury and the gold fields, does, however, create a strong presumption that the idea may have been transferred from the south. It is true that water races for irrigation purposes had been known for thousands of years, and their use for hydraulic mining had a long history before 1862, but the appearance of the first stock water races in Canterbury in the year following those for mining in Otago is, at the least, a very remarkable coincidence.

These earliest beginnings had no sequels upon the higher plains, apparently because of a deeply ingrained belief that the porous gravels of the plains would not carry the water any distance without sustaining a complete loss by seepage. Yet any Canterbury man who had visited Central Otago and seen the several miles of successful water races running along gravel terraces bordering the rivers should have perceived its fallacy.

The next known experiment with water races in Canterbury is recorded in the station diaries kept by Reed of Westerfield.[37] He had races in operation in 1871. Others quickly followed suit. A monument has been erected at Kirwee, a mid-plains station on the Canterbury-Greymouth Trans-island Railway, to one Colonel de Renzie James Brett, who had become familiar with irrigation races in the northwest of British India and had settled, in 1867, in this tussock and gravel country between the Selwyn and Waimakariri Rivers. He and his neighbors, though attempting nothing but extensive sheep farming, found the need for water rather acute. In 1877 he proposed a scheme for watering the greater part of this interfluve, and by dogged promotional effort the scheme was undertaken. By 1880 water was flowing. In 1882, twelve miles of main race, twenty-seven miles of branch race, and thirty-four miles of subsidiary races were in operation, providing ninety thousand acres with eighteen million gallons per day. This does appear to have been the first extensive project and deserves a great deal of acclaim. If there is any value in establishing such priorities, however, it seems doubtful that the popular veneration of Brett as the man who introduced water races in Canterbury is justified.

The water races spread rapidly, from the higher plains to the lower. Closer settlement succeeded the water races: new villages were established, and old villages grew in size. The initial splurge of wheat-growing made possible by this supply of water for the working animals, subsided with the advance of mixed farming; but the even greater need for water caused by the increasing density of sheep and cattle, resulted in a steady extension of the water-race system until the great majority of plains farms were so supplied. Today visitors are more impressed with the new irrigation projects in Ashburton County than with the stock water races, some of which are more than sixty years old. But the former remain an essential cornerstone of mixed farming economy, a fact

Fig. 66. Stock water race near Mayfield, Canterbury; one of the earliest on the high plains, this one is in need of cleaning.

ahc

Fig. 67. A well-kept stock water race on the low plains, which even in an area of high-water table, is economically superior to pumping.

which the great public controversy on the "pros" and "cons" of irrigation has tended to obscure (figs. 66 and 67).

The reasons advanced for the currently expanding irrigation schemes [38] which have developed from the stock water races, include the counteraction of variable rainfall, the abnormal evaporation loss of soil moisture, and the possibility of utilization of much more moisture than the rainfall supplies during the warmest part of the year. In all, about half a million acres should be able to take advantage of irrigation water in South Island within a few years.* The initial cost of the irrigation scheme to the farmers is largely a matter of ditching and leveling; the government's experts insist that the increased yield of the pastures should pay current water costs and leave a substantial margin of profit. To repay the initial costs, some experiments have suggested the feasibility of taking a year or two of wheat before laying down to grass, the increased yield of wheat, with the additional water, just about counterbalancing the first costs.[39]

---

* In 1942 there were less than a hundred thousand acres irrigated in Otago, and only a few thousand acres south of Ashburton County in Canterbury (Red Cliff's area and Level's area). The water for the Red Cliff scheme was drawn from the Waitaki, for the Level's scheme from the Opihi, and for the several Ashburton County schemes from the Rangitata. The main race required a siphon over the nose of the Surrey hills.

The most extensive use of the plains for wheat-growing came in the late eighties and early nineties, the greatest acreage of all being sown in the season of 1891-1892, when the island had 380,115 acres under crop.[40] Yields had declined from the spectacular, and possibly inaccurate, figures reported in the early fifties. The average for Canterbury, which had nearly 75 per cent of the island's acreage in this peak year, was under 23 bushels per acre. This can be attributed not only to the more extensive methods of farming, and the much lighter land onto which wheat growing had encroached, but also to progressively declining yields everywhere, as land was sown too frequently to this cash crop. With the spread of a mixed farming economy, yields improved in the first decade of the new century, as much of the lighter land was left in pasture for several years between successive wheat crops. The increase of dairying, however, on the heavier coastal lands from which the highest yields of wheat had always come led to a further decline in yields. The number of dairy cattle in Canterbury, for example, increased from thirty-six thousand to eighty thousand between 1900 and 1920,[41] while sheep, in the same land district, increased in number only from four million to four and a half million. Wheat had moved back into some of the lands abandoned in the nineties and the earliest years of the new century. The means of reported average yields of wheat for New Zealand as a whole, for successive five-year periods from 1890-1891 to 1939-1940, is shown in table LXIV;[42] of the total for this period Canterbury contributed from 65 to 80 per cent.

TABLE LXIV

QUINQUENNIAL MEANS OF AVERAGE ANNUAL YIELDS OF WHEAT
IN NEW ZEALAND

Quinquennium *	Bushels per Acre
1890 to 1895	22.2
1895 to 1900	26.9
1900 to 1905	32.9
1905 to 1910	29.9
1910 to 1915	29.4
1915 to 1920	26.7
1920 to 1925	27.6
1925 to 1930	33.4
1930 to 1935	29.9
1935 to 1940	32.9

* A quinquennium includes five seasons as 1890-91 to 1894-95.

The somewhat higher yields since 1925 are possibly associated with the general decline in wheat acreage and the probable abandonment of lands which were marginal for wheat production. However, the fluctuations in yield from year to year are considerable; as these must be largely due to variation in climatic conditions, they may completely obscure other trends. The yields in the individual years of the 1930-1931 to 1934-1935 period, as shown in table LXV [43] is one example of this. If the trend toward larger yields during the past twenty years is principally due to cultural factors, these might include, besides the concentration of production on better lands: the heavier fertilization of the land, including that of the grass or roots which precede the wheat in the rotations; the use of new machinery; and the introduction of new clovers such as "Subterranean," which have raised the content of available nitrogen on the lighter lands.

TABLE LXV

ANNUAL WHEAT YIELD PER ACRE IN NEW ZEALAND (1930-1935)

	Yield per acre
1930-1931	30.44 bu.
1931-1932	24.49 "
1932-1933	36.54 "
1933-1934	31.56 "
1934-1935	26.32 "

For the period from 1926 to 1936, Hilgendorf [44] has some interesting comparisons of New Zealand yields with those of other wheat-growing areas (table LXVI).

Increased yields, again assuming these to be chiefly culturally induced, might also be ascribed to the use of new varieties of wheat. Little reliable information, it must be remembered, is available about varieties of wheat in use before the nineties. There were white and red wheats, and spring and winter wheats; and names like Velvet and Pearl recur frequently. Fuller mentions English varieties of white-chaffed white and red wheats.[45] But how many kinds of wheat may have been covered by such generic terms, or from what areas the early wheats arrived, are matters of almost complete uncertainty. In the *Official Handbook for New Zealand* for 1892 the whole scope of wheat production is reviewed; and it is stated that Hunters White, Pearl, and Velvet chaff were the chief kinds sowed in late fall or early winter. Red and white Tuscan were favored for spring sowing. In the threshing returns collected by the government during the nineteen-thirties, over forty varieties were named, but Hilgendorf states that many of the names are merely local designations for a variety otherwise named in other places.[46] Thus, in various areas, Hunters, he says, was called College Hunters, Bell's Hunters, Hunters White, or Red Chaff. In other cases the old names have survived and are applied to new wheats long after all trace of the original varieties have disappeared. Thus the New Zealand Wheat Research Institute found both Talavera and Marshall's White to be actually identical with Solid Straw Tuscan. Sorting out these inaccuracies, the government statistician fitted the accepted varieties into three groups for the 1940-1941 season (table LXVII).[47]

TABLE LXVI

COMPARISON OF WHEAT YIELDS IN NEW ZEALAND WITH THOSE OF OTHER COUNTRIES (1926-1936)

Countries with Small Production and High Yields	millions of acres in wheat	bushels per acre
Holland	0.4	43.5
Denmark	0.3	41.7
Belgium	0.4	38.4
United Kingdom	1.8	32.6
New Zealand	0.3	32.4
Germany	5.2	30.8
Sweden	0.7	28.8
Egypt	1.5	27.2
Japan	1.7	26.9
Countries with Large Production and Low Yields		
China	50.9	16.4
Canada	25.6	14.6
U. S. A.	50.0	13.6
Argentina	15.9	13.6
Australia	12.7	11.5
India	34.0	10.5
U. S. S. R.	92.6	9.9

Tuscan was the leading variety grown for most of this century up to the 1938-1941 period when Cross Seven passed it in rank. It is a solid-straw wheat which, as both Hilgendorf and Frankel of the Wheat Research Institute suggested to this writer, probably came from Spain or Portugal; varieties like Tuscan they thought may have originated from crosses between the bread and macaroni wheats. It seems to have appeared in New Zealand no later than the eighties, and to have taken the name of an older hollow-strawed variety; it was called solid-straw Tuscan to distinguish it from (though it soon largely replaced) the variety whose name it assumed. Its particular value to Canterbury farmers was its resistance to the threshing action of strong hot winds. The stookers named it "barbed wire wheat" in honor of its stiff awns. The straw, solid or semi-solid, is weak, and tends to lodge badly in heavy land. It is inferior in baking quality to most of the other wheats grown, but it blends well with many of them. There seems no doubt that it was the introduction of Tuscan, whenever and wherever that event took place, which allowed wheat to be grown so largely on the high tussock plains in the eighties and nineties, where most other varieties known at the time threshed out very badly in the wind.

TABLE LXVII

PROPORTIONATE AREAS AND YIELDS OF DIFFERENT VARIETIES OF WHEAT FOR NEW ZEALAND (1940-1941)

Varieties	Percentage of total yield (bushels)	Percentage of total area (acres)
Tuscan types:		
Cross Seven	43.57	41.63
Tuscan	33.31	38.44
Dreadnaught	8.25	6.59
Tainui	0.61	0.56
Others	0.54	0.47
Total (Tuscan types)	86.28	87.69
Hunters types:		
Hunters	9.80	8.39
Major	0.37	0.38
Others	0.20	0.16
Total (Hunters types)	10.37	8.93
Pearl types:		
Jumbuck	2.32	2.12
Marquis	0.78	1.01
Others	0.25	0.25
Total (Pearl types)	3.35	3.38

Hunters Wheat was almost certainly introduced before 1860,[48] and this variety accounted for a large share of Canterbury's production up to 1890, if we can be sure the older references are to the grain now known by that name. Its origin, too, is obscure. It apparently is not the "Hunter's White" of the area around the North Sea which had white chaff, for this wheat has red chaff; it probably came from northwestern Europe. It has a stronger straw than Tuscan and has more tillers (though fewer of these survive to form heads), but it is much more heavily damaged by shaking. It is thus grown chiefly on heavier lands in more protected areas and, sown in the autumn, is fed off by sheep in many cases for a short time before being allowed to come away. Its straw is valuable in the diet of dairy cattle.

While the milling and baking qualities of Hunters were much higher than those of Tuscan, it still was necessary to import up to half a million bushels of Australian and Canadian hard wheats for blending purposes in the nineteen-twenties. The low yield of Canadian varieties when grown in New Zealand made them unattractive to the farmer. An Australian variety, Jumbuck,* gave as good a quality of flour as the locally grown Canadian wheat, and although it far exceeded it in yield, that yield was still too low to recommend it widely to New Zealand farmers, especially since it threshed readily in high winds and had a weak straw. Other similar wheats were tried without contributing any more effectively to the solution of the problem of producing in New Zealand some variety whose yields would make it a satisfactory money-crop and obviate the need for importing such large quantities of blending wheats. The solution of the problem was finally found by crossing Tuscan with a series of the Canadian and Australian wheats. The work of Hilgendorf and Frankel in the development of one of these crosses resulted in perhaps as successful a solution to a cross-breeding problem as has ever been made. The result was called Cross Seven (White Fife x Solid-straw Tuscan), after a testing name by which it had been known through many years of its development. Its yield is slightly lower than that of Tuscan, and being somewhat shorter, it matures from two to six days earlier; it does not lodge as easily, and it resists wind threshing equally well. While it is about equal to Tuscan in suscepti-

* This wneat was produced by Ferrer of New South Wales about 1895 and was first introduced into New Zealand in 1901. Its breeding, as given by Hilgendorf [49] was as follows:

Improved Fife x Tardents Blue
↓
Unnamed x Lambrigg Talavera
↓
Jumbuck

bility to rust, it shows a somewhat greater damage from loose smut. Of most importance is that it allows a slightly higher flour-extraction in milling, and is decidedly superior in baking tests.[50] By 1937 its expectations had been proved in commercial growing, milling, and baking. The increase of acreage showed phenomenal rapidity from eighty-four acres in 1934-1935 to thirty-four thousand acres in 1937-1938, and to the ninety thousand acres (42 per cent of all the New Zealand wheat area) of 1940-1941.[51] It should be pointed out that both Tuscan and the Cross Seven which is replacing it got an artificial fillip in the thirties with the increased use of "headers" (harvester-threshers) to which they proved more suitable than did the Hunters varieties. For example, Amuri County, as late as 1936, had 33 per cent of its area in Hunters; in 1940 less than 2 per cent was in this variety.[52]

Wheat has been a cornerstone of agricultural and mixed farming during the whole century of farming occupance, and it still is of great though undoubtedly diminishing importance in South Island. Its story has been told in some detail in order to illustrate the introduction, invention, and spread of plants and techniques. The growth of wheat seems to have been at first chiefly of English varieties of white-chaffed white and red wheats, and undoubtedly English methods of husbandry were in general use. But English implements were cumbersome and very expensive; rough and ready adaptations more suitable to local conditions were quickly made. As the century progressed, there was less dependence on English tradition and experience, and more on local ideas and machines, or on those imported from Australia or North America. One characteristic, however, remained much more typical of English than of Australian or American wheat production: the growth of wheat as an intensively cultivated crop in rotation with grass (and sometimes roots) in an animal-dominated mixed farming economy. For its leading variety of wheat today, however, as for many of its wheat farming techniques, South Island is in debt only to the ingenuity of its own people.

CHAPTER XIII

THE BRASSICAS, GRASSES, AND CLOVERS

THE BRASSICAS

The turnip and cabbage family, the *Brassicas*, have an areal importance in South Island comparable with all of the other root, grain, and pulse crops combined. As with wheat and potatoes, most of New Zealand's *Brassicas* are grown in South Island. The acreage in different classifications for each land district in the 1940-1941 season is shown in table LXVIII and figures 68 and 69.[1] The relatively greater importance of *Brassicas* in Southland can be directly correlated with the need for supplementary feeding in the much more severe winter. Though some of the turnips may be dug, the *Brassicas*, green feed and roots alike, are usually fed off in the fields.

We may neglect here most of the varieties of *Brassica oleraceae*, notably the garden cabbages and cauliflowers, though their importance in truck-gardening and, in total, in kitchen gardens, may be considerable. Two of the varieties derived from *B. oleraceae* are, however, important: kale and choumoellier which, along with rape (*B. napus*), are being sown more and more widely for green feed. The root varieties, turnips (*B. rapa*) and rutabagas or Swedish turnips (*B. napobrassica* or *B. campestris*) occupy a much larger place in the island's agriculture, both areally and economically. The beets, which are usually associated with the turnips, occupy but small acreages. Mangolds are grown a bit,

Fig. 68. Distribution of *Brassica* roots acreage (1940-1941).

SOUTH
ISLAND
NEW ZEALAND

ONE DOT = 500 ACRES IN
RAPE & KALE (GREEN FEED)
SEASON 1940-41

ahc

Fɪɢ. 69. Distribution of *Brassica* green-feed acreage (1940-1941).

but the growing of sugar beets is still in a very early experimental stage, and it is likely to remain so while cheap sugar from Australia or southeastern Asia is available.

TABLE LXVIII

BRASSICA ACREAGE IN NEW ZEALAND (1940-41)
(IN THOUSANDS OF ACRES)

	Green Fodder		Roots			
	rape and/or kale	chou-moellier	turnips [a]	turnips and rape [b]	Total Brassicas	All Grain and Pulse Crops
Marlborough	5.1	—	2.1	0.8	8.0	28.8
Nelson	1.4	—	3.8	0.4	5.6	7.5
Westland	0.1	—	0.6	0.1	0.8	0.3
Canterbury	99.6	3.9	103.1	12.3	218.9	418.3
Otago	35.1	0.8	66.6	11.9	114.4	90.8
Southland	20.7	2.5	85.6	24.3	133.1	52.7
Total for South Island	162.0	7.2	261.8	49.8	480.8	598.4
Total for North Island	36.0	11.8	79.6	12.5	139.9	52.0
Total for New Zealand	198.0	19.0	341.4	62.3	620.7	650.4

[a] Swedish turnips (*Brassica napobrassica*) are not distinguished from ordinary turnips (*B. rapa*): no mangolds or other beets are included.

[b] These returns are thought to be predominantly turnips.

The *Brassicas* had an early start in South Island, but made slow progress as compared with wheat or potatoes. Cabbages, for example, are presumed to have been sown by Cook and Furneaux in their gardens at Dusky and Queen Charlotte Sounds in 1773. Cook mentions the good condition of the cabbages and turnips in that year and the following.[2] Cabbages were reported as persisting in the area of Queen Charlotte Sound when a call was made on the third voyage, and Bellinghausen, visiting at Motuara, not only discovered large quantities of the cabbages but also introduced some more.[3] Dieffenbach,[4] Wakefield,[5] and D'Urville[6] commented on the wide dispersal of cabbages around Cook Strait. There is also considerable evidence of cabbage-growing in North Island at any early date; Cruise[7] mentions turnips in North Island in 1820. D'Urville reported turnips as common in all of the island's whaling stations which he visited, an observation confirmed by the subsequent visits of Smith, Shortland, Tuckett, Monro, and Selwyn. Indeed one would have expected turnips to have been among the first vegetables planted by Englishmen or Scotsmen establishing themselves in a new land. They were certainly among the first vegetables planted at Riccarton,[8] at Akaroa,[9] at Nelson,[10] and at Waitohi (that is, Picton).[11]

The early days saw little need of supplementary fodder for animals, and *Brassicas* were used almost entirely as garden vegetables. As all of the *Brassicas* did serve as such, however, we may assume a considerable early experimentation with varieties and methods of culture. Paul,[12] an early observer in Canterbury, remarked that root crops did well enough but that the swedes, especially, exhausted the soil and he advised against their cultivation on land intended for grain unless they were manured. Fuller,[13] commenting on conditions in the same period, suggested that a rotation of crops, as conducted in England, was not likely to be followed in South Island for some years, because of the high cost of labor in manuring and of the low demand for root crops. Another objection to the rotation of wheat with roots, he says, was that grain did not ripen well on newly turned land, and that just as unevenly ripened wheat milled indifferently, so unevenly ripened barley malted poorly.[14]

It is difficult to find definite statistics of early turnip growing. In 1855, in all of Otago there were but forty-five acres in turnips out of some thirty-six hundred acres in crop or grass.[15] It was to be in the Taieri valley that field cultivation of turnips really began in South Island, presumably to winter animals or fatten them for the Dunedin butchers. Sowing the seed broadcast, with cross-harrowing for thinning, seems to have been the earliest technique used. The costs of hand-hoeing must have helped to keep the acreage down. Andersen [16] has shown the extent of the increase of turnip acreage in the section of Canterbury south of the Rangitata River from 1867 until 1910. The following ratios for five-year periods have been calculated from his figures to show the percentage of the total land under cultivation which was devoted to the roots:

1867:	0.6%	1882:	28.7%	1897:	27.6%
1872:	1.5	1887:	29.1	1902:	30.8
1877:	13.2	1892:	27.7	1907:	36.6

On the average, South Canterbury had slightly more land in turnips than in wheat through this forty-year period. One might suppose that the introduction of refrigeration would have sharply increased the proportion of land in turnips, to satisfy the demands for fattening sheep. Yet nearly 30 per cent of the land in cultivation was in turnips by 1882 when refrigerated shipments of meat began, and the percentage of land in turnips changed very little thereafter. The explanation of this apparent anomaly is, I believe, to be found in the fact that between 1882 and 1907 the total amount of land in cultivation in South Canterbury increased from a hundred and seventy-one thousand acres to two hundred and thirty-three thousand acres, and that many other additional supplementary feed crops besides turnips, especially some of its *Brassica* relatives, were also grown in increasing quantity.

South Canterbury, Otago, and Southland had, however, by far the most intensive cultivation of the *Brassicas*. Nearly 70 per cent of Canterbury's *Brassicas* are today grown in the five counties of Ashburton, Geraldine, Mackenzie, Levels, and Waimate, and turnip cultivation is negligible in the land districts of Nelson, Marlborough, and Westland. Some differences appeared between cultivation on Canterbury's lighter land, and in her drier climate, as compared with practices in the Taieri valley and through the Southland plain (figs. 70 and 71). It rapidly became apparent that while broadcast sowing would work satisfactorily in Canterbury, row-sowing with intensive horse-hoeing, if not hand-hoeing, was needed in the south; the rainier climate made the hilling-up of

Fig. 70. Sheep feeding on turnips in Canterbury on level plains at the foot of the mountains. Here, near Methven, in the rain-shadow of the Southern Alps, turnips are rarely hilled-up.

New Zealand Farmer

the roots almost imperative. They required more manuring in the north in the early years, but very shortly fairly heavy manuring was required everywhere.

The first references to any very specific types being grown extensively are for the decade of the eighties. The most favored then were called "Purple-top," for early winter sowing, or "Green-top Aberdeens" or "Green-top yellows" for spring sowing. "Devonshire Greys" or "Devonshire Grey Stones" were also used for both early and late sowing. There was very little growing of rutabaga varieties which were attacked very severely by the cabbage aphid; those that were grown were principally used for winter feed for pigs. Gradually more and more variety was introduced as the *Brassicas* were integrated into a complex mixed-farming system. For sheep, soft turnips were ready by mid-autumn, yellow turnips in early winter, Swedes in June or July, and rape, kale, or choumoellier in early spring.

It was estimated in the nineties that one acre of good turnips, supplemented with hay, chaff, and a little grass, would finish off eight to fourteen sheep for the freezing works. Similar ratios still hold good. Rape was sown from the first as a supplementary feed, either immediately after harvest or in early spring on skim-

FIG. 71. Sheep feeding on turnips in the downs country of coastal Otago. Here, as in Southland, heavier rainfall requires expensive hilling-up of the roots, usually unnecessary in Canterbury.

New Zealand Farmer

plowed stubble, and was usually fed off, in either case, in time
for a crop of oats or barley to be sown. The root crops were ideally,
though not sufficiently often to this day, combined with dry feed
in the form of chaff, hay, or even straw. With sheep eating at the
rate of twenty pounds per day apiece, and with average crops of
fifteen to twenty tons, an acre would handle about one hundred
sheep for a fortnight, being roughly equivalent to twenty or
twenty-five acres of sown pasture during the period of low pasture
productivity in the winter months. Animals were allowed on turnips for only short periods at first, to prevent bloating. The management of a turnip field was, and is, effected by temporary fences,
called "breaks," which are moved as needed. In sheep flocks the
sequence is usually: hoggets and old ewes for the tops, then fattening animals for the best of the roots, then flock ewes to clean
up. Great care is necessary with the young animals on hard turnips
lest their mouths become deformed, a disability which may easily
impair their competence to feed on grass for the remainder of
their lives.

Most of the higher-country wool farms grow turnips in what
little arable country they have for wintering purposes, and in
Central Otago, notably in the Ida Valley, irrigation water is used
for this purpose. In various other places, in a small way, turnips
appear to serve special purposes for fattening or for winter-
carrying of animals. A considerable part of the arable, even in
North Island, carries *Brassicas* of one kind or another. But their
most important place is in mixed farming south of the Rakaia
River. It was suggested to this writer many times that the Scottish
influence in the south of the island contributed considerably to
this concentration. Even if this important cultural influence had
not been exaggerated, and I believe it has been, a colder, wetter
climate to the south would provide enough reason for this pattern
of distribution.

THE ENGLISH GRASSES AND CLOVERS

Important as are the crops of grain, pulse, green-fodder and
roots in the contemporary scene, exotic grasslands occupied more
than 80 per cent of the land which was listed as "under cultivation" * in the *Agricultural and Pastoral Statistics* for 1940-1941

* That is, most of the "improved" land on the basis of which grassland percentages were calculated on page 287.

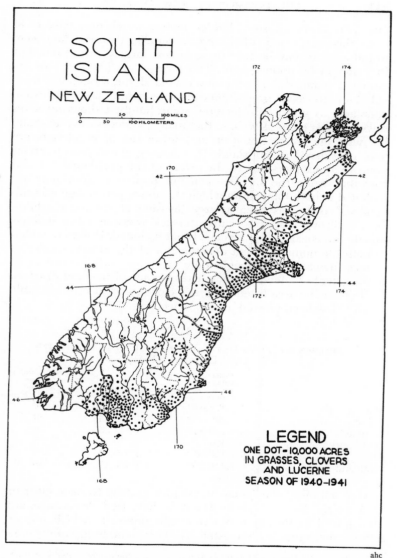

SOUTH
ISLAND
NEW ZEALAND

LEGEND
ONE DOT = 10,000 ACRES
IN GRASSES, CLOVERS
AND LUCERNE
SEASON OF 1940–1941

ahc

FIG. 72. Distribution of acreage of grasses, clovers, and
lucerne (alfalfa), 1940-1941.

(fig. 72). There are some hidden factors which may operate to make this percentage either larger or smaller than the data seem to indicate. It may be that these factors largely cancel out, but they should be noticed here. The acreage of "hay cut," for example, is assumed to be all exotic grassland, but though undoubtedly high, the exact proportion cannot be determined. The exotic grassland, as given, also includes some hundred thousand acres sown to other crops as well, so that many paddocks sown to grain, but with the grass coming on as a lower tier of vegetation, are here considered as grassland. If, however, these considerations point to an exaggeration of the extent of the grassland, it is also true that while the surface-sown but unplowed grasslands are included in both totals from which the above percentage was calculated,* there has been a large invasion of volunteer exotics, such as Brown Top, into native tussock areas, and this indeterminate but considerable acreage is not included. If it were added to both the numerator and denominator of the ratio it would, of course, increase it. Although there are some surface-sown areas to the extent of a few thousand acres in each of the land districts, the bulk of the area listed as "grass, clover, and lucerne" in table LXIX [17] has been plowed at least once.

TABLE LXIX

COMPARISON OF "SOWN GRASS" WITH TOTAL AREA CULTIVATED
BY LAND DISTRICTS (1941)

	Total area in grasses, clover, and lucerne (acres)	Total area cultivated (acres)	"Grass" percentage of total area cultivated (per cent)
Marlborough	374,670	417,856	90
Nelson	299,364	354,343	84
Westland	140,934	147,286	96
Canterbury	2,030,716	2,720,520	75
Otago	1,336,869	1,578,803	85
Southland	1,246,270	1,400,152	89

That not all of the "grass" is used for grazing is made clear in table LXX.[18] Some of the areas cut for hay, seed, or ensilage, are also grazed in the same twelve-month period in which one or more of such crops are harvested. The considerable size of the area

* Unlike the North Island's exotic pastures, most of which were, initially at least, sown on such bush-burn, those of South Island, and especially those of the regions of the great grassland areas (Otago, Southland, Canterbury) were principally sown on arable.

of grassland which was allowed to ripen and was cut for seed is partly attributable to local demands arising from the need to sow fairly large acreages to grass each year in rotational farming. The growing of grass seed is of course not all for domestic consumption. In 1936 nearly four thousand long tons, and in 1940 over 2,287 long tons, were exported chiefly to the United Kingdom, Australia, and the United States of America. Cocksfoot was for many decades the chief seed harvested but in recent years Rye grass has forged well ahead. Southland led in the production of seed until complaints about the lack of persistence and poor germination of its product became general. While Southland has thus lost the lead in Rye-grass seed production, it has forged ahead in the production of Brown Top and Chewings Fescue for lawn seed in the United States and England. The chief grasses harvested for seed in 1940 were Perennial Rye grass, White clover, Italian Rye grass, Chewings Fescue, Red clover and Cow grass, Cocksfoot, Brown Top, and Crested Dogstail, approximately in that order of importance.

TABLE LXX

NUMBER OF GRASSLAND ACRES CUT FOR HAY, SEED, OR ENSILAGE
BY LAND DISTRICTS (1941)

	M	N	W	O	C	S
Grasses and Clovers:						
Cut for seed..	4,118	851	8	75,239	20,250	34,937
Cut for hay...	4,713	10,064	2,172	33,802	17,535	23,111
Cut for ensilage	167	421	636	388	277	490
Lucerne cut for hay or ensilage	3,587	1,064	59	10,801	9,069	77
Total grassland cut	12,585	12,400	2,875	120,230	47,131	58,615
Total acres in sown grassland	374,670	299,364	190,934	2,030,716	1,336,869	1,246,270
Per cent of total grassland cut.	3.4	4.1	2.0	5.9	3.5	4.7

M = Marlborough; N = Nelson; W = Westland; C = Canterbury; O = Otago; S = Southland.

The proportion of the grassland area which is renewed each year is fairly low in general, but equals or exceeds 10 per cent in Canterbury in most years. The proportions of grassland renewed in a recent fourteen-month period are given in table LXXI.[19]

Despite the fact that pastures are increasing in permanency over many parts of the wetter areas of heavier land, it is still true that over the greater part of the Canterbury plains it is unusual for a field to stay ten years in grass without being plowed or re-sown. In Southland where the leys could have a longer life, the necessity for growing root and other supplementary feed crops results in many of the pasture paddocks still being regularly plowed in turn, as the rotation pattern moves about on individual farm holdings.

TABLE LXXI

NUMBER OF ACRES OF GRASSES, CLOVERS, AND LUCERNE SOWN FROM JANUARY 31, 1940 TO MARCH 31, 1941, BY LAND DISTRICTS

	M	N	W	C	O	S
Grassland renewed [a] on:						
Land not previously plowed ...	1,133	1,513	809	4,571	3,830	5,675
Land previously plowed ...	7,322	4,416	3,310	207,071	57,646	68,731
Total acres renewed in season	8,455	5,929	4,119	211,642	61,476	74,406
Total acres in sown grassland	374,670	299,364	140,934	2,030,716	1,336,869	1,246,270
Per cent of total grassland renewed	2.3	2.0	2.9	10.0	4.6	6.0

M = Marlborough; N = Nelson; W = Westland; C = Canterbury; O = Otago; S = Southland

[a] The amount of land sown to grass for the first time was insignificant in this fourteen-month period.

Perennial Rye grass (*Lolium perenne*) and Italian Rye grass (*Lolium multiflorum*) are, together, by far the most important members of the exotic grasslands, as originally sown. Trouble with "false Perennial" seed has long been a problem in New Zealand, and certification of Perennial seeds has been progressively advanced since the late twenties. Southland's seeds had been gaining a reputation among farmers for failure to persist, and certification was an essential measure if any of that land district's seed production business was to be saved, as well as to protect the buyers and users of seed. Actually one of the greatest needs on South

Island's rotational farms is a type of Rye grass intermediate between true Perennial and Italian. The false Perennial was certainly not this. It did not come away a bit faster than the true Perennial, and persisted little longer than the Italian; it had, in other words, the worst points of both. One possible solution to the problem of earlier feed from the more persistent species lies in vernalization of the seed, and investigations with Perennial Rye grass, White clover and Red clover had reached the stage of field experiments in 1940-1942.[20]

In what are called "temporary" pastures, the more short-lived species, which are often more quickly productive of feed, are used. Intended to last only for a season or two, such pastures are sown to Italian Rye grass and Broad Red clover (*Trifolium pratense*) more frequently than to anything else, but Alsike (*T. hybridum*) may replace the Red clover. The Rye grass usually makes up about five-sixths of the seed. In pastures which Levy [21] calls "Short Rotation," a type very common in the mixed-farming country of Canterbury, Otago, and Southland, a mixture dominated by Perennial Rye grass is used, this seed forming some five-eighths of the mixtures. The remainder would, typically, be Italian Rye grass, White clover (*T. repens*), or Red clover, though a variety of other types may be included. For example, the hay grass invader, Timothy (*Phleum pratense*), which has never been widely used in the island, does appear in this type of pasture in Southland.

In the "permanent" pastures, which are usually better described as "Long Rotation," although some may be truly permanent, a greater variety is used. Included among these are species which will die out soon after the first flush of growth, but which will provide food while the longer-lived plants are becoming established. Besides the Rye grasses, Cocksfoot (*Dactylis glomerata*), or Orchard grass, has been important on such areas. The growing of Cocksfoot, however, has met with many difficulties. Cheap Danish seed, poor selection and insufficient care in the certification of seed, have contributed to the increase of less desirable strains, and Cocksfoot seed heads have suffered sharp attack from midge larvae. The problems created by attacks of various insects on the more desirable grasses in New Zealand have been becoming more serious; especially harmful in South Island are the grass grub (*Odontria zealandica*) and the grass caterpillar (*Oxycanus* or *Porina* spp.). Some progress in control has been made with poison using a Paris-green base.[22]

For special purposes, in different regions other grasses and one or more clovers may be added to the grasses mentioned above. On wetter soils Timothy and Meadow Foxtail (*Alopecurus pratensis* or *Poa trivialis*) are often included; on rolling downlands, Crested Dogstail (*Cynosurus cristatus*) has been found satisfactory for sheep. In the lighter lands of the Canterbury plains, where the complex of climate and soils imposes severe seasonal strains which are inimical to the sustained growth of the plants, a number of free-seeding annuals have been tried, to lengthen the life of short-rotation pastures. The most successful currently in use is Subterranean clover (*Trifolium subterraneum*). It covers a range of habitat suitability from the areas of medium to low fertility where Suckling clover thrives, to much superior conditions in the habitat range of the short-lived strain of White clover.* This is illustrated [23] in pastures where, when the fertility is built up by careful management and top-dressing, the Subterranean first crowds out the Suckling but in turn yields place to the White. The agronomic significance of its use lies principally in the fact that, when Subterranean clover is introduced, it becomes profitable to top-dress large areas which formerly did not repay the costs of such treatment.

The true extent and variety of the exotic introductions is realized only when the great number of volunteer grasses, clovers, and weeds in the grasslands are examined. Of the volunteers, Brown Top (*Agrostis tenuis*) and Yorkshire Fog (*Holcus lanatus*) are the most widespread. The former volunteers particularly on poorer soils which are heavier and wetter than the average, and appears as the dominant on thousands of acres of shady hill-country and run-out rotational pastures on the island, especially in Southland, South Otago, and the foothills of the Canterbury plains. The latter, more common on still wetter, peaty areas, has a much more limited distribution. On the drier country, no exotic volunteer is as common as the native *Danthonia pilosa*, but some dozens of volunteers including several *Trifolium* species do appear with it, especially Goose grass, Hair grass, and Sweet Vernal. Some ex-

---

* The common annual clovers in New Zealand grasslands include: [23] Haresfoot Trefoil, Striated clover, Clustered clover, Suckling clover, Hop Trefoil, Reversed clover, Subterranean clover, Spotted Burr clover, and Toothed Burr clover, approximately in that order from the most infertile to the most fertile soils. If this series were continued, on a scale of increasing fertility of habitats, it would be found that the perennial species like White, Red Strawberry, etc., replaced the annuals.

perienced grassland men estimate that the areas dominated by Brown Top and *Danthonia* are as extensive as those sown to the good herbage types of English grasses. Certainly the end of a long rotation on "permanent" pasture is often the plowing under of a sward of nearly pure Brown Top or *Danthonia*.

Only a few of the exotic weeds which occur through the grasslands need be mentioned here.* Rushes (*Juncus effusus* and other species) are common wherever there are springs or water seepages. The Scotch thistle (*Cirsium lanceolatum*) and the so-called Californian or Canadian thistle (*Cnicus arvensis*) are very general on more poorly managed areas. On rough hill-country, notably on the West Coast and Banks Peninsula, the fox-glove (*Digitalis purpurea*) makes spectacular splashes of white and purple. Ragwort (*Senecia jacobea*) and the ox-eye daisy (*Chrysanthemum leucanthemum*) appear particularly on dairy pastures. The more shrubby weeds of the neglected grasslands are associated with the gorse, the broom, and the blackberry discussed below.

In all, ninety-two species of exotic grasses have been identified, apart altogether from the clovers, weeds, and other occupants of the grasslands.[25] Of these, sixty-five probably come from Europe and most of them seem to have been introduced purposely. The Americas supplied nine, Australia was the original home of six, South Africa of one, and there are another ten the present distribution of which is so wide as to make students despair of ever identifying hearth regions. The use of the term "English grasses" does not necessarily imply an ultimate origin within the British Isles, but it is peculiarly appropriate here, since most of the grasses seem to have been brought from England or Scotland especially for the purpose of creating pastures like those of the homeland. Recent introductions such as Subterranean clover, which arrived in New Zealand from Australia but is thought to be of ultimate Mediterranean origin, do not invalidate this general viewpoint.

* Levy [24] selected a few others for special mention including Catsear (*Hypochaeris radicata*), Rib grass (*Plantago lanceolata*), and Pennyroyal (*Mentha pulegium*). We should perhaps also give some attention here to an immigrant from Argentina: the Nasella tussock (espec. *Nassela trichotoma*) which, in the late thirties, seriously infested the native tussock lands of North Canterbury. Apparently completely unpalatable to sheep, and more aggressive than its competitors, it is still spreading rapidly. There is no agreement as to any effective methods of control, but legislation was being prepared in 1942 (Christchurch *Press,* August 7, 1942) for local control boards which, in policy and organization, would parallel the existing Rabbit Boards.

The most important of the English grasses, through the grass-land history of South Island, have been Cocksfoot and the Rye grasses, the former being of greatest importance in the more nearly permanent leys, the latter in the shorter-lived rotational pastures. Cocksfoot has been losing ground in recent years to mixed swards of Rye grass and clover, but there are areas where pastures domi-nated by Cocksfoot have remained for many decades; Banks Pen-insula contains many such fields. *

Italian Rye grass, with almost no rival in its flush of early spring growth, was a constituent of most grassland seed mixtures, but its rather short life kept its proportion in such mixtures low un-less the ley was intended to be a very short one. The Perennial varieties are slower-starting and longer lived, while Cocksfoot, the most persistent of the three, may not become well established until the second year. The last-named was, however, unexcelled as a late summer grass and, indeed, the rapidity of its late summer growth made the problem of maintaining its juvenility acute. Its tussocky habit of growth suggested combination with more turfy types, and Crested Dogstail was first introduced to mix with Cocksfoot for this purpose. The chief difficulty with Italian Rye grass is that its early flush of growth tends to depress later comers, and often leads to an undesirably heavy stocking early in the season.

In their function as the principal base of wool, mutton, and butterfat production, all the grassed areas require careful man-agement. To this end, thorough examination has been made of the findings of such famous grassland experiment stations as those at Rothampstead and Aberystwyth, and a great deal of local work has been done in investigating and improving various phases of this difficult branch of plant husbandry. The over-all aim is of course to obtain the maximum growth of young, palatable herbage over the longest possible period. The juvenility of the growth is maintained by careful pruning through grazing. Great care must be taken to see that the pruning is of the right closeness for the species which it is desired to encourage. Some of the best species

---

* The harvesting of Cocksfoot seed was long a minor industry of Banks Peninsula, though it is fast declining in importance today. Milligan [26] has pointed out that the peninsular forest was largely gone by 1900, and that the lowest land flanking the bays is now covered with a mixture of Cocksfoot, Rye grasses, and clover, which blends upslope into *Danthonia;* the latter forms almost pure stands on the highest land. The replacement of Cocksfoot by *Danthonia* is chiefly due to de-cline in soil fertility to which various forms of soil erosion are actively contributing.

are intolerant of close and continuous grazing, especially in dry weather, and Perennial Rye grass, Cocksfoot, or Red and White clovers may die out if sheep are left too long on a paddock. On the other hand, pasture which is allowed to "get away" may cause Perennial Rye grass, Crested Dogstail, and White clover to be smothered out, or eaten out by selective grazing as ranker, rougher growth is avoided.

A. H. Cockayne [27] emphasized that the essential feature which determines whether a pasture is of a milk-producing nature or not, for either cow or ewe, is the actual age of the herbage itself. If young, it is ideal for the most intensive cattle and sheep farming. If allowed to get rough, the pasture becomes, essentially, one for "store" animals. Rotational grazing offers the ideal method of achieving the desired end of permanent juvenility, but this requires a most precise balance between animals and pastures, a balance which may be upset by even slight variations in climatic factors. On the drier areas of South Island, as we have noted above, there may be considerable deviation in any year from the normal regime of precipitation. Even if a normal season of temperature and moisture conditions is experienced, the natural variation in productivity with seasonal variations in these climatic factors necessitates a careful balance of supplementary feeding. Thus a skillful farmer may manipulate the fertility of the soil and the type of herbage by his type of fertilization, his choice of original pasture mixtures, and his timing of the buying and selling of animals.

There are too many factors involved to allow any simple solution of the problems of grassland management (fig. 73). All Canterbury farmers, for example, cannot buy extra animals in a highly favorable season, nor can they all sell animals in a drought period. For one reason or another most pastures sooner or later become rank, the best species disappear or are replaced by less desirable ones within a few years, and paddocks must be plowed under and re-sown. Thus the relationship of grassland farming to cropping in the mixed farming economy becomes clear. By use of rotations, lack of skill in management or climatic accidents can be overcome or counterbalanced. Everywhere of course the urge is to create pastures of progressively longer life, and it is probably generally true that mixed arable and grassland farming not only involves too many different occupations to allow one farmer to be an expert in all of them, but it also requires a great variety of machinery

ahc

Fig. 73. Contrast in pasture management in Marlborough. Grazing too heavily invites erosion (*left*); grazing too lightly, or at wrong times, invites invasion of second-growth or exotic nuisances like gorse (*right*).

and other equipment which is idle through the greater part of the year. Really permanent pastures would simplify the management and probably increase the profit of farming much of South Island's land. New types of grasses and clovers, together with careful selection and certification of seed, will undoubtedly contribute to this end. For example, irrigation is about to end the drought hazard on much of Ashburton County, which has long been the chief cropping county of the island. The necessity for supplementary feed in the slow-growth periods will, however, remain.

Perhaps the greatest contribution to pasture longevity has been made by the application of fertilizers, most usually "dusted" (that is, broadcast) over the grass. The areas to which top-dressing for all purposes was applied in South Island during one recent year is shown in table LXXII.[28] The lime is especially important in Southland, and ground limestone is the principal form in which it is applied. Superphosphate (or "super") was the most important type of artificial fertilizer while the Nauru deposits were available before the dislocations of World War II. Most of it was shipped by rail to consumers between the months of August and December. Hudson and Scrivener indicate that in the early nineteen-thirties phosphate fertilizer was principally used on the island as an application to special green-feed and fodder crops.[29] Besides "super," a certain amount of basic slag was used, though possibly little of it in South Island. One of the attempts to extend the limited supplies of "super" during the war (chiefly made by some New Zealand scientists) was the mixing of three parts of "super" with one part of serpentine, an experiment about which opinions differ widely.[30] The serpentine may slow down release of the usable phosphorus by converting the bulk of the water-soluble phosphates into water-soluble form, may improve the mechanical condition of the "super," and may reduce the severity of its destruction of bags. The magnesium content of the serpentine (a Hydrogen-Magnesium silicate) is also thought to be potentially valuable where a magnesium deficiency has been noted.[*]

TABLE LXXII

ACREAGES OF LAND TOP-DRESSED IN SOUTH ISLAND
(FEB. 1, 1940 TO JAN. 31, 1941)

Nature of top-dressing	Acres
Artificial fertilizers only	311,824
Lime only	131,020
Both	411,939
Total	854,783

While it is true that the Rye grasses and Cocksfoot are generally suited to the prevalent condition of a moist but freely aerated soil, they cannot maintain themselves in competition with less exacting members of the association which is formed (including individuals both sown and volunteering) unless depletion of fertility is prevented by top-dressing. This of course must be carefully prescribed for the needs of local areas. Thus, while potash has been found to give very little response over much of the island's grassland (and the nitrogen needs vary greatly), phosphorus gives excellent responses nearly everywhere.

From the early forties there are constant references to the laying down of English grasses in the island. The low-carrying ca-

---

[*] Some of the most important experimental work on deficiencies in iron, copper, magnesium, and the trace-elements (such as cobalt and boron), which markedly affect the condition of animals grazing on herbage which grows on the deficient soils, has been done in New Zealand.

pacity of tussock grasslands compared with those of remembered pastures in England or Scotland, must have suggested the procedure at once. The Deans at Riccarton did not, apparently, sow any paddocks to grass until the 1847-1848 season, although some alfalfa for the horses had been grown earlier.[31] The grasses did so well, and the production of meat and dairy products at the very door of the projected capital of Canterbury promised so favorably, that they planned thereafter to put all the land they broke into grass after taking one crop.[32] In 1851 they had plans for sowing thirty to forty acres to English grasses and clover seed. In the second year of the Otago settlement 19½ out of the 219¾ acres planted had been sown to grass.[33] It is probable that the Victorian gold rushes stimulated a demand for cash crops which kept the acreages sown to grass low in the early fifties, but progress was nevertheless steady. In 1854 the Marlborough area had 42½ acres in grass,[34] and Canterbury 289 acres, approximately 10 per cent of the area sown.[35] In the same year the Waikouaiti region had 320 acres, out of 605½ sown, in "hay."[36] This suggests the possibility that much of the sown grassland was used to produce hay as a supplementary winter feed, though amid quite full information about animals and other crops there is a surprising lack of such specific information about grasses. Apparently they were used much more extensively in the other settlements than in Canterbury. The Otago statistics for 1855[37] listed more than a third of the cultivated area, over thirteen hundred out of nearly thirty-six hundred acres, as artificial grassland. A comparison of the acreages in sown grasslands with total acreage in cultivation in 1856 is given in table LXXIII.[38]

TABLE LXXIII

PROPORTIONATE AREAS OF CULTIVATED LAND IN SOWN GRASSES IN 1856

	Nelson	Canterbury	Otago
Total cultivated area (acres)	13,869¾	8,006½	5,022
Sown grasses area (acres)	5,041¾	1,383¾	1,718
Per cent in sown grasses	36	17	34

About this time Paul[39] reported that English grasses were doing very well in Canterbury. Although all the early references examined are to Rye grass and Cocksfoot, one may assume the introduction of a wide variety of other species with the use of cheap and weedy seed. White Clover was certainly an important early addition to this duo; Thomson [40] mentions its rapid spread through Central Otago in the sixties. One of the most interesting side-trails which has been followed in the search for origins is the investigation of the failure of repeated introductions of Red clover. It grew for a season and then in every instance quickly faded out. Since hive-bees were present in considerable number from 1839-1840 on, it was not at first suspected that an insect necessary to its fertilization was absent. Finally the problem was solved with the introduction of the bumblebee * in 1885.[41] By the nineties most of the present exotic grasses and weeds seem to have been widespread.[42]

The sown pastures of the fifties, sixties, and seventies were used for a wide variety of purposes. Near the towns dairying and the fattening of stock for the butchers accounted for a considerable acreage. Elsewhere, through the sheep country, the superior carrying power of sown pastures over tussock, even for wool production alone, had led to the establishment of rotational pastures over ever larger acreages. The fact that grain yields soon declined unless grass was used in rotations encouraged this practice even among farmers whose primary aim was the production of cash crops. The new grasses were almost essential for lambing paddocks, for station dairying, and for the grazing of working bullocks and horses.

On the bigger stations, as has been noted before, a common practice was to let the tussock land to contractors who would plow, sow roots or wheat, take a crop or two, and lay down to grass; by this method very large acreages indeed were converted to sown pastures. By the year 1874, the provincial districts had the following acreages [43] in grass: Nelson, 43,650; Marlborough, 20,308; Westland, 2,121½; Canterbury, 245,518; and Otago (including Southland), 227,985. In the previous year (1873) Canterbury's sown grassland compared in area with other parts of its plowed or improved land as shown in table LXXIV.[44]

The increasing areas of English grasses contributed to the advancing proportions of crossbreds and half-breds in the sheep population, as has been noted, and when refrigerated shipments of meat to England became practicable in the early eighties, both the necessary grassland base and the types of sheep required had largely completed the process of adaptation to cultural and environmental requirements. The refrigerated meat trade led to a

---

* In usage common to England and New Zealand the "humble-bee."

very sudden acceleration of sown grassland acreage and of numbers of crossbred animals in the eighties, but contrary to the implications of many writers on the subject, there seems to have been no sudden revolution in patterns or practices of land use on the island. For example, in 1873 Canterbury had 62 per cent of sown land in grass, and in 1891-1892 only the slightly higher percentage of 68 per cent; other data for the 1891-1892 season are given in table LXXV.[45] In table LXXVI,[46] the acreage of New Zealand under artificial grasses in 1892 is compared with similar acreages of the seven Australasian colonies for the same year.

TABLE LXXIV

USE OF CULTIVATED LAND IN CANTERBURY IN 1873

Type of Use	Acreage
Sown grasses and hay	195,420¼ °
Wheat	68,462¾
Oats (threshed)	40,357
Barley (threshed)	6,810
Potatoes	1,883
Other (incl. *Brassicas*)	5,725¼
Total acres sown	*318,658¼*

Grass percentage of total acreage sown = 62%

° Hay cut from only 10,492 acres.

TABLE LXXV

RELATIVE IMPORTANCE OF LAND SOWN TO GRASS ° IN THE "CULTIVATED LAND" † OF SOUTH ISLAND IN 1892

Type of Land	Marlborough	Nelson	Westland	Canterbury	Otago (incl. Southland)
Total acreage of "cultivated land"	246,324	275,529	14,353	2,047,993	1,866,546
Acres sowed to grass on land:					
Plowed at least once	51,181	65,303	8,084	1,139,179	1,157,246
Never plowed	168,644	175,880	4,933	241,590	180,502
Total in grass	*219,825*	*241,183*	*13,017*	*1,380,769*	*1,337,748*
Per cent of "cultivated land" in grass on land:					
Plowed at least once	21%	24%	57%	55%	62%
Never plowed	68‡	64‡	34	12	10
Total	*89*	*88*	*91*	*67*	*72*

° Regardless of whether the land was previously plowed or not.

† Including all sowed grassland, whether plowed or not, and all other plowed land whether in crop or not.

‡ These proportions of surface-sown grassland were later considerably reduced for Marlborough and Nelson because of reversion or subsequent plowing.

TABLE LXXVI

ACREAGE UNDER ARTIFICIAL GRASSES IN AUSTRALASIAN COLONIES IN 1892

	Acres		Acres
South Australia	17,519	Tasmania	208,596
Queensland	20,921	New South Wales	333,238
Western Australia °	23,344	South Island, N. Z.	3,192,542
Victoria	174,982	North Island, N. Z.	4,211,339

° Figures are for 1891.

South Island's sown pastures were still largely seeded with Cocksfoot and the Rye grasses in 1892; in that year New Zealand as a whole produced 1,436,936 bushels of grass seed, of which 864,511 bushels were Rye grass and 572,425 bushels were Cocksfoot. The production of the two from the different provincial districts of South Island in 1892 is shown in table LXXVII.[47] No other grass seed is recorded as being produced. It will be noted that Canterbury produced more Cocksfoot seed than all the rest of New Zealand, and that Canterbury and Otago together produced some 78 per cent of all the Rye grass seed in the country. There was a fairly large production of clover seed, a business which developed rapidly after the introduction of the bumblebee, but no detailed figures are available.

TABLE LXXVII

PRODUCTION OF TWO PRINCIPAL TYPES OF GRASS SEED IN
SOUTH ISLAND IN 1892

	Rye grass (bushels)	Cocksfoot (bushels)
Marlborough	12,181	4,392
Nelson	1,904	4,054
Westland	—	1
Canterbury	303,573	300,245
Otago (including Southland)	355,107	8,408
Total South Island	672,765	317,100
Total North Island	191,746	255,325
Total New Zealand	864,511	572,425

In summary it may be reiterated that: the farming practices of South Island, from the second decade of organized settlement until the present, were concerned especially with sheep, cattle, and English grasses; that the animals and techniques especially associated with this husbandry came to South Island from Australia;

and that the English grasses derived from Great Britain, as did many of the methods of managing the pastures on which these animals became more and more dependent. While the greatest part of the immigrant population from that country had little knowledge of any pastoral or agricultural techniques and was almost certainly all but completely ignorant of the early Australian methods of sheep-farming used in South Island, it may have possessed, here and there among its individual members, some skill in the management of rotational grasslands which were based on familiar grasses.

CHAPTER XIV

EXOTIC TREES AND SHRUBS

A visitor to the principal farming and pastoral areas of the island, today, is impressed with the dominance in the landscape of two Californian trees and one English hedge-plant: Monterey pine, Monterey cypress, and gorse (fig. 74). These are only three of hundreds of woody plants which have been established there since Cook's first visits; yet there is, I believe, nothing more characteristic of South Island's occupied rural landscape than this ubiquitous trio. It represents a selection from a long series of trials to find quick-growing shelter for man and beast from the winds, hot or raw, which whip across the open plains and downs. The establishment of these three plants was primarily the solution to a practical problem of environmental circumstance, and if the hedge-plant has a long history of similar service to man, the two conifers found in New Zealand their first major utility to the techniques of pastoral production.

Here and there one may find individuals, groves, or hedges which, taken together, represent a vast catalogue of introductions from all parts of the world. Most interesting among these in the landscape are the trees and shrubs which were planted in remembrance of the homeland: oaks, birches, elms, rose bushes, and hundreds of others common on the English, Scottish, and Irish countrysides. Scarcely a river valley is not lined, at least in its lower course, with weeping willows (fig. 75). Scarcely a country drive can be taken where a towering row of lombardy poplars is

ahc

Fɪɢ. 74. A quartet of the most successful and ubiquitous of the exotic invaders: gorse (*center*) flanked by broom in the foreground; behind are Monterey cypress (*left*) and Monterey pine (*right*).

not silhouetted against one point or another of the horizon, or where splashes of yellow-flowering broom, as well as gorse, do not occur.

The interest of early visitors and residents in the trees and shrubs provides a rich mine of information about the time and circumstance of many introductions. Lady Barker,[1] living near Christchurch in 1866, remarked on the preference then for quick-growing lombardies, willows, and blue gums. Crawford[2] observed that the plantations were generally of European, American, Himalayan, or Australian trees, because the native trees took so long to grow. Potts,[3] in his delightful book of the nature lore of South Island, gives a clear picture of the succession of fashions in the plantings of trees of rapid growth on the plains. The willows and

ahc

Fig. 75. Willow at a ford high in a mountain valley. Willows have worked their way upstream to line many of the river banks. Fords must replace bridges in the thinly populated back country.

poplars of the late forties and fifties were replaced in popular esteem by the Australian eucalypts in the next decade, while these, in turn, gave way in the late sixties and seventies to the pair of California conifers.

There is really no need to document the story further. The files of the contemporary press are crammed with information from advertisements of seeds and seedlings for sale, of reports of the proceedings of acclimatization societies, and of general editorial discussion of introductions. In any event, the best evidence is easily seen in the landscape. No reference to oak plantings in the Deans' letters could be half so impressive as the towering trees still growing at Riccarton, and no documentary date is as certain as a ring-count from the bole of a freshly felled tree. Mr. E. C.

Studholme of *Te Waimate* had no need to tell of his father's planting of English trees on that pioneer estate in South Canterbury; as one approaches the station house one walks through flocks of English sheep grazing on English grasses under the spreading limbs of English oaks (fig. 49).

Canterbury's plains are crisscrossed today with hedges of gorse (*Ulex europaeus*) as are the fields of Devonshire or Hampshire; river valleys and abandoned cultivations or clearings are yellow with its blossoms in nearly every month of the year, as the shrub has become almost perpetually flowering in its new habitat. Though there are districts such as Central Otago and the West Coast where gorse is rare, it appears to some degree in every settled part of the island. Here and there it is accompanied by broom, but while broom too has often run wild, it is nowhere as widespread as gorse, and it is so much more easily eradicated that, where it has gotten away, it does not rank with gorse as a noxious weed. Since gorse seed was advertised for sale constantly in the earliest issues of the Dunedin, Christchurch, and Nelson papers, one must suppose it to have been almost the first hedge plant established, though hawthorn hedges were also very early. At any rate, gorse became the unrivaled shelter fence for agricultural areas and later for the mixed farming units or small grazing runs which followed the break-up of the great estates at the turn of the century. Frequently planted at first on the banks of "ditch-and-bank" fences, it gradually replaced the "post-and-rail" which had often provided a more expensive but more immediate barrier to stock. Today, on the areas which were once native tussock and are now used for mixed farming, it is almost universal. Its chief rival is barbed wire, or box-wire, fencing, but such fencing does not supply the all-important shelter for the sheep. Today gaps in old hedges are commonly blocked by posts and wire, and sometimes two or three strands of barbed wire are run through the old hedges to guard against unexpected breaks. Occasionally other exotics, like Monterey cypress, are interplanted in the gaps.

The trimming of the hedges is a matter of great time, worry, and expense; yet the well-trimmed hedge is such an accepted criterion of good husbandry that pride combines with prudence to keep most of the hedges neatly cut back each year. Unfortunately neither of these compulsions is universal, and here and there, despite ordinances, public opinion, and self-interest, hedges have spread out over road allowances and pastures. In the wide valleys of all the great, braided, eastern streams, gorse has displaced nearly all other vegetation. In dozens of localities it has spread from chance seedings in gullies far over adjacent hill slopes. Two particularly badly infested areas are the foothills of Geraldine County in South Canterbury and the hill pastures of Banks Peninsula. It occurs as a weed even in such unlikely places as the Okarito beach in Westland and just east of the mouth of the Waiau river in Southland. But the reputation of gorse as a noxious weed is so well established, and the spread of the plant is so generally accepted as a serious problem in South Island, that it will be sufficient to state the fact without further illustration. The few hiatuses in the distribution of gorse show an interesting correlation with great drought and winter cold (as in Central Otago where it is rare) and with areas which were formerly, or still are, near sections of fairly thick bush. There the forest supplied the posts for fences as well as a good deal of the needed shelter. While well-trimmed gorse hedges are as ubiquitous a feature in the landscape on the plains of Southland as they are in Canterbury, and are probably functionally even more important there as a means to shelter the animals from the raw winds off the Antarctic Ocean, the hedges seemed much younger than those to the north, especially near the areas where patches of native bush had longer persisted. Hedges appear around the seaward fringe of Clutha county only where bush has been cleared for some time. The same generalization holds for most of the land districts of Nelson and Westland, although some of the marshy pakihi lands, which may never have supported even the swamp-loving kahikatea forest, are playing unfortunately welcome hosts to gorse.

It is impossible to strike a balance between the positive and negative contributions of gorse to the rural economy of the island during the past century of settlement, and to arrive at conclusions that are certainly valid. In the earliest decades it filled a great need and, with mechanical gorse-cutters likely to become general after World War II, its maintenance of a position as the most satisfactory of all combined fence-and-shelter hedges seems assured. Yet thousands of acres of potentially productive grazing land have now succumbed to its invasion, and scores, if not hundreds, of acres are added to its realm each year (fig. 76). The farmers consulted on the problem were all but unanimous in the opinion that cutting and grubbing the gorse-covered areas does not pay, as

ahc

FIG. 76. Gorse is exceedingly aggressive and has occupied thousands of potentially productive acres. In this picture, taken near Geraldine in South Canterbury, its spread from hedgerows into the adjoining fields is well illustrated.

most of them are relatively low in potential productivity.* One possible long-term solution, which is being tried in Geraldine County, is the planting of quick-growing pines in the gorse areas, in the expectation that, by shading the sun-loving gorse as well as by competing with its root systems for water, the pines might smother it. This must be a labor of love by the farmers, or a large-scale program assisted by the government, if it is to succeed.

Biological control of both animal and vegetable pests is actively advocated by a large group of practical entomologists in the Dominion, notably those at the Cawthron Institute in Nelson. Gorse has not escaped their attention. The Department of Scien-

---

* One resident of Banks Peninsula advocated burning and intensive grazing of gorse as a satisfactory substitute for cutting and grubbing. He estimated the relative cost of this method to be 6s.8d. an acre (plus some facial eczema on his sheep) as compared with £12 10s. an acre for cutting and grubbing at the prevailing wage of ten shillings a day. He also pointed out the impossibility of grubbing gorse on much of the very strong soil it has occupied. Few other farmers thought his solution a practical one for their own problems.

tific and Industrial Research conducted a project over a period of several years to try to acclimatize *Apion ulicis* for the purpose, without much success at first, due to the out-of-season flowering of the gorse and the high percentage of sterile weevils arriving in New Zealand.[4] In 1933 the insect was extensively liberated in Otago, but there was no evidence, a decade later, that it had had any significant effect. There seems to be no doubt at present that another parasite, the cottony "cushion" or "fluted" scale (*Icerya purchasi*), once a serious pest in the fruit orchards, is attacking and killing gorse in the Waimakariri River bed. Spraying of orchards is now such a standard practice, for a variety of reasons, that the further dissemination of the scale may do no harm.

The broom (*Cytisus* spp. esp. *scoparius*) owes far less to man in its distribution, and it can scarcely have spread one-hundredth as much as gorse. Much more serious a problem than broom is the common blackberry (*Rubus* spp. especially *fructicosus*), which has spread widely in northwestern Nelson and elsewhere in the districts of heavier rainfall. Fortunately it does not act as a vigorous colonizer where the rainfall is less than fifty inches a year. The casual traveler in Nelson and Westland will see thousands of acres dominated by this pest, not only on roadsides and river banks, but also in the second-growth on neglected pastures which had once been laboriously cleared from the bush. Successful burning of this thorny tangle is almost precluded by the amount and persistence of the rainfall. On the west coast south of Greymouth, for example, the occurrence of four or five successive days without rain would be a rare phenomenon indeed. Any type of destruction other than burning involves extremely costly, unpleasant, and tedious work.

It is no problem to account for the introduction of the blackberry. Stapledon, in a humorous speculation, laid it to west-country men desirous of eating their "clotted cream with the familiar pie of that delectable fruit." [5] Its rapid dissemination in a country so well endowed with birds is no more difficult to explain. As in the case of gorse, various biological controls have been attempted, so far with little success. The parasites which attack the blackberry have proven, in every case, too catholic in their tastes, and to protect the fruit industry of the Dominion, none of them was released.

In discussing the primitive vegetation in an earlier chapter, some reference was made to the character and distribution of

ahc

Fig. 77. A giant blue-gum on the Blenheim-Picton highway in Marlborough. Somewhat less successful than the California conifers, the Australian "eucalypts" are, nevertheless, extremely common in the island.

the forests at the time of the first European contacts. While there
were stands of excellent softwood timber where the podocarps
(*Podocarpus* and *Dacrydium* spp.) were frequent, there were few
of these east of the principal watershed through which the agricultural and pastoral occupation quickly spread. The absence of
farm wood lots was felt in a lack of firewood as much as in the
need to import building timber. Above all, there was no shelter
for the homesteads or for the flocks and herds. The urgent need for
some quick-growing tree, or trees, which would solve this problem
led first to the planting of the willows and Lombardy poplars,
either of which had very limited virtues in providing shelter or
timber except in special environmental situations. The Lombardy
poplar is one of the more frost-resistant among the trees of rapid
growth and it does well under a fairly low rainfall; the willow,
in contrast, "likes to have its feet in the water." The next trees
planted on any considerable scale to meet the need were Aus-

tralian eucalypts and wattles, especially Blue Gum (*Eucalyptus globulus*), Red Mountain Ash (*E. gigantea*), and Cider Gum (*E. gunnii*).* The Blue Gum has suffered very severely recently from the Eucalyptus scale (*Eriococcus coriaceus*), and it is usually now successful only in the extreme south of the island, although it was once common everywhere (fig. 77). Though the ladybird beetle (*Rhizobius ventralis*) was introduced to combat the scale, and though other Australian insects which attack the scale have been acclimatized, it is still not safe to hope for successful maturity of Blue Gum plantings in Canterbury or Marlborough.† The "Ash" and the Cider Gum are each much more resistant to both insects and frost than the Blue Gum. The "Ash" grows so rapidly that it is one of the few trees which can be used interspersed with Monterey pine in shelter belts. The Cider Gum is the most frost-resistant of the eucalypts which are valuable for shelter purposes, and it is successful even in Central Otago. The only other hardwoods introduced from Australia in any numbers, the wattles (*Acacia* spp.), have been of very little importance in South Island, *A. decurrens* and *A. dealbata* being the only ones of which more than a few individuals are known. The few small blocks planted to the latter are chiefly used to provide firewood today. In general the Eucalypts have not been a very successful solution to the shelter-belt problem in South Island, and while their introduction in the late fifties was a rather natural result of the close cultural and economic relationships between South Island and the Australian colonies, it may well be that, in this event, the association was unfortunate. Indeed, it is probable that the fashion for planting the Australian Gums delayed for ten years the introduction of the more suitable conifers on a wide scale.

The idea of planting conifers for farm wood lots and shelter belts would not have been a revolutionary one to the emigrants. East[7] points out that Scotch firs had been widely planted throughout England in the eighteenth century. There were many early residents of South Island who, possibly by remembrance of these, thought the conifers might meet the demands. The Deans, for example, sent home in 1850 not only for haw bushes and seeds of alder and birch, but also for seven pounds of Scotch fir seed.[8]

* Other species of *Eucalyptus* which have done fairly well include *E. obliqua, E. amygdaline, E. viminalis,* and *E. regnans.*[6]
† Another pest, the leaf-weevil (*Gonipterus scatellatus*) has been checked with a small mymarid fly (*Anaphoidea nitens*).

The most reasonable assumption which can be made about the "insignis" * (Monterey pine or *Pinus radiata*) and "macrocarpa" (Monterey cypress or *Cupressus Macrocarpa*) is that seeds or seedlings arrived almost simultaneously in New Zealand and in the Australian colonies during the fifties and sixties, and it would be equally reasonable to suppose that this had some connection with the gold-rush traffic across the Pacific. The rôle of the spectacularly large insignis cones as souvenirs may have contributed to this transfer. It is certain that the first introductions were a small representation in a large group of immigrant conifers which were tried; mixed with these as well as with the large number of hardwoods, the California trees had to wait through the trial period to have their virtues recognized. Not until the seventies is this pair mentioned at all frequently by observers, and only in that decade were their seedlings advertised for sale by nurseries in Christchurch and Dunedin.

Foweraker[9] lists forty-seven of the more important conifers which had been introduced into Canterbury alone up to 1925, including species of *Pinus, Picea, Abies, Cupressus, Chamoecyparus, Araucaria, Sequoia,* and *Pseudotsuga.* Some of these he is able to identify as having been planted in the fifties and sixties, among them a Douglas Fir (*Pseudotsuga taxifolia,* known popularly as Oregon Pine or simply "Oregon" in Australasia) introduced in 1859 as a seedling, and another seedling of the larger redwood (*Sequoia gigantea,* known in British forestry circles as "Wellingtonia") which was imported from Exeter in 1862 and successfully established on the Acland estate at Mount Peel, where it has grown to be a magnificent tree today. Moreover, he has definite evidence of importation in pots of seedlings of Wellingtonia, insignis, and macrocarpa from the Australian colonies to Christchurch in the summer of 1864-1865. Between 1868 and 1870 individuals of these three, together with Western yellow pine (*P. Ponderosa,* locally called "Pondosa pine"), "Oregon," and European larch (*Larix decidua*), were planted out in a block of seven acres at the Albury homestead in South Canterbury. Many fine specimens of most of the conifers, as well as various of the hardwoods, which were planted in the seventies or before, can be seen today on dozens of old homesteads throughout the island (fig. 78).

* This popular name derives from an earlier specific classification of the tree as *Pinus insignis.*

Joyce Finney

FIG. 78. Station homesteads (*above*) near Burke's Pass—the northern gateway to the Mackenzie country; and (*below*) in the upper Awatere valley. These station homesteads in the tussock country are set off vividly from the dun-colored grassland by the deep green of the exotic conifers which are universally planted. One is reminded of the origin of the name "Black Hills" in South Dakota, where a conifer-clothed mountain stood out so strikingly against the yellow grasslands.

ahc

It is fairly generally agreed among the farmers questioned that macrocarpa had been the most useful of all from the point of view of shelter alone. It has no rival as a thick, quick-growing, house-high hedge. There are certain limiting climatic and edaphic factors to its successful growth, so that it does not occur as widely as does insignis. It likes a free and well-drained soil, and it prefers a rainfall in excess of twenty inches a year; neither of these factors, however, excludes it from any considerable areas. It has no equal among the exotics in its ability to withstand wind; on the open southern coastal plains of Southland as well as in lowland Canterbury and coastal Marlborough, it has been of extraordinary value. If planted as single trees, or in groups of three or four, the branches of mature individuals have an enormous spread, and the heaviest or most persistent rain rarely penetrates to the ground beneath them. A few such scattered clumps will protect a great many sheep. In its more general use as a constituent of farm hedges it has the special advantage that it survives trimming exceptionally well, is comparatively long-lived, and retains its lower branches better than any other conifer suitable to this purpose. Other uses for macrocarpa are as underplantings in native forests (because of its shade tolerance), for producing a timber which is free-splitting and more durable in the ground than any other exotic conifer, and for yielding a satisfactory firewood.[10]

Insignis has been more widely grown than macrocarpa, until quite recently at least. It became the fashion in the seventies when experimental plantings proved that its rate of growth was greater than that of any other tree suitable for use in shelter belts (fig. 79). It spread rapidly through the scattered homesteads of the sixties, from sea level to elevations above twenty-five hundred feet, and from one end of the island to the other. When the period of closer settlement from 1880 to 1910 demanded the smaller divisions of fields in mixed farming practice, and multiplied many times the need for farm shelter, insignis seemed the ideal tree for the purpose; moreover, due to the widespread earlier plantings, its seeds were generally available.

A consideration of future timber supplies does not seem to have played a very great rôle in the choice of trees planted on farms. Experience over three-quarters of a century has shown that the insignis is a poor tree to plant where drainage is bad, and that it is not very profitable in areas above fifteen hundred feet in elevation, or with less than twenty inches of rainfall. Since

New Zealand State Forest Service

Fig. 79. The rate of growth of *Pinus radiata* in New Zealand is truly amazing. These trees in Dusky State Forest are twenty-one years of age.

it reaches maturity in forty to forty-five years, the problem of replacement of over-age trees is a considerable one. Plantations allowed to become senile are particularly liable to damage from wind, and in many instances there has been damage to stock and buildings from falling trees.

Of more importance than the trees planted for shelter, both in numbers and in relation to general timber supplies on the island, have been the plantations of considerable blocks here and there of various exotics, especially conifers (fig. 80) but including some eucalypts and wattles. Some of these were private ventures inspired by special land regulations, which granted title or preemptive rights to land in proportion to areas planted to timber trees. In Canterbury, in the seventies, as many as two acres of Crown lands were granted for one acre planted with trees.[11] Turner and Beasley [12] state that the first plantation by any local authority was that of the Selwyn Plantation Board, in mid-Canterbury. As nearly as records and memories agree, this was in 1879, and since that date this Board has had some sixteen thousand acres granted to it for tree-planting purposes. Another

New Zealand Aerial Mapping, Ltd.

Fig. 80. Conifers flourish with a minimum of care in the former grass-land areas, and such plantations as these (the dark patches in the photograph) in North Canterbury contribute a substantial amount of timber to supplement the dwindling natural supply.

type of semi-public afforestation was undertaken by the Railway Department of the central government which started its own plantations, again in Canterbury, between 1884-1891.[13] Finally the central government formed its own authority, an afforestation branch of the Lands and Survey Department, in 1896. Official government nurseries were started at Tapanui and Eweburn in Otago and, gradually, the afforestation programs were expanded, especially in areas of pre-European tussock-grassland (fig. 81).

The scope of the combined plantings by individuals, afforestation companies, local authorities, and the central government is best seen by a comparison of figures given in recent government publications. The situation in 1940 is shown in table LXXVIII.[14] The natural forests of South Island still furnish the major supplies of timber produced within the whole country, and of this cutting the major concentration is now in Westland (fig. 81), which has produced more timber since the turn of the century than all of the rest of South Island together.

TABLE LXXVIII

A COMPARISON OF AREAS IN STANDING NATIVE BUSH AND EXOTIC PLANTATIONS IN SOUTH ISLAND IN 1940

	Standing Native Bush	Exotic Plantations conifers	hardwoods *
	(acres)	(acres)	(acres)
Marlborough	130,581	3,155	468
Nelson	279,706	31,972	516
Westland	448,348	3,347	45
Canterbury	122,728	72,894	5,072
Otago	245,171	37,877	884
Southland	120,763	7,103	257

* Chiefly eucalypts.

FIG. 81. Remnants of original native forests and plantations of exotic trees (1938).

Table LXXIX [15] indicates for all New Zealand the proportion of different timbers cut in the 1939-1940 season. Most of the Rimu cut comes from Westland, Nelson, and the Marlborough Sounds. The "beech" (*Nothofagus* spp.) was cut chiefly in Southland. Most of the insignis was cut in the great plantations of North Island; in South Island it was most important from Canterbury. Turner [16] made the assertion in 1937 that, outside of the state exotic plantations (that is, on those of private companies or local bodies) 99 per cent of plantation trees were insignis.* The bulk of the commercial afforestation ventures was, however, in the North Island on the volcanic plateau near the big lakes, as only eight of thirty-two companies which operated in 1939-1940 were in South Island (five in Nelson, two in Southland, and one in Otago). [18] There are of course many privately owned plantations in Canterbury which are not included with the areas attributed to commercial companies.

TABLE LXXIX

ALL TIMBER CUT IN NEW ZEALAND (1939-40)

Species of Timber	Quantity Cut (millions of feet b.m.)	Percentage of Total Cut
Rimu	207.1	61.6%
Insignis	46.8	13.9
Kahikatea	33.0	9.9
Matai	21.2	6.3
Totara	10.9	3.3
"Beech"	9.0	2.7
Other	8.0	2.3
Total	336.0	100.0%

Although it is true that, in 1940, outside of the state forests the insignis did monopolize most of the planted areas on the island, the government was not satisfied that this tree is the single answer to the problem of future timber supply, which is growing more and more critical to those who look ahead even a decade or two. In table LXXIX it should be noted that four of the five leading indigenous timber trees are species of *Podocarpus* (that is, softwoods). It is the shortage of hardwoods and partly the deficiencies in quality, as well as quantity, of locally produced softwoods, whether indigenous or exotic, which has left New Zealand with a

* In 1940, of 310,441 acres in commercial plantations, only 279,810 were in insignis or Monterey pine, which indicates that recent practice has moved toward the later-maturing but more valuable conifers. [17]

net deficit in value in its imports and exports of timber products. In 1940 New Zealand exported over seventeen million board feet (worth £194,370) chiefly to Australia, of which two-thirds was rimu; it imported in the same year £293,968 worth of such products, notably Australian hardwoods, oak, and Douglas Fir.[19] While it seems unlikely that New Zealand can ever supply its own hardwood needs, it can reduce these by using more creosoted softwoods, and it should be able to both counterbalance declining indigenous softwood production, and reduce the necessity for such large importations of Douglas Fir as more and more of its present plantations reach maturity.

As a result, the government has experimented in South Island's state afforestation projects with a large number of conifers. In 1921, of New Zealand's 38,640 acres of government plantings, 12,392 acres were in South Island; of these 3,952 acres were in northern Canterbury; 1,977 acres in Central Otago; 5,984 in south Otago; and the remaining 594 acres were scattered in experimental plots. Even at that time several other imported conifers were being used more widely than insignis in such plots; the relative acreages of the five leading conifers are shown in table LXXX.[20]

TABLE LXXX

AREAS IN GOVERNMENT PLANTATIONS OF PRINCIPAL EXOTIC CONIFERS
IN 1921

Species	Acres
Corsican pine (*Pinus laricio*)	2,764
Larch (*Larix decidua*)	2,597
Insignis (*Pinus radiata*)	1,507
Western Yellow pine (*P. ponderosa*)	1,117
Mixed, Corsican and Western Yellow pine	1,395
Pinus austriaca	1,004

In 1925 the program of government planting was rapidly accelerated. While the largest areas selected were in North Island, South Island's acreage increased more than fivefold between 1921 and 1930, or to 66,186 acres; of this, Balmoral and Eyrewell plantations in Canterbury had 18,671 acres and 12,008 acres, respectively, and the Blue Mountain reserve near Tapanui in south Otago had 18,713 acres. The chief species had changed little; they were, in order of areal importance: western yellow pine, larch, Douglas Fir, and insignis. The principal South Island nurseries were, and still are, at Golden Downs in Nelson, Hanmer Springs in north

Canterbury, Naseby in Central Otago, and at Tapanui in south Otago. Since then there has been little planting of exotics in South Island's state forests, but the introduction of Lodgepole pine (*P. murrayana*) and of Western Red Cedar (*Thuja plicata*) has added still more representation from the forest flora of the American West. The quick-growing southern pines (*P. palustris, P. taeda,* and *P. caribaoa*) apparently find the climate of South Island too cool. Various spruces, including both Norway (*Picea excelsa*) and Sitka (*P. sitchensis*), have been fairly extensively planted at one time or another, but have been so severely attacked by the spruce aphis that they have all but disappeared.

The Douglas Fir is the most valuable timber tree of the group, but the Corsican, Western Yellow, and Lodgepole pines have provided the most significant recent competition for insignis and macrocarpa in farm woodlots or shelter belts, due to their less exacting demands as to soil and climate. They are also more suitable for planting in mixed stands, both as among themselves and with larch. The fairly extensive plantings of this last tree are a bit hard to rationalize. Its deciduous habit makes it much less suitable for shelter and it makes indifferent timber. The facts that it thrives well and has a decorative value, enhanced in the minds of the oldest generation of residents by its European associations, may account for its relatively high acreage. There seems to be little choice between the different pines in terms of relative resistance to pests. The three chief insect enemies are the wood wasp (*Sirex juvencus* or S. *noctilis*), white blight (*Pineus pini,* or *Chermes pini*) and the European bark-beetle (*Hylastes ater*). These are kept fairly well in hand by both silvicultural techniques and biological controls.[21]

This review of the introduction and spread of exotic trees emphasizes the lines of inheritance reaching to South Island from Australia and North America. In its immigrant trees South Island has reproduced less of the characteristics of the British countryside than in almost any other features of its present landscape; these trees are much the most significant of all landscape features which may have been derived from the United States. Of the American trees, Monterey pine is still the most significant exotic introduced, and it, with the cypress which come from the same area, forms one of the best examples of an expatriated plant which played a very much more important rôle in an alien habitat than it ever had at home. The introduction and spread of gorse might have been easily predicted by a shrewd prophet in the mid-nineteenth century, but the unexpectedly rapid adoption of trees very little used elsewhere in the world, and of very limited range in their own home areas, to the exclusion of so many available and well-known alternatives, is of very great significance to the general problems of cultural influences in plant migrations. To assume, in the absence of evidence to the contrary, that the more likely of several alternatives did occur, is often necessary in historical analyses of cultural development; it remains, however, nothing but an assumption, and, had such been made in this case, it must have proved disastrous to subsequent reasoning.

V

CONCLUSION

CONCLUSION

A major purpose of this book has been to introduce students to some problems in the historical geography of the South Island of New Zealand. Perhaps as significant as any of these are the striking similarities and differences between the rural landscapes of the island and those of Great Britain whence most of its present population came. An explanation of these comparisons and contrasts, based on an analysis of the course of the invasion of men and their floral or faunal camp-followers, has been attempted, and a serious effort to emphasize the significance of plant and animal migrations to changes in regional character has been made.

South Island, as we have seen, has almost the same size as Czechoslovakia or Illinois, just under sixty thousand square miles. Largely mountainous, it has, still, quite a bit of hill-and-down country and some fairly extensive plains. Its soils are probably everywhere quite immature, and are certainly nowhere of great natural fertility. In climate the island is very similar to the principal island of Great Britain, but there is much more variety arising from great differences of exposure to the principal trajectories of incoming air masses. The extremely heavy rainfall of the western coasts and their adjoining mountain slopes is balanced against annual means of little more than ten inches in some of the rain-shadowed intermont basins. Rarely is the journey long in winter from the snowfree coasts to well-covered skiing slopes in the mountains. But where most of the settlement has occurred, extremes of temperature show distinct maritime moderation, and by the use of shelter belts of various exotic trees and shrubs it has proved unnecessary to provide winter housing for stock. The vegetation associations of the island, as they appeared to explorers in the nineteenth century, included two areally dominant types. A rain forest, somewhat anomalous under the existing annual regime of air temperature, lay chiefly to the west of the mountains and near to the sea. Over most of the larger areas east of the principal watershed, the land was covered with tall waving grasses which grew in bunches, or tussocks.

In this area lived a few thousand Maori at the time of Cook's first visit. Partly agricultural, they derived their living largely from the resources of fish in the rivers, lakes, and oceans, from the hunting of birds and from the gathering of fruits, roots, and other plant food. While this primitive Polynesian people contributed materially to the success of the earliest whaling and sealing stations established on the coasts, they neither greatly aided, hindered, or otherwise affected the subsequent course of European settlement. By 1850 they were, as they remain today, of little more significance in the region than are the gypsies in Great Britain. The unimportance of the Maori population of the island is in vivid contrast to the profound influence of this people in the North Island, and it may need additional emphasis to those whose knowledge of New Zealand has been in any way acquired through the reading of travelogues.

Of European plants and animals, potatoes and pigs were introduced and widely disseminated over the island by the early part of the nineteenth century. Before 1840, scores of sealing, whaling, and trading ships had visited the island's shores, and dozens of permanent or seasonal settlements had been made in its bays and coves. Many European crops besides potatoes had been tried and had succeeded: goats, cattle, fowl, dogs, and rats had been established here and there on the island, chiefly by the activities of the shore-whaling industry before the first organized settlement occurred in 1841.

This planned series of settlements, as initiated, was conceived as an exemplification of colonizing theories widely held in Great Britain at the time, the greatest proponent of which was Edward Gibbon Wakefield. It was intended that there should be transferred to the new country a cross-section of English rural life; that there should be constituted, at the very antipode of the center of the burgeoning British Empire, a reproduction of its most admirable characteristics.

In the course of fifty years the island was occupied almost to the extent that it is today, although the total population has since markedly increased. The main constituents of the population were the urban poor from the British Isles, who can have had little if any of agricultural or pastoral experience in the homeland. As it turned out, the character of the colony, and its lines of development in terms of the use of the land, bore little resemblance to the plans of those who had worked so hard for its foundation.

At first the relative location of South Island with respect to the earlier settlements in Australia, and the route of sailing vessels to New Zealand by way of that continent, exerted a profound influence on the shape taken by the activities of the agricultural and pastoral entrepreneurs. In South Island were thousands of grassy acres, whose use, if not ownership, it quickly developed, could be had virtually for the asking. In New South Wales, Victoria, and Van Diemen's Land, flocks of Merino sheep which grew the premium wool of the entire world, were rapidly increasing in size. There, too, were herds of Shorthorn cattle admirably adapted to the triple needs of the butcher, the dairy, and the plow. New Zealand was sufficiently close that sheep could be transported with an average loss in transit of less than a quarter of the animals shipped. Moreover, in New South Wales, in the eighteen-forties, a depression had bankrupted or seriously embarrassed many of the squatters. Of these, some moved to New Zealand; others sold sheep at prices as low as a shilling a head to those who wished to obtain them to ship there. Across the Tasman Sea came the sheep in a steady stream, and with them the skills for their management to absorb the energies of the immigrant laborers and capitalists alike in the new colony.

When the gold rushes of the fifties attracted hundreds of shiploads of men from all parts of the world to New South Wales, South Island lost a few of its more adventurous, or least successful, people, but it gained a market for general farm produce which helped to establish firmly an essential agricultural cornerstone for the great pastoral industry. When the gold seekers flocked in turn to South Island itself, a decade later, it received not only a lusty, if motley, addition to its people, but also a wide variety of new skills, not the least of which was knowledge of the management of hydraulic races. The Australian influence also helped to generate a breezy self-confidence and an impatience with tradition which were clearly reflected in the development of new techniques of land use.

From the eighteen-seventies until the end of the century the influences from the British Isles became relatively stronger than they had been in earlier years. The beginning of refrigerated shipments of meat and dairy products to Great Britain served to consolidate earlier experiments in the husbandry of English sheep and cattle, which fed on pastures of English grasses or upon green-feed and roots grown in rotations following British practice; virtually all of the techniques which then became the central interest of the farming industry had, however, been tried out in one place or another on the island in the course of the first forty years of settlement. Similarities of climate made the establishment of patterns and practices familiar in the homeland easy to a degree that was impossible in Australia. South Island was, in its cultural rural landscape in the eighteen-nineties, very much the "Britain of the South" as visitors from the center of the empire frequently and fondly dubbed it. Not only were the plants, animals, and patterns of a familiar rotational grassland farming to be seen everywhere throughout the settled areas, but in the mountains were thousands of antlered stags which rivaled those of Scotland. If Britain now had few wild pigs, the memories of boar hunting were fresh enough in the memories of the people, in song and legend, that the presence of this animal among the big-game resources of the new land did not seem an alien one. Into the sides of countless hillsides were tunneled the rabbit warrens, and through the grainfields hopped and pecked the English sparrows, to provide two less pleasant reminders of home. Even transplanted British salmon could be taken in the boisterous rivers.

Yet there were profound and obvious enough differences. While the endless gorse hedges were familiar, the new barbed wire fences were not. English oaks and elms there were, but they were hard to find amid the regiments of Australian and Californian trees. The slated and thatched roofs of English houses were everywhere replaced by those of the new corrugated iron. If English sheep were already beginning to oust the Merino from the best land, or at least to dilute its blood there, the latter still had no rival in the back country, and the great half-bred flocks obviously showed their descent from this great Australian gift of the earliest years. Oxen had all but disappeared as draft animals, but the dairy and beef herds were still largely formed from selected descendants of the earlier Shorthorn herds of New South Wales. Wheat-growing was the leading agricultural activity, and the techniques of its production, indeed often the wheats themselves, came as largely from Australia or North America as from Great Britain.

The new century was to see the further dilution or replacement of Merino blood in the sheep and the gradual retreat of the Shorthorn before the Hereford and the Jersey. English grasses spread still more widely as did various animal and vegetable pests of British origin. But, in the new century, the people of the island with their co-citizens in the later but more quickly developed island to the north, depended ever more on their own initiative instead of upon borrowing from elsewhere. Quick to adopt the new developments of other lands, they probably gave to the world more than they received in inventiveness directed toward the improvement of use of the land. The basic techniques and patterns established by the turn of the century have experienced, however, little fundamental change; the last half century has seen consolidation and improvement rather than any notable shift in direction.

South Island's inheritances from Great Britain in terms of major directives of land use must, one supposes, almost inevitably have been great, because of the predominant origins of its people in those islands and because of the remarkable climatic similarity of the new habitat to the old. Apart from the proximity of the Australian colonies and the considerable contrasts in habitat characteristics other than climatic, the most important differences from Britain which do exist can, I believe, be traced to the fact that the population, as it arrived, was one largely unskilled in the practices of British farming. It must have had to go to school to *any* system of husbandry and it was able to master the necessary fundamentals without having to unlearn, or to break the chains of old prejudice. The learning was easier because there were so many familiar touches of home in general manners and customs. If the methods of managing cattle and pastures, and of processing butter and cheese were unfamiliar, it was still true that the butter was packed in 56-pound boxes, because half a hundred-weight was a convenient, known size in the English market to which it was destined. So it was with many another item: a greater or less degree of familiar things, the rest borrowed from elsewhere or autochthonous in the island.

The South Island is facing serious problems of land management today toward the solution of which British practice can make only small contributions. To its own initiative and to the experience of resource deterioration in other new, raw lands it must largely look for help. To a considerable degree, however, both islands of New Zealand seem to have finished borrowing from any source. Perhaps a new influx of population in some postwar reshuffling of the world's peoples will bring with it some cultural urges to new directions for the rural economy of the country. If the people who came should be largely from the British Isles, or largely of urban background, this would hardly be likely. A greater probability for change would be that the demand for New Zealand's present pastoral products should greatly decrease, which might happen if the standard of living in the British Isles in postwar years should materially decline, or if the prices of wool, butterfat, or mutton should otherwise be forced to levels which would make their highly organized production in New Zealand unprofitable. As the chemists create cheaper and more acceptable substitutes for wool or butter, New Zealand's farmers may, again, be forced to radically alter their production program. But whatever the future may have in store there seems no immediate prospect of alteration of basic rural patterns in the island.

APPENDIX

A. Administrative Divisions and "Regions" of South Island (*see* figs. 2 and 3)

Some reference to the larval stage of British government in New Zealand was made in chapter III. In the course of several fumbling attempts to create some administrative order in the islands, an act was passed by the Imperial Government in 1846 [*] which, on paper, gave New Zealand a very elaborate system of government with municipalities, provinces with bi-cameral legislatures, and a general colonial assembly, also of two chambers. The incumbent governor, Grey, an arbitrary if generally benevolent despot, succeeded in having the plan revoked, and a somewhat less ambitious scheme did not become operative until 1852. Grey did, however, set up two areas for administrative purposes in 1848 which he called provinces. The province of New Munster included Stewart Island, South (or Middle [†]) Island, and a section of southern North Island; New Ulster comprised the rest of North Island.

The New Act of 1851, which came into effect the next year, created six individual provinces. Three of these were in South Island, each of which in the course of its existence underwent a politico-areal fission which resulted in the existence, at one time or another, of the six provinces shown on the map (fig. 2). As indicated thereon, not all of

[*] 9 and 10 Vict. Cap. 103.

[†] Throughout the nineteenth century the South Island was more popularly known as the Middle Island, and is so labeled on maps of the New Zealand Department of Lands and Survey; the name is still recognized in statutes.

these existed at one time, Southland rejoining Otago before Westland deserted Canterbury, but remembrance of things past has given some separate identity to the six areas in popular consciousness. As divisions for administrative purposes, they have had no function since 1876, but the census continues to use their boundaries, with one exception, as census report units. The exception is the boundary between Southland and Otago, which for census purposes is taken as roughly the same as the boundary between the new administrative areas called land districts. These latter have the same names as the provincial districts, but they have different boundaries (fig. 2). Westland's boundary had been advanced north and Canterbury land district is made to include a considerable area of southeastern Nelson province, approximately the territory of the two present counties of Amuri and Cheviot (fig. 3).

The constitution of town districts and boroughs began early in the course of settlement, and continued very rapidly in Otago during the gold-rush boom of the sixties. Of thirty-six boroughs in existence in all of New Zealand in 1876, nineteen were in Otago, which at that time included Southland. The comatose state of many of these boroughs at present ° has too many parallels in longer-settled parts of the world to call for comment here. The powers of the boroughs are not in any important degree different from usual municipal powers in Canada, Australia, and the United States, deriving from acts of the General Assembly.

Other types of local bodies set up early were road boards, and, beginning with the creation of the first in 1863, all of occupied South Island was divided into road districts within a decade. These elected their own councils and had power to levy on real property, even to borrow against expectable tax income. More rating districts followed in rapid succession for such purposes as river control, land drainage, water supply, and rabbit control; provision of electric power and tramways; and the support and administration of hospitals and harbor areas. Rarely did the boundaries of one district coincide with those of others, and an individual, not unusually, could be subject to rates of many boards with widely varying constituencies.

The present existence of counties suggests the possibility that these various local boards could have been consolidated under county councils, but this has rarely been done. In some cases, especially in the highly "rural" counties like Awatere, the County Council has a good deal of work and authority; in others, particularly in counties containing one or more dominant towns, it may have little importance. The county organization was relatively late in appearing. Though among the instructions given to Hobson, upon his appointment as first

° Arrowtown, Naseby, Clyde, and Hampden are outstanding examples, and these were to be followed by other "ghost-boroughs" in Westland.

governor of New Zealand, were some relative to the establishment of counties and hundreds, the first administrative county in South Island was not set up until 1867, when Westland County was created within Canterbury Province and given a system of local government in the following year.

The Counties Act (1876) was passed to provide a comprehensive system of local government upon the abolition of the provinces in that year. The Councils are elective and have powers to rate for a wide variety of purposes. They were creations from without, rather than from within, however, and there is no county-consciousness in New Zealand, a parallel to the situation in most of the western states and provinces of the United States and Canada. Few South Islanders think of themselves as men of Halswell, of Vincent, or of Awatere. Regional consciousness tends rather to be related to the earlier provincial divisions, or parts thereof. A map (fig. 3) has been presented in this volume, which attempts to indicate a division of the island into those areas which have some reality in the consciousness of the people there resident and of their neighbors. These boundaries are of course elastic. "The Mackenzie Country" is also in a sense part of "The Lake Country"; "The Hakataramea" is also a part of South Canterbury. Similarly most of "The Lake Country" is thought of as, at times, part of Central Otago or Southland, and the southern Lake Country is often grouped with "The Fiords" as Fiordland. So we might run through the list, suggesting other combinations and divisions.

It is a truism, surely, that the conscious reality of the regions is greatest near their centers and fades rapidly toward the margins. The people of Christchurch rather think of Rangiora as in North Canterbury; the people of Rangiora generally do not, and the people of Hanmer Springs almost certainly would not so describe the location of the former town. The most easily recognizable areal consciousness exists on the west coast. A "Coaster," as he is and wishes to be known, has still some of the independent swagger of the "digger" in his attitude; this applies from Karamea in the north to Bruce Bay in the south. Otherwise the Scottish elements in Southland and Otago seem to evidence greatest local pride of birthplace. So rapidly does the population shift about, however, that what consciousness of locality may have developed before 1900 seems now to be gradually dying away.

B. Types of Farms

SHEEP FARMS

1. *A mixed dairy and sheep farm of 250 acres in the lower Mataura valley of Southland.* Eighty cows were milked and, though the young cattle were pastured on another area, the farm carried 650 ewes in

addition. The manager cropped fifty to seventy-five acres a year in rotation about his farm, putting down new English grasses with each move. In an average year (the variations were great) there were twenty-five acres in Swedes, fifteen in *choumoellier* (narrow-stemmed kale), and twenty to thirty acres in oats sown down with the new grasses. To maintain heavy grass production, the farmer was forced to top-dress all his grass with 3 cwt. of lime and 2 cwt. of superphosphate per acre per year; his newly sown grasses getting a ton of lime and 3 cwt. of "super" the first year. (Until such heavy liming was resorted to, it proved impossible to develop heavy grass production in Southland's heavy rainfall area.) Though most of the oats grown in Southland are utilized by being fed off by the stock, cut as hay, or chopped as chaff, after ripening, this farmer sold his, ripened and threshed, to an oatmeal factory at Gore. Such a combination of dairying, sheep farming, and cash-crop production is by no means unique. The farmer had excellent mechanical equipment, including a full set of plows, discs, harrows, etc., and a 20-40 American tractor. Yet the necessity for growing turnips on ridges in Southland (fig. 71) involved considerable labor in hoeing and thinning by hand. The *Brassicas*, both roots and tops, took up the pasture-slack in the winter for both sheep and cattle, and as usual were fed off in the fields.

The sheep were all pure Romneys (the most usual breed on the Southland plains). The ewes are brought in each year, about half the flock being replaced, and half the ewes and all the lambs are sold each year as fats after making maximum use of the early flush of spring growth in the pastures. The first draft goes to the freezing works just before Christmas, the lambs after mid-January, the three hundred ewes left maintaining themselves on the reduced pasture yields.

The ewes come off near-by hill country (in the main from the Hokonuis to the northwest and the hills to the east of the Mataura valley) and are usually full six-tooth ewes of four or five years of age. The greatest danger, foot-rot, is carefully watched.

The pastures although comprising nearly 80 per cent Rye-grass, include as well White clover, Sweet Vernal, Brown Top, Yorkshire Fog, and Dogstail.

2. In sharp contrast was the farmer on *a small area of flat land and low hills, west of the Clutha (between Alexandra and Clyde) in Central Otago.* His father came up to the Dunstan in 1863 from the Bendigo diggings in Victoria, and remained to take up land for sheep. He had applied the water for hydraulic mining to grow gardens in Bendigo; here he, with others, used it to grow fruit trees and English grasses under ten to fifteen inches of rainfall. At the present time the son and grandson of the pioneer run adjacent farms in the area; the original holding of six hundred acres has been subdivided and we may consider

one of the subdivisions, a 170-acre farm, as an example. (It may need to be emphasized again that there are no typical examples even in this small area, which is the reason for avoiding greater use of statistical averages which have even less significance in South Island than elsewhere.) The farm is entirely devoted to grass-farming for sheep; it is all irrigated by systems inherited from, or developing out of, the old mining water races, and the irrigation is all by wild flooding. The water is turned on once a fortnight: about one head (that is, one cusec for twenty-four hours, but the old alluvial mining term remains in use) per fifty acres. It is used only in summer, beginning with late October or early November, and usually continuing until March, though on occasion it has not been used after the end of January. It is easy to overdo the watering, which results in swampiness, the encouragement of the growth of unpalatable rushes, and the inducement of foot-rot in the sheep. The pastures are as permanent as possible; one ley has been down for forty years. A variable acreage is in alfalfa, however, and here it goes out in six years, necessitating replowing and resowing. The alfalfa gives two to three crops of hay a year, which suffices for winter surplus feed. The grass pastures are all harrowed in spring and top-dressed with 2 cwt. of "super" per acre per year. Though the pasture mixture contains the usual dominance of Rye grasses, the manager attempts to keep up the clover content by careful rotational pruning in an attempt to keep any part of it from getting away.

The farm carries some six hundred ewes a year. In the 1940-1941 season the farmer obtained 770 lambs from 540 ewes. Like the last-mentioned farmer, he buys five-year-old Romney half-breds from higher country and puts Southdown rams (imported from Canterbury) to them. The rams are put out in the second week of April; lambing is in mid-September, docking the first week in October. His wool check is of secondary importance to his sales of fat lambs and fat ewes, but he clips over five thousand pounds a year—some nine pounds per ewe—of high-grade half-bred wool. The ewes, as in Farm No. 1, are kept only two years. His chief trouble is foot-rot, and the greatest care is exercised in keeping sheep off the most recently flooded fields (the irrigation of paddocks is in rotation), and in the inspection, paring, and dressing of the feet.

3. Another farm in Central Otago, this also being devoted entirely to sheep, is *a high-country station of twenty-one thousand acres, mostly on the hills.* It is a subdivision of one of the great squatting runs of the early days which was some three times its size. The subdivision was bad, especially in terms of relative allotments of winter and summer country. (This is unfortunately true of entirely too much of the subdivision of the old high-country runs, and, besides reducing carrying capacity in general, the practice may actually be advancing vege-

tation deterioration by excessively heavy grazing of different areas at the wrong times of the year.) This farm, however, is exceptionally well situated by having, in the upper Clutha valley, nearly all of the winter country (that is, low-lying areas where supplementary feed can be grown and where sheep can be protected from the snow) of the former run. Most of the run is, however, clothed with deteriorated native tussock, on the western slopes of the Dunstan mountains at elevations of from a thousand feet (in the upper Clutha valley) to over five thousand feet. The flat consists of three hundred acres, all irrigated, for hay and winter feed.

Though the farmer has from thirty-two hundred to thirty-five hundred sheep, only three men, except for the shearing gang, work the whole place. Each has a pair of horses and four dogs, breaking in two new dogs each year. This manager is sure that, in his area, English setter blood is replacing that of the Scottish collies in the working dogs. His main income is from sales of wool, but he has occasionally been able to supplement this from the sale of surplus ewes. Until recently he ran a pure Merino flock. Difficulty of disposing of the ewes, however, has led him to introduce long-wool and Corriedale blood, and he is moving gradually to the establishment of a half-bred flock. The number of sheep carried has fallen from thirty-five hundred to thirty-two hundred as a result of this shift.

The depredations of rabbits here constitute a severe problem, though it is now less serious than formerly, and the manager feels that, on his run, there has been some improvement in an area which includes the most badly mutilated associations of native tussock vegetation in South Island. So well has he kept rabbits under control that he has part-time work for only one man on the strychnine-with-carrot lines. The increase in stoats, ferrets, and wild cats has helped, he believes. Rabbit fences are very expensive even though, in dry Central Otago, they last very much longer than in wetter areas, and he has not been able to use as many as he would like.

4. One more example should be sufficient to indicate the variety of husbandry types; this time *a combination of fat-lamb raising and agriculture in the Ashburton area in the heart of the Canterbury plains* will be described. The working area of the farm is 440 acres of which fifteen consist of unplowable light shingle. Grain and pulse crops were sown on 180 acres in this particular year, thirty acres were in alfalfa, twenty in rape (for green fodder), two in mangel-wurtzels, and two hundred in "permanent" pasture. Another forty-five acres are taken up with buildings and useless river-bed (chiefly gone to gorse). We may neglect, temporarily, the farmer's full complement of machinery, his dozen horses, his tractor, truck, and combination harvester-thresher, his five dairy cows and his one sow—though such additional items are

as typical here as elsewhere. His total gross income, in 1939, with a slightly different arrangement of fields than that described above, was:

Dairy	£ 90
Sheep sales (including fat lambs, fat ewes and stud sheep)	756
Wool sales	350
Sales of wheat	400
Sales of peas	670
Sales of barley (to maltsters) ..	260
Sales of grass seed	130
Total	*£ 2,656*

If his expenses (including wages of management, depreciation, etc.) were set at seventeen hundred pounds, the margin of profit would have been a thousand pounds. Professor E. H. Bevin of Canterbury Agricultural College, who knows something of this farm and supplied these income figures, suggests that one-half of the margin was due to a good season and an exceptionally shrewd manager.

To get back to the sheep, which bring in about 40 per cent of this farmer's gross income, he had, in this year, 440 ewes and 150 ewe hoggets (mainly Corriedales), as well as a private stud of 120 Southdowns. He carries his own Corriedale rams, raises his own breeding ewes (therefore the 150 ewe hoggets listed), replacing about one-third of his breeding ewes each year in this way. For fat lambs he has his own Southdown stud (from which he also sells stock) to provide rams to put on these ewes. It is perhaps typical of this enterprising gentleman that he is at the same time experimenting with improved Leicester rams for this purpose. He sells all the three-quarter-bred lambs as well as one-third of his Corriedale ewes as fats each year. Half of the lambs are fattened off their mothers and half on rape. The rape, with alfalfa hay and mangel roots, helps to take up the slack in the pastures in late summer and winter, with supplementary feed for the sheep. His "permanent" pastures stay down five to nine years on the average, gradually working around the farm in rotation with the crops.

CATTLE FARMS

1. The first farm is on the shores of Lake Ellesmere, a holding of forty-four acres all on the flat. The soil is a once swampy, silty loam. The area is divided into thirteen paddocks. There is no shelter whatever except in the lee of the house or the milk shed. The cattle are crossbreds, mainly types of milking Shorthorns. In 1941 there were twenty cows, seven heifers, and one Shorthorn bull on the place. The skim-milk was utilized by the litters got by a Tamworth boar out of four sows

(Tamworth and Berkshire cross). The milk from the cows was separated on the farm, the cream being shipped to Christchurch. There was a new four-cow milk shed with an automatic milking machine, cream separator, and other up-to-date equipment. As in most parts of South Island, the accommodation for the pigs was very poor.

All the land was in "permanent" pasture, not plowed and resown until absolutely necessary. The swards had a good thick growth of Cocksfoot, Rye grass, and White clover in the spring.

The gross income per cow was about fifteen pounds—that is, some fifty to sixty dollars per year or twenty to twenty-five dollars an acre. The pigs added another three hundred and fifty to four hundred dollars a year, also gross. This is a fairly typical small dairy plant in the dairying areas; its management requires constant care of the cows and pigs, and the net return for the heavy work is not great. Better stock would undoubtedly have increased the cream check, otherwise there was little improvement which could be suggested.

2. The next farm was within three miles of one of the big cities—a hundred acres of first-class, very productive, heavy land. The basis of the farm economy was a dairy herd for the supply of liquid milk to the city; occasionally some potatoes, garden vegetables, or grain were also grown as cash crops. The dairy herd was continually changing and continually fluctuating in numbers. The farmer did no breeding of cattle, buying in third- to fourth-calvers, keeping them four or five years, and then selling them for what they might bring as fats. His herd averaged about thirty-two cows from June to November; and about twenty-eight through the rest of the year. Though the animals were far from highly bred, he obtained an average of about seven hundred gallons per cow per year; some seventy-five gallons a day from the herd.

His division of land indicates the necessity for a lot of extra winter feed to keep up the production of milk in winter. In 1941 there were in: potatoes, 13 acres; wheat, 6 acres; oat and vetch hay, 6 acres; oats (grain), 3 acres; mangels, 5 acres; green feed (barley and Italian Rye grass), 10 acres; alfalfa, 20 acres; grass, 30 acres. Continual hand feeding and all the care needed on any dairy farm made the work heavy and the off-hours few. Management had to be skilled not only in dairy techniques but also in the carefully planned rotation of the paddocks. The yields per acre in this year were: wheat, 55 to 60 bushels; oat and vetch hay, 3 tons; oats, 60 bushels; potatoes, 7 to 9 tons; mangels, 5 tons; alfalfa (3 cuts), 4 to 5 tons average.

His mechanical equipment was junky, and though he plowed his land with his own plows and harrow, he had nearly all the rest of the farm work, such as hoeing, drilling, discing, cutting, digging, and topdressing, done by contract.

3. A sheep and cattle farm in one of the bays of Banks Peninsula is the last to be described here. It consists of fifteen hundred acres and has been in continuous operation since the sixties. Cleared by both cutting and fire, it has a sward chiefly of Cocksfoot and Rye grass today. With twenty-five hundred head of sheep, the farm carries as well about two hundred fifty head of cattle. The manager breeds many of his own sheep, but buys all of his cattle (all beef steers) at eighteen months, and sells them as fats to Christchurch at about three years. The steers he buys come off the high, back-country of Amuri County as a rule.

The management of the sheep and cattle is a full-time occupation for the farmer and his two sons; two additional hands are occasionally hired at the seasons of heaviest work. Some twelve horses (hacks) are kept, as there is constant riding to be done over fairly steep slopes. A good many dogs are used in the working of the flocks and herds.

Only fifty acres of the whole area have ever been plowed, and there are never more than ten acres in any sort of crop. The grazing of the animals is kept adjusted to the available feed by careful rotational grazing and by timing the buying, selling, and breeding to make maximum use of available grass at all seasons without overgrazing. Apart from the sale of wool, fat sheep, and fat cattle (which contribute to the revenue of the farm in the proportion of 22 per cent, 47 per cent and 31 per cent, respectively), this manager, following a general practice of the Banks Peninsula stations for many decades, cuts as much as fifty acres a year of ripened Cocksfoot to thresh for seed.

Over-all expenses, not including wages of management, run to about 60 per cent of the gross revenue. These expenses include the purchase of cattle, general wages and supplies, and a small item of extra wages for grubbing gorse (one of the most vicious of the exotic weeds (*see* pp. 362-65)), a practice necessitated by the invasion of gorse from a neighboring station of two thousand acres, at least half of which is gorse-covered. As this shrub is much too aggressive to be allowed to exist for shelter purposes, and shelter is of great importance on the bleak peninsular hills, long since deforested, some sixteen thousand trees have been planted, chiefly *Cupressus macrocarpa*, in blocks of three chains square (that is, roughly 200 ft. x 200 ft.). The manager rides over the hills in bad weather, notes where the animals tend to congregate of their own accord, and plants the trees in those spots.

REFERENCE NOTES

CHAPTER I

1. A. H. Clark. "Historical Explanation of Land Use in New Zealand." *Journal of Economic History,* vol. 5, no. 2, Nov. 1945, pp. 215-30.
2. There is no regional descriptive geomorphologic work which deals with as much as one of the major islands of New Zealand. This brief introduction to the subject thus depends heavily upon reports of field work as these have appeared in print, some personal interpretations made in the field, and, though he has not seen this manuscript and no responsibility can be assessed to him, upon the advice and judgment of Professor George Jobberns of Canterbury University College, Christchurch.
3. Before 1930 there were less than twenty stations in South Island recording 24-hour maximum and minimum temperatures and daily totals of precipitation. To supplement such works as Kidson, it was necessary to calculate ten-year means for a variety of climatic values and for a large number of new stations for which records had been kept in the decade 1930-1940. The maps (figs. 12, 13, and 14) are based upon these new calculations, except where the long-term means of the few older stations suggested slight corrections. Observations relative to wind velocity and intensity of precipitation are also referred to these calculations. (For works by E. Kidson, *see* Bibliography.)
4. C. W. Thornthwaite, 1933: "The Climates of the Earth." *G. R.,* vol. 23, no. 3, pp. 433-40.
5. A number of botanists and two geographers, Holmes and Cumberland, have attempted simplified maps and generalized descriptions

398 THE INVASION OF NEW ZEALAND

for the vegetation of all of New Zealand. Cumberland's map entitled "Primitive Vegetation, 1840" is much the most useful yet prepared, and it makes careful use of earlier work. The map (fig. 16)
differs from Cumberland's partly because of different local interpretations, but chiefly in terms of greater generalization, to avoid the
impression of claim to accurate knowledge in many areas of the
situation in the eighteenth century. (J. M. Holmes, 1935: "The
Vegetation of New Zealand," *Scot. Geog. Mag.*, vol. 51, no. 2,
pp. 89-97; *and* K. B. Cumberland, 1941: "A Century's Change:
Natural to Cultural Vegetation in New Zealand," *G. R.*, vol. 31,
no. 4, pp. 529-54.)

6. O. Schmieder, 1928: "The Pampa—A Natural or Culturally Induced
Grassland," *University of California Publications in Geography*,
vol. 2, no. 8, pp. 255-70.

7. H. H. Allan, 1937: "Some Ecological Features of the Main Islands,"
Handbook for New Zealand, A.N.Z.A.A.S., p. 41.

8. L. Cockayne and E. P. Turner, 1928: *The Trees of New Zealand*,
p. 6.

9. This section on soils is based somewhat on personal notes and observations, but chiefly upon the written reports of the few serious
pedologists who have been at work in the island, particularly L. I.
Grange, first director of the New Zealand Soil Survey, and his associates. The excellent summary provided as an appendix to Cumberland has also been drawn upon. (K. B. Cumberland, 1946: *Soil
Erosion in New Zealand: A Geographic Reconnaisance*.)

CHAPTER II

1. P. H. Buck has provided the most lucid and convincing discussion
of ultimate Polynesian origins (P. H. Buck, 1938: *Vikings of the
Sunrise;* and 1946: *An Introduction to Polynesian Anthropology*,
Bernice Bishop Museum *Bulletin*, no. 187).

2. I. L. G. Sutherland, editor, 1940: *The Maori People Today, A Gen-
eral Survey*, chap. 11.
E. W. Durward, 1933: "The Maori Population of Otago," *J.P.S.*,
vol. 42, no. 166.
E. Dieffenbach, 1843: *Travels in New Zealand*.
F. D. Fenton, 1859: *Observations on the State of the Aboriginal
Inhabitants of New Zealand*.
H. D. Skinner, 1933: "The Maoris," chap. 2 of *C.H.B.E.N.Z.*

3. E. Best, 1924b: *The Maori As He Was*, p. 108.

4. Sources are extremely varied and will be cited only as they are vital
to an unusual or important point. Most helpful of general interpretations are: *The Cambridge History of the British Empire*, vol. VII,
part 2, "New Zealand," 1933; Condliffe's *New Zealand in the Making*,
1930; and Marais' *The Colonisation of New Zealand*, 1927. Among

secondary sources, J. C. Beaglehole's many works have perhaps
contributed most to this interpretation of the character of the
invading people.

5. In H. Belshaw, editor, 1947: *New Zealand* (United Nations Series,
Univ. of Calif. Press).
6. J. E. Heeres, 1898: *Abel Janszoon Tasman (His Life and Labours)*;
and J. C. Beaglehole, 1939: *The Discovery of New Zealand*, p. 32.
7. T. M. Hocken, 1898: *Contributions to the Early History of New
Zealand (Settlement of Otago)*, p. 9.
8. J. R. Muir, 1939: *The Life and Achievements of Captain James
Cook*, p. 70.
9. J. C. Beaglehole (1939: *The Discovery of New Zealand*) gives a
photostatic reproduction of Cook's chart of New Zealand from the
British Museum Add. MS. 7085.16. An earlier chart, probably the
work of Cook's own hand, exists (*B.M. Add. MS.* 7085.17), from
which Hawkesworth's engraving and the Admiralty publications
are copied. Beaglehole also reproduced a chart of Cook Strait and
Queen Charlotte Sound as published in Hawkesworth's *Voyages*,
vol. II, and a reproduction of a chart of Dusky Bay from the engraving of W. Whitchurch, in 1776, of the chart made by Cook
in 1773, and published in his *Voyage Toward the South Pole and
Round the World* (1777), vol. I. (*See also* end papers of this
volume.)
10. R. McNab, 1914b: *From Tasman to Marsden.*
11. J. Hight and H. D. Bamford, 1914: *The Constitutional History and
Law of New Zealand*, part I. Chapter III interprets this period.
12. R. McNab. *op. cit.*
13. *Historical Records of New South Wales*, vol. V, p. 832.
14. All records of such trips of Australian-owned vessels to the New
Zealand or other nearby fisheries must be gleaned from the press
of the day. The Naval Custom House records at Port Jackson
(Sydney) took no cognizance of their movements. Undoubtedly
there was much sealing in South Island waters which was not reported in the Sydney or Hobart Town press. Even for those ships
mentioned as coming from New Zealand (a list appears for the
years 1803 ff. in the *Historical Records of New Zealand*, vol. I), it is
not specified what part of New Zealand was visited, and we have
to infer that it was the best known area of northern North Island
which was referred to in general.
15. *Sydney Gazette*, April 1, 1804.
16. J. Hight and H. D. Bamford, 1914: *The Constitutional History and
Law of New Zealand*, part I, p. 28.
17. In *Historical Records of New Zealand*, vol. I, a very complete accounting of this trade may be found; the number of ships, the
catches, and the price of skins and oil being given for each year.

18. Capt. B. Morell, 1832: *A Narrative of Four Voyages to the South Sea.* . . .

19. The report appears in full in *H.R.N.Z.*, vol I, pp. 457 ff.

20. *Oriental Navigator* for 1816 (table, pp. 87-90) quoted R. McNab, 1909: *Murihuku*, p. 160.

21. One of the best documents supporting the thesis of an unfriendly coastal environment as a discouragement to permanent settlement is contained in an account of the journal of the small sloop *Snapper* (29 tons) in 1822-23 recounted by Jules de Blosseville in *Annales des Voyages*, Paris, 1826, Tome XXIX, pp. 145-61.

22. Jerningham Wakefield and Shortland have some of the best material. Of greatest utility is the only partly digested collection of statistics, quotations from documents, newspapers, ships' logs, customs' reports, and government papers assembled by McNab. Most of the sources from which McNab liberally quotes may still be examined in the original, and many of the obvious gaps in his accounts can be filled in from contemporary diaries, letters, and logs scattered through the archives of New Zealand. (E. J. Wakefield, 1845: *Adventure in New Zealand* (1908 edition); E. Shortland, 1851: *The Southern Districts of New Zealand;* and R. McNab, 1913: *The Old Whaling Days.*)

23. For an extremely well-written account of this expedition, see J. C. Beaglehole, 1939: *The Discovery of New Zealand*, pp. 120-31.

24. R. Carrick, 1903: *Historical Records of New Zealand South, Prior to 1840*, p. 12. We may note, also, a reference to over a hundred runaways "known to be living in New Zealand" (*ibid.*, p. 17, from the *Hobart Town Gazette*, Sept. 9, 1826).

25. R. McNab, 1913: *op. cit.*, p. 12.

26. R. McNab, *ibid.*, pp. 3, 9, and 10.

27. A. D. McIntosh, editor, 1940: *Marlborough: A Provincial History*, p. 26.

28. R. McNab, 1913: *op. cit.*, p. 155.

29. J. C. Andersen, 1927a: *Place Names of Banks Peninsula*, p. 57.

30. Evidence of W. B. Rhodes in 1849 quoted by J. C. Andersen, 1927a: *Place Names of Banks Peninsula*.

31. The *Piraki Log* was also published in London in 1910, edited by Anson.

32. For the source of much of the detail in this section, see R. McNab, 1913: *op. cit.*

33. J. C. Andersen, 1927a: *Place Names of Banks Peninsula*, pp. 92 and 158. Also: E. J. Wakefield, 1848: *Handbook of New Zealand by a Late Magistrate of the Colony*, p. 294.

34. J. C. Andersen, 1927b: "Early History of Canterbury," in Speight *et al.*, 1927: *Natural History of Canterbury*, pp. 24-5.

35. T. L. Buick, 1928: *The French at Akaroa, An Adventure in Colonisation.*
36. T. L. Buick, *op. cit.,* p. 11.
37. *Ibid.,* p. 55.
38. Editors of *Akaroa Mail,* 1940: *Akaroa and Banks Peninsula,* p. 100.
39. R. McNab, 1913: *op. cit.,* chap. 20.
40. T. L. Buick, *op. cit.,* pp. 61 and 65.
41. J. C. Andersen, 1927a: *Place Names of Banks Peninsula,* p. 213.
42. The detailed statistics and other data about the southern stations are chiefly those gathered by Edward Shorthand, officer of the New Zealand government, who traveled through the area in 1843-44, that is, less than fifteen years after the founding of the first whaling station. The statistical summary is given in the appendix of his report on that trip (*The Southern Districts of New Zealand,* London, 1851).
43. R. McNab, 1913: *op. cit.,* p. 35.
44. E. Shortland, 1851: *The Southern Districts of New Zealand.*
45. R. McNab, 1913: *op. cit.,* p. 89.
46. J. Bradshaw, 1888: *New Zealand of Today,* p. 63.
47. G. Clarke, 1903: *Notes on Early Life in New Zealand,* pp. 62 and 63.
48. E. W. Durward, 1933: "The Maori Population of Otago," *J.P.S.,* vol. 42, no. 166.
49. R. McNab, 1913: *op. cit.,* p. 97.
50. *Ibid.,* p. 98.
51. *Ibid.,* p. 99.
52. *Ibid.,* p. 179.
53. *Ibid.,* pp. 177-8.
54. W. H. S. Roberts, 1890: *History of Oamaru....*
55. J. C. Andersen, 1916: *Jubilee History of South Canterbury,* p. 45.
56. E. Shortland, *op. cit.,* p. 223.
57. R. McNab (*The Old Whaling Days*) is the source of details in this section.
58. *Ibid.,* pp. 324-27.
59. *Ibid.,* p. 326.
60. The most useful sources are: E. J. Wakefield; 1845: *Adventure in New Zealand* (1908 edition); and W. H. Thorp, *Reminiscences* (Turnbull Library).
61. E. J. Wakefield, 1845: *op. cit.,* pp. 32-3.
62. A. D. McIntosh, 1940: *op. cit.,* pp. 49-51 and 70.
63. J. S. C. Dumont D'Urville, 1841-46: *Voyage de la Corvette l'Astrolabe....* (*See* R. McNab, 1913: *op. cit.,* p. 330.)
64. T. M. Hocken, 1898: Contributions to the *Early History of New Zealand* (*Settlement of Otago*), p. 34 and appendix.

65. The information as to more precise locations of many of these whaling settlements, i.e., both the conditions of site and the agricultural development as distinct from the general situation of each which we know, is in existence in the *Old Land Claim* files of the New Zealand Department of Lands and Surveys. All claims of land purchase from the Maori prior to January 14, 1840, had to be reviewed by special commissions. The evidence presented has been kept from the public during the succeeding hundred years or so because of some very embarrassing lawsuits brought against the government from time to time by heirs of old claimants. It is to be hoped that the government archivist can soon edit, or arrange for the editing of, this material.

CHAPTER III

1. E. J. O'Brien, 1936: *The Foundation of Australia, 1786-1800.*
2. *Ibid.* See also E. O. G. Shann, 1930: *An Economic History of Australia;* S. H. Roberts, 1935: *The Squatting Age in Australia, 1835-1847;* B. Fitzpatrick, 1939: *British Imperialism and Australia, 1783-1833;* and B. Fitzpatrick, 1941: *The British Empire in Australia. An Economic History, 1834-1939.*
3. B. Fitzpatrick, 1939: *op. cit.,* p. 366.
4. There are a number of authorities on the character of the "digger" population as well as of the earlier population in both New South Wales and Victoria. Coghlan discusses especially the importance of "convict blood" in the settlements; Shann writes of the diggers in particular; and Newling's "The Gold Diggers" is helpful. (T. A. Coghlan, 1918: *Labour and Industry in Australia,* pp. 561-2, 874-6; E. O. G. Shann, 1930: *An Economic History of Australia,* 439, chap. XI; *and* C. B. Newling: "The Gold Diggers," *Journal of the Royal Australian Historical Society,* vol. XI, pp. 262-80.)
5. The political history of the different Australasian colonies has been given a thorough treatment in volume VII of the *Cambridge History of the British Empire,* where the succession of settlements in New South Wales, Norfolk Island, Van Diemen's land, and Victoria, and the gradual entanglement of New Zealand within the developing economic and political organization, are very tersely and clearly described.
6. His first and best-known work, *A Letter from Sydney* (1829), was written while he was in jail for abduction following a highly publicized elopement. Harrop is the most complete and authoritative study of Wakefield and his position in the social and political life of England and Australasia. Mills and Fitzpatrick give the best accounts of his Australian connections. (A. J. Harrop, 1928: *The Amazing Career of Edward Gibbon Wakefield;* R. C. Mills, 1915:

The Colonisation of Australia (1829-42); and B. Fitzpatrick, 1941: *The British Empire in Australia. An Economic History. 1834-1939*, especially pp. 259-62.)

7. *Parliamentary Papers*, 1836, xi, p. 499 (quoted in A. J. Harrop, 1928: *The Amazing Career of Edward Gibbon Wakefield*, pp. 85-6).

8. J. S. Marais, 1927: *The Colonisation of New Zealand*, p. 26, N. 3.

9. Backhouse to Stephen, 15th Nov., 1839 (encl.): *Parliamentary Paper*, 1840, xxiii, pp. 652-4. These references are taken severally from: *Historical Records of New Zealand*, vol. I, in which McNab collected some of the more important documents concerned with New Zealand's political history; Hight and Bamford, 1914: *The Constitutional History and Law of New Zealand; C.H.B.E.N.Z.*; and Marais, 1927: *The Colonisation of New Zealand*. Some of the Acts concerned with the sovereignty situation in New Zealand are: 57 Geo. III cap. 53; 4 Geo. IV cap. 96, sec. 3; 9 Geo. IV cap. 83, sec. 4 (Hight and Bamford).

10. All the evidence cannot be summarized here, but attention is called to two proclamations of Governor King in 1804 referring partly to New Zealand: to the description of the missionary Kendall in 1814 as, officially, "the resident magistrate in the Bay of Islands"; and to the description, in 1819, of the settlement of New Zealand as a "dependency of the said territory," i.e., New South Wales.

11. W. P. Reeves, 1925: *Aotea-roa, The Long White Cloud*, p. 131.

12. E. G. Wakefield, 1849: *A View of the Art of Colonisation*, pp. 87-95.

13. J. S. Marais, 1927: *op. cit.*, p. 2 and chap. III.

14. The lengthy official correspondence on this matter is given in *Historical Records of New Zealand*, vol. I, pp. 729 ff.

15. The quotations are from correspondence printed in the *Historical Records of New Zealand*, vol. I.

16. G. H. Scholefield, 1909: *New Zealand in Evolution*, p. 172.

17. *New Zealand Gazette*, Oct. 9, 1841.

18. J. S. Marais, 1927: *op. cit.*, p. 57.

19. A. Saunders, 1896 and 1899: *History of New Zealand* (1642-1893), vol. I, p. 172.

20. Notably W. Pratt, 1877: *Colonial Experiences in New Zealand, by An Old Colonist;* and A. Saunders, 1896: *History of New Zealand* (1642-1893), vol. I.

21. *Fourteenth Report of the New Zealand Company*, 1844.

22. A. Saunders, *op. cit.*, p. 174.

23. A. D. McIntosh, editor, 1940: *Marlborough: A Provincial History*, p. 133.

24. J. S. Marais, 1927: *The Colonisation of New Zealand*, p. 141.

25. W. Pratt, 1877: *Colonial Experiences in New Zealand by An Old Colonist*, p. 55.

26. W. Fox, 1851: *The Six Colonies of New Zealand*, p. 11.

27. F. Wakefield, 1849: *Colonial Surveying*, pp. 70 ff.

28. These figures are from the early government papers and Blue Books published as the *Statistics of New Zealand for 1853-6, 1857,* etc. after 1858.

29. Lady A. Lovat, 1914: *The Life of Sir Frederick Weld.*

30. G. B. Earp, 1849: *Handbook for Intending Emigrants to the Southern Settlements of New Zealand,* chap. 9.

31. *Nelson Examiner*, March 31, 1855.

32. *Nelson Examiner*, Aug. 8, 1855.

33. A. D. McIntosh, editor, 1940: *Marlborough: A Provincial History,* chap. VIII.

34. Quoted in *ibid.*, pp. 180-2.

35. The Hocken Library, in Dunedin, has a great literature on the early years, some of which, from his own large personal collection which became the nucleus of the library, Dr. Hocken himself collected and partially edited (T. M. Hocken, 1898: *Contributions to the Early History of New Zealand*). Like McNab's works it is an invaluable source of documentary and early newspaper records; since Hocken was a very early settler, it contains many useful eyewitness observations and judgments.

36. T. M. Hocken, 1898: *Contributions to the Early History of New Zealand* (*Settlement of Otago*), pp. 4-5.

37. *Ibid.*, pp. 15-6.

38. E. Shortland, 1851: *The Southern Districts of New Zealand*, pp. 172-3.

39. T. M. Hocken, *op. cit.*, appendix. The reports of Dr. Monro also were condensed by Hocken (*ibid.*, app.) and are to be found in full in the 1844 issues of the *Nelson Examiner.*

40. T. M. Hocken, *op. cit.*, p. 83.

41. T. M. Hocken, *op. cit.*, p. 148.

42. Fitton contrasts the position of the region which became the province of Otago in 1852, as between the first year of settlement in 1849 and the sixth year, 1855. For 1849 his figures, which refer only to the Otago block, have been used, but for 1855 those published in the *Otago Provincial Gazette*, as quoted in the *Otago Witness*, Aug. 23, 1856, were preferred, though it is uncertain which is the more nearly accurate. (E. B. Fitton, 1856: *New Zealand. Its Present Condition, Prospects and Resources*, chap. 7.)

43. T. M. Hocken, *op. cit.*, p. 158.

44. H. Beattie, 1909: *Pioneer Recollections*, p. 10.

45. A. R. Dreaver, 1929: "Southland Province of New Zealand in the Days of Dr. J. A. Menzies (Superintendent 1861-1864)." U.N.Z.T. (M. A.)

46. W. H. S. Roberts, undated: *Southland in 1856-7.*
47. J. S. Marais, 1927: *The Colonisation of New Zealand,* p. 318.
48. Some of the best secondary sources are: J. Hay, 1915: *Reminiscences of Earliest Canterbury (Principally Banks Peninsula) and Its Settlers; Akaroa Mail,* editors of, 1940: *Akaroa and Banks Peninsula;* J. C. Andersen, 1927a: *Place Names of Banks Peninsula;* and J. Deans, editor, 1937: *Pioneers of Canterbury: Deans Letters 1840-1854.* Much of the early history of the Hays and the Sinclairs is so clouded by hazy recollection and doubtful anecdote that it is hard to be sure of the essential facts.
49. J. Deans, *op. cit.*
50. E. J. Wakefield, editor, 1869: *Founders of Canterbury,* p. 1.
51. R. Speight *et al.,* 1927: *Natural History of Canterbury,* pp. 60-87.
52. The report is given in full in *Canterbury Papers,* 1850, a brochure of the Association.
53. S. H. Roberts, 1935: *The Squatting Age in Australia,* chap. VII.
54. *Ibid.,* p. 232.
55. A. E. Woodhouse, 1937: *George Rhodes of the Levels and His Brothers.*
56. J. B. Condliffe, 1930: *New Zealand in the Making,* chap. VII.
57. R. B. Paul, 1857: *Letters from Canterbury, New Zealand.*
58. There are a great many sources of information about Canterbury in the fifties. Besides the *Lyttelton Times,* the *Canterbury Provincial Gazette* (especially the issue of July 1, 1854) and the official statistics of the colony, Paul and Fitton have been used. (R. B. Paul, 1854: *Some Account of the Canterbury Settlement; ibid.,* 1857: *Letters from Canterbury, New Zealand;* and E. B. Fitton, 1856: *New Zealand. Its Present Condition, Prospects and Resources.*)
59. R. B. Paul, *op. cit.,* appendix C, p. 130.
60. J. B. Condliffe, 1930: *New Zealand in the Making; C.H.B.E.N.Z.;* W. P. Reeves, 1925: *Aotea-roa, The Long White Cloud;* and G. H. Scholefield, 1909: *New Zealand in Evolution.*
61. The best sources for information about the earlier gold fields are the local newspapers. Vincent Pyke in his "Report on the Gold Discoveries in Otago," *A.J.H.R.* (1863), has most authoritative contemporary data, but it is not easily come by. His story is, however, only slightly condensed in the *New Zealand Handbook of Mines* for 1876, which is readily available. W. P. Morrell's classic study of the gold rushes (*The Gold Rushes,* 1940) has a section on New Zealand; and J. B. Condliffe, 1930: *New Zealand in the Making,* pp. 27-31, has a useful and brief summary.
62. *Otago Witness:* July 28, 1855; March 7, 1857; March 13, 1858; August 6, 1859; and April 6, 1861.

63. V. Pyke, 1863 (see Note 61, above).
64. J. McIndoe, undated pamphlet: "A Sketch of Otago." Complete figures given in this pamphlet have been used as the basis for the chart (fig. 31); some of the figures occur in footnote, p. 103.
65. See also F. von Hochstetter, 1863: *Neu-Seeland.*
66. A. D. McIntosh, editor, 1940: *Marlborough: A Provincial History,* p. 239.
67. W. G. McClymont, 1940: *The Exploration of New Zealand.*
68. A. J. Harrop, 1923: *The Romance of Westland, the Story of New Zealand's Golden Coast.*
69. E. I. Lord, 1940: *Old Westland.*
70. I. Faris, 1941: *Charleston: Its Rise and Decline.* For discussion of the evidence of Brunner and Heaphy as to a supposed wreck in 1825 of an early wool ship from Van Diemen's Land and the massacre of the crew by the local Maori, see also A. J. Harrop, 1923: *The Romance of Westland, the Story of New Zealand's Golden Coast,* p. 24; and E. I. Lord, 1940: *Old Westland.*
71. Details of the involved land alienation proceedings, in transference from the Maori to the Crown, have not been thoroughly studied, but Harrop (*op. cit.,* p. 24) and Lord (*op. cit.,* p. 37) have some useful comments.
72. *Nelson Examiner,* April 17, 1858.
73. A. J. Harrop, *op. cit.,* p. 59.
74. The figures for gold production are readily available in the *New Zealand Mining Handbook* (1906, p. 574) and in many editions of the *Official Year Book.*
75. J. B. Condliffe, 1930: *New Zealand in the Making,* p. 30.
76. *Statistics of New Zealand* for 1881.
77. J. T. Critchell and J. Raymond, 1913: *History of the Frozen Meat Trade.* This is still considered the standard work on the development of refrigeration techniques and the resulting trade.
78. W. R. Jourdain, 1925: *History of Land Legislation and Settlement in New Zealand.*

CHAPTER IV

1. Population data in this chapter depend very largely on the following sources: (1) official census returns and reports (the New Zealand *Population Census,* 1936, vol. I, p. 11, which lists dates on which various censuses were taken); (2) the annual *New Zealand Official Year Book* (the first issue in 1892 was titled *Handbook for New Zealand*); (3) other handbooks such as: Sir J. Vogel, 1875: *Handbook of New Zealand;* and J. Hector, 1883: *A Handbook of New Zealand;* (4) official statistical returns which list census data, as *Statistics of New Zealand* for 1853-56, 1858, 1861, etc.

2. The definitions of such terms as "provincial district," "land district," and "county," are discussed in Appendix A, pp. 387-9. Data for figure 36 have been calculated from data in: A. S. Thomson, 1859: *The Story of New Zealand*, vol. II, pp. 59, 329; *Statistics for New Zealand* for 1891; and *Population Census* 1936, vol. I.

3. *C.H.B.E.N.Z.*, p. 175.

4. Manuscript in preparation in 1942: *Social History of Canterbury*, by G. T. J. Wilson and N. Barker.

5. *General Report*, 1921 census, p. 1. (The *Report* gives no information concerning the process involved in "random sampling.")

6. J. S. Marais, 1927: *The Colonisation of New Zealand*, p. 65. This ignores the Akaroa French and some others.

7. *Ibid.*, p. 66.

8. A. Charlton, 1935: "Contributions of Germans and Scandinavians to the History of New Zealand," U.N.Z.T. (M.A.).

9. W. Pratt, 1877: *Colonial Experiences in New Zealand, by an Old Colonist*, p. 84.

10. E. B. Fitton, 1856: *New Zealand. Its Present Condition, Prospects, and Resources*, pp. 295, 310, 343.

11. R. B. Paul, 1854: *Some Account of the Canterbury Settlement*, p. 21.

12. *Southland Gazette*, vol. I, p. 164: *Otago Witness*, April 5, 1862.

13. J. C. Crawford, 1880: *Recollections of Travel in New Zealand and Australia*, p. 252.

14. *General Report*, 1921 Census, p. 118.

15. J. C. Andersen, 1916: *Jubilee History of South Canterbury*, chap. x.

16. J. Hector, 1883: *A Handbook of New Zealand*, p. 78.

17. *Official Handbook* of 1892, p. 51.

18. Manuscript in preparation in 1942: *Social History of Canterbury*, by G. T. J. Wilson and N. Barker.

19. J. Lyng, 1939: *The Scandinavians in New Zealand, Australia, and the Western Pacific*.

20. A. Charlton, 1935: "Contributions of Germans and Scandinavians to the History of New Zealand," U.N.Z.T. (M.A.), appendix B.

21. J. C. Andersen, 1916: *Jubilee History of South Canterbury*, pp. 358-9.

22. *Ibid.*, p. 374.

23. Quoted in J. Hector, 1883: *A Handbook of New Zealand*, pp. 86-7.

24. *General Report*, 1921 Census, p. 138.

25. *General Report*, 1926 Census, vol. 17, p. 68.

26. F. G. Fuller, 1859: *Five Years Residence in New Zealand*, p. 96.

27. J. C. Beaglehole, 1936: *New Zealand, A Short History*, p. 48.

28. Quoted in Marais, 1927: *The Colonisation of New Zealand*, p. 329.

29. R. B. Paul, 1857: *Letters from Canterbury, New Zealand*, pp. 27-30.

CHAPTER V

1. Lord Ernle, 1912: *English Farming, Past and Present.*
2. H. C. Darby, editor, 1936: *An Historical Geography of England, before A.D. 1800,* chap. 13.
3. In Defries' *Sheep and Turnips* (1938), a biography of Arthur Young, there is a pithy and useful summary of early agricultural "revolutions." Young, himself, wrote some two hundred and fifty volumes, and while secretary to the Board of Agriculture contributed to and assisted in promoting the extremely valuable series of pamphlets by the appointed commissioners, *General View of the Agriculture of....* (any one of a great many counties), for the period of 1795 to 1810. For a later period, some additional hints and information appear in J. F. Burke, 1834: *British Husbandry,* vol. I.
4. Lord Ernle, *op. cit.,* p. 149.
5. H. C. Darby, editor, 1936: *An Historical Geography of England, before A.D. 1800,* p. 465.
6. Lord Ernle, *op. cit.*
7. For a lucid and full discussion of the situation, see G. Slater, 1907: *The English Peasantry and the Enclosure of the Common Fields.*
8. For an excellent contemporary account of the practical effects of this attitude on retarding the introduction of new techniques and machines, see J. Burke, 1834: *British Husbandry,* vol. I, chap. 8.
9. A. Defries, 1938: *Sheep and Turnips,* p. 73.
10. Sir R. G. Stapledon, 1928: *A Tour in Australia and New Zealand, Grasslands and Other Studies.*
11. *Ibid.,* p. 18.

CHAPTER VI

1. R. O. Buchanan, 1935: *The Pastoral Industries of New Zealand,* Inst. of Brit. Geographers, publication no. 2.
2. These include (*ibid.,* pp. 92, 294, 296, and 297) dot density maps of distribution of sheep (one dot per five thousand sheep); actual numbers of sheep per thousand occupied acres; carrying capacity of land in terms of sheep per thousand occupied acres; sheep percentage of total grazing (the last three are on a county basis).
3. Statistics used here are nearly all directly from either the *Statistical Report of Agricultural and Pastoral Production of New Zealand* (published for each season) or from the summaries of these in the annual *Official Year Books.* In citing data, the abbreviations A. and P. Statistics, 1940-41 (or whatever season), or *N.Z.O.Y.B.,* 1940 (or whatever year), will be used.

4. H. Belshaw, *et al.*, 1936: *Agricultural Organization in New Zealand.*
5. A. Defries, 1938: *Sheep and Turnips*, p. 184.
6. At least a half dozen other official figures of the area of the island are given. The *N.Z.O.Y.B.* (1938), p. 47, gives 37,528,960 acres (by calculation).
7. A. and P. Statistics, 1940-41.
8. *Ibid.* R. O. Buchanan (*op. cit.*, p. 23) gives a 1925-29 average of under twelve million.
9. E. J. Fawcett, 1929: "Livestock Production of the Period 1901-2 to 1926-7, Based on Standard Values and Units," *N.Z.J.A.*, vol. 28, no. 6. (Fawcett contributed many articles on sheep economy in *N.Z.J.A.*, vols. 25, 28, and 40.)
10. W. B. Sutch, 1936: *Recent Economic Changes in New Zealand*, chap. X.
11. *N.Z.O.Y.B.*, 1938, p. 226. Figures for exports are taken for a period between the great wars to avoid any abnormalities due to dislocation of trade associated with unique wartime conditions.
12. *N.Z.Y.O.B.* for 1938, pp. 413-14, 420, and 422.
13. Calculated from figures in *ibid.*, pp. 490 and 866.
14. *Ibid.*, p. 403.
15. Calculated from figures in A. and P. Statistics, 1940-41.
16. For many contributions of fact and judgment, the author is indebted to Professor Hudson and his staff at Canterbury Agricultural College, and to the Dominion's Department of Agriculture. Good and detailed description of the localization of types of sheep can be found in R. O. Buchanan, 1935: *The Pastoral Industries of New Zealand*, Inst. of Brit. Geographers, publication no. 2, chaps. III, IV, and V; and from Fawcett (writing in: H. Belshaw *et al.*, 1936: *Agricultural Organization in New Zealand*).
17. The percentages in tables XXX and XXXI have been calculated from the date (as of April 30, 1941) given in A. and P. Statistics, 1940-41.
18. Capt. J. Cook, 1777: *A Voyage Towards the South Pole and Round the World* ..., vol. 1, p. 131. In other editions of Cook's *Journal* this passage is variously changed from the text here quoted, but it may be assumed that this is an account, substantially, of what happened.
19. Capt. J. Cook, 1784: *A Voyage to the Pacific Ocean, Undertaken by the Command of His Majesty, for Making Discoveries in the Northern Hemisphere.* ... vol 1, p. 131.
20. A. D. McIntosh, editor, 1940: *Marlborough: A Provincial History*, p. 34.
21. R. McNab, 1913: *The Old Whaling Days*, chap. XIII.

22. R. Carrick, compiler and editor, 1903: *Historical Records of New Zealand South, Prior to 1840*, p. 79.

23. See pages 21-22 of this volume, and Elizabeth Lawrence's articles in the *Australian Geographer*, especially vol. 3, no. 3, for comparative unreliability of rainfall in New South Wales.

24. See Lord Ernle, 1912: *English Farming, Past and Present*, chap. VIII.

25. G. B. Earp, 1849: *Handbook of Intending Emigrants to the Southern Settlements of New Zealand*, p. 123.

26. G. A. Brown, 1904: *Australian Merino Studs*.

27. E. W. Cox, 1936: *The Evolution of the Australian Merino*.

28. E. O'Brien, 1936: *The Foundation of Australia, 1786-1800*, p. 213.

29. E. W. Cox, *op. cit.*

30. A letter by Fox to Dillon in 1850 discussing some of these yields is quoted in: A. D. McIntosh, 1940: *Marlborough, A Provincial History*, p. 108.

31. See note 28 of chapter III of this volume.

32. The files of the *Nelson Examiner* clearly record the large influx of sheep toward the end of the decade. On July 22, 1848, it reported that 5,500 sheep with cattle and horses had been imported and dispersed since Nov. 25, 1847. The issue for March 10, 1849, reported that of 36,673 bales of wool auctioned at one sale in London, 83 were from New Zealand, bringing prices of from 8d. to 1s. per pound. (This was 2d. to 3d. lower than Australian wool was selling.) On Sept. 29, 1849, large numbers of sheep from New South Wales were offered for sale, but through the early fifties greater and greater stress in advertising was laid on "acclimated" sheep.

33. See pages 25 and 26 of this volume.

34. J. Deans, editor, 1937: *Pioneers of Canterbury: Deans Letters 1840-1854*, p. 67.

35. Edward Shortland, 1852: *The Southern Districts of New Zealand*, pp. 257-60.

36. J. Deans, *op. cit.*, p. 100.

37. E. O. G. Shann, 1930: *An Economic History of Australia*, p. 120.

38. J. Deans, *op. cit.*, pp. 160 and 285.

39. J. Deans, *ibid.*, appendix, p. 284.

40. J. Deans, *ibid.*, p. 68.

41. Edward Shortland, 1851: *The Southern Districts of New Zealand*, p. 191.

42. R. M. Burdon, 1938: High Country: *The Evolution of a New Zealand Sheep Station*, p. 78.

43. J. Deans, *op. cit.*, pp. 124, 135.

44. W. Fox, 1851: *The Six Colonies of New Zealand*, p. 9.

45. F. G. Fuller, 1859: *Five Years' Residence in New Zealand*, p. 148.
46. A. S. Thomson, 1859: *The Story of New Zealand*, vol. 2, p. 331.
47. A. D. McIntosh, editor, 1940: *Marlborough: A Provincial History*, p. 164 (quoting from the *Nelson Examiner*).
48. R. B. Paul, 1857: *Letters from Canterbury, New Zealand*, p. 106.
49. W. G. McClymont, 1940: *The Exploration of New Zealand*, p. 99.
50. R. B. Paul, 1857: *Letters from Canterbury, New Zealand*, appendix.
51. E. B. Fitton, 1856: *New Zealand. Its Present Condition, Prospects, and Resources*, p. 118.
52. J. C. Andersen, 1916: *Jubilee History of South Canterbury*, p. 86.
53. The map (fig. 45) is based upon official surveys, information contained in Browning's map of 1863, and local sources. A similar map appears in: A. E. Woodhouse, 1937: *George Rhodes of the Levels and His Brothers*.
54. J. C. Andersen, *op. cit.*, p. 85 ff. gives the figures quoted in tables XXXIII and XXXIV, and in this paragraph.
55. R. B. Paul, 1857: *Letters from Canterbury, New Zealand*.
56. R. M. Burdon, 1938: *High Country: The Evolution of a New Zealand Sheep Station*, pp. 52 and 53.
57. T. M. Hocken, 1898: *Contributions to the Early History of New Zealand (Settlement of Otago)*, p. 169.
58. Quin and Rodger, editors of the *Tapanui Courier*, tell this story in *Tapanui Station* (undated), a rather disjointed series of reminiscences about the early sheep days in Otago, which was examined in the museum of the *Otago Early Settlers Association*, Dunedin.
59. His shepherd, G. H. Hussing, made a log of this journey from memory, which is available in the museum of the *Otago Early Settlers Association*, Dunedin.
60. R. M. Burdon, *op. cit.*, pp. 93-4.
61. The description herein of the management of sheep runs and the general techniques of sheep farming is based on so much varied evidence that it is almost impossible to give proper credit. A good deal is from remembrance of things past by the old pioneers. Some diaries in the Canterbury Museum and diaries and early pamphlets in the Hocken and Turnbull libraries were read. Then a great series of articles in the contemporary press, and the work of first-hand reporters like Fitton, Fox, Paul, and others was checked. Two of the best contemporary sources are: F. G. Fuller, 1859: *Five Years Residence in New Zealand;* and F. A. Weld, 1860: "Hints to Intending Sheep Farmers in New Zealand" (a pamphlet).
62. R. B. Paul, 1854: *Some Account of the Canterbury Settlement*, p. 24.
63. *Ibid.*, p. 91.
64. Samuel Butler, 1863: *A First Year in the Canterbury Settlement*, chap. IV.

65. *Nelson Examiner*, Dec. 4, 1852.
66. W. Perry, *et al.*, 1924: *Sheep Farming in New Zealand*.
67. A. D. McIntosh, editor, 1940: *Marlborough: A Provincial History*, p. 108, quoting a letter from Fox to Dillon.
68. *Otago Witness*, April 19, 1851.
69. See especially R. M. Burdon, 1938: *High Country: The Evolution of a New Zealand Sheep Station*, chap. 8.
70. James Adam, 1874: *Twenty-five Years of Emigrant Life in the South of New Zealand* (pamphlets); and J. S. Marais, 1927: *The Colonisation of New Zealand*.
71. *Otago Witness*, May 29, 1858.
72. J. C. Andersen, 1916: *Jubilee History of South Canterbury*, p. 91.
73. *Nelson Examiner*, Apr. 17, 1858; and A. J. Harrop, 1923: *The Romance of Westland, the Story of New Zealand's Golden Coast*, p. 35.
74. R. M. Burdon, 1938: *High Country: The Evolution of a New Zealand Sheep Station*.
75. J. T. Critchell and J. Raymond, 1912: *History of the Frozen Meat Trade*.
76. K. B. Cumberland, 1941: "A Century's Change: Natural to Cultural Vegetation in New Zealand," *G. R.*, vol. 31, no. 4, especially p. 536.
77. *Ibid.*, p. 549. See also K. B. Cumberland, 1946.
78. A. H. Clark, 1947: "Physical and Cultural Geography," in Belshaw, editor, 1947: *New Zealand*.
79. V. D. Zotov, 1938a: "Some Correlations between Vegetation and Climate in New Zealand," *N.Z.J.S.T.*, vol. 19, no. 8; *ibid.* 1938b: "Survey of The Tussock-Grasslands of The South Island, New Zealand," *N.Z.J.S.T.*, vol. 20A, no. 4A, pp. 212A-44A; and *ibid.*, 1940: "Certain Types of Soil Erosion and Resultant Relief Features on the Higher Mountains of New Zealand," *N.Z.J.S.T.*, vol. 21B, no. 5B, pp. 256B-62B.
80. L. Cockayne: 1919-1922: "An Economic Investigation of the Montane Tussock Grassland of New Zealand," *N.Z.J.A.*, vol. 18, no. 1 to vol. 25, no. 3.
81. *Maintenance of Vegetative Cover in New Zealand, with Special Reference to Land Erosion*, N.Z.D.S.I.R. *Bull.* no. 77. (This study is strongly recommended to any student of the New Zealand scene.)
82. A. D. McIntosh, editor, 1940: *Marlborough: A Provincial History*, p. 278.
83. Figures to 1921 from R. O. Buchanan; 1935: *The Pastoral Industries of New Zealand*, Inst. of British Geographers, publication no. 2, p. 74; figures for 1941 from A. and P. Statistics, 1940-41.
84. J. B. Condliffe, 1930: *New Zealand in the Making*.
85. J. C. Andersen, 1916: *Jubilee History of South Canterbury*, p. 334.

86. W. R. Jourdain, 1925: *History of Land Legislation and Settlement in New Zealand*, pp. 26-35 and 91-151.
87. J. B. Condliffe, *op. cit.*, chap. VIII.
88. Lord Ernle, 1912: *English Farming, Past and Present*, p. 178.

CHAPTER VII

1. A. and P. Statistics, 1940-41 (source of basic data).
2. This proportion for the whole of New Zealand is obtained by deduction from figures in *N.Z.O.Y.B.*, 1938, p. 410.

   In percentages of total cattle:

Bulls 2 years and over for dairy purposes	1.3%
Cows and heifers 2 years and over for dairy purposes	44.1
Heifers 1 to 2 years for dairy purposes	6.7
Bulls 1 to 2 years for dairy purposes	.5
Heifer calves for dairy purposes	7.5
Bull calves for dairy purposes	.7
Total (ignoring steers of dairy breeds)	60.8%

   Thus, roughly, for every 44 dairy cows there are some 61 cattle in all devoted to dairying purposes. So if 100 cattle were all part of the dairy cattle group, some 73 would be, on the average, dairy cows. The degree to which the *Dairy Cow per 100 Total Cattle* ratio is less than 73 is a measure of the local importance of beef cattle.
3. A. H. Cockayne, 1916a: "Conversion of Fern-land into Grass," *N.Z.J.A.*, vol. 12, no. 6, pp. 421-39.
4. *N.Z.O.Y.B.* 1918; A. and P. Statistics 1940-41.
5. Figures are from *N.Z.O.Y.B.*, 1918 and 1928.
6. Many of the details in this footnote were supplied by: Lord Ernle, 1912: *English Farming, Past and Present.*
7. M. H. Ellis, 1932: *The Beef Shorthorn in Australia.*
8. R. Dawson, 1831: *The Present State of Australia*, p. 426.
9. H. C. Philpott, 1937: *A History of the New Zealand Dairy Industry 1840-1935*, chap. I.
10. *Historical Records of New South Wales*, vol. II, p. 95.
11. R. McNab, 1913: *The Old Whaling Days*, p. 71.
12. J. Buchan, 1926: "Short History of Waikouaiti from the Maori Occupation to 1860," *U.N.Z.T.* (M.A.), pp. 10, 15.
13. See p. 69 of this volume.
14. A. D. McIntosh, editor, 1940: *Marlborough: A Provincial History*, p. 53. Dieffenbach (1843: *Travels in New Zealand*) mentions a man driving cattle from Port Underwood to the Wairau about this time.

15. E. J. Wakefield, 1908 edition: *Adventure in New Zealand*, p. 40.
16. Volume I of the *Canterbury Herd Book* (1871) contains a letter by Rhodes to the editor, describing this importation.
17. A. E. Woodhouse, 1937: *George Rhodes of the Levels and His Brothers*, p. 11.
18. W. Pratt, 1877: *Colonial Experiences in New Zealand, by an Old Colonist*, p. 20.
19. *Twelfth Report of the New Zealand Company*, appendix, pp. 139, 141.
20. A. D. McIntosh, *op. cit.*, p. 91.
21. *Nelson Examiner*, July 22, 1948.
22. A. D. McIntosh, *op. cit.*, p. 107.
23. T. L. Buick, 1928: *The French at Akaroa, An Adventure in Colonisation*, p. 186.
24. Besides Buick, the greatest collection of information and legend about Banks Peninsula was made by the editors of the *Akaroa Mail* for a centenary volume called *Akaroa and Banks Peninsula*, published in 1940. Much of the material is legendary beyond doubt, but the general picture seems to be true, and I have used only such of the material as seemed to me to be substantially in accord with more carefully documented sources. Edward Shortland, 1851: *The Southern Districts of New Zealand*, p. 253, reported of the Hay establishment (Shortland spelled it Hayes, but it is undoubtedly the same family) at Pigeon Bay: "He had now eighteen head of cattle, nine of them cows, which run at liberty in the bush, and yielded, as he said, from twenty-five to thirty pounds of butter a week." Not until 1846 was the first beef butchered at Purau—probably some two-year old steers. (Buick, *ibid.*)
25. J. Deans, editor, 1937: *Pioneers of Canterbury: Deans Letters 1840-1854*, p. 72.
26. *Canterbury Herd Book*, vol. II, 1873, Introduction.
27. J. Deans, *op. cit.*, pp. 78-80.
28. See Lyttelton Harbour on the map of Banks Peninsula (fig. 27).
29. J. Deans, *op. cit*, p. 110.
30. *Ibid.*, p. 91.
31. *Ibid.*, p. 113.
32. *Ibid.*, p. 124.
33. *Ibid.*, pp. 166 ff.
34. T. M. Hocken, 1898: *Contributions to the Early History of New Zealand (Settlement of Otago)*, appendix.
35. *Ibid.*, chaps. XII and XVI.
36. An advertisement in the *Nelson Examiner*, June 5, 1852.
37. *Nelson Examiner*, Aug. 8, 1855.

38. E. B. Fitton, 1856: *New Zealand. Its Present Condition, Prospects, and Resources,* p. 140.
39. J. Hay, 1915: *Reminiscences of Earliest Canterbury (Principally Banks Peninsula) and Its Settlers,* pp. 113-14.
40. *Lyttelton Times,* Dec. 30, 1855.
41. See table VI, p. 116 of this volume.
42. Figures for 1851 from: A. S. Thomson, 1859: *The Story of New Zealand,* vol. II, p. 331; figures for 1855 from *Statistics of New Zealand* for 1853, 1854, 1855, and 1856; and for 1861 *ibid.* for 1861.
43. *Otago Witness* for July 14, 1855.
44. F. G. Fuller, 1859: *Five Years' Residence in New Zealand,* p. 169.
45. Notably the MS. of the Chudleigh Diary in the Canterbury Museum.
46. Andreas Reischek described one such cattle station in the eighties, as well as the existence of others dotted along the southern Westland Coast from Ross to Jackson Bay. His book, translated and published in English in 1930 as *Yesterdays in Maoriland,* is so highly colored and dramatic that one is tempted to doubt its accuracy in details.
47. Collier has a rather journalistic account of the early Australian stockmen and bullock drivers. Roberts in his excellent work on squatting life in Australia in its fullest bloom (1835-1847) has a good deal of material about this. (J. Collier, 1911: *The Pastoral Age in Australia,* chaps. XVI and XVII; and S. H. Roberts, 1935: *The Squatting Age in Australia.*)
48. R. M. Burdon, 1936: *High Country: the Evolution of a New Zealand Sheep Station,* p. 47.
49. This conclusion concerning the spurt of cattle importations is reached by the frequency of offerings of cattle by advertisement in the *Otago Daily Times,* the *Lyttelton Times,* and the *Nelson Examiner,* the files of which newspapers were searched from their beginnings (in 1861, 1850, and 1842, respectively) until the seventies for information for this study.
50. H. G. Philpott, 1937: *A History of the New Zealand Dairy Industry, 1840-1935,* p. 24.
51. Breeders like Thomas McKay of Nelson, H. P. Hall and Rev. J. G. Bluett of Christchurch, for example, were pioneers. The New Zealand Jersey Cattle Association, like most other groups concerned with particular cattle and sheep breeds in the Dominion, has issued a little historical booklet called *The Jersey in New Zealand* (1932), the facts of which I take to be correct.
52. Manuscript in preparation in 1942: *Social History of Canterbury,* by G. T. J. Wilson and N. Barker.
53. H. G. Philpott, *op. cit.,* while weak on the early period, is very detailed in his descriptions from 1870 onward.

54. J. B. Condliffe, 1930: *New Zealand in the Making;* R. O. Buchanan, 1935:*The Pastoral Industries of New Zealand,* Inst. of Brit. Geographers, publication no. 2; and H. G. Philpott, *op. cit.*
55. Some farms on which cattle figured are described in the appendix, pp. 393-95.
56. H. G. Philpott, *op. cit.,* pp. 213-14.
57. G. H. Scholefield, 1909: *New Zealand in Evolution,* p. 145.

CHAPTER VIII

1. J. R. Fleming, 1938: "Farm Management Survey (Plains Area, Ashburton County, New Zealand)," N.Z.D.S.I.R. *Bull.,* no. 58, p. 21.
2. From issues of *N.Z.O.Y.B.*
3. A. and P. Statistics for 1941; *N.Z.O.Y.B.,* 1938, p. 403.
4. Lord Ernle, 1912: *English Farming, Past and Present,* p. 181 ff.
5. J. Buchan, 1926: "Short History of Waikouaiti from the Maori Occupation to 1860," U.N.Z.T. (M.A.).
6. J. Deans, editor, 1937: *Pioneers of Canterbury: Deans Letters 1840-1854,* pp. 67 and 68.
7. *Ibid.,* appendix.
8. These figures are all from the different years of the official statistics of New Zealand. There were also many figures given in the newspapers from year to year, often quoting the *Provincial Gazette.* Thus the *Canterbury Provincial Gazette* quoted 564 horses for Canterbury for 1854; the *Otago Provincial Gazette* gave 717 for Otago in 1855. These figures are both quoted in the *Otago Witness* for September 23, 1854, and August 23, 1856, respectively.
9. R. B. Paul, 1857: *Letters from Canterbury, New Zealand,* pp. 43 ff.
10. J. Bradshaw, 1888: *New Zealand of Today,* p. 150.
11. For an excellent analysis of the New Zealand pig industry of two decades ago, see F. R. Callaghan, 1930: "The Pig Industry of New Zealand," N.Z.D.S.I.R. *Bull.* no. 17, pp. 38-62.
12. H. Belshaw et al., editors, 1936: *Agricultural Organization in New Zealand,* p. 475; and F. R. Callaghan, *op. cit.,* pp. 43-4.
13. Figures for 1938 from *N.Z.O.Y.B.* for 1938; figures for 1941 from A. and P. Statistics for 1940-41.
14. A. and P. Statistics for 1940-41.
15. *N.Z.O.Y.B.* for 1937, p. 413.
16. Banks' *Journal,* Ed. Hooker, 1896, chap. X.
17. Capt. J. Cook, 1777: *A Voyage Toward the South Pole and Round the World . . . ,* vol. I, p. 123.
18. The quotations in this paragraph are from *ibid.,* vol. II, pp. 154, 155, and 159.
19. Capt. J. Cook, 1784: *A Voyage to the Pacific Ocean . . . ,* vol. I, p. 131.

20. R. McNab, 1914b: *From Tasman to Marsden,* pp. 85, 88.
21. The evidence is given in Captain Haven's Report to Governor King, *Historical Records of New South Wales,* vol. II, p. 95; also quoted in R. McNab, 1909: *Murihuku.*
22. R. McNab (1909: *Murihuku*) cites examples of reports of presence of pigs.
23. R. McNab, 1913: *The Old Whaling Days,* p. 87.
24. *Ibid.,* p. 7.
25. The log was copied by McNab in the library of the *Nantucket Historical Society,* Nantucket, Massachusetts, and is reproduced as an appendix in *ibid.,* pp. 433 ff.
26. E. Dieffenbach, 1843: *Travels in New Zealand.*
27. E. J. Wakefield, 1845: *Adventure in New Zealand* (1908 edition).
28. J. C. Crawford, 1880: *Recollections of Travel in New Zealand and Australia.*
29. R. McNab, 1913: *op. cit.*
30. E. J. Wakefield, *op. cit.,* p. 35.
31. Editors of *Akaroa Mail,* 1940: *Akaroa and Banks Peninsula,* p. 136.
32. J. D. Peart, 1937: *Old Tasman Bay,* p. 99.
33. T. M. Hocken, 1898: *Contributions to the Early History of New Zealand (Settlement of Otago),* appendices.
34. Edward Shortland, 1851: *The Southern Districts of New England,* p. 19.
35. T. M. Hocken, *op. cit.*
36. D'Urville's voyage of 1827 is described at length in his *Voyage de la corvette l'Astrolabe* (Paris, 1830-35). One of the most industrious of New Zealand's Maori scholars, S. Percy Smith, translated several extracts from it; that dealing with the landings in Tasman Bay was published in the *Transactions of the New Zealand Institute,* vol. 40, 1907, pp. 416-47.
37. J. Deans, editor, 1937: *Pioneers of Canterbury: Deans Letters 1840-1854,* pp. 49 and 50.
38. E. Dieffenbach, 1843: *Travels in New Zealand,* vol. I, p. 30.
39. *Twelfth Report of the New Zealand Company,* p. 121.
40. W. Pratt, 1877: *Colonial Experiences in New Zealand, by An Old Colonist.*
41. J. Deans, 1937: *op. cit.,* p. 72.
42. *Ibid.,* p. 79.
43. *Otago Witness* for Nov. 10, 1849.
44. J. Buchan, 1926: "Short History of Waikouaiti from the Maori Occupation to 1860," U.N.Z.T. (M.A.).
45. A. R. Dreaver, 1929: "Southland Province of New Zealand in the Days of Dr. J. A. Menzies, Superintendent (1861-1864)," U.N.Z.T. (M.A.), quoting *Otago Provincial Gazette.*

46. Statistics in the *New Zealand Gazette*, June 27, 1862.
47. R. M. Burdon, 1936: *High Country: The Evolution of a New Zealand Sheep Station*, pp. 75 and 76.
48. F. von Hochsetter, 1867: *New Zealand, Its Physical Geography, Geology, and Natural History*, p. 162.
49. E. Dieffenbach, 1843: *Travels in New Zealand*, vol. II, p. 50.
50. G. M. Thomson, 1922: *The Naturalisation of Plants and Animals in New Zealand*, p. 36.
51. A. Saunders, 1896 and 1899: *History of New Zealand (1642-1893)*, vol. I, p. 178.
52. *N.Z.O.Y.B.* for 1918, pp. 552-53.
53. F. R. Callaghan, 1930: "The Pig Industry of New Zealand," N.Z.D.S.I.R. *Bull.*, no. 17, p. 59.
54. J. R. Fleming, 1938: "Farm Management Survey (Plains Area, Ashburton County, New Zealand)," N.Z.D.S.I.R. *Bull.*, no. 58.
55. The figures in this paragraph are from the *N.Z.O.Y.B.*, 1942, p. 810, with the exception of those for 1918 which are from *N.Z.O.Y.B.*, 1918, p. 554.
56. Capt. J. Cook, 1777: *A Voyage Towards the South Pole and Round the World* . . . , vol. I, p. 123.
57. Capt. J. Cook, 1784: *A Voyage to the Pacific Ocean* . . . , vol. I, p. 131.
58. T. M. Hocken, 1898: *Contributions to the Early History of New Zealand (Settlement of Otago)*, appendix.
59. E. Dieffenbach, 1843: *Travels in New Zealand*, vol. I, p. 41.
60. J. C. Crawford, 1880: *Recollections of Travel in New Zealand and Australia*, p. 33.
61. Editors of *Akaroa Mail*, 1940: *op. cit.*, p. 136.
62. *Otago Witness* for Nov. 10, 1849, and April 6, 1850.
63. A. C. Barker (manuscript letters of Mr. and Mrs. A. C. Barker written in 1849-50, in Canterbury Museum).
64. A. S. Thomson, 1859: *The Story of New Zealand*, vol. II, p. 331.
65. *Statistics of New Zealand* for 1861 and 1886.
66. E. B. Fitton, 1856: *New Zealand. Its Present Condition, Prospects, and Resources*, p. 11.
67. These figures are from the *Annual Reports* of the Department of Internal Affairs for the years following the seasons mentioned.

CHAPTER IX

1. J. C. Andersen, 1916: *Jubilee History of South Canterbury*, p. 108.
2. J. Hector, 1883: *A Handbook of New Zealand*, third edition, p. 100.
3. S. Sidney, 1853: *The Three Colonies of Australia*, second edition, p. 27.
4. P. Cunningham, 1827: *Two Years in New South Wales*.

5. G. H. Haydon, 1846: *Five Years Experience in Australia Felix.*
6. H. M. Suttor, 1925: *Australian Milestones.*
7. *Illustrated Sydney News,* May 16, 1865.
8. D. G. Stead, 1935: *The Rabbit in Australia.*
9. G. M. Thomson, 1922: *The Naturalisation of Plants and Animals in New Zealand,* p. 21.
10. A very full history of the Otago Acclimitisation [*sic*] Society is given in the *Otago Daily Times* issue of May 6, 1867.
11. R. M. Burdon, 1938: *High Country: The Evolution of a New Zealand Sheep Station,* p. 136.
12. T. M. Hocken, 1898: *Contribution to the Early History of New Zealand (Settlement of Otago),* appendix.
13. Editors of *Akaroa Mail,* 1940: *Akaroa and Banks Peninsula,* p. 120 ff.
14. A. D. McIntosh, editor, 1940: *Marlborough: A Provincial History,* p. 278; and G. H. Scholefield, 1909: *New Zealand in Evolution,* p. 84.
15. G. M. Thomson, *op. cit.,* pp. 85 ff.
16. A. D. McIntosh, *op. cit.,* p. 279 (based on contemporary newspapers).
17. Of chief importance in unraveling the story of rabbit menace have been: R. M. Burdon (*op. cit.*) and G. T. J. Wilson and N. Barker (manuscript in preparation in 1942: *Social History of Canterbury*). Other sources of information have been old newspaper files, diaries, letters, and memories of old settlers. Some of the statements herein may contain factual errors of detail, but the picture as a whole is as nearly correct as is likely to be obtained.
18. D. G. Stead, 1935: *The Rabbit in Australia.*
19. *Ibid.*
20. G. M. Thomson, *op. cit.,* p. 96.
21. *Annual Reports* of the Department of Internal Affairs, *Appendix to Journals,* House of Representatives, paper H-22.
22. G. M. Thomson, *op. cit.,* p. 41.
23. J. Deans, editor, 1937: *Pioneers of Canterbury: Deans Letters 1840-1854,* p. 244.
24. G. M. Thomson, *op. cit.*
25. E. Hardcastle, 1907: *The Deer of New Zealand,* a pamphlet.
26. A. N. Perham, 1922: "Deer in New Zealand," *A. J. H. R.,* paper C-3A.

CHAPTER X

1. Data in table calculated from A. and P. Statistics, 1940-41.
2. Percentages were calculated from data in *N.Z.O.Y.B.,* 1942, p. 774.
3. From *N.Z.O.Y.B.,* 1942, p. 324.
4. *Ibid.,* p. 329.

CHAPTER XI

1. Capt. J. Cook, 1777: *A Voyage Toward the South Pole and Round the World* . . . , vol. I, p. 123.
2. *Ibid.*, p. 122.
3. *Ibid.*, p. 152.
4. G. Forster, 1777: *A Voyage Around the World.* . . .
5. Capt. J. Cook, 1784: *A Voyage to the Pacific Ocean* . . . , vol. II.
6. Bellinghausen's *Log* is given in full as an appendix in: R. McNab, 1909: *Murihuku.*
7. E. Dieffenbach, 1843: *Travels in New Zealand*, vol. I, pp. 31, 41, and 58.
8. *Ibid.*, vol. I, p. 31.
9. E. J. Wakefield, 1845: *Adventure in New Zealand.*
10. R. McNab, editor, 1908: *Historical Records of New Zealand*, vol. I, p. 213 ff.
11. J. S. C. Dumont D'Urville, 1830-5: *Voyage de la Corvette l'Astrolabe.*
12. J. Buchan, 1926: "Short History of Waikouaiti from the Maori Occupation to 1860," U.N.Z.T. (M.A.), pp. 18-26.
13. T. M. Hocken, 1898: *Contributions to the Early History of New Zealand (Settlement of Otago.)*, appendix, p. 213.
14. Edward Shortland, 1851: *The Southern Districts of New Zealand*, p. 175.
15. J. Hay, 1915: *Reminiscences of Earliest Canterbury (Principally Banks Peninsula) and Its Settlers.*
16. T. L. Buick, 1928: *The French at Akaroa, An Adventure in Colonisation*, p. 139.
17. *Ibid.*, pp. 184-86.
18. *Ibid.*, pp. 206-07.
19. *Nelson Examiner*, April 30, 1842.
20. W. Pratt, 1877: *Colonial Experiences in New Zealand by An Old Colonist*, pp. 100 ff., 134, and 137.
21. W. Fox, 1843: "Letters to Colonel Wakefield . . . ," in appendix to *Thirteenth Report of the New Zealand Company*, p. 121.
22. J. Deans, editor, 1937: *Pioneers of Canterbury: Deans Letters 1840-1854*, pp. 81, 207, 216, 221, appendix.
23. *Otago Witness*, July 14, 1855.
24. *Statistics of New Zealand* for the years 1853-56.
25. Data for 1890-91 from *Handbook of New Zealand* for 1892; for 1940-41 from A. and P. Statistics for 1940-41.
26. Data for 1929-30 season from *N.Z.O.Y.B.*, 1931, p. 46; for the 1940-41 season from A. and P. Statistics for 1940-41.
27. *N.Z.O.Y.B.*, 1942, p. 338.
28. R. Speight *et al.*, editors, 1927: *Natural History of Canterbury*, p. 269.

CHAPTER XII

1. *Statistics of New Zealand* for 1861; *Handbook of New Zealand* for 1892; and A. and P. Statistics, 1940-41.
2. *The New Zealand Official Handbook,* 1892.
3. A. and P. Statistics for 1940-41.
4. F. W. Hilgendorf, 1939: *Wheat in New Zealand,* pp. 17-18.
5. R. MacNab, 1914b: *From Tasman to Marsden.*
6. E. J. Wakefield, 1848: *Handbook for New Zealand by a Late Magistrate of the Colony.*
7. T. M. Hocken, 1898: *Contributions to the Early History of New Zealand (Settlement of Otago.),* appendix, p. 237.
8. J. Deans, editor, 1937: *Pioneers in Canterbury: Deans Letters 1840-1854.*
9. R. B. Paul, 1857: *Letters from Canterbury, New Zealand,* appendix C, p. 130.
10. R. B. Paul (*ibid.;* and 1854: *Some Account of the Canterbury Settlement*) has a number of references to such practices, and F. G. Fuller (1859: *Five Years Residence in New Zealand,* pp. 135-37) has a catalogue of part-time occupations for the poor man thus seeking to acquire land.
11. R. B. Paul, 1857, *op. cit.,* pp. 96-7.
12. Wilson and Barker's manuscript, which has been so helpful in this study, mentions the use of big logs taken from the Alford forest for this purpose in Ashburton. Many of the technical details and trends in the development of the wheat industry were suggested from this manuscript and from talking to the authors individually. There are a few other helpful studies such as that of B. L. Evans ("History of the Wheat Industry in New Zealand," U.N.Z.T. (M.A.)), and many useful references to machinery and techniques in: R. Wallace, 1891: *The Rural Economy and Agriculture of Australia and New Zealand.* Perhaps most of the information came from early papers, diaries, reports, and above all from interviews with older farmers and implement dealers.
13. J. C. Andersen, 1916: *Jubilee History of South Canterbury,* p. 137.
14. Manuscript in preparation in 1942: *Social History of Canterbury,* by G. T. J. Wilson and N. Barker.
15. J. C. Andersen, *op. cit.*
16. G. T. J. Wilson and N. Barker, *op. cit.*
17. R. Wallace, 1891: *The Rural Economy and Agriculture of Australia and New Zealand,* p. 257.
18. B. L. Evans, *op. cit.*
19. G. T. J. Wilson and N. Barker, *op. cit.*
20. J. C. Andersen, *op. cit.,* p. 138.

21. B. L. Evans, *op. cit.;* and J. Ridley, 1866: in Adelaide *Register*, May 6 (an article on the origin of the "stripper" or "header-harvester").

22. *Otago Daily Times*, July 19, 1862, and Oct. 10, 1867.

23. G. T. J. Wilson and N. Barker, *op. cit.*

24. H. Guthrie-Smith, 1926: *Tutira.*

25. L. G. D. Acland, 1946: *The Early Canterbury Runs;* P. S. E. Hereford in *Cyclopaedia of New Zealand*, 1903, vol. III, pp. 801-2, 804-5; and R. Wallace, 1891: *The Rural Economy and Agriculture of Australia and New Zealand.*

26. Figures for table LXIII are given by R. Wallace (*op. cit.*, p. 256) for the 1889-90 season. By that time much of the original freehold of the company had been sold.

27. P. S. E. Hereford in *Cyclopaedia of New Zealand*, 1903, vol. III, p. 801.

28. P. S. E. Hereford, *op. cit.*, p. 102; and R. Wallace, 1891: *The Rural Economy and Agriculture of Australia and New Zealand*, p. 103.

29. P. S. E. Hereford, *op. cit.*, p. 855; and G. T. J. Wilson and N. Barker, *op. cit.*

30. *Cf.* Argentinian practice as discussed in: Mark Jefferson, 1926: *Peopling the Argentine Pampas.*

31. G. T. J. Wilson and N. Barker, *op. cit.*

32. J. C. Andersen, 1927a: *Place Names of Banks Peninsula*, p. 588.

33. G. T. J. Wilson and N. Barker, *op. cit.*

34. R. Gilkison, 1930: *Early Days in Central Otago.*

35. J. C. Crawford (1880: *Recollections of Travel in New Zealand and Australia*), for example, describes such irrigation.

36. V. Pyke, 1887: *History of the Early Gold Discoveries in Otago.*

37. G. T. J. Wilson and N. Barker, *op. cit.*

38. Very little has been written about irrigation in Canterbury. The following sources just about complete the list: M. F. Davies, 1940: "Irrigation in the Canterbury Plains," *Geography*, no. 128, vol. 25, part 2, pp. 68-75; a paper read at the Sixth Annual Conference of the New Zealand Grassland Association, Dunedin, Aug. 10-12, 1937, by W. C. Stafford (pp. 128-31 in the mimeographed proceedings of the Conference); and A. A. Copeland, 1939: "Farms Under Irrigation," *N.Z.J.A.*, vol. 58, no. 6, pp. 478-83.

39. New Zealand Department of Scientific and Industrial Research, *Annual Report*, 1941, *A.J.H.R.*, H-34, p. 40.

40. *New Zealand Official Handbook*, 1892.

41. Figures are from *New Zealand Official Year Books* for the various years.

42. Calculated from data in *N.Z.O.Y.B.*, 1942, p. 809.

43. *N.Z.O.Y.B.*, 1942, p. 809.

44. F. W. Hilgendorf, 1939: *Wheat in New Zealand*, p. 22.
45. F. G. Fuller, 1859: *Five Years' Residence in New Zealand*, p. 130.
46. F. W. Hilgendorf, 1939: *op. cit.*, p. 27.
47. A. and P. Statistics for 1940-41.
48. F. W. Hilgendorf, *op. cit.*
49. *Ibid.*, p. 34; see also W. S. Campbell, 1911: "William Ferrer's Work in Connection with His Improvements of Wheat for Australian Conditions," Report of the A.N.Z.A.A.S., vol. 13.
50. O. H. Frankel, 1934: "'Cross 7' Wheat," N.Z.D.S.I.R. *Bull.*, no. 46.
51. A. and P. Statistics for 1940-41.
52. A. and P. Statistics for 1936-37 and for 1940-41.

CHAPTER XIII

1. A. and P. Statistics for 1940-41.
2. Capt. J. Cook, 1777: *A Voyage Towards the South Pole and Round the World . . .*, vol. I, p. 123 and vol. II, p. 152.
3. R. McNab, 1909: *Murihuku* (Bellinghausen's Log in the appendix).
4. E. Dieffenbach, 1843: *Travels in New Zealand.*
5. E. J. Wakefield, 1845: *Adventure in New Zealand.*
6. J. S. C. Dumont D'Urville, 1841-46: *Voyage au pole sud et dans l'Océanie. . . .*
7. R. Cruise, 1823: *Journal of a Ten Months' Residence in New Zealand.*
8. J. Deans, editor, 1937: *Pioneers of Canterbury. Deans Letters 1840-1854*, p. 81.
9. Editors of *Akaroa Mail*, 1940: *Akaroa and Banks Peninsula*, p. 128.
10. *Nelson Examiner*, March 19, 1842.
11. *Nelson Examiner*, March 29, 1845.
12. R. B. Paul, 1857: *Letters from Canterbury, New Zealand.*
13. F. G. Fuller, 1859: *Five Years Residence in New Zealand*, p. 128.
14. *Ibid.*, p. 129.
15. *Otago Gazette* for 1855, quoted in the *Otago Witness*, Aug. 23, 1856.
16. J. C. Andersen, 1916: *Jubilee History of South Canterbury*, p. 126.
17. Data taken from and calculated from A. and P. Statistics, 1940-41.
18. *Ibid.*
19. *Ibid.*
20. *Annual Reports* of the N.Z.D.S.I.R. (*A.J.H.R.*, H-34) especially for 1940; and D. Cairns, 1940: *N.Z.J.S.T*, vol. 22A, no. 2A, pp. 86A-96A.
21. H. Belshaw *et al.*, 1936: *Agricultural Organization in New Zealand*, chap. 18.
22. The N.Z.D.S.I.R. *Annual Reports* (*A.J.H.R.*, H-34) have continual progress reports on this problem; it is also discussed in: D. Miller, L. J. Dumbleton, and J. F. Clark, 1936: "Biological Control of Noxious Insects and Weeds in New Zealand," *N.Z.J.S.T.*, vol. 18,

no. 7, pp. 579-93. See also L. J. Dumbleton, 1941: "The Grass Grub and Subterranean Grass Caterpillar," *N.Z.J.A.*, vol. 62, p. 180.
23. E. B. Levy and L. W. Gorman, 1936: "Strain in Subterranean Clover," *Proceedings in the Fifth Conference of the New Zealand Grassland Association*, pp. 19-32.
24. H. Belshaw *et al.*, 1936: *"Agricultural Organization in New Zealand,"* chap. 18.
25. H. H. Allan, 1936: "An Introduction to the Grasses of New Zealand," N.Z.D.S.I.R. *Bull.*, no. 49, p. 144.
26. P. S. Milligan, 1941: "An Historico-Geographic Survey of Banks Peninsula," U.N.Z.T. (M.A.).
27. A. H. Cockayne, 1937: Presidential Address to the Sixth Annual Conference of New Zealand Grass Association.
28. A. and P. Statistics, 1940-41.
29. H. Belshaw *et al.*, 1936: *Agricultural Organization in New Zealand*, chap. 18.
30. *Annual Reports* of the N.Z.D.S.I.R. (*A.J.H.R.*, H-34), especially the *Report* for 1941, pp. 36-7.
31. J. Deans, editor, 1937: *Pioneers of Canterbury: Deans Letters 1840-1854*, pp. 67, 148.
32. *Ibid.*, p. 157.
33. *Otago Witness* for April 6, 1850.
34. *Nelson Examiner*, Aug. 8, 1855.
35. *Canterbury Provincial Gazette* for July 1, 1854, quoted in *Otago Witness*, Sept. 23, 1855.
36. J. Buchan, 1926: "Short History of Waikouaiti from the Maori Occupation to 1860," U.N.Z.T. (M.A.), chap. IX.
37. *Otago Witness*, Aug. 23, 1856.
38. Data taken from and calculated from *Statistics of New Zealand*, 1853-56.
39. R. B. Paul, 1857: *Letters from Canterbury, New Zealand*, p. 100.
40. G. M. Thomson, 1922: *The Naturalisation of Plants and Animals in New Zealand*, p. 398.
41. *N.Z.J.S.*, vol. I, pp. 550-54, 1883.
42. F. W. Hilgendorf, 1932: *Pasture Plants and Pastures of New Zealand*.
43. Sir J. Vogel, 1875: *Handbook of New Zealand*, p. 69 ff. of second edition.
44. *Ibid.*, p. 125.
45. Figures taken from and calculated from *New Zealand Official Handbook*, 1892, pp. 95, 100.
46. *Ibid.*
47. *Ibid.*, p. 134.

CHAPTER XIV

1. Lady Barker, 1870: *Station Life in New Zealand,* p. 47.
2. J. C. Crawford, 1880: *Recollections of Travel in New Zealand and Australia,* p. 68.
3. T. H. Potts, 1882: *Out in the Open,* pp. 33 ff.
4. N.Z.D.S.I.R. *Annual Reports (A.J.H.R.,* H-34) 1929, 1933.
5. Sir R. G. Stapledon, 1928: *A Tour in Australia and New Zealand, Grasslands and Other Studies,* p. 72.
6. R. Speight *et al.,* 1927: *Natural History of Christchurch,* p. 255.
7. R. C. Darby, editor, 1936: *An Historical Geography of England Before A. D. 1800,* p. 491.
8. J. Deans, editor, 1937: *Pioneers of Canterbury: Deans Letters 1840-1854,* p. 167.
9. R. Speight *et al., op. cit.,* p. 249 ff.
10. W. J. Dolamore, in a paper read at the Sixth Annual Conference of the New Zealand Grasslands Association (1937, pp. 119-27), made an excellent statement on farm shelter in New Zealand, with special reference to Southland-Otago; he discusses in this paper all the common farm shelter trees.
11. *N.Z.O.Y.B.* 1921-22, p. 347.
12. H. Belshaw *et al.,* editors, 1936: *Agricultural Organization in New Zealand,* p. 570.
13. *Ibid.,* p. 569.
14. Data from A. and P. Statistics for 1940-41.
15. *N.Z.O.Y.B.,* 1942, p. 369.
16. A.N.Z.A.A.S., *Handbook of New Zealand,* p. 54.
17. *N.Z.O.Y.B.,* 1942, p. 375.
18. *Ibid.,* p. 73.
19. *Ibid.,* p. 370.
20. *N.Z.O.Y.B.,* 1921-22, p. 349.
21 D. Miller, L. J. Dumbleton, and J. F. Clark, 1936: "Biological Control of Noxious Insects and Weeds in New Zealand," *N.Z.J.S.T.,* vol. 18, no. 7, pp. 579-93.

NOTES ON SOURCES OF STATISTICAL DATA

A specially useful treatment of the statistics of the Colony and the Dominion may be found in E. P. Neale, 1938: *Guide to New Zealand Official Statistics.* Neale describes the pitfalls and limitations of the current statistics in the *N.Z.O.Y.B.* (1942, pp. 27-32) and in the *General Report* of the *Population Census* of 1926 (pp. 1-6). Official statistical records of New Zealand began to be compiled in 1841, the year following its proclamation as a British colony. These were sent as reports to the Colonial Office in London combined with various other reports, where they were traditionally known as "Blue Books." Transcriptions or copies of these are available in some of the New Zealand archives.

The first statistics printed in New Zealand were the *Statistics of New Munster* for 1841-48 (Wellington, 1849). Other similar and partial publications appeared from time to time. Statistical reports were also published occasionally in the *New Zealand Government Gazette* (Auckland, 1840-47), and in the *Gazettes* of New Ulster (Auckland, 1848-53) and of New Munster (Wellington, 1848-53), entitled *New Zealand Government Gazette* (*Province of New Ulster*—or *Munster*).

After the provinces, established in 1852, began effective operations in 1853, and until they were abolished in 1876, the Provincial Councils were active in the collection of local statistics which were published in the various official *Provincial Gazettes*. It was not until 1858, however, that the first edition of statistics for the colony as a whole was published in New Zealand. Then the *Statistics of New Zealand* covering the four years 1853-56 were published, and the *Statistics* thereafter appeared annually until 1920. Since 1920, the omnibus annual publication, which in that year ran to four weighty volumes, has been discontinued in favor of the publication of statistics in nine sub-groupings, such as the A. and P. Statistics, the *Statistical Report on Population and Buildings,* and so forth.

With each issue of the *Statistics* there appeared a *Report,* which became

427

lengthier and leaned more to interpretation with each succeeding year. For various purposes, these *Reports,* together with extracts from the *Statistics,* were compiled into a succession of *Handbooks of New Zealand,* such as Sir Julius Vogel's *Handbook* of 1875 entitled *The Official Handbook of New Zealand, A Collection of Papers by Experienced Colonists on the Colony as a Whole and on the Separate Provinces.* This was published for the purpose of stimulating immigration and general interest in the colony and circulated principally in Great Britain. Sir James Hector issued a similar *Handbook* for the Melbourne International Exposition, 1880, which he revised and republished in a number of subsequent years. For the first time in 1889, and again in 1890, the *Report* on the *Statistics* was published separately from the data. In 1891, its place was taken by the *Report* of the census of that year, but in 1892 a new publication was issued, this time with much additional descriptive material, which was called "The Handbook of New Zealand for 1892." Its title was changed in 1893 to the *New Zealand Official Yearbook,* and the title has remained unchanged for the annual publications since that time. Up until 1921 the *Year Book* was published in the year following its title date; the title date referred to the year to which the most recent of its statistics applied. A change was made in 1922, when the title date was given as 1921-22, and the date since has referred to the year of publication.

After each census, from 1858 until 1916, in the first four instances as part of the volume of the *Statistics* for that year, but thereafter separately, volumes of the *Census Statistics* appeared. After 1891, a *Report* on each census was also published separately from the census figures themselves. In the last three censuses, the *Census Statistics* and the *Report* have been combined in a series of volumes, and for these years, 1921, 1926, and 1936, the most convenient summaries are given in the last volume of the *Report,* called the "General Report." Most references for 1936 are to volume I of the *Report,* "Increase and Location of Population." Only a few preliminary statistics for the 1945 census are available as this book is being written.

The *New Zealand Gazette* (officially the *New Zealand Government Gazette* or the *New Zealand Official Gazette*) is published monthly, and contains many useful statistics, especially current meteorological records. Besides the *Gazette,* the *N.Z.O.Y.B.* and the annual issues of the *Statistics* in the new departmentalized form, statistics of interest to the study were found in: "Meteorological Observations," published monthly by the New Zealand Meteorological Office; in *N.Z.J.A.,* and in *N.Z.J.S.T.* Of the last two journals, the former is an official publication of the N.Z.D.A., the latter of the N.Z.D.S.I.R. For variations in different quantities through the course of a year, the best source is the "Monthly Abstract of Statistics" published by the N.Z.D.C.S.

BIBLIOGRAPHY

Three standard bibliographical guides to the literature of New Zealand are easily available: J. Collier, 1889: *Literature Relating to New Zealand;* T. M. Hocken, 1909: *Bibliography of New Zealand Literature;* and A. H. Johnstone, 1927: *Supplement to Hocken's Bibliography of New Zealand Literature.* The most useful bibliographical summary, though biased towards the needs of the institutional historians, is to be found in the *Cambridge History of the British Empire,* vol. 7, part 2, "New Zealand," pp. 259-90; its listing of the various New Zealand archives, of early newspapers, and of government documents, is particularly good. Part 1 of the same volume, dealing with Australia, has a similar section. G. H. Scholefield, 1929: *New Zealand in Evolution,* is another good introduction to the New Zealand source material.

Because of the frequency of reference, the following abbreviations of certain journals, government publications, government departments, and standard references have been used throughout this volume. All other source material may be found in the usual alphabetical listing by author which immediately follows this list of abbreviated titles.

ABBREVIATED TITLES

A.J.H.R.   *Appendices to the Journals of the House of Representatives* in Wellington. These are frequently referred to in the literature also as *New Zealand Parliamentary Papers (N.Z.P.P.). Annual Reports* of government departments most frequently so appear. They are identified by year, letter and number, as: *A.J.H.R.* H-35.

A. and P.   *Statistical Report on the Agricultural and Pastoral Pro-*
Statistics   *duction of New Zealand.* Published for each season, usually from May 1 to April 30, thus citations are for parts of two years as, for example, A. and P. Statistics, 1940-1.

A.N.Z.A.A.S.   *Australian and New Zealand Association for the Advancement of Science.*

D. M. Bull.   *Dominion Museum Bulletin,* Wellington.

C.H.B.E.   *Cambridge History of the British Empire,* vol. 7, Cambridge, 1933.

C.H.B.E.N.Z.   *Ibid.,* part 2, *New Zealand.*

B.N.Z.G.S.   *Bulletin of the New Zealand Geological Survey,* Wellington, New Series, 1906—.

G.J.   *The Geographical Journal,* London, 1893—.

G.R.   *The Geographical Review,* New York, 1916—.

G.S.N.Z.R.   *Geological Survey of New Zealand, Reports,* Wellington, 1864-95.

H.R.N.S.W.   *Historical Records of New South Wales,* Sydney, 7 vols., 1762-1811.

H.R.N.Z.   *Historical Records of New Zealand,* (vol. 1: McNab, 1908; vol. 2: McNab, 1914a).

J.P.S.   *Journal* of the Polynesian Society, New Plymouth, New Zealand, 1892—.

J.R.G.S.   *Journal* of the Royal Geographical Society, London, 1831-1881.

N.Z.D.A.   New Zealand Department of Agriculture.

N.Z.D.C.S.   New Zealand Department of Census and Statistics.

N.Z.D.I.A.   New Zealand Department of Internal Affairs.

N.Z.D.L.S.   New Zealand Department of Lands and Survey.

N.Z.D.P.W.   New Zealand Department of Public Works.

N.Z.D.R.   New Zealand Department of Railways.

N.Z.D.S.I.R.   New Zealand Department of Scientific and Industrial Research.

N.Z.G.   *New Zealand Geographer,* Auckland.

N.Z.J.A.   *New Zealand Journal of Agriculture,* Wellington, 1912—.

N.Z.J.S.   *New Zealand Journal of Science* (vols. 1-2, Feb. 1882 to Nov. 1885; vol. 1 (new issue) Jan. to Nov. 1891).

N.Z.J.S.T.   *New Zealand Journal of Science and Technology,* Wellington, 1918—. (Beginning with vol. 20, no. 1 July, 1938, published in two parts, the volumes, numbers, and pages of the Agricultural section being given the

BIBLIOGRAPHY 431

suffix A, the General section references having the suffix B.)

N.Z.M.D.   New Zealand Mines Department.

N.Z.O.Y.B.   *New Zealand Official Year Book,* Wellington, 1893–.

N.Z.P.P.   See *A.J.H.R.*

N.Z.S.F.S.   New Zealand State Forest Service.

T.N.Z.I.   *Transactions and Proceedings of the New Zealand Institute,* Wellington, 1868-1933,

later changed to:

T.R.S.N.Z.   *Transactions and Proceedings of the Royal Society of New Zealand,* 1934–. (References to this series are sometimes given as T.N.Z.I. for dates after 1933.)

U.N.Z.T.(M.A.)   University of New Zealand, Thesis for degree of Master of Arts, unpublished.

BIBLIOGRAPHY

Acland, L. G. D., 1946: *The Early Canterbury Runs* (2nd edition), Christchurch.

Adam, James, 1874: *Twenty-five Years of Emigrant Life in the South of New Zealand.* (In pamphlets.) Edinburgh.

Adams, T. W., 1916: "The Species of the genus *Pinus* now growing in New Zealand with some notes on their Introduction and Growth," *T.N.Z.I.,* vol. 48, pp. 216-23.

Adams, W. C., 1853: *A Spring in the Canterbury Settlement,* London.

Akaroa Mail, editors of, 1940: *Akaroa and Banks Peninsula,* Akaroa.

Allan, H. H., 1929: "A List of Supposed Wild Hybrids Among Naturalised Plants of New Zealand," *N.Z.J.S.T.,* vol. 11, no. 5, pp. 255-61.

——, 1936: "An Introduction to the Grasses of New Zealand," *N.Z.D.S.I.R. Bull.* no. 49, Wellington.

——, 1937a: "Some Ecological Features (Botanical) of the Main Islands," *Handbook for New Zealand,* A.N.Z.A.A.S., Auckland.

——, 1937b: "Indigenous Grasslands of New Zealand," *Handbook for New Zealand,* A.N.Z.A.A.S., Auckland.

——, 1946: "Tussock Grassland or Steppe," *N.Z.G.,* vol. 2, no. 1, pp. 223-34.

Argus, newspaper, Melbourne, 1840–.

Andersen, J. C., 1916: *Jubilee History of South Canterbury,* Christchurch.

——, 1927a: *Place Names of Banks Peninsula,* Wellington.

——, 1927b: "Early History of Canterbury," in Speight *et al.*

Armstrong, J. B., 1883: "Fertilisation of Red Clover in New Zealand," *N.Z.J.S.,* vol. I, no. 11, pp. 500-4.

Aston, B. C., 1911: "Some Effects of Imported Animals on Indigenous Vegetation," *T.N.Z.I.,* vol. 44, pp. 19-24.

Atkinson, J., 1826: *An Account of the State of Agriculture and Grazing in New South Wales* (Part I), Sydney.

432   THE INVASION OF NEW ZEALAND

——, 1844: *An Account of the State of Agriculture and Grazing in New South Wales* (Part II), Sydney.
A.N.Z.A.A.S., 1937: *Handbook for New Zealand*, Auckland.
Australian (newspaper), 1842-8, Sydney.
Baker, N., 1932: *A Surveyor in New Zealand*, 1857-96, (the recollections of John Holland Baker, edited by Noeline Baker), Auckland.
Banks, Sir J., 1896: *Journal (1768-1771)*. Edited by Sir J. D. Hooker, London.
Barker, A. C.: Manuscript letters of Mr. and Mrs. A. C. Barker written during a voyage to New Zealand in 1849-50, and during their first years in the Canterbury Settlement. Canterbury Museum, Christchurch.
Barker, Lady, 1870: *Station Life in New Zealand*, London.
Barnett, M. A. F., 1942: "The Climate of New Zealand," *N.Z.O.Y.B.*, pp. 10-16.
Bartrum, J. A., 1916: "Highwater Rock-platforms: a Phase of Shore-line Erosion," *T.N.Z.I.*, vol. 48, pp. 132-4.
——, 1938: "Shore Platforms," *Journal of Geomorphology*, vol. 1, no. 3, pp. 266-8.
Bathgate, A., 1876: *Colonial Experiences,* Dunedin.
——, 1922: "Some changes in the Fauna and Flora of Otago in the Last Sixty Years," *N.Z.J.S.T.*, vol. 4, no. 6, pp. 273-83.
Beaglehole, E., 1937: "New Zealand Anthropology Today," *J.P.S.*, vol. 46, no. 3, pp. 154-72.
——, 1938: "Anthropology in New Zealand," *J.P.S.*, vol. 47, no. 4, pp. 152-62.
Beaglehole, J. C., 1934: *The Exploration of the Pacific*, London.
——, 1936: *New Zealand, A Short History*, London.
——, 1939: *The Discovery of New Zealand*, Wellington.
——, 1947: "Discovery," chapter 1 of Belshaw, ed.
Beattie, H., 1909: *Pioneer Recollections*, Gore.
Bell, J. M., Clarke, E. de C., and Marshall, P., 1911: "Geology of the Dun Mountain Subdivision, Nelson," *B.N.Z.G.S.*, no. 12.
Bellinghausen, T., 1909: "Log" of the expedition to the Antarctic of the Russian ships, *Mirny* and *Wostok* given as an appendix to McNab, 1909.
Belshaw, H., 1927: "The Dairying Industry of New Zealand," *Econ. Geog.*, vol. 3, no. 3, pp. 281-97.
Belshaw, H., *et al.*, editors, 1936: *Agricultural Organization in New Zealand*, Melbourne.
Belshaw, H., editor, 1947: *New Zealand*, United Nations Series, University of California Press, Berkeley.
Benson, W. N., 1922: "An Outline of the Geology of New Zealand," *Journ. of Geol.*, vol. 30, no. 1, pp. 1-17.
——, 1935a: "Notes on the Geological Features of Southwestern New Zealand," *G.J.*, vol. 86, no. 5, pp. 393-401.
——, 1935b: "Some Landforms in Southern New Zealand," *Australian Geographer*, vol. 2, no. 7, pp. 3-22.
——, Bartrum, J. A., and King, L. C., 1934: "Geology of the Region About Preservation and Chalky Inlets; Part II, Evolution of Modern Topography," *T.R.S.N.Z.*, vol. 64, no. 1, pp. 51-85.

Best, E., 1916: "Maori Storehouses and Kindred Structures," *D. M. Bull.*, no. 5.
——, 1924a: *The Maori*, Wellington, 2 vols.
——, 1924b: *The Maori as He Was*, Wellington.
——, 1925a: "The Maori Canoe," *D. M. Bull.*, no. 7.
——, 1925b: "Maori Agriculture," *D. M. Bull.*, no. 9.
——, 1929: "Fishing Methods and Devices of the Maori," *D. M. Bull.*, no. 12.
Black, J. M., 1932: "The History and Development of the Port of Timaru," U.N.Z.T. (M.A.)
Blanchard, E., 1882: "La Nouvelle-Zélande; la Colonisation, etc." *Revue des Deux Mondes*, vol. 49, pp. 355-94.
Blosseville, J. de, 1826: in *Annales des Voyages*, Tome 29, pp. 145-61, 173-4, Paris.
Bradshaw, J., 1888: *New Zealand of Today*, London.
Broad, L., 1892: *The Jubilee History of Nelson from 1842-1892*, Nelson.
Brodie, W., 1845: *The State of New Zealand*, London.
Brown, G. A. ("Bruni"), 1904: *Australian Merino Studs*, Melbourne.
Bruce, A., 1877: *The Livestock and Pastures of New South Wales*, Sydney.
Brunner, T., 1848 and 1850: "Journal of an Expedition to Explore the Interior of the Middle Island of New Zealand," *Nelson Examiner*, Sept. 30-Oct. 21, 1848. (Also in *J.R.G.S.*, vol. 20, pp. 344-78, 1850.)
Buchan, J., 1926: "Short History of Waikouaiti from the Maori Occupation to 1860," U.N.Z.T. (M.A.)
Buchanan, J., 1875: "The Botany of Otago," *T.N.Z.I.*, vol. 1, pp. 181-212, 1868. (Published in Wellington, 1875.)
Buchanan, R. O., 1930: "Geographical Influences on the Dairying Industry of New Zealand," *Geography*, vol. 15, pp. 630-40.
——, 1935: "The Pastoral Industries of New Zealand," *Inst. of Brit. Geographers*, publication no. 2, London.
Buck, Sir Peter (Te Rangi Hiroa), 1924: "The Passing of the Maori," *T.N.Z.I.*, vol. 55, pp. 362-75.
——, 1925: "The Coming of the Maori," *Cawthron Lectures*, vol. 2, no. 1, Nelson.
——, 1938: *Vikings of the Sunrise*, New York.
——, 1946: *An Introduction to Polynesian Anthropology*, Bernice Bishop Museum, *Bulletin*, no. 187.
Buick, T. L., 1900: *Old Marlborough, or the Story of a Province*, Palmerston North, N.Z.
——, 1928: *The French at Akaroa, An Adventure in Colonisation*, Wellington.
Buller, J., 1878: *Forty Years in New Zealand*, London.
Burdon, R. M., 1938: *High Country: The Evolution of a New Zealand Sheep Station*, Christchurch.
Burfitt, C. T., 1913: *The History of the Founding of the Wool Industry of Australia*, Sydney.
Burke, J. F., 1834: *British Husbandry*, vol. 1, London.
Butler, S., 1863: *A First Year in the Canterbury Settlement*, London.
Cairns, D., 1940: "Vernalization and Photo-periodic Induction: I. Perennial Rye-grass (*Lolium perenne*)," *N.Z.J.S.T.*, vol. 22A, no. 2A, pp. 86A-96A.

Calder, J. W., 1946: "Trends of Wheat Production in New Zealand," *Rural Education Bulletin*, Canterbury Agricultural College, vol. 1, no. 4.

Callaghan, F. R., 1930: "The Pig Industry of New Zealand," *N.Z.D.S.I.R. Bull.*, no. 17, pp. 38-62.

Cambridge History of the British Empire, 1933; vol. VII, part I, *Australia;* vol. VII, part II, *New Zealand*, Cambridge.

Campbell, M. B., 1935: "A Period of the Early Settlement of Canterbury (1868-73)," U.N.Z.T. (M.A.).

Campbell, R. L., 1927: "The Exploration of Otago," U.N.Z.T. (M.A.).

Campbell, W. S., 1911: "William Ferrer's work in connection with his improvements of wheat for Australian conditions," *Report* of the *A.N.Z. A.A.S.*, vol. 13, Sydney.

Canterbury Chamber of Commerce, 1942: "Cocksfoot Seed Production," *Bulletin*, no. 142.

Canterbury Herd Book, Wilkin, R., editor, 1871 and 1873: vol. I, 1871; vol. II, 1873. Christchurch.

Canterbury Ordinances, 1853-75: Published legislation of the Canterbury Provincial Council.

Canterbury Papers, 1850 and 1862: First Series issued by the Canterbury Association, London, 1850; Second Series issued by the Canterbury Provincial Government, London, 1862.

Canterbury Provincial Gazette, 1853-76: Official Publication of Canterbury Provincial Council (1853-75).

Carrick, R., compiler and editor, 1903: *Historical Records of New Zealand South, Prior to 1840*, Dunedin.

Carrington, H., 1949: *Life of Captain Cook*, London.

Chapman, F. R., 1891: *The Exploration of Western Otago*, Dunedin.

——, 1893: *Notes on the Depletion of the Fur Seal in the Southern Seas*, Dunedin.

Charlton, A., 1935: "Contributions of Germans and Scandinavians to the History of New Zealand," U.N.Z.T. (M.A.).

Childe-Pemberton, W. S., 1909: *Life of Lord Norton*, London (quoted by J. S. Marais, 1927, *The Colonisation of New Zealand*, p. 329).

Cholmondeley, T., 1854: *Ultima Thule—Thoughts Suggested by a Residence in New Zealand*, London.

Christchurch Press (newspaper) 1861—. Christchurch.

Chudleigh, E. R., *Ms.;* "Diary" for 1862 ff. in the Canterbury Museum, Christchurch.

Clark, A. F., 1932a: "Insects Infesting *Pinus radiata* in New Zealand," *N.Z.J.S.T.*, vol. 13, no. 4, pp. 235-43

——, 1932b: "The Pine-bark Beetle (*Hylastes ater*) in New Zealand," *N.Z.J.S.T.*, vol. 14, no. 1, pp. 1-20.

Clark, A. H., 1945: "Historical Explanation of Land Use in New Zealand," *Journal of Econ. History*, vol. V, no. 2, pp. 215-30.

——, 1946: "Field Work in Historical Geography," *The Professional Geographer*, (old series), vol. 4, no. 1, pp. 13-22.

——, 1947a: "Physical and Cultural Geography," in Belshaw, H., editor, *New Zealand*, Berkeley.

——, 1947b: "South Island, New Zealand, and Prince Edward Island, Canada: A Study of 'Insularity'," *N.Z.G.*, vol. 3, no. 2, pp. 137-50.

Clarke, G., 1903: *Notes on Early Life in New Zealand*, Hobart.

Clayden, A., 1885: *A Popular Handbook to New Zealand*, London.

Clayton, H. H., *et al.*, editors, 1927: *World Weather Records. Smithsonian Miscellaneous Collections*, vol. 79, pp. 123-5.

———, 1934: *World Weather Records* (continued). *Smithsonian Miscellaneous Collections*, vol. 90, pp. 75-8.

Cockayne, A. H., 1910: "The Effect of Burning on Tussock Country," *N.Z.J.A,.* vol. 1, no. 1, pp. 7-15. (Part 1 of "The Natural Pastures of New Zealand.")

———, 1914: "Monterey Pine—the Great Timber Tree of the Future," *N.Z.J.A.*, vol. 8, no. 1, pp. 1-26.

———, 1915: "Some Economic Considerations Concerning Montane Tussock Grasslands," *T.N.Z.I.*, vol. 48, pp. 154-65.

———, 1916a: "Conversion of Fern-land into Grass," *N.Z.J.A.*, vol. 12, no. 6, pp. 421-39.

———, 1916b: "*Danthonia* in New Zealand," *N.Z.J.A.*, vol. 13, no. 5.

———, 1918: "The Grasslands of New Zealand," (a series of five articles), *N.Z.J.A.*, vol. 16, no. 3 to vol. 17, no. 3.

———, 1927: "New Zealand Agriculture; its Trend in the Past Quarter Century," *N.Z.J.A.*, vol. 32, no. 2, pp. 88-92.

———, 1930: "The Evolution of Grassland Farming in New Zealand," *N.Z.J.A.*, vol. 40, no. 4, pp. 219-25.

———, 1937: Presidential Address to the Sixth Annual Conference of New Zealand Grassland Association. From "Papers Read at Sixth Annual Conference," (mimeographed).

Cockayne, L., 1885: "A Brief List of Some British Plants (Weeds) Lately Noticed, Apparently of Recent Introduction into This Part of the Colony; with a Few Notes Thereon," *T.N.Z.I.*, vol. 18, pp. 288-90.

———, 1919: *New Zealand Plants and Their Story*, Wellington.

———, 1919-1922: "An Economic Investigation of the Montane Tussock Grassland of New Zealand," (fourteen articles), *N.Z.J.A.*, vol. 18, no. 1 to vol. 25, no. 3.

———, 1920: *The Distribution of the Vegetation and Flora of New Zealand*, Nelson.

———, 1926: "Ecology of the Forests and Taxonomy of the Beeches," Part 1 of *Monograph on the New Zealand Beech Forests*, Wellington.

———, 1928a: "The Vegetation of New Zealand," *Die Vegetation der Erde*, vol. 14, no. 2, Leipzig.

———, 1928b: "Forests from the Practical and Economic Standpoints," Part 2 of *Monograph on the New Zealand Beech Forests*, Wellington.

Cockayne, L., and Turner, E., 1928: *The Trees of New Zealand*, Wellington.

Cockayne, L., Simpson, G., and Thomson, J. G., 1932: "The Vegetation of South Island, New Zealand," *Vegetationsbilder*, vol. 22, Reihe Heft 5/6.

Coghlan, Sir T. A., 1894: *Statistical Account of the Seven Colonies of Australia*, Sydney.

———, 1918: *Labour and Industry in Australia*, London, 4 vols.

Collier, J., 1889: *Literature Relating to New Zealand*, Christchurch.

———, 1911: *The Pastoral Age in Australia*, Christchurch.

Commission on Southern Pastoral Lands, 1920: "Report," *A.J.H.R.*, C-15.

Condliffe, J. B., 1930: *New Zealand in the Making*, London.

——, 1932: "Problems of Land Settlement in New Zealand," in *Pioneer Settlement*, American Geographical Society Special Publication, no. 14, pp. 418-33, New York.

——, 1933: "Economic Development," chap. 8, *C.H.B.E.N.Z.*, pp. 149-71.

Congreve, Sir W., 1858: "Comparative Statement Showing the Number and Condition of the Sheep in the Province of Canterbury, 1 January 1855, to 31 December 1857," Paper Laid on the Table by the Provincial Council, no. 10, session IX.

Connell, R. P., 1939: "Land Deterioration," *N.Z.J.A.*, vol. 59, no. 1, pp. 4-12.

Cook, Capt. J., 1777: *A Voyage Towards the South Pole and Round the World:* "Performed in. . . . 1772, 1773, 1774 and 1775. . . . In which is included. . . . Furneaux's Narrative. . . . during the Separation of the Ships," 2 vols., "Printed for W. Strahan and T. Cadell in the Strand," London.

——, 1784: *A Voyage to the Pacific Ocean Undertaken, By the Command of His Majesty, for Making Discoveries in the Northern Hemisphere:* "Performed. . . . in the years 1776, 1777, 1778, 1779, and 1780," 3 vols.: I and II, by Cook; III by Capt. James King. "Published by Order of the Lords Commissioners of the Admiralty. . . . Printed by W. and A. Strahan, for G. Nicol . . . and T. Cadell," London.

Copland, A. A., 1939: "Farms under Irrigation," *N.Z.J.A.*, vol. 58, no. 6, pp. 478-83.

Copland, D. B., 1930: *Wheat Production in New Zealand*, Christchurch.

Cotton, C. A., 1913a: "The Physiography of the Middle Clarence Valley," *G.J.*, vol. 42, no. 3, pp. 225-46.

——, 1913b: "Tuamarina Valley: Note on the Quaternary History of the Marlborough District," *T.N.Z.I.*, vol. 45, pp. 316-22.

——, 1914: "Preliminary Note on the Uplifted East Coast of Marlborough," *T.N.Z.I.*, vol. 46, pp. 286-94.

——, 1916a: "Block Mountains and a 'fossil' Denudation Plain in Northern Nelson," *T.N.Z.I.*, vol. 48, pp. 59-75.

——, 1916b: "Structure and Later Geological History of New Zealand," *Geol. Mag.* (New Series), vol. 3, no. 6, pp. 243-49 and 314-20.

——, 1916c: "Fault Coasts in New Zealand," *G.R.*, vol. 6, no. 1, pp. 20-47.

——, 1917a: "Block Mountains in New Zealand," *American Journal of Science*, vol. 44, pp. 249-93.

——, 1917b: "The Fossil Plains of North Otago," *T.N.Z.I.*, vol. 49, pp. 429-32.

——, 1918a: "The Outline of New Zealand," *G.R.*, vol. 8, no. 6, pp. 320-40.

——, 1918b: "River Terraces in New Zealand," *N.Z.J.S.T.*, vol. 1, no. 3.

——, 1922: *Geomorphology of New Zealand*, Part I. Systematic, Wellington (3rd edition, 1942, Rev.).

——, 1945: "Geomorphic Provinces in New Zealand," *N.Z.G.*, vol. I, no. 1, pp. 40-47.

Cowan, J., 1930: *The Maori Yesterday and Today*, Christchurch.

——, 1940: *Settlers and Pioneers*, Wellington.

Cox, E. W., 1936: *The Evolution of the Australian Merino*, Sydney.

Crawford, J. C., 1880: *Recollections of Travel in New Zealand and Australia*, London.

Critchell, J. T., and Raymond, J., 1912: *History of the Frozen Meat Trade*, London.

Cruise, R., 1823: *Journal of a Ten Months' Residence in New Zealand*, London.

Cumberland, K. B., 1940: "Canterbury Landscapes: A Study in New Zealand Geography," *G.R.*, vol. 30, no. 1, pp. 19-40.

———, 1941: "A Century's Change: Natural to Cultural Vegetation in New Zealand," *G.R.*, vol. 31, no. 4, pp. 529-54.

———, 1943: "A Geographic Approach to Soil Erosion in New Zealand," *The Australian Geographer*, vol. 4, no. 5, pp. 121-31.

———, 1944a: "Contrasting Regional Morphology of Soil Erosion in New Zealand," *G.R.*, vol. 34, no. 1, pp. 77-95.

———, 1944b: "High Country Run. . . . ," *Economic Geography*, vol. 20, no. 3.

———, 1945: "Burning Tussock Grassland: a Geographic Survey," *N.Z.G.*, vol. 1, no. 2, pp. 149-64.

———, 1946: *Soil Erosion in New Zealand: A Geographic Reconnaissance*, Wellington.

Cunningham, G. H., 1946: "The Introduction of Plant Diseases into New Zealand," *N.Z.G.*, vol. 2, no. 1, pp. 247-52.

Cunningham, P., 1827: *Two Years in New South Wales*, London.

Dacre, J. C., 1947: "Climatology and Meteorology of the New Zealand Area: A Bibliography," *N.Z.G.*, vol. 3, no. 2, pp. 129-38.

Darby, H. C., editor, 1936: *An Historical Geography of England, before A. D. 1800*, Cambridge.

Davies, M. F., 1940: "Irrigation in the Canterbury Plains," *Geography*, no. 128, vol. 25, part 2, pp. 68-75.

Dawson, R., 1831: *The Present State of Australia*, Sydney.

Dean, J., 1946: "The Lowburn Run, North Canterbury," *N.Z.G.*, vol. 2, no. 2, pp. 345-54.

Deans, J., editor, 1937: *Pioneers of Canterbury: Deans Letters 1840-1854*, Dunedin.

Deem, J. W., and Jenkinson, G. H., 1914: "The Rabbit Pest; Control by Effective Fencing," *N.Z.J.A.*, vol. 9, no. 1, pp. 62-6.

Defries, A., 1938: *Sheep and Turnips* (a biography of Arthur Young), London.

Dick, R. B., 1940: "Observations on Insect-life in Relation to Tussock-grassland Deterioration (Preliminary Report)," *N.Z.J.S.T.*, vol. 22, no. 1A, pp. 19A-29A.

Dieffenbach, E., 1843: *Travels in New Zealand*, London, 2 vols.

Diels, L., 1896: "Vegetations-Biologie von Neu-Seeland," *Botanischer Jahresbericht*, vol. 22, pp. 202-30, Berlin.

Dolamore, W. J., 1937: "Farm Shelter in New Zealand," Paper read at the Sixth Annual Conference of the New Zealand Grasslands Association, (mimeographed).

Donne, T. E., 1924: *Game Animals of New Zealand,—an Account of their Introduction, Acclimatisation and Development*, London.

Dreaver, A. R., 1929: "Southland Province of New Zealand in the Days of Dr. J. A. Menzies, (Superintendent, 1861-1864)," *U.N.Z.T.* (M.A.).

Duff, R., 1940: "The South Island Maori," chap. 11 of: Sutherland, I. L. G., editor: *The Maori People Today, A General Survey*, Christchurch.

Dumbleton, L. J., 1941: "The Grass Grub and Subterranean Grass Caterpillar", *N.Z.J.A.*, vol. 62, p. 180.

D'Urville, J. S. C. Dumont, 1830-5: *Voyage de la Corvette l'Astrolabe*, Paris, 25 vols. (Parts of vols. 2 and 3, which refer to his New Zealand visits of the first voyage, have been translated by S. Percy Smith and published in *T.N.Z.I.*, vol. 40, 1908, pp. 416-47.)

——, 1841-6: *Voyage au pôle sud et dans l'Océanie sur les Corvettes l'Astrolabe et la Zelée, executé par Ordre au Roi pendant les Annees 1837-40*, Paris. 10 vols. (Parts of vols. 8 and 9 deal with the second New Zealand visit.)

Durward, E. W., 1933: "The Maori Population of Otago," *J.P.S.*, vol. 42, no. 2.

Earp, G. B., 1849: *Handbook for Intending Emigrants to the Southern Settlements of New Zealand*, London.

——, 1853: *New Zealand—Its Emigration and Gold Fields*, London.

East, W. G., 1936: "England in the Eighteenth Century," chap. 13 of Darby, 1936.

Easterfield, T. H., Rigg, T., and Bruce, J. A., 1929: "Pakihi Lands of the Nelson Province," *N.Z.J.S.T.*, vol. 11, no. 4, pp. 231-41.

Edie, E. G., Seelye, C. J., Raeside, J. D., 1946: "Notes on the Canterbury Floods of February, 1945," *N.Z.J.S.T.*, vol. 27, p. 397.

Elder, J. R., 1929: *Pioneer Explorers of New Zealand*, London.

——, 1930: *Goldseekers and Bushrangers in New Zealand*, London.

——, 1933: "Later Exploration," *C.H.B.E.N.Z.*, pp. 31-44.

Ellis, L. M., 1922: "The Progress of Forestry in New Zealand," Address to the Sixteenth Meeting of the A.N.Z.A.A.S. Jan. 1923. Published, Wellington.

——, 1923: "Forests and Forestry in New Zealand," *Proceedings of the Imperial Forestry Conference*, Ottawa.

Ellis, M. H., 1932: *The Beef Shorthorn in Australia*, Sydney.

Epps, W., 1894: *Land Systems of Australasia*, London.

Ernle, Lord (Prothero, R. E.), 1912: *English Farming, Past and Present* (New edition, 1936, Sir A. D. Hall, editor), London.

Evans, B. L., 1938: "History of the Wheat Industry in New Zealand," U.N.Z.T. (M.A.).

Faris, I., 1941: *Charleston: Its Rise and Decline*, Wellington.

Fawcett, E. J., 1929: "Livestock Production of the Period 1901-2 to 1926-7, Based on Standard Values and Units," *N.Z.J.A.*, vol. 28, no. 6.

——, 1936a: "Sheep Farming," in Belshaw, *et al.*, pp. 408-37.

——, 1936b: "Dairy Farming," in Belshaw, *et al.*, pp. 438-71.

Fell, A., 1926: *A Colonist's Voyage to New Zealand* (Diary of a voyage in the eighteen-forties not previously published). Exeter.

Fenton, F. D., 1859: *Observations on the State of the Aboriginal Inhabitants of New Zealand*, Blue Book, Auckland.

Fereday, R. W., 1872: "On the Direct Injuries to Vegetation in New Zealand by various Insects, especially with Reference to Larvae of Moths and

Beetles feeding upon the Field Crops; and the Expediency of introducing Insectivorous Birds as a remedy," *T.N.Z.I.*, vol. 5, pp. 289-94.

Ferrar, H. T., 1929: "The Soils of Irrigation Areas in Central Otago," N. Z. Ecol. Surv. *Bulletin*, no. 33.

Finney, J. K., 1941: "The Progress of Land Utilisation in Waimari County, Canterbury, New Zealand," U.N.Z.T. (M.A.).

Firth, R., 1929: *The Primitive Economics of the New Zealand Maori*, London.

Fitton, E. B., 1856: *New Zealand. Its Present Condition, Prospects and Resources*, London.

Fitzgerald, J. E., editor, 1863: *Writings and Speeches of J. R. Godley*, Christchurch.

Fitzpatrick, B., 1939: *British Imperialism and Australia, 1783-1833*, London.
——, 1941: *The British Empire in Australia. An Economic History. 1834-1939*, Melbourne.

Fleming, J. R., 1938: "Farm Management Survey. (Plains Area, Ashburton County, New Zealand)," N.Z.D.S.I.R., *Bull.* no. 58, Wellington.

Ford, R. J., 1933: "Some Changes in Occupational and Geographical Distribution of Population in New Zealand, 1896-1926," U.N.Z.T. (M.A.).

Forster, G., 1777: *A Voyage Round the World in H.B.M.S. "Resolution" during the Years 1772, 1773, 1774, and 1775*, London. 2 vols.

Foweraker, C. E., 1927: "Forestry—Native and Introduced Timber Trees," in Speight *et al.*, *Natural History of Canterbury*.

Fox, W., 1843: Letters to Col. W. Wakefield: 1. Nelson. Oct. 24, 1843. Appendix to *12th Report of the N. Z. Co.*, pp. 101-2; 2. Nelson. Dec. 1, 1843. Appendix to *13th Report of the N. Z. Co.*, p. 121.
——, 1849: *Report on the Settlement of Nelson*, London.
——, 1851: *The Six Colonies of New Zealand*, London.

Frankel, O. H., 1934: " 'Cross 7' Wheat," N.Z.D.S.I.R. *Bull.* no. 46.

Frazer, Sir F. V. *et al.*, 1940: *Report of a Commission Appointed to Investigate the Sheep Farming Industry*, Wellington.

Fuller, F. G., 1859: *Five Years' Residence in New Zealand*, London.

Gardner, R., 1944: *The Industrial Development of New Zealand*, Wellington.

Garnett, R., 1898: *Edward Gibbon Wakefield; Colonisation of South Australia and New Zealand*, London.

Garnier, B. J., 1946: "The Climates of New Zealand according to the Thornthwaite Classification", *Annals of the Association of American Geographers*, vol. 36, no. 3, pp. 151-77.

Geisler, W., 1931: *Allgemeine Länderkunde von Australien und Ozeanien*, Hannover.

Gibbs, H. S., Raeside, J. D., *et al.*, 1945: "Soil Erosion in the High Country of the South Island," N.Z.D.S.I.R. *Bull.* no. 92, Wellington.

Gilkison, R., 1930: *Early Days in Central Otago*, Dunedin.

Gill, T. N., 1893: "A Comparison of Antipodeal Faunas," *National Academy of Sciences*, Memoir, Washington.

Goldie, J., *Ms.:* "Diary" of a tour of exploration with J. McKerrow, in Western Otago in 1853. Hocken Library, Dunedin.

Grange, L. I., 1935: "The Soils of Ashburton County in Relation to Irrigation," N.Z.D.S.I.R., *Annual Report, A.J.H.R.*, H-34, p. 56.

——, 1938: "Soil Survey," N.Z.D.S.I.R. *Bull.*, no. 69, pp. 52-9.

——, 1944: "A Basic Scheme for Land Classification," *N.Z.J.S.T.*, vol. 26, sec. A, no. 3.

Grattan, C. H., editor, 1947: *Australia*, United Nations Series, University of California Press, Berkeley.

Gregory, J. W., 1907: *Australia and New Zealand*, London.

Grimstone, S. E., 1847: *The Southern Settlements of New Zealand* (Pamphlet in Hocken Library, Dunedin), Wellington.

Guthrie-Smith, H., 1926: *Tutira*, London, second edition.

——, 1936: *Sorrows and Joys of a New Zealand Naturalist*, Dunedin.

Haast, H. F., 1948: *The Life and Times of Sir Julius von Haast*, Wellington.

Haast, Sir J. von, 1861: *Report of a Topographical and Geological Exploration of the Western Districts of Nelson Province*, Nelson.

——, 1864: "Notes on the Mountains and Glaciers of Canterbury Province," *J.R.G.S.*, vol. 34, pp. 87-95.

——, 1879: *Geology of the Provinces of Canterbury and Westland, New Zealand*, Christchurch.

Hamilton, W. M., 1945: "The Dairy Industry in New Zealand," N.Z.D.S.I.R. *Bull.* no. 89.

——, 1947: "The Farming Industries," a chapter in Belshaw, 1947.

Hardcastle, E., 1907: *The Deer of New Zealand*, Wellington (Undated but catalogued as 1907 in Turnbull Library, Wellington).

Harris, C. S., and Harris, A. C., 1939a: "Soil Survey of Duvauchelle Bay, Wainui District, Banks Peninsula," N.Z.D.S.I.R. *Bull.* no. 65. (Soil Survey Division, publication no. 1.)

——, 1939b: "Soil Survey of Westport District," N.Z.D.S.I.R. *Bull.* no. 71. (Soil Survey Division, publication no. 3.)

Harris, C. S. and Birrell, K. S., 1939: "Soil Survey of the Wairau Plains, Marlborough", N.Z.D.S.I.R. *Bull.* no. 72. (Soil Survey Division, publication no. 4.)

Harrop, A. J., 1923: *The Romance of Westland, the Story of New Zealand's Golden Coast*, Christchurch.

——, 1928: *The Amazing Career of Edward Gibbon Wakefield*, London.

——, 1933: "The Companies and British Sovereignty, 1825-50," chap. 5 in C.H.B.E.N.Z., pp. 61-91.

Hay, G. H. L., 1901: *Annandale, Past and Present. (A History of the Occupation of Pigeon Bay by the Hay Family; published privately.)* Christchurch.

Hay, J., 1915: *Reminiscences of Earliest Canterbury (Principally Banks Peninsula) and Its Settlers*, Christchurch.

Haydon, G. H., 1846: *Five Years Experience in Australia Felix*, London.

Healy, A. J., 1945: "Nasella Tussock . . . ," N.Z.D.S.I.R. *Bull.* no. 91.

Heaphy, C., 1842: *Narrative of a Residence in Various Parts of New Zealand—with a Description of the Present State of the Company's Settlements*, London.

——, 1846: "Exploring Expedition to the South West of Nelson," *Nelson Examiner*, Mar. 7 and 14.

Hector, J., 1863: "Geological Expedition to the West Coast of Otago," *Otago Provincial Gazette*, no. 274. Also *J.R.G.S.*, vol. 34, pp. 96-111, 1864; and

Proc. of the Roy. Geog. Soc., vol. 8, pp. 47-50, 1863; vol. 9, pp. 32-3, 1864.

——, 1883: *Handbook of New Zealand,* Wellington. (First edition 1881. Quotations from third edition, 1883.)

Heeres, J. E., 1898: *Abel Janszoon Tasman: His Life and Labours.* Bound with "Tasman's *Journal* and Other Notes," Amsterdam.

Henderson, J., 1911: "On the Genesis of the Surface Forms and Present Drainage-systems of West Nelson," *T.N.Z.I.,* vol. 43, pp. 306-15.

——, 1918: "Notes on the Geology of the Murchison District," *N.Z.J.S.T.,* vol. 1, no. 2, pp. 108-12.

——, 1921: "Notes to accompany a Map of the Cheviot District," *N.Z.J.S.T.,* vol. 4, no. 1, pp. 24-30.

——, 1924: "The Post-Tertiary History of New Zealand," *T.N.Z.I.,* vol. 55, pp. 592 ff.

——, 1929: "The Faults and Geological Structure of New Zealand," *N.Z.J.S.T.,* vol. 11, no. 2, pp. 93-7.

Herbertson, A. J., and Howarth, O. J. R., editors, 1914: *Oxford Survey of the British Empire,* vol. 5, "Australasia," Oxford.

Hereford, P. S. E., editor, 1902-08: *Cyclopaedia of New Zealand,* Wellington, 6 vols.

Hight, J., 1933: "Introduction," chap. I, *C.H.B.E.N.Z.,* pp. 3-7.

Hight, J., and Bamford, H. D., 1914: *The Constitutional History and Law of New Zealand,* part 1, Christchurch.

Hilgendorf, F. W., 1927: "Agriculture of the Province," Speight *et al.,* pp. 257-72.

——, 1932: *Pasture Plants and Pastures of New Zealand,* Christchurch.

——, 1935: "The Grasslands of South Island, New Zealand," N.Z.D.S.I.R. *Bull.* no. 47.

——, 1939: *Wheat in New Zealand,* Christchurch.

Hochstetter, F. von, 1863: *Neu-Seeland,* Stuttgart.

——, 1867: *New Zealand, Its Physical Geography, Geology and Natural History.* Translated from the German original, 1863, by Edward Sauter (this edition considerably revised by Hochstetter and Sauter jointly previous to translation), Stuttgart.

Hochstetter, F. von, and Petermann, A., 1864: *The Geology of New Zealand,* Auckland.

Hocken, T. M., 1898: *Contributions to the Early History of New Zealand (Settlement of Otago.)* London.

——, 1909: *Bibliography of New Zealand Literature,* Wellington.

Holford, G. H., 1919: "The Primary Industries of Canterbury," *Canterbury Progress League, Bull.* no. 1, Christchurch.

——, 1925: "The New Zealand Corriedales," (pamphlet issued by the *Corriedale Sheep Society, Inc.*), Christchurch. (See also: "The Corriedale, New Zealand," issued by the same society, *circa* 1938, Christchurch.)

Holman, E. H., 1928: *The American Whaleman,* New York.

Holmes, J. M., 1934: "Geographical Factors in the Foundations of New Zealand's Wealth," *The Australian Geographer,* vol. 2, no. 3.

——, 1935: "The Vegetation of New Zealand," *Scot. Geog. Mag.,* vol. 51, no. 2, pp. 89-99.

Homs, J., 1918: "Agricultural Implements, and Machinery in Australia and New Zealand," *Bulletin of the Bureau of Foreign and Domestic Commerce,* Washington.

Hudson, A. W., and Hopewell, H. G., 1941: "Mole Drainage in New Zealand," N.Z.D.S.I.R. *Bull.* no. 86.

Hudson, A. W., and Scrivener, F. L. C., 1936: "Fertilizers and Manures in New Zealand," chap. 19, Belshaw, *et al.,* Melbourne.

Hudson, A. W., Doak, B. W., and McPherson, G. K., 1933: "Investigations into Pasture Production," N.Z.D.S.I.R. *Bull.* no. 31.

Hunt, W. D., 1917: *Land Tenure in New Zealand,* (pamphlet), Dunedin.

Huntington, E., 1931: "Early Days in the Marlborough Sounds," U.N.Z.T. (M.A.).

Hursthouse, C., 1857: *New Zealand: The Britain of the South,* London.

Hussing G. M., (undated): "The Memory Log of G. M. Hussing," (Regarding a journey to Lake Wakatipu from Oamaru in the eighteen-fifties). In the Museum of the *Otago Early Settlers' Association, Inc.,* Dunedin.

Hutton, Capt. F. W., and Drummond, J., 1909: *The Animals of New Zealand.* (First edition, 1904; citations from third edition, 1909; other editions, 1905, 1923.) Christchurch.

Hutton, F. W., and Ulrich, G. H. F., 1875: *Report on the Geology and Goldfields of Otago,* Dunedin.

Illustrated Sydney News (newspaper), 1853-94: Sydney.

Irving, R. F., and Alpers, O. T. J., 1902: *The Progress of New Zealand in the Century,* Toronto and Philadelphia.

Jay, Captain, 1913: "Log of the *Mary Mitchell,*" McNab, 1913, appendix, pp. 43 ff.

Jefcoate, H. C., 1922: "The History of the Early Gold Discoveries in the Province of Otago, 1851-1863," U.N.Z.T. (M.A.).

Jefferson, M., 1926: *Peopling the Argentine Pampa,* New York. (No. 16 in American Geographical Society's Research Series.)

Jobberns, G., 1926: "Raised Beaches in the Teviotdale District, North Canterbury," *T.N.Z.I.,* vol. 56, pp. 225-6.

——, 1927: "The Canterbury Plains, Their Origin and Structure," Speight *et al.,* pp. 88-96.

——, 1928: "The Raised Beaches of the North East Coast of the South Island of New Zealand," *T.N.Z.I.,* vol. 59, pp. 508-70.

——, 1932: "The Puhi Puhi Valley and the Seaward Kaikoura Mountains," *N.Z.J.S.T.,* vol. 13, no. 6, pp. 341-52.

——, 1935: "Physiography of Northern Marlborough," *N.Z.J.S.T.,* vol. 16, no. 6, pp. 349-59.

——, 1937: "The Lower Waipara Gorge," *T.R.S.N.Z.,* vol. 67, pp. 125-32.

——, 1946: "The Marlborough Coast Route of the South Island Main Trunk Railway," *N.Z.G.,* vol. 2, no. 1, pp. 235-46.

Jobberns, G., and King, L. C., 1933: "The Nature and Mode of Origin of the Motunau Plain, North Canterbury, New Zealand," *T.N.Z.I.,* vol. 63, pp. 355-69.

Johnstone, A. H., 1927: *Supplement to Hocken's Bibliography of New Zealand Literature,* Christchurch.

Jourdain, W. R., 1925: *History of Land Legislation and Settlement in New Zealand*, Wellington.

Keesing, F. M., 1928: "The Changing Maori," *Memoirs of the Board of Maori Ethnographical Research*, vol. 4, New Plymouth.

Kendrew, W. G., 1922: *The Climates of the Continents*, Oxford.

Kidson, E., 1931a: "The Annual Variation of Rainfall in New Zealand," *N.Z.J.S.T.*, vol. 12, no. 5.

——, 1931b: "Dry Years in New Zealand," *N.Z.J.S.T.*, vol. 13, no. 2.

——, 1932a: "The Climate of New Zealand," *Australien und Neu-Seeland. Handbuch der Klimatologie*. Band IV. Teil 5. pp. 109-38, Berlin.

——, 1932b: "The Frequency of Frost, Snow and Hail in New Zealand," *N.Z.J.S.T.*, vol. 14, no. 1.

——, 1932c: "The Canterbury Nor'wester," *N.Z.J.S.T.*, vol. 14, no. 2.

——, 1936: "Climate" (of New Zealand), chap. 8 of Belshaw *et al.*, 1936.

King, B. E., 1947: "The Pastoral Age," *N.Z.J.A.*, vol. 74, no. 3.

King, L. C., 1934: "Geology of the Lower Awatere District," *N.Z.D.S.I.R. Geol. Memoirs*, no. 2, pp. 1-48.

——, 1937: "The Structure of Northeastern Marlborough," *T.R.S.N.Z.*, vol. 67, pp. 33-46.

King, L. C., and Jobberns, G., 1934: "Shore-line changes on the New Zealand Coast," *Proceedings* of the Fifth Pacific Science Congress, vol. 2, pp. 1285-95, Toronto.

Kissel, F. T. M., 1918: "The Distribution of Population in New Zealand," (with map based on 1916 *Census Report*), *N.Z.J.S.T.*, vol. 1, no. 4, pp. 210-12.

Köppen, W., 1923: *Die Klimate der Erde*, Berlin.

——, 1931: *Grundriss der Klimakunde*, Berlin.

Laing, R. M., 1924: "Vegetation of Banks Peninsula," *T.N.Z.I.*, vol. 55, pp. 438-44.

Laing, R. M., and Blackwell, E. W., 1906: *Plants of New Zealand*, Christchurch.

Levy, E. B., 1936: "Pastures of New Zealand," chap. 18 of Belshaw *et al.*, 1936.

Levy, E. B., and Gorman, L. W., 1936: "Strain in Subterranean Clover," *Proceedings in the Fifth Conference of the New Zealand Grassland Association*, 1936, pp. 19-32. Wellington.

Linton, R., 1926: "Ethnology of Polynesia and Melanesia," *Field Museum of Natural History Guide*, part 6, Chicago.

Lord, E. I., 1940: *Old Westland*, Christchurch.

Lovat, Lady A., 1914: *The Life of Sir Frederick Weld*, London.

Lovell-Smith, E. M., 1931: *Old Coaching Days*, Christchurch.

Lyng, J., 1939: *The Scandinavians in Australia, New Zealand and the Western Pacific*, Melbourne.

Lyttelton Times (newspaper) 1851-1929 (Lyttelton, 1851-63, and Christchurch, 1863-1929).

McClymont, W. G., 1940: *The Exploration of New Zealand*, Wellington.

McGillivray, R., 1929: "The Mackenzie Country Grasslands," *N.Z.J.A.*, vol. 39, no. 2, pp. 73-8.

McIndoe, J., (undated): *A Sketch of Otago*, (pamphlet), Hocken Library, Dunedin.

McIntosh, A. D., editor, 1930: *Marlborough: A Provincial History*, Blenheim.

McIvor, C., 1893: *History and Development of Sheep Farming from Antiquity to Modern Times* (part II has many references to Australasia), Sydney.

McKay, A., 1890: *Reports of Geological Explorations During 1888-9*, Wellington.

McKenzie, R. M., 1933: "Gold in Otago," U.N.Z.T. (M.A.).

Mackenzie, Sir T., 1896: *Exploration between Dusky Sound and Lake Manapouri*, Dunedin. (Reprinted from the *Otago Daily Times*.)

McKerrow, J., 1863: "Reconnaissance Survey of the Lake Districts of Otago and Southland, New Zealand," *Otago Provincial Gazette*.

——, 1870: "On the Physical Geography of the Lakes Districts of Otago," *T.N.Z.I.*, vol. 3, pp. 254-63.

McNab, R., 1906: *Agriculture in New Zealand*, Wellington.

——, editor, 1908: *Historical Records of New Zealand*, vol. 1, Wellington.

——, 1909: *Murihuku*. "A History of the South Island of New Zealand and the Isles Adjacent. . . . from 1642-1835." Wellington.

——, 1913: *The Old Whaling Days*, Christchurch.

——, editor, 1914a: *Historical Records of New Zealand*, vol. 2, Wellington.

——, 1914b: *From Tasman to Marsden*, Dunedin.

Macpherson, J. A., 1910: "Condition of the Mackenzie Plain and Runs in Central Otago," *N.Z.J.A.*, vol. 1, no. 1, pp. 15-17. (Part 2 of "The Natural Pastures of New Zealand." *See* Cockayne, A. H., 1910.)

Macpherson, E. O., 1942: "Discussion of Phosphate Deposits in New Zealand," in N.Z.D.S.I.R., *Annual Report, A.J.H.R.*, H-35, p. 29.

Madden, E. A., Lambert, J. P., and Suckling, F. E. T., 1940: "Pasture Survey, Banks Peninsula," *Canterbury Progress League Report*, pp. 1-10, Christchurch.

Makereti (Maggie Papakura), 1938: *The Old-time Maori*, London.

Marais, J. S., 1927: *The Colonisation of New Zealand*, Oxford.

Marlborough Provincial Gazette, 1860-76 (official publication of the Marlborough Provincial Council, Blenheim).

Marshall, F. R., 1915: *Features of the Sheep Industries of the United States, New Zealand, and Australia Compared*, Washington.

Marshall, P., 1912: *New Zealand and Adjacent Islands*, Heidelberg.

Martin, H. B., 1884: "Objections to the Introduction of Beasts of Prey to destroy the Rabbit," *T.N.Z.I.*, vol. 17, pp. 179-82.

Mason, B. H., 1941: "The Geology of the Mount Grey District, North Canterbury," *T.R.S.N.Z.*, vol. 71, pp. 103-26.

Matthews, H. J., 1905: *Tree Culture in New Zealand*, Wellington.

Maxwell, E., 1919: "Rate of Growth of Indigenous and Exotic Trees in New Zealand," *N.Z.J.S.T.*, vol. 2, no. 6, pp. 371-76.

Maynard, F., 1937: *The Whalers*. (The first English edition of *Les Balinières*, edited by A. Dumas, translated by F. W. Reed.) London.

Miller, D., 1936: *Garden Pests in New Zealand*, Nelson.

Miller, D., Dumbleton, L. J., and Clark J. F., 1936: "Biological Control of Noxious Insects and Weeds in New Zealand," *N.Z.J.S.T.*, vol. 18, no. 7, pp. 579-93.

Milligan, P. S., 1941: "An Historico-Geographic Survey of Banks Peninsula," U.N.Z.T. (M.A.).

Mills, R. C., 1915: *The Colonisation of Australia, 1829-42.* London.

Mitchell, J., 1850: "Report of Expedition for finding an Inland Route from the Wairau to Port Cooper Plains, April 1850," *New Munster Gazette,* p. 62.

Monro, D., 1844: Letters to the editor of the *Nelson Examiner,* July 20 to Oct. 23. (Also given, Hocken, 1898, appendix, pp. 230-63.)

Morgan, P. G., 1922: "Notes on the Geology of New Zealand," (to accompany geological sketch maps), *N.Z.J.S.T.,* vol. 5, no. 1, pp. 46-57.

——, 1927: "Minerals and Mineral Substances of New Zealand," *B.N.Z.G.S.,* no. 32, New Series.

Morrell, B., 1832: *A Narrative of Four Voyages to the South Seas, etc. (From the year 1822 to 1831),* New York.

Morrell, W. P., 1933: "The Constitution and the Provinces, 1850-76," chap. 6 in *C.H.B.E.N.Z.,* pp. 95-119.

——, 1935: *New Zealand,* London.

——, 1940: *The Gold Rushes,* London.

Morton, P. H., 1930: *The Cattle of New South Wales, from 1788, more especially the Cattle of the Illawarra, from 1804-1930,* Sydney.

Muir, J. R., 1939: *The Life and Achievements of Captain James Cook,* London.

Mulgan, A., 1946: *Pastoral New Zealand, Its Riches and Its People,* Christchurch.

Munro, D., 1917 and 1923: "The Rabbit Pest," *N.Z.J.A.,* vol. 15, no. 4, pp. 206-9; vol. 26, no. 2, pp. 81-4.

Myers, J. G., 1923: "The Introduced Birds of New Zealand," *N.Z.J.S.T.,* vol. 6, no. 1, pp. 40-41.

Neale, E. P., 1938: *Guide to New Zealand Official Statistics,* (pamphlet), Auckland.

Neill, W. T., 1925: *Surveys and Maps,* Wellington.

Nelson Examiner (newspaper), 1842-73, Nelson.

Nelson Provincial Gazette, 1853-76 (official publication of the Nelson Provincial Council).

Newling, C. B., 1925: "The Gold Diggers," *Journ. Roy. Aust. Hist. Soc.,* vol. 11, pp. 262-80.

New South Wales Herd Book, 1876: vol. II, Sydney.

N.Z.D.I.A., *Annual Reports* of: *A.J.H.R.,* H-22.

N.Z.D.S.I.R., *Annual Reports* of: *A.J.H.R.,* H-34.

New Zealand Jersey Cattle Association, 1932: *The Jersey in New Zealand,* (pamphlet), Wellington.

New Zealand Journal, 1840-1852 (official organ of the New Zealand Company, published in London, Feb. 8, 1840 to Nov. 6, 1852).

New Zealand Meteorological Office, "Meteorological Observations," Annual Publication.

N.Z.M.D., 1887: *Handbook of New Zealand Mines,* Wellington.

——, 1898: *Report on Water-Conservation for Mining, Irrigation, Domestic Use.... etc.,* Wellington.

——, 1906: *The New Zealand Mining Handbook,* Wellington.

New Zealand Mines Statement. Annual Report of the N.Z.M.D., *A.J.H.R.,* C-2.

New Zealand Official Handbook, 1892: (See "Notes on Sources of Statistical Data," above).

New Zealand *Statistical Report on Trade and Shipping,* 1921—.

New Zealand *Population Censuses.* (See "Notes on Statistics Sources" above).

Nicholl, S. R., (no date): *Notes on Sheep and Wool in New South Wales, 1787-1825* (in Mitchell Library, Sydney).

O'Brien, E., 1936: *The Foundation of Australia, 1786-1800,* London.

Otago Daily Times (newspaper), 1861—, Dunedin.

Otago News (newspaper), 1848-51, Dunedin.

Otago Provincial Gazette, 1862-76 (official publication of the Otago Provincial Council), Dunedin.

Otago Witness (newspaper), 1851–, Dunedin. (Later merged with *Otago Daily Times.*)

Packard, W., 1947: "Lake Coleridge Catchment Basin: A Geographic Survey of its Problems," *N.Z.G.,* vol. 3, no. 1, pp. 19-40.

Park, J., 1910: *Geology of New Zealand,* Christchurch.

Parsons, F., 1904: *The Story of New Zealand,* Philadelphia.

Paul, R. B., 1854: *Some Account of the Canterbury Settlement,* London.

——, 1857: *Letters from Canterbury, New Zealand,* London.

Peart, J. D., 1937: *Old Tasman Bay,* Nelson.

Perham, A. N., 1922: "Deer in New Zealand," (Report on the Damage Done by Deer in the Forests and Plantations of New Zealand), *A.J.H.R.,* C-3A.

Perry, W., *et al.,* 1924: *Sheep Farming in New Zealand,* Christchurch.

Petre, H. W., 1842: *The Settlements of the New Zealand Company,* London, fourth edition.

Philpott, H. G., 1937: *A History of the New Zealand Dairy Industry, 1840-1935,* Wellington.

Piraki Log. Ms.; The log of a whaler, Hempleman, who began operations around Banks Peninsula in the year 1835, 1836, or 1837. Canterbury Museum, Christchurch. (Also published in London, 1910, edited by Anson.)

Popplewell, D. L., 1929: "Some Ecological Effects of Acclimatisation in New Zealand," *N.Z.J.S.T.,* vol. II, no. 2, pp. 125-27.

Port Phillip Patriot (newspaper), 1853-8, Melbourne.

Potts, T. H., 1882: *Out in the Open,* Christchurch.

Pratt, W., 1877: *Colonial Experiences in New Zealand, by An Old Colonist,* London.

Prothero, R. E. *See* Ernle, Lord.

Pyke, V., 1863: Report on the Gold Discoveries in Otago, *A.J.H.R.* (Most of which is contained in N.Z.M.D., *Handbook of New Zealand Mines,* 1876 and 1887 and in Pyke, 1887).

——, 1887: *History of the Early Gold Discoveries in Otago,* Dunedin.

Quin and Rodger (editors of the *Tapanui Courier*), 1910, *Tapanui Station,* Tapanui. In library of *Otago Early Settlers' Association, Inc.,* Dunedin.

Raven, Captain, 1796: Letter, dated Nov. 2 quoted in *H.R.N.S.W.,* vol. 2, pp. 94-6.

Reeves, W. P., 1925: *Aotea-roa, The Long White Cloud* (third edition) London. (First edition published in London, 1898.)

Reid, R. C., 1884: *Rambles on the Golden Coast of the South Island of New Zealand,* Hokitika.

Reischek, A., 1930: *Yesterdays in Maoriland,* London. Translated by H. E. L. Priday from: *Sterbende Welt, zwölf Jahre forscherleben aus Neu-seeland.* (Herausgeben von seinem Sohn.) Leipzig, 1924.

Report of Committee of Inquiry, 1939: "Maintenance of Vegetative Cover in New Zealand, with Special Reference to Land Erosion," N.Z.D.S.I.R. *Bull.* no. 77.

Reports of the New Zealand Company, 1840, 1844: Reports of the Court of Directors, published in London from time to time. Referred to are: *First Report:* May 14, 1840; *Twelfth Report:* Apr. 26, 1844; *Thirteenth Report:* June 29, 1844.

Ridley, J., 1866: Article on the origin of the "stripper" or "header-harvester," (the Australasian terms for a combined harvester and thresher), Adelaide *Register* (newspaper), May 6.

Roberts, S. H., 1933: "The Wool Trade and the Squatters," chap. 7 of *C.H.B.E.,* vol. 7, part I, *Australia,* pp. 185-205.

——, 1935: *The Squatting Age in Australia, 1835-1847,* Melbourne.

Roberts, W. H. S. (undated): "Southland in 1856-7," Hocken Library, Dunedin.

——, 1890: *History of Oamaru and North Otago, New Zealand, from 1835 to the end of 1889,* Oamaru.

Rochfort, J., 1852: "Journal of Two Expeditions to the West Coast of the Middle Island in 1859," *J.R.G.S.,* vol. 32, pp. 294-303.

Rogers, J. D., 1925: *Historical Geography of the British Dominions,* vol. 6, *Australasia,* second edition revised by R. N. Kershaw, Oxford.

Rose, J. H., 1933: "Captain Cook," *C.H.B.E.N.Z.,* pp. 23-9.

Rusden, G. W., 1883: *History of New Zealand,* London.

Russell, H. L., and Macklin, T., 1925: "Intensive Dairying in New Zealand and Wisconsin," *Univ. of Wis. Agr. Exp. Sta., Bull.* no. 377.

Saunders, A., 1896 and 1899: *History of New Zealand (1642-1893):* vol. I (1642-1861), vol. II (1861-1893), Christchurch.

Schlich, Sir W., 1918: "Forestry in the Dominion of New Zealand," *Quarterly Journal of Forestry,* vol. 12, no. 1, pp. 1-28.

Scholefield, G. H., 1909: *New Zealand in Evolution,* London.

——, 1929: "Historical Sources and Archives in New Zealand," *N.Z.J.S.T.,* vol. 11, no. 3, pp. 129-41.

——, 1930a: (pseud. "Annalist"), "The Makers of Canterbury," *Christchurch Press,* 39 articles from Jan. to Nov.

——, 1930b: "The Makers of Otago," *Otago Daily Times,* a series of articles, Jan. to Oct.

Schmieder, O., 1928: "The Pampa—A Natural or Culturally Induced Grassland," *University of California Publications in Geography,* vol. 2, no. 8, pp. 255-70.

Scott, E., 1933: "British Settlement in Australia," 1783-1806, and "The Extension of Settlement," 1806-1825, chaps. 3 and 4 of *C.H.B.E.,* vol. 7, part 1, *Australia,* pp. 55-119.

448   THE INVASION OF NEW ZEALAND

Scott, R. H., 1947: "Cereal Production," *N.Z.J.A.*, vol. 74, no. 4.
Sears, P. D., 1945: "The Regional Variety of Pasture Growth in New Zealand," *N.Z.G.*, vol. 1, no 1, pp 57-82.
Seelye, C. J., 1946: *Maps of Average Rainfall in New Zealand*, New Zealand Meteorological Office, Wellington.
Segar, H. W., 1900: "The Population of New Zealand," *T.N.Z.I.*, vol. 33, p. 445 ff.
Shann, E. O. G., 1930: *An Economic History of Australia*, Cambridge.
Shortland, Edward, 1851: *The Southern Districts of New Zealand*, London.
Shrimpton, A. W., and Mulgan, A. E., 1930: *Maori and Pakeha, A History of New Zealand*, Christchurch, second edition (first edition 1921).
Sidney, S., 1853: *The Three Colonies of Australia*, second edition, London.
Simmonds, J. H., 1927: *Trees from Other Lands for Shelter and Timber in New Zealand*, Auckland.
Sinclair, H. I., 1944: *Population: New Zealand's Problem*, Dunedin.
Skinner, H. D., 1912: "Maori Life on the Poutini Coast Together with Some Traditions of the Natives," (based on notes taken in 1897 by G. J. Roberts), *J.P.S.*, vol. 21, no. 4, pp. 141-51.
——, 1921: "Culture Areas in New Zealand," (with map), *J.P.S.*, vol. 30, no. 2, pp. 71-8.
——, 1933: "The Maoris," chap. 2 in *C.H.B.E.N.Z.*, pp. 9-21.
Skinner, W. H., 1912: "Ancient Maori Canals, Marlborough, New Zealand," (with map), *J.P.S.*, vol. 21, no. 3, pp. 105-8. (Based largely on Annual Report of the N.Z.D.L.S., Appendix 8, 1902-3, by C. W. Adams, which included a map.)
Sladen, F. W. L., 1912: *The Humble Bee*, London.
Sladden, D., 1894: "The Frozen Meat Trade," *N.Z.O.Y.B.*
Slater, G., 1907: *The English Peasantry and the Enclosure of the Common Fields*, London.
Smith, H. B., 1914: *The Sheep and Wool Industry of Australasia*, Christchurch.
Smith, W. M., 1936: *Marketing of Australian and New Zealand Primary Products*, London.
Soljak, P. J., 1946: *New Zealand, Pacific Pioneer*, New York.
Somerset, H. C. D., 1938: *Littledene: A New Zealand Rural Community*, Christchurch.
Southland Provincial Gazette, 1864-70 (official publication of Southland Provincial Council, 1861-70), Invercargill.
Southy, R., 1851: *The Rise, Progress and Present State of Colonial Sheep and Wools to 1851*, London.
Speight, R., 1908: "Some Aspects of the Terrace-development in the Valleys of the Canterbury Rivers," *T.N.Z.I.*, vol. 40, pp. 16-43.
——, 1915: "Intermontane Basins of Canterbury," *T.N.Z.I.*, vol. 47, pp. 336-53.
——, 1916a: "The Orientation of the River Valleys of Canterbury," *T.N.Z.I.*, vol. 48, pp. 137-44.
——, 1916b: "The Physiography of the Cass District," *T.N.Z.I.*, vol. 48, pp. 145-53.
——, 1917: "The Geology of Banks Peninsula," *T.N.Z.I.*, vol. 49, pp. 365-92.

——, 1918: "Structural and Glacial Features of the Hurunui Valley," *T.N.Z.I.*, vol. 50, pp. 93-105.

——, 1927: "Geology of the Province," (Canterbury), Speight, *et al.*, pp. 60-87.

——, 1928: "Geological Features of the Waimakariri Basin," *Records of Canterbury Museum, Christchurch*, series III, no. 3, pp. 199-229.

Speight, R., Wall, A., and Laing, R. M., editors, 1927: *Natural History of Canterbury*, Christchurch. (Quoted as Speight, *et al.*, 1927.)

Stafford, W. C., 1937: "Irrigation in South Island," *Papers Read to the Sixth Annual Conference of the New Zealand Grasslands Association*. Mimeographed.

Stapledon, Sir R. G., 1928: *A Tour in Australia and New Zealand, Grasslands and Other Studies*, Oxford.

Statistics of New Zealand. (See "Note on Sources of Statistical Data," above.)

Stead, D. G., 1935: *The Rabbit in Australia*, Sydney.

Stewart, W. D., 1909: "Land Tenure and Land Monopoly in New Zealand," *Journ. of Pol. Econ.*, vol. 17, nos. 2 and 3, pp. 82-91 and 144-52.

Stout, Sir R., 1886: *Notes on the Progress of New Zealand, 1864-1884*, Wellington.

Studholme, E. C., 1940: *Te Waimate*, Christchurch.

Sutch, W. B., 1936: *Recent Economic Changes in New Zealand*, Wellington.

Sutherland, I. L. G., editor, 1940: *The Maori People Today, a General Survey*, Christchurch.

——, 1947: "Maori and Pakeha," chapter in Belshaw, editor.

Sutherland, L. E., 1931: "The Settler and Surveyor—Explorers of Otago," U.N.Z.T. (M.A.).

Suttor, H. M., 1925: *Australian Milestones*, Sydney.

Swainson, W., 1859: *New Zealand and Its Colonisation*, London.

Sydney Gazette (newspaper), 1803-42, Sydney. (A government gazette as well as a newspaper, 1803-32.)

Sydney Herald (newspaper), 1831-42, Sydney. (Then *Sydney Morning Herald*, 1842—.)

Tasman, A., 1898: *Journal of his Discovery of Van Diemen's Land and New Zealand, 1642; with documents relating to his exploration of Australia, 1644*, Amsterdam. Translated by J. E. Heeres. (*See* Heeres, 1898).

Taylor, G., 1941: *Australia and New Zealand*, New York.

Taylor, N. H., 1938: "Land Deterioration in the Heavier Rainfall Districts of New Zealand," *N.Z.D.S.I.R. Bull.* no. 62, also, *N.Z.J.S.T.*, vol. 19, no. 11, pp. 657-81.

Teviotdale, D., 1937-9. (A series of articles on sites occupied by the hunters of the moa.) *J.P.S.*, 1937, vol. 46, no. 3; 1938a, vol. 47, no. 1; 1938b, vol. 47, no. 3; 1939, vol. 48, no. 4.

Thomson, A. S., 1859: *The Story of New Zealand*, 2 vols., London.

Thomson, G. M., 1874: "Some of the Naturalised Plants of Otago," *T.N.Z.I.*, vol. 7, pp. 370-76.

——, 1884: "The Rabbit Pest," *N.Z.J.S.*, vol. 2, pp. 79-80.

——, 1891: "On some Aspects of Acclimatisation in New Zealand," *Report of third meeting of the A.N.Z.A.A.S.*, Christchurch.

——, 1922: *The Naturalisation of Plants and Animals in New Zealand*, Cambridge.

——, 1923: "Naturalised Animals and Plants," *N.Z.J.S.T.*, vol. 6, pp. 223-31.

Thomson, J. T., 1858: "Extracts from a Journal Kept During the Performance of a Reconnaissance Survey of the Southern Districts of the Province of Otago," *J.R.G.S.*, vol. 28, pp. 298-332.

Thornthwaite, C. W., 1933: "The Climates of the Earth," *G.R.*, vol. 23, no. 3, pp. 433-40.

Thorp, W. H., *Ms.*, "Reminiscences," in Turnbull Library, Wellington.

Travers, W. T. L., 1869: "On the Changes Effected in the Natural Features of a New Country by the Introduction of Civilized Races," *T.N.Z.I.*, vol. 2, pp. 299-330.

Trollope, A., 1874: *New Zealand*, London.

Troup, R. S., 1932: *Exotic Forest Trees in the British Empire*, Oxford.

Tuckett, F., 1898: "Diary" (of a journey along the eastern and southern coasts of South Island, Mar. 28-June 1, 1844). Published in appendix A to Hocken, 1898, pp. 203-25.

Tull, J., 1773: *Horse-hoeing Husbandry*, London.

Tunzelman, N. von, *Ms.*, "Reminiscences and Troubles of a Wakatipian Pioneer," Hocken Library, Dunedin.

Turner, E. F., 1935: "The Foundations of the Otago Settlement with Some Experiences of the Emigrants from 1848 to 1850," U.N.Z.T. (M.A.)

Turner, E. P., 1937: "Forestry in New Zealand," A.N.Z.A.A.S., *Handbook of New Zealand*, pp. 50-54, Auckland.

Turner, E. P., and Beasley, A., 1936: "Forestry in New Zealand," chap. 27, Belshaw *et al.*, pp. 562-606.

Turner, F. J., 1930: "Physiographic Features of the Lower Cascade Valley and the Cascade Plateau, Westland," *T.N.Z.I.*, vol. 61, pp. 524-35.

Turner, G. M. D., 1921: "History of the Rangiora District," U.N.Z.T. (M.A.)

Turner, H. T., 1919: "Sheep and the High Country Runs," *N.Z.J.A.*, vol. 18, no. 1, pp. 90-2.

U. S. Weather Bureau, 1930: *Climatic Summary of the United States, 1930*, Washington.

U. S. Weather Bureau, 1941: "Climatological Data for the United States by Sections," vol. 28, no. 13, "Year," Washington.

Vogel, Sir J., 1875?: *Handbook of New Zealand*, London (second edition).

Waite, R., 1869: *The Discovery of the West Coast Gold Fields*, (pamphlet), Nelson.

Wakefield, E. G., 1829: *A Letter from Sydney*, London.

——, 1849: *A View of the Art of Colonisation*, London.

Wakefield, E. J., 1845: *Adventure in New Zealand*, London. (Many later editions, including Christchurch, 1908, from which quotations for this study were taken.)

——, 1848: *Handbook for New Zealand by a Late Magistrate of the Colony*, London.

——, editor, 1869: *Founders of Canterbury* (Letters of E. G. Wakefield, *et al.*), London. (Republished, Wellington, 1937.)

——, 1889: *New Zealand After Fifty Years*, London.

Wakefield, F., 1849: *Colonial Surveying*, London.

Wallace, R., 1891: *The Rural Economy and Agriculture of Australia and New Zealand*, London.

Watts, I. E. M., 1947: "The Relation of New Zealand Weather and Climate," *N.Z.G.*, vol. 3, no. 2, pp. 115-28.

Walsh, P., 1892: "The Effect of Deer on the New Zealand Bush, a Plea for the Protection of our Forest Reserves," *T.N.Z.I.*, vol. 25, pp. 435-38.

Webb, L., 1940: *Government in New Zealand*, Wellington.

Weld, F. A., 1860: *Hints to Intending Sheep Farmers in New Zealand*, (pamphlet), London, third edition.

Wentworth, W. C., 1819: *Statistical, Historical and Political Description of New South Wales*, Sydney (?).

Westland County and Provincial Gazette, 1868-76. (Official publication of the Westland County Council, 1868-72, and of the Westland Provincial Council, 1873-76.)

Weston, I. W., 1936: "Arable Farming," chap. 24 in Belshaw, *et al.*

White, T., 1890: "On Rabbits, Weasels and Sparrows," *T.N.Z.I.*, vol. 23, pp. 201-7.

Wild, L. J., 1915: "Notes on the Soils of the Wairau Plain," *T.N.Z.I.*, vol. 47, pp. 413-16.

Williams, G. J., 1936: "The Geomorphology of Stewart Island, New Zealand," *G.J.*, vol. 87, no. 4, pp. 328-37.

Williamson, J. A., 1933: "The Exploration of the Pacific," chap. I, *C.H.B.E.*, vol. 7, part I, *Australia*, pp. 25-53.

Wilson, E., 1936: *Land Problems of the Forties* (pamphlet), Dunedin.

Wilson, G. T. J., 1930: "The Golden Grey (An Historical Treatise on the Grey District during the Provincial Period, 1854-76)," *U.N.Z.T.* (M.A.)

Wilson, G. T. J., and Barker, N. (*Ms.*), *Social History of Canterbury*, (in preparation in 1942. Seen only in *ms.* form).

Wilson, J., editor, 1912: *Reminiscences of the Early Settlement of Dunedin and South Otago*, Dunedin.

Wilson, J. P., 1918: "The Rabbit Nuisance in Central Otago," *N.Z.J.A.*, vol. 17, no. 5, pp. 291-4.

Wöhlers, J. F. H., 1895: *Memories of the Life of J. F. H. Wöhlers; Missionary at Ruapuke*, Dunedin. (Translated from the German by J. Houghton, 1895; original place or time of the German publication unknown.)

Wood, F. L. W., 1944: *Understanding New Zealand*, New York.

Woodcock, J. W., 1947: "Farming in Otago," *N.Z.J.A.*, vol. 74, no. 1.

Woodhouse, A. E., 1937: *George Rhodes of the Levels and His Brothers*, Christchurch.

Young, A., 1784-92: *Annals of Agriculture and Other Useful Arts*, London. 17 vols.

——, 1799-1809: *General View of the Agriculture of the County of* ... *Lincoln*, 1799; *Hertfordshire*, 1804; *Norfolk*, 1804; *Suffolk*, 1804; *Essex*, 1807 (2 vols.); *Sussex*, 1808; *Oxfordshire*, 1809.

Zotov, V. D., 1938a: "Some Correlations between Vegetation and Climate in New Zealand," *N.Z.J.S.T.*, vol. 19, no. 8, pp. 474-87.

——, 1938b: "Survey of the Tussock-grasslands of The South Island, New Zealand," N.Z.D.S.I.R., *Bull.* no. 73. (Also in *N.Z.J.S.T.*, vol. 20A, no. 4A, pp. 212A-44A).

——, 1940: "Certain Types of Soil Erosion and Resultant Relief Features on the Higher Mountains of New Zealand," *N.Z.J.S.T.*, vol. 21B, no. 5B, pp. 256B-62B.

INDEX

ST. MARY'S COLLEGE OF MARYLAND LIBRARY
ST. MARY'S CITY, MARYLAND

33833

DATE

8/7/72

MAR 2 1 1983

GAYLORD